AF429463

Consciousness-Based Psychology

SRI AUROBINDO'S VISION OF YOGA, HEALTH AND
TRANSPERSONAL GROWTH

By

Soumitra Basu, M.D.
Michael Miovic, M.D.

"Yoga is nothing but practical psychology"

Sri Aurobindo

INSTITUTE OF INTEGRAL YOGA PSYCHOLOGY
INDIA

Acknowledgment

Sri Aurobindo Ashram Trust, Dr. A. S. Dalal

Consciousness-Based Psychology
Sri Aurobindo's Vision of Yoga, Health and Transpersonal Growth

Copyright : Paulette Hadnagy
Author : Dr. Soumitra Basu and Dr. Michael Miovic

Second edition 2023

ISBN 978-93-95460-67-5 (Paperback
ISBN 978-93-95460-95-8 (ebook)

BISAC Code:
PSY000000, PSYCHOLOGY / General
PSY031000, PSYCHOLOGY / Social Psychology
PSY036000, PSYCHOLOGY / Mental Health
REL062000, RELIGION / Spirituality
HEA055000, HEALTH & FITNESS / Mental Health
OCC010000, BODY, MIND & SPIRIT / Mindfulness & Meditation
OCC026000, BODY, MIND & SPIRIT / Yoga see HEALTH & FITNESS / Yoga

Thema Subject Category:
VXA, Mind, body, spirit: thought and practice
VX, Mind, body, spirit
QRYM2, Spiritualism
JBCC, Cultural studies
JB, Society and culture: general
JM, Psychology
JMT, Psychology: states of consciousness
VSPD, Mindfulness

Cataloging-in-Publication Data for this title is available from the Library of Congress.

Published by:
PRISMA, an imprint of Digital Media Initiatives
PRISMA, Aurelec / Prayogshala,
Auroville 605101, Tamil Nadu, India
www.prisma.haus

Contents

Preface

This book presents a consciousness-based approach to psychology and psychiatry based upon the worldview of Sri Aurobindo (1872-1950), the great Indian yoga philosopher and spiritual teacher. The author, Dr. Soumitra Basu, is a psychiatrist in Kolkata, India, who has developed this approach over more than three decades of clinical practice. The co-author, Dr. Michael Miovic, is a colleague and psychiatrist from the United States who has also written about the relevance of Sri Aurobindo's work to psychology and psychiatry.

Since Sri Aurobindo's thought is complex, the authors have attempted to make this book accessible to a variety of readers who are interested in yoga, transpersonal psychology, spirituality and mental health. To achieve this goal, we have included many case studies from both India and the United States, and we have directly quoted certain passages from the works of Sri Aurobindo and the Mother that illustrate particular points especially well. Note that since Sri Aurobindo considered "the Mother" (aka Mirra Alfassa) to be his equal and collaborator in developing their integral yoga, her statements are cited often in this book to illustrate his point of view. Also, since understanding Sri Aurobindo's model of consciousness is an experiential process, rather than an intellectual activity that relies primarily on analyzing information, this book is intended for both lay and professional readers, although it addresses content from the professional discourse of psychology and psychiatry.

Part 1 of this book reviews the main themes and concepts from Sri Aurobindo's yogic worldview that frame the discussion of consciousness and consciousness-based psychology (CBP). In Chapter 1, Dr. Miovic presents the philosophy of Sri Aurobindo and Indian yoga, with an eye towards readers outside of India who may have a limited background in this tradition of thought. In Chapter 2, Dr. Basu then reviews the history of Western psychology as seen through the lens of Indian yoga and the consciousness perspective. Chapters 3-9 proceed to present the core concepts of CBP, with a focus on the relationship between CBP and the biopsychosocial model of psychology and psychiatry. These chapters address key issues such as the psychic being (evolving soul), karma, rebirth, the relationship between the soul and the ego, occultism, the possession model of illness, the communal and social dimensions of CBP, and higher and deeper orders of cognition. This survey of Sri Aurobindo's detailed and disciplined approach to what is loosely called "intuition" culminates in an extraordinary case study of how the Mother used supramental cognition to experience LSD without actually ingesting the substance.

Part 2 addresses advanced topics in CBP, beginning with Sri Aurobindo's yogic map of the planes and parts of the being (Chapter 10), and his description of the levels and causes of disharmonies in consciousness (Chapter 11). Chapters 12-18 review the planes of consciousness from the Superconscous down to the Inconscient, with case studies of clinical problems that can arise at each level, plus practices for yogic growth and self-development. Note that in CBP growth is a fluid process in which both the client and clinician are evolving in consciousness across the lifespan, and each may be more developed in certain planes and parts of the being than the other at a given point in time. Thus, there is not a fixed division between growth and treatment, nor an assumption that the clinician has to be more "advanced" than the client. Finally, the Appendix contains an essay that examines how Western psychology and culture have unfairly pathologized mystics in the past, and explains why current diagnostic criteria for mental illness now view spirituality as potentially healthy. This problem is illustrated with reference to misguided interpretations about the etiology of Sri Aurobindo's interest in mysticism.

Historically, the current book builds upon the work of prior scholars—notably Dr. Indra Sen, Dr. Haridas Chaudhuri and Dr. A. S. Dalal—who have applied insights from Sri Aurobindo's Integral Yoga to the concerns of psychology. Indeed, the present book began in the late 1990s as a research project named "Implications of Sri Aurobindo's Thought in psychology and psychiatry," which was carried out by Dr. Basu with guidance from Dr. Dalal at Sri Aurobindo Ashram. Over time, the work expanded to include clinical applications, and along the way benefitted from valuable inputs by Dr. Matthijs Cornelissen and Professor Arabinda Basu.

In the last 20 years, the field of integral yoga psychology (which we call CBP in this book) has grown further, and now compasses a small community of scholars and clinicians, many of whom have contributed their time and expertise to this book. The authors thank Dr. Susan Curtiss for her suggestions and contribution of case studies on trauma therapy (Chapter 17). Dr. Don Salmon corrected the history of CBP (Chapter 2), and Dr. Debashish Banerji contributed his expertise to the discussion of post-modernism as it relates to integral yoga and CBP. Dr. Banerji has also edited a journal issue on Sri Aurobindo's relevance to transpersonal psychology (1), which he has expanded to serve as a source book for Integral Yoga Psychology.(2) Dr. Cornelissen has organized conferences on integral psychology, and has a small training institute in Pondicherry, India, that conducts courses on Indian psychology from the integral perspective (www.ipi.org.in). Dr Anand Reddy established The Sri Aurobindo Centre for Advanced Research (SACAR)in 1998 and has been conducting courses on Integral Yoga Psychology. These and other important developments in the field are also reviewed in Chapter 2.

For readers who are interested, we recommend going to the source of the wisdom in this book. Sri Aurobindo and the Mother's collected works are available for free online, through the Sri Aurobindo Ashram, at sriaurobindoashram.org. Among Sri Aurobindo's many works, The Letters on Yoga are often written in shorter passages and a conversational style that can be more approachable than his formal writings. The Mother's Agenda, which is the record of her exploration of the body's consciousness, is also conversational in style and fascinating to read. It is available online via the Auroville website at www.auroville.org.

Although this book focuses on the work of Sri Aurobindo and the Mother, nonetheless CBP provides a flexible framework that is open to insights from a variety of cultures, traditions, teachers, disciplines of study, and approaches to the exploration of consciousness. Also, while the yogic tradition has always maintained that one can experience a consciousness that is infinite and free from conditioning, yogis are pragmatic and recognize that time passes, cultures change, and teaching has to be adapted to specific contexts. One example of how culture has already changed since the time of Sri Aurobindo and the Mother is new feelings about the use of gendered terms in language. Both Sri Aurobindo and the Mother used the words "man" and "men" to refer to all human beings, in accordance with the conventions of their time. However, everything about their lives suggests this was only a linguistic convention and not reflective of gender bias or prejudices about sexual orientation. They viewed all genders as equal, and in Chapter 9 we discuss their futuristic vision of non-gendered, non-sexual supramental life forms on Earth.

On the other hand, it is worth noting that Sri Aurobindo understood other secrets of language with which the rest of the world has yet to catch up. He was a superb poet and writer, and he made extensive use of the printed word.In the past, great yogis were not writers and their teachings were transmitted orally, sometimes for centuries, before others finally wrote them down. This is why the Buddha's eightfold path was succinct, and why Sri Ramana Maharshi boiled that already compact teaching down to a single question ("who am I?") that can be remembered anytime and anywhere. In contrast to this classical method, Sri Aurobindo adapted his teaching to a modern world with much higher rates of literacy and access to printed material. Now, sitting quietly and reading is a very different activity from conversing. Sri Aurobindo understood that the written word can, if handled artistically, create a meditative or mantric effect, and he leveraged these more subtle qualities of language in his work. That is why we include many passages in his own words—because how he says something is just as important as what he says.He knew how to convey not only information, but the *consciousness* of that which he evoked.

References

1. International Journal of Transpersonal Studies, Vol.37:1, 2018

2. Integral Yoga Psychology: Metaphysics & Transformation

as Taught by Sri Aurobindo, edited by Debahsish Banerji, Lotus Press, Wisconsin, 2020.

Abbreviations/Short forms of References

CWSA: Collected Works of Sri Aurobindo, Sri Aurobindo Ashram, Puducherry

CWM: Collected Works of The Mother, Sri Aurobindo Ashram, Puducherry

Agenda: Mother's Agenda, Institut de Recherches Evolutives, Paris, 1981

Evening Talks: Evening Talks with Sri Aurobindo, Recorded by A.B. Purani, 4th Edition, Sri Aurobindo Ashram, Puducherry, 2007

Verses quoted at the beginninig and end of each chapter are taken from Sri Aurobindo's epic poem, *Savitri* (CWSA 33-34)

PART 1

CORE CONCEPTS

1
Consciousness and the Need for a New Psychology

> *There is no last certitude in which thought can pause*
> *And no terminus to the soul's experience.*
> *A limit, a farness never wholly reached,*
> *An unattained perfection calls to him*
> *From distant boundaries in the Unseen:*
> *A long beginning only has been made.*
>
> Savitri, *pg. 69*

Two factors are driving psychology and psychiatry inexorably towards a tryst with destiny: the spread of yoga and meditation around the globe and into healthcare, and the decolonization of thought that has unleashed the power of indigenous perspectives. In the last 20 years, these two forces have lead to the rebirth of Indian psychology as a valid field and complementary approach to the conventional Western model of mental health. And with yoga and Indian psychology comes that destined meeting which was always inevitable: Sri Aurobindo.

Sri Aurobindo (1872-1950) is the most important Indian thinker in over two thousand years, and he was a master of the English language. To give an analogy that most should understand, he was like a combination of Einstein, Shakespeare, and the Buddha all in one. Not only was he a profoundly original and creative thinker, but he also expressed his insights in some of the finest English prose and poetry ever written. For psychology, Sri Aurobindo's revolutionary interpretation of the evolution of consciousness is a paradigm shift not seen since the Buddha created what we now call Buddhism, and the purpose of this book is to show the far-reaching implications of this work. Sri Aurobindo considered himself to be a yogi, not a psychologist, but because yoga is so focused on personal experience of different states or capacities of consciousness, it is by its nature highly psychological. In the West, the word "yoga" has come to mean primarily the physical exercises of hatha yoga, but in India this has always been yoga's least important branch. For Sri Aurobindo, yoga meant much more than simply a method of exercise or stress reduction: it is a direct, first-person exploration of the infinite potentials of consciousness. In 1934, he wrote a statement for public dissemination that summarized his approach to yoga and specifically referred to it as "psychological discipline":

> "The teaching of Sri Aurobindo starts from that of the ancient sages of India that behind the appearances of the universe there is the Reality of a Being and Consciousness, a Self of all things one and eternal. All beings are united in that One Self and Spirit but divided by a certain separativity of consciousness, an ignorance of their true Self and Reality in the mind, life and body. It is possible by a certain psychological discipline to remove this veil of separative consciousness and become aware of the true Self, the Divinity within us and all."(1)

This paragraph summarizes the traditional goal of Indian yoga, which was the realization of the "Self," meaning a non-dual awareness of an absolute Reality that transcends any form of conditioning. Like many yogis and spiritual teachers, Sri Aurobindo interpreted this liberation in a psychological sense as a living experience or state of awareness, not in a religious sense as a sort of "heaven" where one goes after death. This is the old news, and it has been dealt with extensively in transpersonal psychology and writings about the perennial philosophy. However, from here Sri Aurobindo goes on to deliver some new news. In the second paragraph of this statement, he proposes that the evolution of consciousness on Earth is directional and moving towards a supramental manifestation:

> "Sri Aurobindo's teaching states that this One Being and Consciousness is involved here in Matter. Evolution is the method by which it liberates itself; consciousness appears in

what seems to be inconscient, and once having appeared is self-impelled to grow higher and higher and at the same time to enlarge and develop towards a greater and greater perfection. Life is the first step of this release of consciousness; mind is the second; but the evolution does not finish with mind, it awaits a release into something greater, a consciousness which is spiritual and supramental. The next step of the evolution must be towards the development of Supermind and Spirit as the dominant power in the conscious being. For only then will the involved Divinity in things release itself entirely and it become possible for life to manifest perfection." (2)

Sri Aurobindo's theory of evolution is so important and so original that we must take some time here to compare it with the ordinary and scientific views of consciousness. Sri Aurobindo was educated at Cambridge and was well aware of the developments of modern science and the heated debates sparked by Darwin's work on the evolution of species. Unlike many religious thinkers, Sri Aurobindo took biological evolution as a settled fact. However, he rejected the reductionistic approach to consciousness expounded by materialistic science, and brought the wisdom of yoga to bear on this question. He arrived at this perspective through a combination of his own yogic experience and the non-dualist philosophy of Vedanta, which is expressed in the Upanishads. In the following letter, he shows that he thoroughly understands the normal view of consciousness—and then he calls this view into question:

"The ordinary view of consciousness is based on normal superficial experience plus science. For physical science consciousness is a temporary phenomenon in an unconscious world, something evolved in an animate organisation that somehow develops in an originally inanimate and unconscious Matter. It is not inherent in life, for the plant has it not, it is rather a growing flicker that, once established, lasts intermittently through sleep and waking while life lasts and disappears with the dissolution of life. The ordinary mind identifies consciousness with human waking consciousness possibly shared by the animal — though that is not certain, for many refuse consciousness to the animal. A man is conscious while he lives, when he is dead consciousness disappears, when he is asleep, stunned, drugged, anaesthetised, in trance, then his consciousness is suspended; he is temporarily unconscious. How far is this scientific-superficial view correct or maintainable? For it raises two fundamental questions — is the waking surface consciousness the only form of consciousness possible? and again, is the consciousness synonymous with mind, is all consciousness mental or are other forms of it, supramental or submental, possible?" (3)

Based on his own experience and the philosophy of yoga, Sri Aurobindo did not think that consciousness is synonymous with mind, and he elaborated his own perspective in thousands of pages of writing spanning many decades of work. In the next passage, he briefly lays out his notion of planes of consciousness, which Wilber and other transpersonal psychologists were to take up again some 50 years later:

"Consciousness is usually identified with mind, but mental consciousness is only the human range which no more exhausts all the possible ranges of consciousness than human sight exhausts all the gradations of colour or human hearing all the gradations of sound — for there is much above or below that is to man invisible and inaudible. So there are ranges of consciousness above and below the human range, with which the normal human has no contact and they seem to it unconscious, — supramental or overmental and submental ranges." (4)

In Chapters 8 and 9 we shall explore in detail exactly what Sri Aurobindo meant by the terms "overmental" and "supramental." For now, it is worth noting the close kinship between Sri Aurobindo's yogic approach to consciousness and the blend of psychology and religion that William James explored in his seminal work on

The Varieties of Religious Experience. Sri Aurobindo actually read one of James's books on psychology (it is not clear which one) and commented that it was "full of valuable suggestions." (5) James did not live to read Sri Aurobindo, but his conclusion to the *Varieties of Religious Experience* was entirely Aurobindonian:

> "The whole drift of my education goes to persuade me that the world of our present consciousness is only one out of many worlds of consciousness that exist, and that those other worlds must contain experiences which have a meaning for our life also; and that although in the main their experiences and those of this world keep discrete, yet the two become contiguous at certain points, and higher energies filter in." (6)

James's memorable phrase about the "many worlds of consciousness that exist" is precisely what Sri Aurobindo spent decades exploring. In the next passage, Sri Aurobindo describes a little bit about his own experience of these other ranges or dimensions of consciousness:

> "Consciousness is not, to my experience, a phenomenon dependent on the reactions of personality to the forces of Nature and amounting to no more than a seeing or interpretation of these reactions. If that were so, then when the personality becomes silent and immobile and gives no reactions, as there would be no seeing or interpretative action, there would therefore be no consciousness. That contradicts some of the fundamental experiences of Yoga, e.g., a silent and immobile consciousness infinitely spread out, not dependent on the personality but impersonal and universal, not seeing and interpreting contacts but motionlessly self-aware, not dependent on the reactions, but persistent in itself even when no reactions take place. The subjective personality itself is only a formation of consciousness which is a power inherent, not in the activity of the temporary manifested personality, but in the being, the Self or Purusha."(7)

The quest for enlightenment, or "Self-realization," is familiar to students of the perennial philosophy and transpersonal psychology, as these concepts have spread around the globe in the last century. However, it is what comes next that is still little understood and defines Sri Aurobindo's real genius: how he connects consciousness as experienced by individuals with the larger evolution of consciousness on Earth. In the following paragraph, he begins to explain his understanding of how Consciousness becomes or "creates" Matter, not vice versa. This is the big paradigm shift, the Aurobindonian point of view that is radically new:

> "Consciousness is a fundamental thing, it is the fundamental thing in existence — it is the energy, the action, the movement of consciousness that creates the universe and all that is in it — not only the macrocosm, but the microcosm is nothing but consciousness arranging itself. For instance when consciousness in its movement, or rather a certain stress of movement, forgets itself in the action it becomes an apparently "unconscious" energy; when it forgets itself in the form it becomes the electron, the atom, the material object. In reality it is still consciousness that works in the energy and determines the form and the evolution of form. When it wants to liberate itself, slowly, evolutionarily, out of matter, but still in the form, it emerges as life, as the animal, as man and it can go on evolving itself still farther out of its involution and become something more than mere man". (8)

This one paragraph distills Sri Aurobindo's worldview into a few sentences. He uses the word *involution* to denote the process of how the transcendent Absolute (i.e. the Sachchidananda of the Upanishads) delimits or defines itself to become Matter, and *evolution* is the sequential process through which the consciousness involved in matter slowly releases itself across time in a series of life forms on Earth. In his magnum opus on philosophy, *The Life Divine*, he carefully explained how this cosmological process creates a graded series of "planes of consciousness" that culminate in the physical plane that we perceive as the material universe. We shall return to this in Chapter 9, but it is this metaphysical frame-work that leads to a metapsychology in which spiritual and mystical experiences of various supra-physical phenomenon can be interpreted as correct perceptions of reality rather than fantasies, illusions, or hallucinations.

In the West, the concept of evolution was founded upon Darwin's work on the evolution of species, and ever since then it has been assumed that evolution is primarily a material process driven by random genetic mutation and selective pressure. In contrast, for Sri Aurobindo evolution is primarily about consciousness. Whereas Western science views the evolution of life-forms as the essence of evolution and any growth in consciousness a second-ary result, Sri Aurobindo views consciousness as the essence and changes in life-forms as the supporting result. When looking at the evolutionary tree as described by science, it is striking that consciousness has grown over time—from the rudimentary sig-naling of single cell organisms, to the development of sensations in lower life forms, to the emergence of a central nervous system, to the expression of emotion in many animals, to the appearance of simple forms of language and thinking in higher primates, to the full florescence of a mental consciousness in human beings. The obvious question to ask is what comes next? According to the dogma of materialism, we are not supposed to ask that ques-tion because evolution has no direction or purpose, as it is all due to random genetic mutation and selective pressure. Today human beings rule the world, tomorrow it may be cockroaches or back to amoeba. Evolution is simply about survival, and consciousness is an epiphenomenon of the struggle to survive.

This materialistic interpretation of evolution may be correct — or not. From the perspective of yoga, it has been known for mil-lennia that there are "planes" of consciousness that lie above that of the reasoning mind and the normal state of human consciousness. Sri Aurobindo made a careful study of the ranges of consciousness that lie above the mental awareness of the average human being. Based on this, he proposed that evolution on Earth is directional and is going to manifest these higher planes of consciousness in an increasing number of individuals. In fact, we already see the beginnings of this evolutionary process in mystics and various types of intuitive people who have had unusual experiences of consciousness or paranormal abilities. But this is only a beginning — more is coming, and as consciousness grows this process could even lead to a physical change in the life-form needed to support the full evolution of consciousness on Earth.

That is a really big idea, and one may well wonder how these speculations about the future have any bearing on the here-and-now concerns of psychology and psychiatry? In the next letter, Sri Aurobindo answers that question by applying his theory of consciousness to the experience of an individual "I", or ego, which is eminently relevant to psychology. Note that in this passage his reference to a "progressive coming down" of consciousness is involution, while evolution is what he explicitly describes:

> "Now that is what consciousness is — it is not composed of parts, it is fundamental to being and itself formulates any parts it chooses to manifest — developing them from above downward by a progressive coming down from spiritual levels towards the evolution in matter or formulating them in an upward working in the front by this process that we call evolution. If it chooses to work in you through the sense of ego, you think that it is the clear-cut individual I that does everything; if it begins to release itself from that limited working, then you too either begin to expand your sense of I till it bursts into infinity and no longer exists or to shed it and flower into spiritual wideness. Of course this is not what is spoken of in modern materialistic thought as consciousness, because that thought is governed by science. Science sees consciousness only as a phenomenon which emerges out of inconscient Matter and consists of certain reactions of the system to outward things. But that is phenomenon of consciousness, it is not consciousness itself, it is even only a very small part of the possible phenomena of consciousness and can give no clue to the true nature of Consciousness, the spiritual Reality which is of the very essence of existence".(9)

That, in brief, is an introduction to Sri Aurobindo's thought in simple terms, and as much as possible in his own words. His voluminous writings expand upon these concepts and insights in complex ways, but this is the essence of how he connects metaphysics, cosmology, consciousness, evolution and psychology in a radically new way. Now let us apply his worldview to psychology in particular.

Definition of Psychology

Although Sri Aurobindo never wrote a formal work on psychology, he left enough comments in his writings to piece together the framework for his views. In a manuscript from 1917-18, he stated his basic definition for the field as, "Psychology is the knowledge of consciousness and its operations" (10). In an incomplete manuscript from 1927, he elaborated this definition further:

> "Psychology is the science of consciousness and its status and operations in Nature and, if that can be glimpsed or experienced, its status and operations beyond what is known as Nature".(11)

Notably, Sri Aurobindo uses the word "science" in his definition of psychology. While he was an avowed mystic, he was very rational and endowed with much common sense. As such, he accepted the findings of science as far as they go. His only caveat was that there are things science cannot know. The scientific method is founded upon testing hypotheses via experiments. It can thus only study phenomenon that are measurable and repeatable, which limits its field of knowledge to a certain range of material phenomenon. It cannot study non-material phenomenon, and it also cannot study material phenomenon that are either not measurable or not repeatable. Thus, science cannot say anything about "God" or other purely spiritual phenomenon, and it must remain forever agnostic about the ultimate nature of reality. Unfortunately, there are many scientists who do not understand the limits of scientific knowledge, including even some of the most brilliant ones, such as Stephen

Hawking who confused science with atheism. Science is a method of inquiry that is agnostic about the ultimate nature of reality. Atheism is a faith in the non-existence of God (or any spiritual reality), which belief has not been proven by any scientific experiment and cannot be. Likewise, materialism is a faith where matter is the only reality, which belief also cannot be proven or disproven by the experimental method. Blaise Pascal, one of the founders of the scientific method, understood these issues and addressed them in his famous "Wager", which points out that agnosticism is correct for the moment—because no human being knows for sure whether or not God exists—but has to be wrong in the end, because ultimately God either does or does not exist. He wagered that it is safer to believe in God than not to, and had a profound mystical experience that lead him adopt the Christian faith. Pascal was thus a rational mystic, as was Sri Aurobindo. Both embraced the scientific study of Nature, but also accepted that there are phenomena "beyond what is known as Nature."

Sri Aurobindo showed that he thoroughly grasped all of these issues in another letter to a student who had questions about the relationship between physics and metaphysics, between scientific knowledge and yogic knowledge:

"The difficulty is that you are a non-scientist trying to impose your ideas on the most difficult because most material field of science — physics. It is only if you were a scientist yourself basing your ideas on universally acknowledged scientific facts or else your own discoveries — though even then with much difficulty — that you could get a hearing or your opinion have any weight. Otherwise you open yourself to the accusation of pronouncing in a field where you have no authority, just as the scientist himself does when he pronounces on the strength of his discoveries that there is no God. When the scientist says that "scientifically speaking God is a hypothesis which is no longer necessary" he is talking arrant nonsense — for the existence of God is not and cannot be and never was a scientific hypothesis or problem at all, it is and always has been a spiritual or a metaphysical problem.

You cannot speak scientifically about it at all either pro or con. The metaphysician or the spiritual seeker has a right to point out that it is nonsense; but if you lay down the law to the scientist in the field of science, you run the risk of having the same objection turned against you.

As to the unity of all knowledge, that is a thing *in posse*, not yet *in esse*. The mechanical method of knowledge leads to certain results, the higher method leads to certain others, and they at many points fundamentally disagree. How is the difference to be bridged — for each seems valid in its own field: it is a problem to be solved, but you cannot solve it in the way you propose. Least of all in the field of physics. In psychology one can say that the mechanical or physiological approach takes hold of the thing by the blind end and is the least fruitful of all — for psychology is not primarily a thing of mechanism and measure, it opens to a vast field beyond the physical instrumentalities of the body consciousness. In biology one can get a glimpse of something beyond mechanism, because there is from the beginning a stir of consciousness progressing and organising itself more and more for self-expression. But in physics you are in the very domain of the mechanical law where process is everything and the driving consciousness has chosen to conceal itself with the greatest thoroughness — so that, "scientifically speaking", it does not exist there. One can discover it there only by occultism and Yoga, but the methods of occult science and of Yoga are not measurable or followable by the means of physical science—so the gulf remains still in existence. It may be bridged one day, but the physicist is not likely to be the bridge builder, so it is no use asking him to try what is beyond his province." (12)

Note how careful Sri Aurobindo is in his thinking. He cautions us not to naively assume that scientific knowledge obviates spiritual knowledge, or vice versa. He is frank about the fact that, practically speaking, there is still a gulf between physics and metaphysics that has yet to be bridged—and he did not claim to have bridged that gulf himself. Such humility is the mark of true intelligence. Because Sri Aurobindo understood the limits of different domains of knowledge and ways of knowing, he was able to say:

> "A complete psychology cannot be a pure natural science, but must be a compound of science and metaphysical knowledge".(13)

He elaborated this point further by stating that:

> "A complete psychology must be a complex of the science of mind, its operations and its relations to life and body with intuitive and experimental knowledge of the nature of mind and its relations to supermind and spirit". (14)

> "Psychology may begin as a natural science, but it deals already with supraphysical and must end in a metaphysical enquiry. If one side of the process it studies and its method of enquiry is physical; the other and more important is non-physical; it is a direct observation of mental operations by mind without any regard to their physiological meaning, support, substratum or instrumentation". (15)

These statements form the theoretical basis for consciousness-based psychology (CBP). Sri Aurobindo did not have anything to add to the scientific side of psychology, as he was not a scientist, but as a yogi he had much to add the spiritual and philosophical aspects of psychology. He took a universalist perspective and thus considered figures from different spiritual traditions to have been great yogis, including the Buddha, Lao Tzu, and Jesus Christ, as well as people from the Hindu tradition such as Ramakrishna Paramahamsa, Swami Vivekananda, and Sri Ramana Maharshi. Indeed, he recognized the Buddha as having been a supremely pragmatic and skilled psychologist, and once said:

> "Thus was it possible for the Buddha to attain the state of Nirvana and yet act puissantly in the world, impersonal in

his inner consciousness, in his action the most powerful personality that we know of as having lived and produced results upon earth". (16)

That is high praise, and it should dissuade us from trying to find division and conflict where he saw none. In fact, Sri Aurobindo described his own initial enlightenment in Buddhistic terms, though he arrived at it through meditating for three days with a yogi from the Hindu tradition:

"Now to reach Nirvana was the first radical result of my own Yoga. It threw me suddenly into a condition above and without thought, unstained by any mental or vital movement; there was no ego, no real world — only when one looked through the immobile senses, something perceived or bore upon its sheer silence a world of empty forms, materialised shadows without true substance. There was no One or many even, only just absolutely That, featureless, relationless, sheer, indescribable, unthinkable, absolute, yet supremely real and solely real. This was no mental realisation nor something glimpsed somewhere above, — no abstraction — it was positive, the only positive reality — although not a spatial physical world, pervading, occupying or rather flooding and drowning this semblance of a physical world, leaving no room or space for any reality but itself, allowing nothing else to seem at all actual, positive or substantial. I cannot say there was anything exhilarating or rapturous in the experience, as it then came to me, — the ineffable Ananda I had years afterwards, — but what it brought was an inexpressible Peace, a stupendous silence, an infinity of release and freedom. I lived in that Nirvana day and night before it began to admit other things into itself or modify itself at all, and the inner heart of experience, a constant memory of it and its power to return remained until in the end it began to disappear into a greater Superconsciousness from above. But meanwhile realisation added itself to realisation and fused itself with this original experience. At an early stage the aspect of an illusionary world gave place to one in which illusion is only a small surface phenomenon with an immense Divine Reality behind it and a supreme Divine Reality above it and an intense Divine Reality in the heart of everything that had seemed at first only a cinematic shape or shadow. And this was no reimprisonment in the senses, no diminution or fall from supreme experience, it came rather as a constant heightening and widening of the Truth; it was the spirit that saw objects, not the senses, and the Peace, the Silence, the freedom in Infinity remained always with the world or all worlds only as a continuous incident in the timeless eternity of the Divine."(17)

In this passage, one gets a sense of the richness of Sri Aurobindo's inner life and that he experienced a continual growth or evolution of consciousness. In the course of exploring consciousness and the constitution of matter, Sri Aurobindo discovered that there are an ascending series of levels or layers of consciousness above the reasoning mind. At the height of this scale, there is a plane of consciousness that mediates between the formless, transcendent Infinite and the many worlds of form and creation. He called this plane the Supermind and explained that it had been hinted at in classical Indian yoga philosophy, but never fully elaborated. In his view, the realization of Nirvana or the Self as described in Buddhism and Advaita Vedanta, respectively, is only an initial and static state that can be followed by a dynamic heightening and widening of consciousness that eventually leads to the Supermind.

It is important to understand that in putting forth his formulation of the supramental transformation, Sri Aurobindo was not a confused dualist who did not really understand non-dualism. The pre-trans fallacy that Wilber described in psychology is mirrored by another pre-trans fallacy in yoga, which confuses pre-enlightenment understandings of transformation from post-enlightenment ones. Sri Aurobindo had a post-enlightenment understanding of yoga and approached transformation from a non-dual consciousness. For readers who wish to know more about the evolution of Sri Aurobindo's thought over time, Banerji has written scholarly summaries of the different iterations and formulations of his yoga. Also, Banerji's introduction to the field of integral yoga psychology is the most sophisticated synthesis to date of the scholarly questions at stake, with reference to contemporary discourse on epistemology, integrality, and post-modern critical theory. (18, 19)

Relevance to "Whole-Person Health"

The relevance of these yogic concepts to clinical practice is that the Buddha's methods of mindfulness and meditation have now become standard in healthcare. Over the last few decades, it has become clear that long-term psychotherapy meanders to meager outcomes and is too expensive to deliver at a population level. As a result, a shift towards more structured and short-term models of therapy emerged in psychology. At the same time, epidemiology has revealed that lifestyle, stress, and behavioral factors have a significant impact on physical health in developed nations. Recently, these two developments converged to make yoga, meditation, and mindfulness central to managing symptoms and promoting well-being in healthcare, because they are tangible interventions that can be taught at a large scale. Much research shows that these so-called "mind-body" approaches are broadly effective for a range of both mental and physical health conditions, including depression, anxiety, pain, somatization, and even psychotic symptoms (20-31). While critical research suggests that publication bias may have over-represented the degree of positive effects for mindfulness-based interventions, this bias towards publishing positive results is no worse here than in other fields. (32) Also, there is no question that dialectical behavior therapy (DBT), which was developed by drawing on Zen ideas and practices, has been a major step forward in treating a variety of mental health conditions characterized by impulsivity and emotional dysregulation, and has stimulated the development of other competing models that often incorporate similar elements.(33, 34)

Precisely because of the strength of all this research, clinical experience, and patient feedback, private insurance in the United

States now pays for training in mindfulness-based stress reduction (MBSR), and government-funded treatment for veterans has set this whole-person approach as the overarching framework for *all* healthcare. (35) This is a dramatic shift in paradigm, and it has brought with it more attention to other aspects of the "whole person" as well, including their culture, values, life-goals, religion, spirituality, gender identity and sexual orientation. In retrospect, it is easy to see why the Buddha's methods have been so easily adapted into clinical settings, and it is because his worldview is agnostic and focused on direct experience, rather than faith or theology, which is an inherently patient-centered approach. Actually, the eightfold path is a masterpiece of existential CBT (cognitive-behavior therapy) that teaches people how to lead a balanced life, and much of contemporary psychotherapy is simply an elaboration and application of these principles to a specific clinical contexts and conditions. However, the widespread diffusion of yoga, meditation, and mindfulness across healthcare settings now raises two interesting issues: first, what happened in yoga in the 2,500 years after the Buddha; and second, what will clients and clinicians do when they start to experience phenomenon of consciousness that are not described in either Western psychology or even in Buddhism? For mindfulness is simply the process of exploring awareness in an open-ended, non-judgmental way but — what is the content that such a process can reveal? Inevitably, such a journey to wholeness must ultimately include *all of consciousness*, the scope of which is potentially not only vast but infinite. This is where Sri Aurobindo enters the picture, because he literally wrote the book on what happened in yoga in the 2,500 years after the Buddha, and what consciousness is and can become.

As we start down this path of learning about Sri Aurobindo's yoga as it relates to the clinical concerns of psychology and psychiatry, a few contextualizing statements are needed. First, Sri Aurobindo's yoga is a growth-oriented approach to living and was never intended to be a treatment for any specific health condition, whether mental or physical. It is thus best understood as a worldview and life-view which can incorporate a wide range of approaches to healing from *both* science and spirituality. Second, because Sri Aurobindo sees Matter as an expression of Spirit, he finds no fundamental contradiction or opposition between the two, and therefore accepts whatever knowledge medical science has to offer the quest for health and wellbeing. As a result, throughout this book we will assume that medications and other neuropsychiatric treatments (such as ECT, TMS, and vagal nerve stimulation) have a valuable role to play in the treatment of mental health conditions, as does research in neuroscience and neurobiology. However, since this is a book about the non-local aspects of consciousness, the focus will be on the latter.

Third, we take it for granted that spiritual and mystical experiences can be normal, healthy, and central to growth. There is an old debate in psychology about mysticism and "madness," but since transpersonal psychology has resolved this at the theoretical level, we have moved this debate to the Appendix, where we explain why Sri Aurobindo was mentally healthy. This topic may be of academic interest to those who wish to know more about the history of psychology and psychiatry, but the main point is that contemporary clinicians have fairly reliable (although not perfect) diagnostic criteria that help them distinguish normal mysticism and spirituality from mental illness. However, it should be acknowledged that people can have a complex mix of *both* mystical experiences and psychiatric symptoms, and this is addressed in Chapter 12.

Once one has been able to put these three contextual factors in the right perspective, then it should be easy to appreciate the genius of Sri Aurobindo's contributions to transpersonal psychology. He had a detailed understanding of the evolving soul and the purpose of rebirth (Chapter 3); a sophisticated description of the ego and its relationship with the soul (Chapter 4); a nuanced model of how occult factors interact with biological and psychosocial mechanisms in possession states (Chapter 5); deep appreciation for the cultural and social dimensions of spiritual psychology (Chapter 6); a complete theory of subliminal and supra-rational forms of cognition (Chapters 7-9); and the most comprehensive yogic map of consciousness developed to date (Chapter 10). Along the way, we will see that he also grasped the importance of emotional and cognitive development in childhood, knew that delirium is an organic brain condition, and even pegged the essence of affect dysregulation decades before this syndrome was accurately defined in Western psychology (Chapter 4). In short, he was an acute observer of human nature who developed a whole system of psychology based on his yogic understanding of consciousness.

Two other areas where Sri Aurobindo excelled were in his conceptualization of mind-body medicine and the psychology of worldview. A lingering weakness in the current "mind-body" paradigm is the implicit suggestion that there is a direct connection between the "mind," or cognitive apparatus, and the "body." Long ago, Sri Aurobindo explained that there is a vital plane of consciousness that mediates between the mind and the body, and this is centrally involved in emotion, motivation, desire, impulses, attachment, basic drives, and even physical health. We shall return to this in Chapters 5 and 15, when we examine how Sri Aurobindo's understanding of the vital describes the meeting point among cognitive-behavior therapy, mindfulness, psychodynamic therapy, and psychosomatic conditions. While the importance of affect and the limbic system may now seem like common sense to clinicians today, note that the terminology of both "mind-body" medicine and DSM diagnoses still omit the word "emotion," which is a mistake in communicating to the public what we mean. Sri Aurobindo had already worked all this out, plus coined the accurate yet inoffensive term of "an unstable vital" to describe affect dysregulation over 100 years ago.

Sri Aurobindo was also far ahead of the West is in the psychology of worldview. That is a relatively new term that takes a broad look at how people make meaning of life. (36-38) This approach appears now to be morphing into a measurement-based reincarnation of older schools such as existential psychology, humanistic psychology, and the psychology of religion. However, if one really wants to look at the issue of worldview, then one has to grapple seriously with India, which has a continuous tradition of exploring metapsychology that dates back at least 3,000 years. Recently, this ancient field of inquiry has finally thrown off the vestiges of colonialism that subjected it to the West, and started to reclaim its own roots. This has lead to a series of academic conferences, several textbooks, and a handful of journal articles that address how Western and Indian psychology can complement each other. (39) The authors of this book have contributed to those efforts, which were initially launched and organized by a colleague, Dr. Cornelissen. (40) While the field of Indian psychology certainly contains more points of view than just that of Sri Aurobindo, there is no single perspective within it that is more innovative and important than that of Sri Aurobindo. Why? Because he is one of those rare thinkers who created a new worldview, complete with a new cosmology, model of consciousness, theory of evolution, and a framework for psychology.

Last but not least, there is one area of life and thought where Sri Aurobindo stands out as absolutely unparalleled, and that is in his support of female-friendly spirituality. Long before Western academia became interested in matriarchal religion, Sri Aurobindo had already formulated a new theology based on the Mahashakti or Supreme Goddess, and he put this into practice by recognizing that human women can be masters of yoga. Indeed, he even let one such woman — Mirra Alfassa, aka "the Mother"— run their co-created ashram. That is why in this book we use statements from the Mother to represent his point of view, because he had done the same. In the Appendix we analyze the history of how Sri Aurobindo's remarkable demonstration of spiritual, psychological and social health was wrongly pathologized by materialist critics who were biased against mystics, but we here we leave that sad past in the past, where it belongs. The world has moved on, and it is evolving in precisely the direction that Sri Aurobindo predicted. Also, humanity is now facing a climate crisis of epic proportions, and increasingly there is a sense that the only way to secure a brighter future for us all is a global evolution and transformation of consciousness. Thus, now more than ever Sri Aurobindo's message of hope, unity, and possibility is sorely needed, and his work deserves to be read as a treasure of humanity that belongs not just to India or people with a Y chromosome, but to everyone everywhere—and to the whole Earth.

> *Masters of living, free from the bonds of Thought,*
> *Who are overseers of Fate and Chance and Will*
> *And experts of the theorem of world-need,*
> *Can see the Idea, the Might that change Time's course...*
>
> Savitri, *pg. 53-54*

References

1. CWSA 36, pg. 547
2. Ibid
3. CWSA 28, pg. 19
4. Ibid, pg. 16
5. CWSA 27, pg. 526
6. James, William: The Varieties of Religious Experience, Penguin, USA, 1902, pg. 519
7. CWSA 28, pg. 15
8. Ibid, pg. 22
9. Ibid, pg. 23
10. CWSA 12, pg. 305
11. Ibid, pg. 316-317
12. CWSA 28, pg. 395-396
13. CWSA 12, pg. 305
14. Ibid.
15. Ibid, pg. 306
16. CWSA 21-22, pg. 33
17. CWSA 35, pg. 249-250
18. Banerjee, Debasish: Seven Quartets of Becoming: A Transformational Yoga Psychology Based on the Diaries of Sri Aurobindo, DK Printworld (P) Ltd, India,1st Edition, 2012.
19. Banerjee, Debasish (editor): Integral Yoga Psychology: Metaphysics & Transformation as Taught by Sri Aurobindo, Lotus Press, Wisconsin, 2020. See pp. 5-26 and 61-82.
20. Hempel, S, Taylor, SL, Marshall, NJ, Miake-Lye, IM, Beroes, JM, Shanman, R, Solloway, MR, Shekelle, PG. Evidence Map of Mindfulness. VA-ESP Project #05-226; 2014
21. The Meeting of Meditative Disciplines and Western Psychology: A Mutually Enriching Dialogue Walsh, et. al., American Psychologist 2006

22. Mindfulness-Based Therapy: A Comprehensive Meta-Analysis Khoury, B., et. al. Clinical Psychology Review, 2013

23. Mindfulness-Based Interventions for Psychiatric Disorders: A Systematic Review and Meta-Analysis Goldberg, S.B., et. al. Clinical Psychology Review, 2018

24. Mindfulness Interventions Creswell, J.D., Annual Review of Psychology, 2017

25. Mindfulness Training and Physical Health: Mechanisms and Outcomes Creswell, J.D., et. al., Psychosomatic Medicine, 2019

26. Mindfulness and Cognitive–Behavioral Interventions for Chronic Pain: Differential Effects on Daily Pain Reactivity and Stress Reactivity Davis, M.C., et. al., Journal of Consulting and Clinical Psychology, 2015

27. Mindfulness Meditation and The Immune System: A Systematic Review of Randomized Controlled Trials Black, D.S., et. al. Annals of the New York Academy of Sciences, 2016

28. Meditation or Exercise for Preventing Acute Respiratory Infection: A Randomized Controlled Trial Barrett, B., et. al., Annals of Family Medicine, 2012 http://www.bpddemystified.com/treatments/psychotherapy/bpd-specific-psychotherapies/

29. The Neuroscience of Mindfulness Meditation Tan, Y.-Y., et. al., Nature Reviews Neuroscience, 2015

30. How Do Mindfulness-Based Cognitive Therapy and Mindfulness-Based Stress Reduction Improve Mental Health and Wellbeing? A Systematic Review and Meta-Analysis of Mediation Studies Gu, J., et. al. Clinical Psychology Review, 2015

31. Effectiveness of Online Mindfulness-Based Interventions in Improving Mental Health: A Review and Meta-Analysis of Randomised Controlled Trials Spijkerman, M.P.J., et. al., Clinical Psychology Review, 2016

32. Coronado-Montoya S, Levis AW, Kwakkenbos L, Steele RJ, Turner EH, et al. Reporting of Positive Results in Randomized Controlled Trials of Mindfulness-Based Mental Health Interventions. PLOS ONE 11(4): e0153220, 2016

33. Linehan MM, Wilks Cr. Course and Evolution of Dialectical Behavior Therapy. Amer J of Psychotherapy, Vol. 69, No. 2, 2015, pp 97-110

34. Choi-Kain LW, Finch EF, Masland SR, Jenkins JA, Unruh BT. What Works in the Treatment of Borderline Personality Disorder, *Curr Behav Neurosci Rep.* 2017;4(1):21-30.

35. See va.gov/wholehealth.

36. Josephson, A. M., & Peteet, J. R. (Eds.). (2004). Handbook of Spirituality and Worldview in Clinical Practice. American Psychiatric Publishing, Inc.

37. Koltko-Rivera, M. E. The Psychology of Worldviews. Review of General Psychology, 8(1), 3–58, 2004.

38. Johnson, K., Hill, E.D., & Cohen, A. Integrating the Study of Culture and Religion: Toward a Psychology of Worldview. Social and Personality Psychology Compass, 5, 137-152, 2011.

39. See www.en.wikipedia.org, Indian psychology.

40. Cornelissen M, Misra G, Varma S, eds. (2014). Foundations and Applications of Indian psychology (2nd ed.). Delhi: Dorling Kindersley.

2
History of Consciousness — Based Psychology

There Mind, a splendid sun of vision's rays,
Shaped substance by the glory of its thoughts
And moved amidst the grandeur of its dreams.
Imagination's great ensorcelling rod
Summoned the unknown and gave to it a home,
Outspread luxuriantly in golden air
Truth's iris-coloured wings of fantasy,
Or sang to the intuitive heart of joy
Wonder's dream-notes that bring the Real close..

Savitri, *pg. 327*

If there is to be a rapprochement between Sri Aurobindo's approach to yoga and contemporary psychology, then we must trace out the various lines of work within Western psychology that are relevant to consciousness-based psychology (CBP). This chapter will review some of these key historical developments, which include the concept of an unconscious or subconscious, the scientific study of meditation, transpersonal psychology, parapsychology, and a more socio-cultural approach to psychology that encompasses post-modern and critical theory.

Sigmund Freud (1886-1939) always looms large in any discussion of the "unconscious," because of the dramatic influence that his school of psychoanalysis had on the theory and practice of Western psychotherapy. However, while Freud's work was undoubtedly significant, and we will return to Sri Aurobindo's comments on it in Chapter 17, it is also important to acknowledge the work of other Western psychologists who were more Aurobindonian in spirit. For example, we have already touched on William James's seminal work on *The Varieties of Religious Experience*, which is entirely consonant with CBP. James (1842-1910) was acquainted with Buddhist thought and the basics of yoga philosophy, and was steeped in the American tradition of transcendentalism. However, even before James there were pre-Freudian psychologists both in the United States and Europe who were strongly influenced by Indian philosophy (in the United States, partially via transcendentalist writers like Emerson, Thoreau and Whitman; in Europe by the German idealists like Hegel). The mid-19th century psychologist and philosopher, Gustav Fechner (1801-1887), who is considered to be the founder of experimental psychology, had a complex understanding of subconscious and superconscious planes of consciousness, as well as an evolutionary worldview. His psycho-physical principles were intended to provide a kind of panpsychist, non-dualistic understanding of the relationship between mind and matter, but by the 20th century were used to bolster materialist ideas instead.

An immediate European precursor to Freud, who is now thought to have had a more profound and neurologically accurate view of the "unconscious," is Pierre Janet (1859-1947). Ernest Rossi, a disciple of hypnotherapist Milton Erickson (1901-1980), studied Janet's work and collected a large amount of neurological research showing its applicability to modern psychotherapy. One of Rossi's major themes is the prevalence of different phases of consciousness throughout the day and night. He makes an analogy to the waking, dream and sleep states (analogous to the surface, subliminal and superconscient of Sri Aurobindo) and notes that we have minor versions of these shifts throughout the day. Ayurveda has similar ideas about phases of consciousness throughout the day, noting times we are more open to subliminal and superconscious influences, as well as gaps such as dawn and twilight when we are more open to the Self. Some of Erickson's healings are related to this understanding, and Rossi documents these in fascinating ways. He was inspired by Janet's notion of dissociation, which in some ways is distantly related to Avidya and provides an understanding of the various levels of consciousness which is closer to that of Indian philosophy than Freud's ideas were.

Transpersonal Psychology

Carl G. Jung (1875-1961), who can be called the first transpersonal psychologist in the West, conceived of growth as a process of shifting the centre of personality away from the "little ego" towards the greater reality of the Self. Roberto Assagioli (1888-1974), who developed psychosynthesis as an unique approach to psychology, went even further and asserted that the direct experience of the self or pure self-awareness is true, and that psychology should study people both as personalities and as souls. Shirazi notes that both Jung and Assagioli considered the soul (Self, Higher/Transpersonal Self) as the cardinal means for integrating the total psyche. Their notions of the "soul" are not as clear as those of Sri Aurobindo, but there is nonetheless a striking parallel in how they attempted to transform the personality using the soul/psyche as the catalyst. (1)

After the pioneering work of Jung and Assagioli, many other critics of mainstream psychology noted that it did not deal with that which is uniquely human — the striving for growth and self-development, and the attainment of the higher values of life. This deficiency lead to the rise of Humanistic psychology whose chief protagonist, Abraham Maslow (1908-1970), distinguished two broad types of human needs — fundamental physiological needs which are the legacy of humanity's atavistic past, and meta-needs that encompass moral, aesthetic, intellectual and other similar needs for self-actualization or the attainment of one's highest potentials. Towards the end of his life, Maslow conceived of human growth even beyond self-actualization:

> "I consider Humanistic, Third Force psychology to be transitional, a preparation for a still 'higher' Fourth Psychology, transpersonal, transhuman, centered in the cosmos rather than human needs and interests, going beyond humanness, identity, self-actualization, and the like". (2)

This higher psychology began to take shape in the form of transpersonal psychology in the late 1960s, and since then has taken up the study of areas such as higher states of consciousness, ultimate values, highest meanings, self-transcendence, mystical experiences, etc. In an overview of Sri Aurobindo's relevance to psychology, A.S. Dalal pointed to three landmark developments beyond the boundaries of traditional psychology that have taken place as a result of the transpersonal perspective (3):

> Psychology is being redefined as the study of consciousness in the deeper sense of a pluridimensional reality that is in consonance with Sri Aurobindo's thought where there are ranges of consciousness above and below the mind;
> The traditional methods of psychology (introspective study of mind, observation and quantification of behavior, analytical probing into the unconscious) have been supplemented by experiential methods like meditative and mystical techniques, use of psychedelic drugs, body techniques and effects of music and sound on the psyche. The new approach is more in the nature of a "self-knowledge psychology" and as such one must proceed in it from the knowledge of oneself to the knowledge of others; and
> The Ego needs to be replaced by a Beyond-Ego principle so that one can discover one's true nature. A dis-identification from the ego leads to an awakening and development of the real personality.

In 1975, transpersonal psychology took a major step forward with the appearance of Ken Wilber's *The Spectrum of Consciousness* (4), which was the first systematic approach to show how the consciousness of mystical states fits in with the consciousness of neurosis and psychosis. Wilber used the analogy of the spectrum of light where many different frequencies make up the totality of visible light. Similarly, Wilber conceptualized that consciousness is composed of many different bands or levels. In Wilber's holarchy, the developmental stages (studied along psychodynamic, object-relational and cognitive lines) described in conventional psychology and "the higher stages of consciousness" described in contemplative traditions such as yoga psychology, each find their distinctive places. In the Wilberian paradigm, the contemplative stages of development are neither sequential, parallel, nor alternative to the conventional stages of development, and there can be complex interactions between the two. Thus, a person who is considered to be outwardly eccentric or even psychotic may at the same time have considerable spiritual development. (5) This divergence means that the oversimplified two-step model of development, which places psychological development first followed by spiritual development, is incorrect.

A necessary corollary of the transpersonal paradigm is that one cannot simplistically generalize the characteristics of one stage to other stages. Unfortunately, this is exactly what psychologists tend to do, creating what Wilber described as a "pre-trans fallacy"— a confusion of pre-personal structures with trans-personal structures just because both are non-rational. Thus, on the one hand we find pre-personal structures (phantasmic, magical, and mythical) being raised to trans-personal status by Jung when he equates them with mystic and spiritual experiences. On the other hand, trans-personal structures including higher mystic experiences were reduced to pre-personal infantilisms by Freud. It has been rightly observed that the pre/trans fallacy is a very significant theoretical construct and is likely to rank as one of Wilber's most enduring contributions to clinical practice. (6)

In contrast to Wilber's structural-hierarchical paradigm, Michael Washburn has formulated a dynamic-dialectical paradigm, which in a way seeks to connect Jungian thought to the wider transpersonal field. He refined Jung's theory to construct a bipolar model of the psyche: the egoic pole and the non-egoic pole, the respective seats of the two poles being the Ego and the dynamic ground (so called as it is the source of all psychic dynamics viz. libido, general psychic energy, spirit and hence is conceptualized to represent the Self). Human development takes place as a result of the dialectical interplay between two psychic poles. Initially, there is a dominance of the dynamic ground (thesis), followed by the dominance of the ego (antithesis), leading finally to an integration (synthesis). Contrary to Wilber, Washburn proposed that the pre-personal and the transpersonal reflect the very same potentials at two different levels. The non-egoic resources (dynamic ground) can be expressed before the ego develops and look pre-egoic or they can be expressed after the ego develops and look trans-egoic. (7)

The perspective on human growth implicit in Sri Aurobindo's thought contains the basic elements of both Wilber's paradigm and Washburn's paradigm, although it also surpasses them as neither Wilber nor Washburn have given the soul its due place in their paradigms. Teklinski describes how in his zeal to give more credence to the Impersonal or Transcendent Reality, Wilber relegated the individual poise of the soul to an inferior mythic status. Similarly, Washburn's non-egoic ground is inherited and universal and cannot be interpreted as being personal in any regard like the soul.(8) In fact, the seed-ideas of Sri Aurobindo's consciousness paradigm lie scattered across the works of a host of transpersonal thinkers including Jung, Wilber, Washburn, Hameed Ali, Assagioli, Stanislav Grof, the modern exponents of body-centered transpersonal approaches, and the practitioners of transpersonal psychoanalytic psychotherapy and existential transpersonal psychotherapy. As Brant Cortright commented: "All of modern psychotherapy may be seen to be an intuitive groping toward a deeper source of wisdom than the surface self". (9)

It is in this context that Aldous Huxley's (1894-1963) notion of the "perennial philosophy" became a core transpersonal terminology that refers to a range of spiritual experiences that have been recorded throughout history and across different cultures. Though different researchers interpret the "perennial philosophy" in different ways, there is a unanimous transpersonal view that a complete concept of mental health must include both psychological and spiritual dimensions. In an overview of transpersonal research, Cortright listed some basic assumptions that define a transpersonal approach, chief of which are:

> Our essential nature is spiritual. The spiritual source supports and upholds the psychological structures of the self;

> Consciousness is multidimensional,
> Human beings have valid urges towards spiritual seeking,
> expressed as a search for wholeness through deepening individual, social and transcendent awareness.(10)

Cortright showed that with the growth of transpersonal psychology, the psychic conflict emphasized by psychoanalysis has been re-contextualized so that it is no longer the central feature of psychological life:

"What is central in transpersonal psychology is the movement and growth of consciousness — its development, vicissitudes, and varied expressions in its divine unfolding. Consciousness then becomes the proper subject of transpersonal psychology. Conventional psychology studies consciousness at various levels and stages of self-development, that is, as consciousness is conditioned, expressed, and modified by the structures of the self. Spiritual systems study consciousness insofar as it transcends or encompasses more than the self, that is, in its unconditioned levels. Transpersonal psychology studies consciousness in all its manifestations, from its origin in the infant and the various developmental derailments and pathological manifestations that may occur in its growth to full consolidation in a mature, cohesive self, all the way through the myriad developments of spiritual realization". (11)

However, despite attempts by transpersonal psychology to shift contemporary interest to consciousness studies, it was really David Chalmers's article on the hard problem of consciousness (published in the December 1995 issue of *Scientific American)* that had more effect on the scientific community in terms of identifying consciousness as a central issue. Other researchers and practitioners outside the school of transpersonal psychology have also had a major influence in promoting spiritual and consciousness-based paradigms. For instance, Jon Kabat-Zinn, founder of MBSR (mindfulness-based stress reduction) earned great popularity with his practice. (12) Similarly, other developments that have expanded the scope of conventional psychology include ACT (acceptance and commitment therapy), DBT (dialectical and behavioural therapy), MCBT (mindful CBT), and other mindfulness based practices that are now popular in mental health centres. Loch Kelly has demonstrated how non-dual therapies are gaining acceptance even outside the transpersonal realm. (13)

Finally, interest in transpersonal psychology and Buddhist practices has lead to other innovative developments, such as Dream Yoga, which works with the phenomenon of lucid dreaming by subjects (stylishly called oneironauts) who are aware they are dreaming in the midst of dreaming, and can even direct their dreams. Research in this field, which was initiated by Keith Hearne in 1970s and later carried to sophistication by Stephen LaBerge, shows that lucid dreaming can be cultivated and may be useful in dream anxiety disorder, insomnia, parasomnias and PTSD. It can also be a useful tool for personal growth. (14)

Neurobiology of Meditation

In a significant development, Western scientists began studying the effects of meditative practices from the 1950s on. In 1973, the Menninger Foundation recorded Swami Rama as proving the existence of consciousness awareness in deep sleep, which is delta wave-dominated sleep. (15) Herbert Benson's seminal work, *The Relaxation Response* (1975) was the first comprehensive document recording the benefits of meditation through changes in metabolism, heart rate, blood pressure, respiration and brain chemistry. In 1977, the American Psychiatric Association officially acknowledged the need for a critical examination of the clinical effectiveness of meditation; and in 1979, Jon Kabat-Zinn founded the Mindfulness-Based Stress Reduction (MBSR) program at the University of Massachusetts, which has greatly stimulated interest in the study of meditation. In India, the Advanced Centre of Yoga at NIMHANS has been working extensively on the clinical benefits of mindfulness meditation, as well as the neurobiology of consciousness along the spectrum from illness to wellbeing.

Since the 1980s, Jonathan Smith has been writing on the need to define meditative states. Through the Mind and Life Conferences and work at universities like UCLA, Brown, Emory and elsewhere (particularly Dan Siegel and his "interpersonal neurobiology") there are now emerging agreements regarding different forms of meditation, which include (a) concentration, (b) open awareness, and (c) compassion or "kind attention". The further state of "non-dual awareness" is also part of this understanding. In 1984, Shapiro articulated a working definition of meditation as "a family of techniques which have in common a conscious attempt to focus attention in a nonanalytical way and an attempt not to dwell on discursive, ruminating thoughts". (16)

The research on meditation has yielded some interesting findings in terms of neurobiology. For instance, alpha waves (8-13 Hz) are considered to signify the gateway to meditation but are *not* increased in cultural trance states (such as tongue-piercing or walking on fire without pain), while theta waves (4-8 Hz) are associated with deeper states of meditation. Delta waves (up to 4 Hz) may represent the bridge to the cosmic consciousness. There have been reports of Tibetan Buddhist monks demonstrating a correlation between gamma waves (25-100 Hz) and transcendental states, though this needs more substantial research to be validated. (17) In the 1990s, Newberg and d'Acquili (18,19) conducted neuroimaging studies of Christian nuns and Tibetan monks who were in the midst of unitive experiences induced by intensive prayer or meditation, and they identified brain circuits that seem to be involved in these states of awareness. Part of this circuitry involves de-activation of an area in the parietal lobe that helps with temporal and spatial orientation. Based on this, Newberg and d'Acquili proposed two sets of "operators" or neural circuits, the causal operators and the holistic operators. While the causal operators allow our usual perception of causality or baseline reality in a world accessed through sensory perception and reason, the holistic operators allow the perception of wholeness in the midst of diversity. Without dismissing one set of operators or the other, both can be considered as representing complementary versions of reality.

These neurophysiological correlates may explain some of the key characteristics of unitive experiences, which are marked by loss of the sense of self, loss of the sense of space and time, the perception of infinity, and the perception of impersonality and/or undifferentiated oneness.(20)

Similarly, since 2008 Zoran Josipovic has been conducting research on how some practitioners achieve non-dual states of awareness. He believes the brain has an extrinsic network that deals with external tasks, and an intrinsic or default network that is active in introspective practices. Usually only one of these networks is active at a given time, but some meditators have the capacity to keep both the networks active during meditation, which may lead to the harmonious feeling of oneness or non-duality.(21). Neuro-scientist and Buddhist teacher John Yates makes another distinction, almost perfectly parallel to the "left mode" and "right mode" of McGilchrist – between "Selective attention" (narrow, detached, conceptual, quantitative, linear, analytic, roughly left hemisphere) and "Peripheral awareness" (wide, immersed, intuitive, qualitative, metaphorical, roughly right hemisphere). (22) This also relates to Ernest Rossi's discoveries about brain rhythms shifting throughout the day and night. In a way, we "shift" between being more outer (selective attention, narrow, detached) and inner (more intuitive, "holistic" etc), with further distinctions being focused more on the "head" brain (mental), "heart" brain (higher vital) and "gut" brain"/enteric nervous system (central vital). (23)

Most recently, Helminiak has written a scholarly reappraisal of the neuropsychological research on spiritual experience, entitled *Brain, Consciousness and God: A Lonerganian Integration*.(24) This work highlights that a variety of neuronal networks are involved in self-referential experience, such as the "default-mode network" identified by Raichle (25), that is involved in the sense of oneself. Helminiak makes the interesting observation that this network is located in the inner regions of the cortex, as if the neuronal basis for the sense of self is stored safely in the inner folds of the cortex. Meditation affects the functioning of this default-mode network and induces lasting changes, so that one can have a more focused and centered state of mind that is calm and free from distractions.

Also, Vago and Silbersweig describe a number of other integrative networks in the brain pertinent to different kinds of meditation, all involved in the experience of self. They view the subtle experience at the high point of meditative practice as a sort of meta-awareness—much like an acquired skill where awareness itself becomes the object of awareness. They summarize the major effects of meditation with the acronym, S-ART: self-awareness, self-regulation and self-transcendence, which means to know oneself, to manage oneself and to move beyond oneself. (26) Yet, Helminiak opines that despite such sophisticated neurological research, what has not yet been touched is the unitive experience itself, i.e., that high point of meditation in which consciousness becomes pure consciousness, a fully non-objectified and non-reflecting self-presence in contrast to consciousness as intentional and directed towards some object. He concludes that while consciousness depends on brain functioning to some degree, consciousness per se is a different kind of reality in comparison to the spatio-temporal array of brain anatomy and physiology. (27)

Finally, the 14th Dalai Lama has also been interested in neuroscience, and since 1987 has engaged in dialogues with groups of scientists organized by the Mind and Life Institute. He has encouraged scientists to examine advanced Tibetan spiritual practitioners to see what effects of their practice could benefit the general mass of humanity.(28) In addition, there have been attempts to relate the non-dual awareness gained in meditation to therapy and personal growth by psychotherapists, such as John Prendergast and Loch Kelly. Prendergast traces the convergence of healing and spiritual awakening in the depths of the heart.(29) Loch Kelly draws from neuroscience, psychology and ancient wisdom traditions to show how to live a life from the foundation of an open heart and peaceful mind.(30)

Parapsychology and Consciousness Studies

A related line of work that has contributed to a larger definition of consciousness is parapsychology. The field has its roots in the 19th century, when no less than William James supported the opening of the American Society for Psychical Research, in 1885. James understood the importance of the attempt to study paranormal phenomenon from a scientific perspective, and his views on such phenomenon were in part influenced by those of his friend, FWH Myers (1843-1901). Myers opined that there is a central core of consciousness beyond mind and body, which survives the death of the physical body, and is potentially the integrative, harmonizing guide of our entire nature. He viewed our individual consciousness as a focalization of universal planes of consciousness, and felt the entire universe is undergoing an evolutionary process. Evidently, this is quite similar to Sri Aurobindo's view. His use of the term "subliminal self," in his treatise "Human Personality and its Survival of Bodily Death," (31) as a deep region of the subconscious mind that accounted for paranormal events, antedated Sri Aurobindo's usage of that term for the inner being. The inner being described by Sri Aurobindo is of course different from the subconscious and is connected with the cosmic consciousness though it is also responsible for many of our paranormal experiences.

Precisely because it threatens the materialist paradigm, no field of psychology has suffered more bias and discrimination than parapsychology. Over the years, parapsychologists have been accused of being frauds and idiots, and their work has been grossly underfunded and heavily over-criticized. While it is true that early parapsychological research had methodological flaws that weakened its findings, these have been addressed over the last 50 years, to the point that parapsychology research is now among the most rigorous fields of science. Salmon and Maslow (2007) wrote an excellent review of parapsychological research from the perspective of CBP, which documents some of the completely unscientific denials of parapsychology that scientists have voiced over the years, as well as reviews that establish contemporary parapsychology research is methodologically sound. (32) Among its valid findings are that "psi" (also called paranormal, anomalous, or non-local) phenomenon such as extrasensory perception (ESP), telepathy, precognition and the direct influence of mind over matter known as psychokinesis (PK), are all scientifically established facts. While science cannot explain *how* such phenomenon occur, rigorous experiments have proven that they *do* happen—at least in small ways and under certain conditions. One of the most convincing and amazing set of findings was described by Braud, in his paper on retro-active intentional influence.(33) The most important conclusion from parapsychological research is that consciousness is non-local, meaning not solely generated by and limited to the brain.

Readers who are interested in learning more about contemporary parapsychology research should study the work of Dean Radin, who is at the Institute of Noetic Sciences in California. (34) However, perhaps the single best work on parapsychology to date is that of Dr. K.R. Rao (2005). (35) Trained at Duke in the early 1960s, he went on to establish the first parapsychology laboratory in India. His work has the advantage of looking at parapsychology both from the perspective of Western science, as well as in light of Indian traditions such as yoga and Buddhism. Rao explains that while parapsychology in Indian parlance can be called the science of *siddhis* (a yogic term for a power or ability, such as the direct influence of mind over matter), in Western description it is the study of cognitive anomalies. (36) The term "cognitive anomalies" finds acceptance because psi phenomena deal with information acquisition and are therefore "cognitive," but as they do not fit with current materialistic notions of cognition are better considered as "anomalies." Rao laments that the sharp distinction between the natural and supernatural, and between subjectivity and objectivity, does not allow for a full exploration of psi phenomena in the West. In contrast, CBP offers a fresh direction for the study of psi phenomena because it does not accept such false dichotomies. For example, Sri Aurobindo's description of the "inner being," or subliminal personality, offers plausible explanations for many psi phenomena, and some of the really anomalous psi phenomena (anomalous in the true sense of the term, like hallucinations and pseudo-intuitions, and not just phenomenon that challenge materialism by being non-local) may be traced to the "intermediate zone" between the subliminal personality and surface personality (see Chapter 11).

Combining the insights of both transpersonal psychology and parapsychology, the Scientific and Medical Network (a worldwide professional community) has advocated that both rational analysis and intuitive insights should be combined in order to deepen understanding in science, medicine and education. In 2001, this group drew up a "Manifesto for an Integral Science of Consciousness," which states that there may be more to consciousness than localized brain processes, and proposed a new framework based on an expanded set of postulates that transcend yet include those of modern science:

> The universe is an organic multileveled interconnected unity with manifest and unmanifest aspects pervaded by life and consciousness.
> The evolving and self-organizing universe reflects intelligence, order, creativity, meaning and purpose.
> Science cannot be separated from metaphysics.
> Knowledge can be acquired not only by means of sense perception but also intuitively - there are degrees of knowing.
> Explanations need not be restricted to the physical realm.
> Consciousness is fundamental and formative - it drives evolution from within.
> Life is experienced by us as energy and consciousness.
> Consciousness can exist independently of physical substrates.
> Human consciousness may in some form survive the death of the brain.
> The universe is participatory (beyond the duality of subject and object) and the human mind is one of the ways in which it knows itself. (37)

In a similar vein, since 1999 Ed Kelly has been conducting a major study with a group of psychologists, parapsychologists, physicists and philosophers (both Eastern and Western). The group is led by Michael Murphy, with yearly meetings at Esalen, and has published two books—*Irreducible Mind* in 2007 (38) and *Beyond Physicalism* in 2015. (39) Eric Weiss had initially suggested the group focus more on Whitehead instead of Sri Aurobindo, as scientists would be more likely to accept a Western philosopher. (40) However, Eric Weiss himself wrote a chapter in *Beyond Physicalism* about Whitehead and Sri Aurobindo, and explained that Sri Aurobindo's work is more profound than that of Whitehead. In that same book, Murphy wrote a chapter on "evolutionary panentheism," which resembles Sri Aurobindo's philosophy of integral non-dualism (Purna Advaita).

Postmodernism and Beyond

The last line of psychological thought that is consonant with CBP concerns itself with the social, political, and cultural dimensions of consciousness. The emergence of post-modern critical theory, championed by French thinkers such as Foucault, sought to deconstruct the hidden power agendas embedded within cultural discourse, and highlight the reality of social and cultural relativity. As Wilber has explained, while modernism dealt with scientific empiricism and logic, postmodernism advocated epistemological pluralism. Postmodernism was a reaction against modernity, or at times a counterbalance to modernity and at times a continuation of modernity by other means. (41) The scientific empiricism of modernity was founded on sensory data and championed by the natural sciences, in the hopes that this would facilitate universal verification. When the reaction against modernity took place, postmodernism attempted to deconstruct scientific empiricism not primarily by surpassing it with mystical wisdom, but by undermining science in its own premise. The denouement of empiricism changed with postmodernism, and it became a broad empiricism (in Wilberian terms) to encompass not only sensory experience but also mental experience (approached by logic, mathematics, semiotics, phenomenology and hermeneutics) and spiritual experience (approached by experiential mysticism). (42) Welwood, in continuity with Wilber, described an "inner empiricism", which would be a hallmark of a "self-conscious psychology". (43) However, extreme postmodernism became too ironical when it deemed all truth to be a subjective preference in the face of an essentially truthless world. (44) Instead of truths, there were only interpretations, and this brought new psychological challenges. If everything is deconstructed and all identities are blurred, a chaotic situation arises. The unique essence of each identity is lost while the ego, which carries a false semblance of uniqueness, persists. The ego is a difficult terrain, and from the perspective of CBP it can only be dealt with effectively via inputs from experiential spirituality, otherwise it simply puts on manipulative disguises. One can also postulate that the zeal of postmodern deconstruction that has flattened unique identities has also lead to a backlash that contributed to the rise of destructive religious fundamentalism in the 21st century, as fundamentalism seeks to preserve old cultural identities. Another manifestation of the fallout of post-modernism is what Alan Kirby has termed as pseudo-modernism: a shallow, superficial existence with social acquaintances who are not true friends in terms of emotion and love, and where life is consumed with phones, clicks, presses, surfs and downloads—all while the mobile device becomes the global bank where one stores both information and money. (45) Pseudo-modernism facilitates newer narcissistic preoccupations like taking selfies, or playing nihilistic web games such as 'Blue Whale,' where vulnerable adolescents are pressured to take the challenge of committing suicide.

This is where CBP offers a path forward. Unlike spiritual traditions that favour a dissolution of the individual in the cosmic consciousness or the Void, Sri Aurobindo advocates for the persistence of individual uniqueness as part of a transformational agenda. Sri Aurobindo was emphatic that individual self-development along the transformational trajectory needs to be completed with a collective transformation. (46) Banerji has traced out how Sri Aurobindo's thought converges with that of other postmodern thinkers, (47) and in terms of individual psychology this evolution of the cognitive consciousness to disclose new supra-rational cognitive matrices is discussed in Chapters 7-9. For CBP, the specter of pseudo-modernism represents an evolutionary crisis where humanity has become stuck at the level of mental cognition resulting in a life of material opulence but spiritual bankruptcy, a life of impermanence of values and imperfection of ideals. The only way out is an evolutionary growth in consciousness beyond the Mind—a transformation of the present human being into a supramental being. Such and evolution would automatically imply the emergence of new support systems, and the foremost of these would be in line with a consciousness-based approach to psychology. This would be in consonance with what Wilber named as *psychologia perennis*, a perennial psychology, but with one modification—it would also encompass an evolutionary transformation of consciousness integrated around a real and enduring center of individual identity, which Sri Aurobindo and the Mother called the *psychic being*, or evolving soul. This is not the ego, but the true spiritual person.

Emergence of CBP

The worldview of CBP accepts and synthesizes all the domains of psychology outlined above—physiological, emotional, cognitive, transpersonal, parapsychological, socio-cultural, post-modern, and beyond post-modern. Sri Aurobindo relates all of these dimensions and domains of psychology to a common substrate, which is the great underlying fact of existence that he identifies as "Consciousness" Consciousness is a fundamental reality that is simultaneously pluridimensional and integral. To be simultaneously pluridimensional and integral, we have to acknowledge that the multiplicity, the Many, actually emerges from a unitary matrix, the One. Sri Aurobindo explains that this emergence takes the form of a cosmic evolution, which is a dynamic and progressive process that has the potential to manifest supra-rational cognitive fields that surpass ordinary cognition at the level of the outer mind of the ego-based personality structure. In other words, the human mind such as it is currently constituted is not the end of the evolutionary process—it is a transition to a higher mode of consciousness.

The aim of CBP is not to neglect the empirical spirit of science but to understand everything in the light of the fundamental truth of existence which is Consciousness. The skeptic might inquire how CBP will deal with empiricism. The answer is that empiricism should remain, but its denouement must change. During the postmodern era, the "scientific empiricism" of modernity that marked psychology as a natural science changed to a "broad empiricism" so that sensory experience could be complemented by mental and spiritual experience. This led to an experiential "inner empiricism" that Welwood described as requisite for a paradigm of "human science" characteristic of a "self-knowledge psychology". Today, the next step in this line of evolution would be a shift towards a consciousness-based psychology whose hallmark could be described as "integral empiricism". CBP integrates science and spirituality, Matter and Spirit. This integral empiricism should accommodate all approaches, both objective and subjective, and integrate them around a Beyond-Ego principle for an evolutionary progression along a transformational trajectory. Richard Hartz demonstrated how Sri Aurobindo himself, from a poise of conscious subjectivity, employed methodological pluralism blending introspectionism, skepticism and faith to construct his logbook of spiritual experience – the "Record of Yoga." (48) In contrast to the concept of the clash of civilizations, Hartz studies the *Clasp of Civilizations*, where in the emergent pluralism that triumphs over exclusivism, intuitive faculties are likely to flower "as Eastern civilizations, which have traditionally cultivated them, assimilate what they have learnt from the West, rediscover their own genius and turn their reviving creative energies towards the future". (49) In continuation of that tradition, CBP should be simultaneously an integral and transformative psychology.

Historically, a number of writers have contributed to the growth of CBP. The first exploration of the psychological insights contained in Sri Aurobindo's thought can be traced to an article entitled "A Psychological Appreciation of Sri Aurobindo's System of Integral Yoga" by Indra Sen, published in 1944. (50) The term "Integral Psychology" as a nomenclature for Sri Aurobindo's psychological perspective first appeared officially (though anecdotal evidence points to its use earlier) in Indra Sen's writings in 1957, when Haridas Chaudhuri and Frederick Spiegelberg held a commemorative symposium on the integral philosophy of Sri

Aurobindo. (51) Indra Sen's book "Integral Psychology" appeared in 1986.(52) Haridas Chaudhuri developed an unique version of Integral Psychology in the 1970s. Shirazi explains that Chaudhuri's triadic principle of uniqueness, relatedness and transcendence were related on the one hand to the domains of personal, interpersonal and transpersonal psychological enquiry, and on the other hand approximately paralleled the three modes of Self described by Sri Aurobindo: Individual, Universal and Transcendent. (53) In 1981, Dr. A.S. Dalal also used the term "Integral Psychology" to refer to Sri Aurobindo's approach to psychology, but he later discontinued this practice as he found that other writers were using the same term to refer to new schools of thought not founded upon Sri Aurobindo's worldview (for instance, Ken Wilber also uses the term "integral psychology" to refer to his own work). In 2001, Dr. Dalal named his landmark book on Sri Aurobindo's psychological perspective *A Greater Psychology*. (54) Also, there have been other variants of the nomenclature, such as "Integral Spiritual Psychology" (Jobst Muhling, 1960), "Integral Yogic Psychology" (Kishore Gandhi, 1966, 1986), "Integral Yoga Psychology" (Madhusudhan Reddy, 1988), and "Global Psychology" (C. Goswami, 1987). (55)

In terms of content, writers interested in Sri Aurobindo's psychological thought have tried to introduce his worldview in a variety of ways, each with its own utility. In the 1980s, Dalal began by summarizing the evolution of Western psychology from Freud and Jung to transpersonal psychology, and showed how Sri Aurobindo's worldview accepts the essential insights of every school of thought while also enlarging the scope of each. (56) In the late 1990s, this author (Basu) presented a paradigm for integral health based on the work of Sri Aurobindo and the Mother (57). In the 2000s, the co-author (Miovic) highlighted how worldview frames all of psychology, using Pascal's wager to understand the philosophical strengths and weaknesses of theism, atheism, and agnosticism (58). Salmon and Maslow covered this same territory from the scientific perspective, giving an informative review of research on consciousness. They encouraged skeptics to adhere to the scientific method of maintaining a curious and open-minded agnosticism, rather than jumping to the unscientific conclusions of reductionistic and atheistic materialism. (59)

Most recently, Cortright has synthesized Sri Aurobindo's Integral Yoga and Western psychology to understand transpersonal psychology, with a special emphasis on depth psychotherapy. (60) Teklinski has employed Shirazi's three broad-spectrum categories of subjective experience – Egocentric (pertaining to the surface personality), the Cosmocentric (pertaining to the realm of the Impersonal Transcendence or Ultimate Reality) and Psychocentric (pertaining to the individual poise of the soul or psychic being)—to demonstrate that the Egocentric and Cosmocentric forces cannot identify a facilitative agent for personal growth. In contrast, an integral psychological perspective can provide this facilitative agent, in the form of a soul-poise known in Integral Yoga as the "psychic being," which is a poise of the Unborn Self projected into the manifestation. The psychic being alone can be the facilitative agent for transformation of the individual consciousness.(61) Margot Esther Borden used the Aurobindonian concepts of diversified unity and pluridimensional reality to construct pillars that uphold the integral framework in her book, *Psychology in the Light of the East*. (62)

In addition, semi-structured research in the field is beginning to emerge. Natalie Tobert, a medical anthropologist, used a combination of questionnaires and subject interviews to study how occult and spiritual approaches can supplement modern therapeutic interventions in mental health settings in India. Presented in her book, *Spiritual Psychiatries*, Dr. Tobert's study included field work in Dr. Basu's clinic in Kolkota, as well as interviews with both patients and a variety of mental health professionals who were practicing consciousness-based approaches to health and psychology, inspired by Sri Aurobindo's vision. (63) Approaching this terrain from a more psychological perspective, Larry Seidlitz has pioneered a semi-structured approach to qualitative research in the field of integral psychology. He selected participants who could provide lived experiences of Integral Yoga and its perceived effects in various fields of work, notably in business, education, health care and the arts. Applying a relatively subjective approach to data analysis, he demonstrated how work, life and spiritual pursuit can merge into one, consistent with Sri Aurobindo's adage, "All life is yoga". (64). Meanwhile, Neeltje Huppes has used her extensive experience with integral education at the Sri Aurobindo Ashram (Delhi Branch) and at the Sri Aurobindo International Centre of Education (Pondicherry) to construct a practical workbook on psychic education that brings out succinctly the psychological perspective of integral education. (65)

Also, Matthijs Cornelissen has worked diligently over the last 20 years to develop the field of integral psychology and Aurobindonian studies. This has included organizing conferences on the topic, and encouraging academic psychologists in India to formulate a perspective on psychology based on the spiritual heritage of India. This is a significant historical development, as prior to Cornelissen's work the majority of academic psychologists in India were stuck in a post-colonial rut of following only the Western model, without acknowledging the accomplishments of indigenous Indian psychology. Partly as a result of Cornelissen's work, the regulatory authority of Indian Universities has now officially recognized Indian psychology as a distinct subject. In addition, Cornelissen established the Indian Psychology Institute in 2006 (www.ipi.org.in) and, along with Professors Girishwar Misra and Suneet Verma, brought out a comprehensive resource book on Indian psychology. (66)

Finally, in 1992, *Namah –The Journal of Integral Health* was launched from Pondicherry, as a platform to explore Integral Health and Integral Psychology. In the last three decades, a wide range of contributors from around the world have published in *Namah*, including A.S. Dalal, Alok Pandey, David Johnston, Arya Maloney, D.B. Bisht, Vandana Gupta, James Anderson, Joachim P. Seckel, and the present authors. (67)

Conclusion

In this book, the authors have decided to use the term "consciousness-based psychology" (CBP) to refer to the approach to psychology that emerges from the work of Sri Aurobindo and the Mother. We have steered away from the old term of "integral psychology," because this can refer to other schools of thought as well. We prefer the designation of CBP because it more clearly describes the essence of this orientation, which is that Consciousness is the most fundamental fact of existence and of human psychology.

This chapter has reviewed the various strands of contemporary psychology that are consonant with CBP, including the physiological, cognitive, transpersonal, parapsychological, socio-cultural, and post-modern perspectives. In CBP, the findings and contributions of each of these sub-fields is understood within a larger meta-psychological framework that includes metaphysics. Sri Aurobindo summarizes his perspective on consciousness, psychology, and evolution as follows:

"Man cannot be final, he is a transitional being. This is very clear from the incompleteness and imperfection of all his powers of consciousness; he can only arrive at some limited form of temporary and unstable perfection by much labour and struggle; and yet the search for perfection is ingrained in his nature. There is something that he is not yet which he has to be; he is reaching always towards the something yet unrealised; his whole life and nature is a preparation, an endeavour of Nature towards what is beyond him". (68)

In a cosmicity's wide formless surge,
A conscious edge of the Transcendent's might
Carving perfection from a bright world-stuff,
It figured in it a universe's sense.
There consciousness was a close and single weft;
The far and near were one in spirit-space,
The moments there were pregnant with all time.

Savitri, *pg.. 301*

References

1. Shirazi,Bahman, A.K: Haridas Chaudhuri's Contributions to Integral Psychology, in Integral Yoga Psychology-Metaphysics and Transformation as Taught by Sri Aurobindo, edited by Debashish Banerji, Lotus Press, USA, 2020

2. Maslow, A.H: Toward a Psychology of Being. New York: Van Nostrand Reinhold, 1968

3. Dalal, A.S: Sri Aurobindo and Modern Psychology, in Psychology, Mental Health and Yoga, 3rd ed, Auroshakti Foundation, Pondicherry, 2012, pg. 3-23

4. Wilber, Ken: "Psychologia Perennis: The Spectrum of Consciousness", Journal of Transpersonal Psychology, 1975, Vol.7, p. 105

5. Cortright Brant: Psychotherapy and Spirit, Theory and Practice in Transpersonal Psychotherapy, SUNY Press, 1997, pg. 72

6. Ibid, pg. 74

7. Ibid, pg. 85-86

8. Teklinski, Elizabeth M: A Matter of Heart and Soul-The Value of Positing a personal Ontological Center for Developmental Psychology, in op.cit Integral Yoga Psychology- Metaphysics and Transformation as Taught by Sri Aurobindo

9. op.cit Psychotherapy and Spirit, pg. 18

10. Ibid, pg. 16-17

11. Ibid, pg. 49

12. Kabat-Zinn, Jon: Full Catastrophe Living: Using the Wisdom of your Body and Mind to Face Stress, Pain and Illness, 15th Anniversary Edition, Random House, 2005

13. Kelly,Loch: Shift into Freedom: The Science and Practice of Open-hearted Awareness, Sounds True, US, 2015

14. Dunning, Brian: Lucid Dreaming, Skeptoid Podcast #632, July 17, 2018

15. Green, Elmer & Alyce : Beyond Biofeedback, Chap. II, Self-Regulation: East and West, Knoll Publishing Co.,1977, pg. 197-218

16. Shapiro, DH, Jr in Introduction, Meditation: Classical and Contemporary Perspectives, Ed by Shapiro, DH,Jr & Walsh,RN; Aldine, New York, 1984, pg. 6

17. www.thoughtmedicine.com/2011/06/b

18. Newberg,Andrew & D'Acquili,Eugene: The neuropsychology of spiritual experience. In: H.G. Koenig (Ed.). *Handbook of religion and*

mental health* (pp. 76-94). San Diego: Academic Press, 1998.

19. Newberg, A & d'Acquili, E. *Why God won't go away: Brain science and the biology of belief.* New York: Ballantine, 2001

20. www.pbs.org/wgbh/questionofgod/voices/newberg.html

21. Danzico, Matt: Brains of Buddhist monks scanned in meditation study, April 24th, 2011, www.bbc.com.

22. Yates, John: The Mind Illuminated:A Complete Meditation Guide Integrating Buddhist Wisdom and Brain Science, Dharma Treasure,USA, 2015

23. Rossi, E.L & Lippincott, B.M: The Wave Nature of Being -Ultradian Rhythms and Mind-Body Communication, www.ernesttrossi.com

24. Helminiak Daniel A: Brain, Consciousness And God, State University of New York, 2015

25. Raichle, M.E et al: A default mode of brain function, PNAS [Proceedings of the National Academy of Sciences of the United States of America], 98(2), 2001,pg. 676-682

26. Vago, David R & Silbersweig, David A: Self-awareness, self-regulation, and self-transcendence (S-ART): A framework for understanding the neurobiological mechanisms of mindfulness. Frontiers in Human Neuroscience, 6, Article 296,2012

27. Op.cit. Brain, Consciousness And God, pg. 92-96

28. Lama, Dalai: A Collaboration Between Science and Religion, January 14th, 2003, www.dalailama.com

29. Prendergast, John J: The Deep Heart—Our Portal to Presence, Sounds True, Boulder, 2019

30. Kelly, Loch: The Way of Effortless Mindfulness – A Revolutionary Guide for Living an Awakened Life, Sounds True, Boulder, 2019

31. Myers, FWH: Human Personality and Survival of Bodily Death, Volumes.I & II, Longmann, Green & Co, London,1903

32. Salmon, Don & Maslow, Jan: Yoga Psychology and the Transformation of Consciousness—Seeing Through the Eyes of Infinity, Paragon House,USA,2007, pg. 60-74

33. Braud W: Wellness Implications of Retroactive Influence: Exploring an Outrageous Hypothesis, Alt Ther Health Med, 2000—pdfs.semanticscholar.org.

34. Radin, Dean: The Conscious Universe: The Scientific Truth of Psychic Phenomena, Harperone, 2000, US.

35. Rao, KR: Consciousness Studies: Cross-cultural Perspectives, McFarland Publishing,2005 pg. 314

36. Rao. KR: Indian psychology, parapsychology and spiritual psychology. International Journal of Yoga Philosophy, Psychology and Parapsychology.Vol.1, No.1, 2013, pg. 4-14

37. Scientific and Medical Network: Manifesto for an Integral Science of Consciousness, UK, 2001

38. Kelley, Edward et al (eds): Irreducible Mind; Towards a Psychology for the 21st Century, Rowman & Littlefield, 2007, US

39. Kelley, Edward et al: Beyond Physicalism: Towards Reconciliation of Science and Spirituality, Rowman & Littlefield, 2015.

40. private communication with Don Salmon

41. Wilber Ken: The Collected Works of Ken Wilber, Vol.8, Shambala, USA, 2000, pg. 122

42. Ferrer, Jorge N: Revisioning Transpersonal Theory, State university of New York, 2002, pg. 53

43. Welwood J (ed): The Meeting of the Ways. Explorations in East/West Psychology, Shocken Books, New York, 1979, pg. 224

44. Op.cit. The Collected Works of Ken Wilber, Vol.3, p.15

45. Kirby, Alan: The Death of Postmodernism and Beyond, Philosophy Now (58), Nov-Dec, 2006

46. Sri Aurobindo: The Arya's Fourth Year, Arya 1918, 15 July (also in CWSA 13, 108)

47. Banerji, D: Introduction, Seven Quartets of Becoming: A Transformational Yoga Psychology: Based on the Diaries of Sri Aurobindo, Nalanda International and D.K. Printworld, New Delhi, 2012, pg. 24

48. Hartz, R; A Larger Self-Sri Aurobindo and the Science and Art of Yoga, in op.cit Integral Yoga Psychology- Metaphysics and Transformation as Taught by Sri Aurobindo

49. Hartz R: The Clasp of Civilizations – Globalization and Religion in a Multicultural World, Nalanda International, USA & D. K. Printworld (P) Ltd, India, 2015, pg. 230

50. Sen, Indra: The Urge for Wholeness in Integral Psychology –The Psychological System of Sri Aurobindo, SAICE, Pondicherry, Ist Ed, 1986, pg.171-174

51. Chaudhury, Haridas & Spiegelberg, Frederic(eds): The Integral Philosophy of Sri Aurobindo—A Commemorative Symposium by Cultural Integration Fellowship, San Francisco, George Allen & Unwin Ltd, UK, 1960

52. Sen, Indra: Integral Psychology –The Psychological System of Sri Aurobindo, SAICE, Pondicherry, Ist Ed, 1986

53. Shirazi, Bahman A.K: op.cit,Integral Yoga Psychology-Metaphysics and Transformation as Taught by Sri Aurobindo

54. Dalal, A.S: A Greater Psychology – An Introduction to the Psychological Thought of Sri Aurobindo, Jeremy P.Tarcher/Putnam, New York,2001

55. Basu, S & Krishnamohan,K: Nomenclature Apropos of Sri Aurobindo's of Sri Aurobindo's Psychological System: A Historical Note and Reappraisal, Mother India,Vol. LVIII, No.10, 2005

56. Dalal, A. S: Mental Health and Sri Aurobindo's Integral Yoga, Sri Aurobindo Circle, No.38, 1982

57. Basu, S: Integral Health, 2nd ed, SAIIIHR, Pondicherry, 2011

58. Miovic,M: Towards a spiritual psychology: bridging psychodynamic psychotherapy with integral yoga in Consciousness and its transformation – papers at the Second International Conference on Integral Psychology, Edited by Matthijs Cornelissen,SAICE,Pondicherry, 2001

59. Op. cit: Yoga Psychology and the Transformation of Consciousness

60. Cortright, Brant: Integral Psychology—Yoga, Growth and Opening the Heart, State University of New York,USA, 2007

61. Teklinski, Elizabeth M: op. cit Integral Yoga Psychology- Metaphysics and Transformation as Taught by Sri Aurobindo

62. Borden, Margot Esther: Psychology in the Light of the East, Rowman & Littlefield, Lanham, Maryland, 2017

63. Tobert, Natalie: Spiritual Psychiatries: Mental Health Practices in India and UK, Aethos, UK, 2014

64. Seidlitz, Larry: Integral Yoga at Work—A Study of Practitioners' Experiences Working in Four Professional Fields, 1st Edition, Indian Psychology Institute & Digital Empowerment Foundation, Pondicherry, 2016; *also* Long-term spiritual growth and its influence on professional endeavour, in op.cit, Integral Yoga Psychology-Metaphysics and Transformation as Taught by Sri Aurobindo

65. Huppes, Neeltje: Psychic Education—A workbook based on the writings of Sri Aurobindo and The Mother, Sri Aurobindo Education Society, New Delhi, 2001

66. Cornelissen, M; Misra Girishwar &Varma Suneet (eds): Foundations and Applications of Indian Psychology, Dorling Kindersley, India, 2014

67. Namah-The Journal of Integral Health, Sri Aurobindo Society, Pondicherry, www.namahjournal.com

68. CWSA 12, pg. 265

3
Rebirth in Consciousness:
The Psychic Being

In an abysmal lapse of all things built
Transcending every perishable support
And joining at last its mighty origin,
The separate self must melt or be reborn
Into a Truth beyond the mind's appeal.

Savitri, pg. 307

Sri Aurobindo and the Mother used the term "psychic being" to refer to the immortal essence of the human being that survives the death of the body, and is reborn from life to life as it grows in consciousness. Since this evolving soul is the foundation of their yoga and stands at the center of CBP, we start here with a detailed study of the psychic being. First for Sri Aurobindo's discussion of the often misunderstand phenomenon of "reincarnation," which starts out on a humorous note and then becomes deeply insightful:

"You must avoid a common popular blunder about reincarnation. The popular idea is that Titus Balbus is reborn again as John Smith, a man with the same personality, character, attainments as he had in his former life with the sole difference that he wears coat and trousers instead of a toga and speaks in cockney English instead of popular Latin. That is not the case. What would be the earthly use of repeating the same personality or character a million times from the beginning of time till its end! The soul comes into birth for experience, for growth, for evolution till it can bring the Divine into matter. It is the central being that incarnates, not the outer personality — the personality is simply a mould that it creates for its figures of experience in that one life. In another birth it will create for itself a different personality, different capacities, a different life and career. Supposing Virgil is born again, he may take up poetry in one or two other lives, but he will certainly not write an epic but rather perhaps slight but elegant and beautiful lyrics such as he wanted to write, but did not succeed, in Rome. In another birth he is likely to be no poet at all, but a philosopher and a Yogin seeking to attain and to express the highest truth — for that too was an unrealised trend of his consciousness in that life. Perhaps before he had been a warrior or ruler doing deeds like Aeneas or Augustus before he sang them. And so on — on this side or that the central being develops a new character, a new personality, grows, develops, passes through all kinds of terrestrial experience.

As the evolving being develops still more and becomes more rich and complex, it accumulates its personalities, as it were. Sometimes they stand behind the active elements, throwing in some colour, some trait, some capacity here and there, — or they stand in front and there is a multiple personality, a many-sided character or a many-sided, sometimes what looks like a universal capacity. But if a former personality, a former capacity is brought fully forward, it will not be to repeat what was already done, but to cast the same capacity into new forms and new shapes and fuse it into a new harmony of the being which will not be a reproduction of what it was before. Thus you must not expect to be what the warrior and the poet were — something of the outer characteristics may reappear but very much changed and new-cast in a new combination. It is in a new direction that the energies will be guided to do what was not done before.

Another thing. It is not the personality, the character that is of the first importance in rebirth — it is the psychic being who stands behind the evolution of the nature and evolves with it. The psychic when it departs from the body, shedding even the mental and vital on its way to its resting place, carries with it the heart of its experiences, — not the physical events, not the vital movements, not the mental buildings, not the capacities or characters, but something essential that it gathered from them, what might be called the divine element for the sake of which the rest existed. That is the permanent addition, it is that that helps in the growth towards the Divine. That is why there is usually no memory of the outward events and circumstances of past lives — for this memory there must be a strong development towards unbroken continuance of the mind, the vital, even the subtle physical; for though it all remains in a kind of seed memory, it does not ordinarily emerge. What was the divine element in the magnanimity of the warrior, that which expressed itself in his loyalty, nobility, high courage, what was the divine element behind the harmonious mentality and generous vitality of the poet and expressed itself in them, that remains and in a new harmony of character may find a new expression or, if the life is turned towards the Divine, be taken up as powers for the realisation or for the work that has to be done for the Divine". (1)

Aside from being beautifully written, this statement about the psychic being answers some of the common questions about rebirth, such as why the process exists at all (to "bring the Divine into matter"), why people generally do not remember past lives, and what the difference is between the psychic being and the outer personality. Conventional psychology studies the surface personality, which revolves around the ego and ends with the death of the body, while the psychic being is an evolving immortal soul-entity that surpasses the ego and is independent of the surface personality. CBP certainly accepts the reality of the surface personality, but it sees this as existing for the sake of the evolving psychic being. In subsequent chapters we shall elaborate further the interaction between the psychic being and the outer personality, but for the moment the point to emphasize is that CBP sees growth as not only the meaning and purpose of one passing human life, but as the entire *raison d'être* of all life and of consciousness itself. This fundamental orientation towards growth of consciousness gives CBP a profoundly positive approach to the human condition.

For example, whereas the older traditions of Buddhism and Hinduism viewed karma and rebirth as problems to be solved by transcending the cycle of reincarnation (via nirvana or moksha), Sri Aurobindo and the Mother viewed the psychic being as a deep potential to be fulfilled via the evolution of consciousness on Earth. In the following letter, Sri Aurobindo explains these yogic issues by way of tracing out the relationship between the psychic being and the Atman or Self of the Vedantic tradition:

"It is necessary to understand clearly the difference between the evolving soul (psychic being) and the pure Atman, self or spirit. The pure self is unborn, does not pass through death or birth, is independent of birth or body, mind or life or this manifested Nature. It is not bound by these things, not limited, not affected, even though it assumes and supports them. The soul, on the contrary, is something that comes down into birth and passes through death—although it does not itself die, for it is immortal — from one state to another, from the earth-plane to other planes and back again to the earth-existence. It goes on with this progression from life to life through an evolution which leads it up to the human state and evolves through it all a being of itself which we call the psychic being. This being supports the evolution and develops a physical, a vital, a mental human consciousness as its instruments of world-experience and of a disguised, imperfect, but growing self-expression. All this it does from behind a veil, showing something of its divine self only in so far as the imperfection of the instrumental being will allow it. But a time comes when it is able to prepare to come out from behind the veil, to take command and turn all the instrumental nature towards a divine fulfilment. This is the beginning of the true spiritual life. The soul is able now to make itself ready for a higher evolution of manifested consciousness than the mental human — it can pass from the mental to the spiritual and through degrees of the spiritual to the supramental state. Till then, till it has reached the spiritual realisation, there is no reason why it should cease from birth, it cannot in fact so cease. If having reached the spiritual state, it wills to pass out of the terrestrial manifestation, it may indeed make such an exit, — but there is also possible a higher manifestation, in the Knowledge and not in the Ignorance". (2)

The last sentence above spells out the fundamental difference between Sri Aurobindo and all other schools of yoga, be they Eastern or Western. Even the Buddhist notion of the Bodhisattva, the enlightened being who returns to Earth out of compassion to help other beings attain Nirvana, still sees the goal of life as for all beings to transcend the cycle of rebirth. In contrast, Sri Aurobindo and the Mother affirm that the cycle of rebirth exists for a profound purpose, which is for the psychic being *to fulfill the evolution of consciousness on Earth*. Thus, in CBP the psychic being is the nexus where psychology, religion, philosophy, and metaphysics meet.

Journey of the Soul

Having thus established why the psychic being stands at the center of CBP, we may now go on to answer a host of questions about the soul and rebirth. To begin with, Sri Aurobindo noted that the term "soul" has developed so many different definitions and connotations in English, which is why he preferred the term "psychic being," which is coined from the Greek root *psyche* (or *psuche*, meaning soul or spirit), and is appropriately embedded in the word "psychology." He learned the term from the Mother (who in turn learned it from European occultists with whom she studied in Algeria), and he equated it with the *caitya purusha* of the Upanishads. As for reincarnation, Sri Aurobindo preferred the term "rebirth" to other terms such as "transmigration", "metempsychosis" and "reincarnation," because

> "...Reincarnation is the now popular term, but the idea in the word leans to the gross or external view of the fact and begs many questions. I prefer "rebirth", for it renders the sense of the wide, colourless, but sufficient Sanskrit term, *punarjanma*, "again-birth", and commits us to nothing but the fun-

damental idea which is the essence and life of the doctrine". (3)

In response to a question about the fear of death, the Mother explained how one can dis-identify the sense of self from the body, and identify instead with the psychic being:

> "There is another, a little more difficult, but better, I believe. It lies in telling oneself: "This body is not I", and in trying to find in oneself the part which is truly one's self, until one has found one's psychic being. And when one has found one's psychic being — immediately, you understand — one has the sense of immortality. And one knows that what goes out or what comes in is just a matter of convenience: "I am not going to weep over a pair of shoes I put aside when it is full of holes! When my pair of shoes is worn out I cast it aside, and I do not weep." Well, the psychic being has taken this body because it needed to use it for its work, but when the time comes to leave the body, that is to say, when one must leave it because it is no longer of any use for some reason or other, one leaves the body and has no fear. It is quite a natural gesture — and it is done without the least regret, that's all.
>
> And the moment you are in your psychic being, you have that feeling, spontaneously, effortlessly. You soar above the physical life and have the sense of immortality. As for me, I consider this the best remedy." (4)

Interestingly, the method of dis-identification with the body the Mother describes here is quite similar to the approach of atmic inquiry ("who am I?") taught by Sri Ramana Maharahsi. However, although the process is similar, there is a subtle difference in goal. The experience of Nirvana or Self-realization leads to a state in which all sense of individual "self" or identity disappears, while the experience of the psychic being leads to the sense of an immortal but evolving individual identity that is a manifestation of the Divine. Whereas classical Buddhist and Vedantic practice did not specifically cultivate the psychic being, or used any experience of it as a step to the realization of Nirvana or the Self, the Mother used the experience of the Self or Nirvana as a stable platform upon which to carry on the evolution of the psychic being and the transformation of the body's consciousness.

The psychic being survives death and carries the deepest and most essential memory-traces of a lifetime forward to serve the evolution of consciousness in future lives. However, it is important to note that the growth of the psychic being happens in life itself, and not between births. The Mother explained that after death, the psychic being:

> "goes into a kind of rest for assimilation where the result of the progress accomplished during its active existence is worked out, and when this assimilation is finished, when it has absorbed the progress it had prepared in its active life on earth, it comes down again in a new body bringing with it the result of all its progress and, at an advanced stage, it even chooses the environment and the kind of body and the kind of life in which it will live to complete its experience concerning one point or another. In some very advanced cases the psychic can, before leaving the body, decide what kind of life it will have in its next incarnation". (5)

The Mother also explained that the withdrawal of energies and consciousness into the psychic being is not the same as attaining Nirvana. A rest of the psychic being between lives does not mean an attainment of Nirvana for "the psychic is something essentially linked to divine manifestation, not to divine nonintervention, not to Nirvana." (6) She further explained that when the psychic being becomes completely formed and conscious:

> "it presides over the formation of the new body, and usually through an inner influence it chooses the elements and the substance which will form its body in such a way that the body is adapted to the needs of its new experience. But this is at a rather advanced stage. And later, when it is fully formed and returns to earth with the idea of service, of collective help

and participation in the divine Work, then it is able to bring to the body in formation certain elements of the mind and vital from previous lives which, having been organized and impregnated with psychic forces in previous lives, could be preserved and, consequently, can participate in the general progress. But this is at a very, very advanced stage." (7)

Thus, it is not the surface personality or character that is of primary importance in the phenomenon of rebirth, but memories and impressions carried forward by the psychic being in its evolutionary journey. In the letter quoted at the beginning of this chapter, Sri Aurobindo noted that "there is usually no memory of the outward events and circumstances of past lives." (8) However, there are exceptions and, in fact, much has been written about cases in which people do have memories of past lives, and this is a topic of perennial appeal to the popular mind. In order to do justice to this topic, one must approach it with a sense of balance, and we must dispense with simplistic notions of "one rule fits all." The process of rebirth is vast and varied, and one must approach it without preconceptions. As Sri Aurobindo explained:

> "There is no rule of complete forgetfulness in the return of the soul to rebirth. There are, especially in childhood, many impressions of the past life which can be strong and vivid enough, but a materialising education and the overpowering influences of the environment most often, but not quite always, prevent their true nature from being recognised. There are even a number of people who have definite recollections of a past life. But these things are discouraged by education and the atmosphere and cannot remain or develop; in most cases they are stifled out of existence. At the same time it must be noted that what the psychic being mainly carries away with it and brings back is ordinarily the essence and effect of the experiences it had in former lives, and not the details, so that you cannot expect the same coherent memory as one has of past happenings in the present existence.
>
> A soul can go straight to the psychic world but that de-

pends on the state of consciousness at the time of departure. If the psychic is in front at the time, this immediate transition is possible. It does not depend on the acquisition of a mental and vital as well as a psychic immortality — those who have acquired that would rather have the power to move about in the different planes and even act on the physical world without being bound to it. On the whole it may be said that there is no one rigid rule for these things; manifold variations are possible depending upon the consciousness, its energies, tendencies and formations, although there is a general framework and design into which all fit and take their place." (9)

The Mother explained that true psychic memories

"are unforgettable moments of life when the consciousness is intense, luminous, strong, active, powerful, and sometimes turning points in life that have changed the direction of one's life. But one will never be able to say what dress one was wearing or the gentleman with whom one spoke and the neighbours and the kind of field where one was".(10)

Or again:

"When you have the psychic memory you remember a set of circumstances at one *moment* of life, particularly of the inner emotion, of the consciousness that acted at that moment. And then that passes into the consciousness along with some associations, with all that was around you, perhaps a word spoken, a phrase heard; but what was most important was the state of the soul in which you were: for that indeed remains very clearly engraved".(11)

The Mother cautions that most people's recollections of "past lives" are the product of fancy and imagination:

"Those who claim to have been such a baron of the Middle

Ages or such a person who lived at such a place and such a time, are fanciful, they are simply victims of their own mental imagination. In fact, what remains of past lives are not beautiful pictures in which you appear as a mighty lord in a castle or a victorious general at the head of an army – that is only romance. What remains is the memory of those instants when the psychic being emerged from the depths of your being and revealed itself to you – that is to say, the memory of those instants when you were wholly conscious.......... At the time when you live such moments of your life, you do not care at all about remembering that you were Mr. X, such a person, living at such a place and in such an epoch; it is not the memory of your civic status that remains. On the contrary, you lose all consciousness of these petty external things, accessories and perishables, so that you may be wholly in the flare of the soul revelation or of the divine contact. When you remember such instants of your past lives, the memory is so intense that it seems to be still very close, still living, and much more living than most of the ordinary memories of our present life. At times, in dreams, when you come into contact with certain planes of consciousness, you may have memories of such intensity, such vibrant colour, so to say, even more intense than the colours and things of the physical world. For there are the moments of true consciousness........ These minutes of contact with the soul are often those that mark a decisive turn of our life, a forward step, a progress in consciousness, and that frequently corresponds with a crisis, an extremely intense situation when there comes a call in the whole being, a call so strong that the inner consciousness pierces the layers of unconsciousness covering it and is revealed all luminous on the surface......... Yet you must not believe that all memories of past lives are those of moments of great crisis, of important mission or of revelation. Sometimes they are moments very simple, transparent, when an integral, a perfect harmony of the being was expressed. And that may correspond to altogether insignificant external situations........Once the privileged moment passes, the psychic being plunges into an inner somnolence and the whole outer life melts into a gray monotony which does not leave any trace".(12)

It is hardly surprising that we only retain the imprints of key moments of past lives, for this also holds true in our present lives. As the Mother also noted, when we look at our current life in retrospect, we find that we recall only essential moments, key lessons, and capacities or skills or understanding that we have built up over time. Most day-to-day details of our lives are forgotten. (13)

Sometimes, individuals claim to have memories of their "animal births". The Mother pointed out that such claims are wholly based on fancy because in the case of animals, "the divine spark......is buried much too deep down to be able to come up consciously to the surface and be associated with the outer life. One must become a wholly conscious being, conscious in all its parts, totally united with one's divine origin before one can truly say that one remembers his past lives". (14)

Another source of confusion is the difference between psychic memories and memories of the vital being, which can also be "true" but are not the same. The ordinary individual is a loose amalgam of disorganized ideas, desires and vital impulses revolving in a disjointed fashion around an ego constructed from these very same elements. When a person dies, these amorphous elements of the surface personality get de-linked, dissipated and scattered in the cosmic consciousness as fringe entities of little importance. However, if a person has one plane of consciousness that is exceptionally well-developed in a particular lifetime, that organization can remain in the cosmic consciousness to inspire subjects in future eras who are ready to receive and benefit. Thus the exceptional vision of Alexander, the mighty courage of Shivaji, or the indomitable determination of Napoleon can still inspire and embolden warriors on the battlefield. Likewise, a brilliant philosophical mind-set can remain in the cosmic consciousness to influence future generations of thinkers.

In the same vein, it can be said that if an individual has a vital consciousness that has indulged in terrible acts, then after death a disembodied fragment of this vital force can persist and maliciously influence susceptible subjects. Sometimes such vital formations can appear or be interpreted as apparitions or "ghosts." In this context, it must be emphasized that not all subtle formations that survive beyond a particular life-span necessarily represent soul-elements. (15) In exceptional cases when a dramatic account of a past life is actually corroborated by cross-checking facts, it is not the memory traces carried by the psychic being but rather a strong vital memory carried by a disembodied vital element that is responsible. Also, the Mother described small vital entities which are:

> "formed by the decomposition of desires that have persisted after a man's death and retained their form; of imaginations that have remained coagulated and try to manifest and reappear. Sometimes they are small beings of the vital world, not very well-disposed; as soon as they see people playing at such things – automatic writing, spirit-communication – they come and play. And as they are in a domain from where it is easy to read human thought, they tell you very well what you have in your head". (16)

When asked about the difference between spectacular past-life events narrated by children and reported in newspapers, and the specific memory imprints carried by the psychic being, the Mother answered:

> "The memories...mentioned in the newspapers, are the memories of the vital being, when exceptionally it has come out of a body in order to enter another. That happens, though not frequently. The memories I am referring to are those of the psychic being, and one is conscious of them only when one is in conscious relationship with one's psychic being". (17)

Things can only be different if all the planes and parts of the being are completely integrated around the psychic being, so as to produce "a completely formed conscious being" that can "pass consciously from one life to another without losing anything of its consciousness". (18) The Mother added that this is a rare occurrence and usually such beings "are not in the least inclined to narrate their adventures." (19)

Finally, apropos the question about when exactly the psychic being enters the body upon rebirth, Sri Aurobindo pointed out that this, too, is variable:

> "As regards the stage at which the soul returning for re-birth enters the new body no rule can be laid down, for the circumstances vary with the individual. Some psychic beings get into relation with the birth-environment and the parents from the time of inception and determine the preparation of the personality and future in the embryo, others join only at the time of delivery, others even later on in the life and in these cases it is some emanation of the psychic being which upholds the life. It should be noted that the conditions of the future birth are determined fundamentally not during the stay in the psychic world but at the time of death — the psychic being then chooses what it should work out in the next terrestrial appearance and the conditions arrange themselves accordingly." (20)

Past Lives and Therapeutic Work

The next question that arises is whether a regression analysis of past life events can be beneficial for psycho-therapeutic work. There are past-life therapies that attempt to trace the effects of karmas from past lives into the present, and work upon them. However, while past-life regression therapy has garnered some popular attention in the West, it is generally not consonant with CBP, where the aim of rebirth is understood as being spiritual progression. The integral vision of Sri Aurobindo and the Mother does not favor past-life regression as this puts one back in touch with things that were already in the process of elimination, and if one is spiritually receptive and open to the Divine Grace, the karmas can be automatically driven away. (21) These principles are illustrated in the following case study:

> An 8-year old girl was having repetitive disturbances in the form of being pushed and physically harassed by invisible forces. Every time she seemed about to suffer a near-fatal outcome, at the last moment she would be saved by an inner voice who cautioned her. This voice identified itself as her mother from a past birth and gave precise descriptions of her supposed past life. At peak moments of her crisis, her distress responded to low doses of anti-psychotics (olanzapine), but her problems recurred repeatedly. She had such misery and agony that everyone was afraid she could not bear such suffering. Her inner guidance from her "other mother" always saved her, but family and clinicians alike were both concerned about the possibility of death or a complete psychotic breakdown.
>
> On questioning, it was found that the girl's estranged father, who did not agree to a legal divorce with her mother, had commissioned a Muslim occultist to create disturbances in the child's behavior. Presumably, the father believed that this would force her mother to seek his help. The girl was then referred to a Sufi occultist and a Hindu Tantrik, both of whom did not explore her past life or deal with her inner voice of a mother from a past life. Instead of giving importance to her "other mother," what both occultists did was to invoke a Higher Light that would free the girl from past attachments as well as from her present predicament. Of course, it was acknowledged that her past life experiences had made her vulnerable to disruptive occult forces in the present life. But the emphasis was to facilitate the forward journey of the soul rather than ruminating on the past. Within six months of these spiritual interventions, the girl gradually recovered from disturbances by "invisible forces."

As this case shows, when a subject in distress talks of past-life experiences, the endeavour of intervening mystics and occultists should not be to dwell on and explore those experiences, but rather to offer these experiences to a higher spiritual truth, so that the past bonds can be outgrown with the help of the Divine Grace. Spiritually, the mission of the psychic being is always to move forward towards the Supramental manifestation, and therefore delving into past-life experiences, much of which are anyway distorted, has limited significance in the growth of consciousness. As Sri Aurobindo explained,

> "Seriously, these historical identifications are a perilous game and open a hundred doors to the play of imagination. Some may, in the nature of things must be true; but once people begin, they don't know where to stop. What is important is the lines, rather than the lives, the incarnation of Forces that explain what one now is — and, as for particular lives or rather personalities, those alone matter which are very definite in one and have powerfully contributed to what one is developing now. But it is not always possible to put a name upon these; for not one hundred-thousandth part of what has been has still a name preserved by human Time." (22)

About the "lines" of spiritual development that Sri Aurobindo alludes to above, the Mother further explained that there are certain lines of consciousness that support different individuals at different points in time: "there is the line of divine consciousness which seeks to manifest from above and upholds a certain series of formations, peculiar to itself, in the universe which is its field of manifestation" (23). Thus, a certain line of consciousness that explores music originating from higher planes might support different musicians (say X, Y and Z) at different eras in history — but that does not mean that X is reborn as Y or Z . Rather, X, Y and Z have the capacity of manifesting a certain higher-order musical tradition through inspiration from higher planes of consciousness, but each composes in accordance with the demands of the Time-Spirit and each has one's own contemporary uniqueness.

Sri Aurobindo also noted that in his approach to yoga, the

future is much more important than the past:

> "It is not of course indispensable to know [*about past lives*].
> It is sometimes a matter of interest for knowing the lines of
> one's past development and how one has come to what one is
> now. But to overpass this outward development is of course
> the main aim of the Yoga. We are not to be tied by our past
> lives.
>
> Too much importance must not be given to past lives.
> For the purpose of this Yoga one is what one is and, still
> more, what one will be. What one was has a minor impor-
> tance." (24)

Another reason that memories of past lives are not pursued in Integral Yoga is because subconscious memory is not carried across
lifetimes, so it is not likely that any clinically significant problems
are propagated through the process of rebirth. Whatever energies
are carried forward should be viewed more as circumstances the
psychic being has chosen for its work and growth in this life:

> "Certainly, the subconscient is formed for this life only and
> is not carried with it by the soul from one life to another.
> The memory of past lives is not something that is active any-
> where in the being – if by memory is meant the memory of
> details…But usually it is only the essence of past lives that
> is activised in the being, not any particular memories".(25)
> "Names, events, physical details are remembered only under
> exceptional circumstances and are of a very minor impor-
> tance. When people try to remember these outward things,
> they usually build up a number of romantic imaginations
> which are not true." (26)

Also, Sri Aurobindo did not ascribe to the notion that rebirth is
traumatic:

> "I know nothing about any terrible suffering endured by the
> soul in the process of rebirth; popular beliefs even when they

have some foundation are seldom enlightened and accurate." (27)

Finally, it is worth noting that antecedents arising in the past should not be confused with the play of subtle physical forces in the present, which can very much cause psychological distress that warrants clinical attention. Sri Aurobindo explains that such forces have nothing to do with predetermination. (28) Thus, even if there seem to be antecedents in the past, it is not necessary that these are invincible causative factors of distress in the present:

> "There is no such thing as an insuperable difficulty from past lives. There are formations that help and formations that hamper; the latter have to be dismissed and dissolved, not to be allowed to repeat themselves". (29)

Finding the Soul

A common question is what contact with the psychic being feels like, or how to know that one is in contact with the psychic being. One sure sign is a feeling of inexplicable sweetness or joy that has no outer cause, but arises spontaneously. The psychic feeling is simple, pure, supra-rational, and immediate. It is not an emotion so much as a subtle tact or feeling that stands behind all emotion. It also has a sense as having existed from and for all eternity. As the Mother described,

> "And the moment you are in your psychic being, you have that feeling, spontaneously, effortlessly. You soar above the physical life and have the sense of immortality…This is a deep experience and you can always get it back as soon as you recover the contact with the psychic being. This is a truly interesting phenomenon, for it is automatic. The moment you are in contact with your psychic being, you have the feeling of immortality, of having always been and being always, eternally. And then what comes and goes — these are life's

accidents, they have no importance". (30)

Also, note that the psychic being may make its presence felt not only in beautiful and harmonious circumstances imbued with peaceful emotions and sensations, but also in dangerous and painful moments of crisis, or when life itself stands in the balance. For if the psychic being were not able to confront the most dire extremes of disaster and death, then it would not be truly immortal. Satprem, who worked closely with the Mother, eloquently expressed the beauty and power of the psychic being as follows:

> "Even in this life, we have all known instants of pure transparency or sudden flowering, and twenty or forty years later we find intact the snapshot, including the exact hue of the sky, even the little pebble on the path or the absurd routine that was unfolding that day, as if it were there for all eternity — it is not "as if," it really *is* for eternity. These are the only moments when we have lived, when a real I has surfaced in us out of these thousands of hours of nonexistence. In tragic circumstances too, the psychic can emerge, when all at once the whole being gathers together in a great poignant intensity, and something is rent: then we feel a kind of presence behind which makes us do things we would normally be quite incapable of doing. This is the other face of the psychic, not only one of joy and sweetness, but also of tranquil power, as though it were forever above every possible tragedy, an invulnerable master." (31)

An example of how the psychic being can come forth to confront danger happened to the author (Dr. Basu) in the 1980s, when he was working with a group of people who were abusing heroin. The drug mafia decided to assault him, as his work interfered with their business, and at the moment that he was attacked by a gang of thugs intent on crippling him, he suddenly felt a deep peace within and a massive inner strength that was oblivious to the blows being inflicted upon him. He felt calm, relaxed and protected — in the very midst of a severe beating — and soon help appeared from unexpected quarters to rescue him. Afterwards he understood that it was the psychic being that had come forward to safeguard the outer being. Further details and exercises to help contact the psychic being are discussed in Chapter 12.

Karma

In the Aurobindonian paradigm, rebirth is viewed from a flexible poise that emerges naturally from the consciousness perspective. Whether one passes after birth into hell or heaven is also psychologically untenable from the integral perspective, as hell and heaven are merely mental formations. However, these formations have been so fed with beliefs and dogmas across religions that they can nonetheless affect people:

> "Hell and heaven are often imaginary states of the soul, or rather of the vital being, which it constructs about it after its passing. What is meant by hell is a painful passage through some vital world or a dolorous lingering there, as for instance in many cases of suicide where one remains surrounded by the forces of suffering and turmoil created by this unnatural and violent exit. There are also, of course, real worlds of mind and vital worlds which are penetrated with joyful or dark experiences, and one may pass through these as the result of things formed in the nature which create the necessary affinities. But the idea of reward or retribution is a crude or vulgar conception and we can disregard it as a mere popular error". (32)

In fact, Sri Aurobindo dismissed simplistic notions of karmic rewards and punishments for purported deeds or misdeeds as "Too symmetrical to be true."(33) He added that:

> "The object of birth being growth by experience, whatever reactions come to past deeds must be for the being to learn and grow, not as lollipops for the good boys of the class (in

the past) and canings for the bad ones. The real sanction for good and ill is not good fortune for the one and bad fortune for the other, but this that good leads us towards a higher nature which is eventually lifted above suffering and ill pulls us towards the lower nature which remains always in the circle of suffering and evil". (34)

In another conversation he commented:

> "The Law of Karma is not mathematical or mechanical: Certain energies are put forward and certain results tend to be produced. Karma is not the fundamental law of consciousness. The basic law is spiritual. Karma is a secondary machinery to help the consciousness to grow by experience. The laws of being are primarily spiritual. It is quite possible to eliminate the Karmic force — it is not absolute. It is the mind that formulates these laws; and the mind always tries to put them as absolute." (35)

Sri Aurobindo also explained that our notions of time-periods between death and rebirth cannot be construed along rigid lines: "the rigid rules of time and of Karmic reaction laid down dogmatically by the Theosophist hierophants are certainly erroneous." (36) The Mother, based on her vast repertoire of experiential knowledge, said that there are no common rules as in some cases there could be immediate rebirth while in others it could take centuries or millennia to find a suitable milieu for rebirth. (37)

Importantly, according to Sri Aurobindo and the Mother there is an intimate connection between the individual and collective evolution of consciousness, such that each new life has a continuity with the cosmic memory. If this continuity were absent, then there could be no evolutionary process, either individually or collectively, and we could never manifest shared universal values and nor be capable of an infinite expansion of knowledge and vision. For example, a highly developed psychic being can transfer its memory traces to other evolving psychic beings, and this sort of inner influence or transmission shows that rebirth should be understood not in only individualistic terms, but also as a cosmic phenomenon that affects the whole evolution of consciousness. In Sri Aurobindo's vision, the old idea of reincarnation errs by an excessive individualism. The psychic being enters into birth not as an isolated being, but as a part in the life of the whole — and therefore the soul inherits the life of the whole. (38, 39) Rebirth is thus an occasion and means of a spiritual evolution that explains all the missing links in the evolution of consciousness on Earth, which biological factors alone do not explain. (40) In Sri Aurobindo's yoga psychology, a major breakthrough occurs when the psychic being comes forward and takes over the ego as the leader of individual identity and growth. The planes and parts of the being can now be organized and harmonized around the psychic being, and this integrated individual is then ready to travel forward and upward along the evolutionary trajectory. (41)

> *The child of the Void shall be reborn in God,*
> *My Matter shall evade the Inconscient's trance.*
> *My body like my spirit shall be free.*
> *It shall escape from Death and Ignorance.*
>
> Savitri, *pg. 406*

References

1. CWSA 28, pg. 543-544
2. Ibid, pg. 536-537
3. CWSA 13, pg. 259
4. CWM 05, pg. 315-316
5. CWM 9, pg. 268
6. Agenda IV, pg. 275
7. CWM 09, pg. 268-269
8. CWSA 28, pg. 544
9. Ibid, pg. 536
10. CWM 05, pg. 36
11. Ibid, pg. 33

12. CWM 15, pg. 340-342
13. Ibid, pg. 342-343
14. Ibid, pg. 343
15. CWSA 21-22, pg. 929
16. CWM 05, pg. 35
17. Agenda VIII, pg. 393
18. CWM 05, pg. 34
19. Ibid
20. CWSA 28, pg. 539
21. Agenda III, pg. 63-64
22. CWSA 28, pg. 553-554
23. CWM 03, pg. 148
24. CWSA 28, pg. 552-553
25. Ibid, pg. 551
26. Ibid, pg. 552
27. Ibid, pg. 538
28. Ibid, pg. 562
29. Ibid, pg. 545
30. CWM 05, p. 316
31. Satprem: Sri Aurobindo or Adventure of Consciousness, English translation by Institut de Recherches Evolutives, Paris, 1993, p. 89
32. CWSA 28, pg. 535-536
33. CWSA 28 pg. 533
34. Ibid
35. Evening Talks, pg. 217
36. CWSA 12, pg. 71
37. CWM 03, pg. 145
38. CWSA 13, pg. 365-366
39. Ibid, pg. 363-364
40. Ibid, pg. 297
41. CWSA 23-24, pg. 150

4
The Ego and the Psychic Being

The landmarks of the little person fell,
The island ego joined its continent.
Overpassed was this world of rigid limiting forms:
Life's barriers opened into the Unknown.

Savitri, pg. 25

While the core of CBP centers upon the discovery and development of the psychic being, CBP is by no means naive about the reality of the ego and its role in human psychology. CBP accepts all that clinical and academic psychology have learned about the structure and function of the ego since the time of Freud, but it interprets this knowledge within a larger understanding of the evolution of consciousness.

To summarize the current state of knowledge in Western psychology, the ego is the central organizing concept in the biopsychosocial model of psychology and psychiatry. In this model, the central functions of the ego are described as reality testing, memory, impulse control, judgment, affect tolerance, defense and executive functioning. Practically, the dominant trend in psychotherapy and psychiatric treatment has been to try to strengthen ego functioning so as to help individuals better cope with both intrapsychic and interpersonal conflicts. Psychotropic medications can be used to support ego functioning, and informed clinicians understand that there is no contradiction between pharmacological and psychological approaches to treatment. While in the past there were disputes between the pharmacological model and psychological ones, those have been resolved, such that now the standard of care is an integrated approach. Also, the contemporary model of "integrative medicine" is in the process of expanding the biopsychosocial model to include spiritual and transpersonal growth as well.

Sri Aurobindo was well aware of the ego, and in fact studied it from more angles and viewpoints than Western psychology has. He examines the ego from three important perspectives: metaphysical, evolutionary, and psychological. The metaphysical perspective examines the role of individual identity in a worldview where a formless, infinite, unitary Reality is the cause of the world of multiplicity that we perceive with our outer senses and material consciousness. The evolutionary perspective examines how the ego is formed during the emergence of the mental and vital consciousness from the material Inconscience, and justifies the phenomenon of ego as a necessary though temporary construct during the evolutionary process. The psychological perspective examines how the ego is too limited to effectively harmonize the parts and planes of the being, and how it can be replaced by a beyond-ego principle, which is the psychic being.

Ego – The Metaphysical Perspective

Sri Aurobindo's metaphysics informs the understanding of consciousness that he uses to frame psychology, and of the ego's role within psychology. As Sri Aurobindo explained, in classical Indian philosophy, spiritual liberation (enlightenment) was pursued as a shift in consciousness from the ego to the Jiva (also termed the Jivatman or Self):

> "That substance is the self of man called in European thought the Monad, in Indian philosophy, Jiva or Jivatman, the living entity, the self of the living creature. This Jiva is not the mental ego-sense constructed by the workings of Nature for her temporary purpose. It is not a thing bound, as the mental being, the vital, the physical are bound, by her habits, laws or processes. The Jiva is a spirit and self, superior to Nature. It is true that it consents to her acts, reflects her moods and upholds the triple medium of mind, life and body through which she casts them upon the soul's consciousness; but it is itself a living reflection or a soul-form or a self-creation of the Spirit universal and transcendent". (1)

In other words, the Individual Self (Jiva), the Cosmic Self, and the Transcendent Self are three different poises of the same Reality. In classical Indian spirituality, the quest for ego-transcendence proceeded via a shift of awareness from the ego to the Individual Self (Jiva), and then usually culminated in "an entire return, loss, immersion or extinction of the Jiva in the Supreme." (2) In contrast, in Sri Aurobindo's approach it is understood that Supermind creates an eternal principle of individuality, the Jiva, which in turns projects an eternal but evolving representation of itself into the evolution of consciousness in Matter. This evolving soul, or psychic being, is thus a fundamental Truth of existence that cannot and should not be dismissed as an ephemeral phenomenon fated to illusion or dissolution. As the Mother explained:

> "This is where the problem arises. Sri Aurobindo says it [the Jiva] is permanent while all the ancient traditions say it disappears with the body. Otherwise there would be no permanent material life – for this [individuality] is the very nature of materialization. Were it destined to disappear, the phenomenon of physical dissolution would become permanent, and there could never be physical immortality, because, after exhausting a certain…basically, a certain number of illusions or disorders or falsehoods, one would return to the Truth. But according to Sri Aurobindo, it isn't like that: this individualization, this individual personalization is the Truth, a real, authentic divine phenomenon – the only falsehood is the deformation of consciousness. Well, when we rediscover the true consciousness of Unity – that Unity which is both in and above the manifest and non-manifest ('above' in that it contains both the manifest and non-manifest equally), well, this Truth includes material personalization…". (3)

Thus, in Sri Aurobindo's system of metaphysics, the ego is a temporary formation of individuality that facilitates the evolution of consciousness in matter. As this evolution shifts from its lower to higher stages, the ego-centric awareness is replaced with the consciousness of the psychic being, which then becomes the center of individual identity that organizes the evolution of consciousness from Mind upwards to Supermind.

Ego — The Evolutionary Perspective

As the evolution of consciousness in Matter proceeds, at some point the possibility of individual identity needs to emerge. Plants do not have a consciousness of individual identity, nor do lower animals. However, in higher animals a sense of individuality starts to emerge, and this becomes pronounced in human beings. Initially, this growth towards individualization out of the indeterminate stuff of the Inconscience proceeds through a gradually developing form of "a constantly self-affirming mental, vital and physical ego". (4) This transient and death-bound ego is initially necessary to achieve the uniqueness of each individual, for by living in division and strife with other egos, each ego is able to better define and thus individualize itself. But eventually a point is reached at which the ego is too limited to allow for a progressive and higher evolution of consciousness: it needs to be replaced by a center of individuality that is eternal and capable of living in the consciousness of Unity with all other beings. Thus, as the evolution of consciousness proceeds towards its higher potentials, the psychic being must emerge from behind the veil of awareness and come forward to lead the further evolution of consciousness. The soul must replace the ego as the true center of individual identity. As Sri Aurobindo explains:

> "It is this ego-sense that gives a first basis of coherence to what otherwise might be a string or mass of floating impressions: all that is so sensed is referred to a corresponding artificial centre of mental consciousness in the understanding, the ego-idea. This ego-sense in the life-stuff and this ego-idea in the mind maintain a constructed symbol of self, the separative ego, which does duty for the hidden real self, the spirit or true being. The surface mental individuality is, in consequence, always ego-centric; even its altruism is an en-

largement of its ego: the ego is the lynch-pin invented to hold together the motion of our wheel of nature. The necessity of centralization around the ego continues until there is no longer need of any such device or contrivance because there has emerged the true self, the spiritual being, which is at once wheel and motion and that which holds all together , the centre and the circumference" .(5)

The ego therefore serves a transitional purpose: it supports the emergence and definition of individuality at one point in evolution, but then needs to be transcended at the next stage of evolution. The ego is necessary to support the emerging, self-affirming individuality which has to sustain itself in a world divided by chaos, strife and competition. However, once this step is achieved, the ego then needs to be surpassed in order for a higher and truer consciousness to emerge.

Ego – The Psychological Perspective

Having studied the ego from the perspective of both metaphysics and evolution, Sri Aurobindo then analyzed the psychological structure and function of the ego. This description will sound more similar to that of Western psychology — although he adds a dimension that Western psychology missed. Sri Aurobindo describes the ego has containing five domains of structure, function and operations: the mental ego, the vital ego, the physical ego, the collective ego, and the substratum ego. The mental and vital egos are the psychological components of the biopsychosocial model, the collective ego is the social aspect, the physical ego is the biological part, and the substratum ego is a root sense of individual identity not clearly articulated in Western psychology.

Mental ego

The mental ego co ordinates our cognitive activities but its action is limited to the surface personality and it has no access to the inner planes of consciousness and has no leverage in supra-rational functions like intuition. It imparts an individual uniqueness to ideas and preferences without which the individuality cannot segregate itself from the mass, cannot be a leader in the usual sense of the term. However it is also responsible for biases, preferences and idiosyncrasies and in the process ushers in the elements of falsehood and ignorance. It is the basis of what is known as "egoism", that self-centered attitude that often accompanies not only professional assertiveness, intellectual excellence, financial success or social status but also the venerated phenomena of altruism, social service and philanthropy. When intellectuals and spiritual seekers abhor physical work, they may be serving the mental ego. As Sri Aurobindo quips, "The idea of giving up physical work for mental self-development is a creation of the mental ego". (6) It should be noted that the true "I" is not the mental ego but "the eternal I which assumes various personalities in various lives".(7)

Vital ego

The vital ego canalizes and imparts an individual uniqueness to the passions, emotions, dynamisms, courage, will-force as well as to desires, lusts, ambitions and anger, attributes that make an individual appear "strong", "weak", "moody" , "aggressive" or "psychopathic" to the common eye. However the vital ego has no access to the inner being which holds the pranic Shakti or energy that is in communion with the Universal Shakti. It is the vital ego that asserts itself in the execution of large tasks, which otherwise would have remained in the realm of ideas, and thus naturally gives rise to pridefulness and boasting. It is the vital ego that in one poise gives an unique turn to romanticism while in another poise allows lust, perversion, and related disturbing attributes of character. On one hand, it can canalize artistic creativity, while on the other hand it can also stamp an individual with the mark of cruelty, hatred and jealousy. While the mental ego can be dealt through morality and ethics and can be transcended through a spiritual discipline, the vital ego is much more difficult to restrain and transform. Sri Aurobindo describes that the vital ego not only justifies self-assertion but also can deceptively indulge in self-depreciation and a morbid exaggerated self-criticism and this supposedly "negative egoism" is also a "poise or pose of the vital ego". (8)

Physical ego

The physical ego is linked with the individual bodily constitution and imparts an uniqueness to each individual's structural and functional repertoire. It has, however, no access to the individual's subtle body-consciousness in the inner being. It modulates our external bodily characteristics, our habitual patterns of living, our individual variations in biochemical and neurophysiological functioning, our genetic and environmental influences. The physical ego transcribes a body-image of the individual that may evoke a wide array of reactions ranging from narcissistic satisfaction to denial and hatred. The physical ego cannot be altered through morality, ethics, or psychological techniques. Generations of mystics and yogis have tried to transcend the physical ego through strict ascetic austerities but the results were always transient. It was only in the 20th century that The Mother undertook a new yoga in the plane of cellular consciousness that paves way to the transformation of the physical consciousness.

Collective ego

The collective ego represents the consciousness of collective humanity which "is only a larger comprehensive edition or a sum of individual egos". (9) The collective ego is a psycho-social entity made of one's identity group, be it family, clan, race, religion, or nation. It is "Made of the same substance, in the same mould of nature, it has not in it any greater light, any more eternal sense of itself, any purer source of peace, joy and deliverance. It is rather even more tortured, troubled and obscured, certainly more vague, confused and unprogressive. The individual is in this respect is greater than the mass and cannot be called on to subordinate his more luminous possibilities to this darker entity. If light, peace, deliverance, a better state of existence are to come, they must descend into the soul from something wider than the individual but also from something higher than the collective ego". (10)

Substratum ego

Even if the practical egoism of our triple nature (mental, vital and physical) is transcended through a psycho-spiritual discipline, there still remains a residual impression of the ego as "a general sense of the separate I". (11) This "indefinable but fundamental ego-sense" is the substratum ego. (12)

> "This substratum ego is something vague, indefinable, elusive; it does not or need not attach itself to anything in particular as the self; it does not identify itself with anything collective; it is a sort of fundamental form or power of the mind which compels the mental being to feel himself as a perhaps indefinable but still a limited being which is not mind, life or body but under which their activities proceed in Nature" (13)

The substratum ego gives the impression of a "self" or "being" behind the ego and separate from the ego, hence it is often mistaken for a spiritual essence, the true self or soul-essence or "true Purusha" or "true Person within" .(14)

From the above is clear that Sri Aurobindo understood all of the essential qualities and characteristics of the ego covered in Western psychology, plus more. However, throughout his analysis of the ego, Sri Aurobindo notes that no part or aspect of the ego has access to the psychic being or spiritual planes of consciousness, thus neither the individual nor the collective can find final fulfillment at the level of the ego. The central insight of transpersonal psychology is that human beings can have valid experiences of supra or trans-egoic states of consciousness, and that there is a whole growth trajectory along this transpersonal dimension. Sri Aurobindo affirms these basic tenets of transpersonal psychology in the following comment:

"In human egoism and its satisfaction there can be no divine culmination and deliverance. A certain purification from egoism is the condition even of ethical progress and elevation, for social good and perfection; much more is it indispensable for inner peace, purity and joy. But a much more radical deliverance, not only from egoism but from ego-idea and ego-sense, is needed if our aim is to raise human into divine nature. Experience shows that, in proportion as we deliver ourselves from the limiting mental and vital ego, we command a wider life, a larger existence, a higher consciousness, a happier soul-state, even a greater knowledge, power and scope. Even the aim which the most mundane philosophy pursues, the fulfillment, perfection, satisfaction of the individual is best assured not by satisfying the narrow ego but by finding freedom in a higher and larger self. There is no happiness in smallness of the being, says the Scripture, it is with the large being that happiness comes. The ego is by its nature a smallness of being; it brings contraction of the consciousness and with the contraction limitation of knowledge, disabling ignorance, -- confinement and a diminution of power and by that diminution incapacity and weakness, -- scission of oneness and by that scission disharmony and failure of sympathy and love and understanding, -- inhibition or fragmentation of delight of being and by that fragmentation pain and sorrow. To recover what is lost we must break out of the worlds of ego. The ego must either disappear in impersonality or fuse into a larger I : it must fuse in the wider cosmic 'I' which comprehends all these smaller selves or the transcendent of which even the cosmic self is a diminished image." (15)

The Interaction Between Soul and Ego

The next question that arises is what is the functional relationship between the psychic being and the ego? The fact that people are growing simultaneously along lines of both ego development in one life, and soul (psychic being) development across multiple births, means that the integral clinician has to distinguish both lines of development and understand the interaction between the two. It is critical to understand that premature attempts to dissociate the seat of individual identity from the ego can lead to confusion and chaos in ordinary circumstances, as happens in a variety of pathological states described in conventional psychiatry and psychology. For instance, in schizophrenia the mental ego loses its consistent power of co-ordination of cognitive processes leading to disorganization of thought structure and functions. In depression or aggression, the vital ego can abdicate its control and fall prey to disruptive vital forces that can compel one to commit suicide or homicide. Also, the vital ego can unduly exaggerate its presence and spawn delusions of grandiosity as well as sexual and/or financial excesses in the manic phase of bipolar disorder. The Mother described how in delirious states accompanying high fever, the lack of support of the material consciousness facilitates attack by negative forces resembling hallucinations. (16) Such phenomena can occur when the physical ego cannot carry out its functions with consistency. That is why in ordinary counseling it is better to deal with egoism rather than advising a dissociation from the ego per se, and why standard medical treatments for delirium can be so helpful and at times even critical.

Before delving further into the interaction between the psychic being and the ego in clinical work, it would be helpful to comment on the powerful mediating effect of what Sri Aurobindo and the Mother call the *vital consciousness* or *vital being*. This was discussed briefly above with reference to the "vital ego," but the reality of the vital is so important to much of human life that it it is worth elaborating at some length.

In integral yoga psychology, the term "the vital" is used to denote the complex of emotion, desire, drive, and motivation that fuels much of human feeling and behavior. In yogic terms, the vital encompass the energies of the chakras from the pelvic or sex-center up through the chest or "heart" center, while in neuroscience this would map to the limbic system and autonomic nervous system, and Western psychology has studied the vital via psychoanalysis and attachment theory. In Buddhist terms, the vital is the root of desire and craving, which are to be overcome with mindfulness. The current construct of "mind-body" medicine makes a mistake by not including the vital in its labelling, for it suggests that there is a direct link between cognition (thoughts or mental imagery) and the body (physiology). In fact, to the degree there is a connection, that link is very strongly mediated by the vital. One example of how this mind-body link can be misconstrued by the public is to think that simply having positive thoughts will cure medical illnesses such as cancer or high blood pressure, while having negative thoughts will lead directly to disease and death. Not only does much medical research contradict such simplistic notions, but so does integral yoga's understanding of the vital.

The Mother lucidly explained the vital in the following talk from September 9, 1953, in response to a question about how to "convert" or change the functioning of the vital. This is central to clinical practice, which often aims to regulate the vital, whether with psychotherapy or medications, or both. In CBP, to "convert the vital" would mean to transform its functioning so completely that it would be placed under permanent mastery by the psychic being. Note how the Mother distinguishes between the mind, the vital and the psychic being in this discussion, and astutely describes the limitations of the mind and the vital:

"Can't the vital be converted?

"Convert the vital? Surely one can. It is a difficult task, but it can be done. If it could not be done, then there would be no hope. But generally the mind is not sufficient. For, I have known very many people who could see very clearly, understand very well, were mentally thoroughly convinced, could even describe to you and tell you extraordinary things, could easily give excellent lessons to others, but their vital was up to all sorts of tricks and would not listen at all to all that. It said, "It is all the same to me, say what you may; as for myself, I go my own way!"

It is only when contact with the psychic has been established that this can convert anything at all — even the worst criminal — in a moment. These are those "illuminations" which seize you and turn you inside out completely. After that, all goes well. There may be slight difficulties of adjustment, but still things go well.

But the mind is a big preacher, that is its nature: it gives speeches, sermons, as it is done in the churches. So the vital usually gets impatient and answers the mind, not very politely: "You are a nuisance! what you say is very good for you, but for me it won't do." Or, at the best, when the mind is gifted with especially remarkable capacities and the vital is of a little higher kind, it may say: "Oh! how beautiful it is, what you tell me (sometimes this happens), but you see, I, I am unable to do it; it is very beautiful, but it is beyond my capacity."

But this vital is a strange creature. It is a being of passion, enthusiasm and naturally of desire; but, for example, it is quite capable of getting enthusiastic over something beautiful, of admiring, sensing anything greater and nobler than itself. And if really anything very beautiful occurs in the being, if there is a movement having an exceptional value, well, it may get enthusiastic and it is capable of giving itself with complete devotion — with a generosity that is not found, for example, in the mental domain nor in the physical. It has that fullness in action that comes precisely from its capacity to get enthused and throw itself wholly without reserve into what it does. Heroes are always people who have a strong vital, and when the vital becomes passionate about something, it is no longer a reasonable being but a warrior; it is wholly involved in its action and can perform exceptional things because it does not calculate, does not reason, does not say "One must take precautions, one must not do this, must not do that." It becomes reckless, it gets carried away, as people say, it gives itself totally. Therefore, it can do magnificent things if it is guided in the right way.

A converted vital is an all-powerful instrument. And sometimes it gets converted by something exceptionally beautiful, morally or materially. When it witnesses, for example, a scene of total self-abnegation, of uncalculating self-giving — one of those things so exceedingly rare but splendidly beautiful — it can be carried away by it, it can be seized by an ambition to do the same thing. It begins by an ambition, it ends with a consecration.

There is only one thing the vital abhors; it is a dull life, monotonous, grey, tasteless, worthless. Faced with that, it goes to sleep, falls into inertia. It likes extremely violent things, it is true; it can be extremely wicked, extremely cruel, extremely generous, extremely good and extremely heroic. It always goes to extremes and can be on one side or the other, yes, as the current flows.

And this vital, if you place it in a bad environment, it will imitate the bad environment and do bad things with violence and to an extreme degree. If you place it in the presence of something wonderfully beautiful, generous, great, noble, divine, it can be carried away with that also, forget everything else and give itself wholly. It will give itself more completely than any other part of the being, for it does not calculate. It follows its passion and enthusiasm. When it has desires, its desires are violent, arbitrary, and it does not at all take into account the good or bad of others; it doesn't care the least bit. But when it gives itself to something beautiful, it does not calculate either, it will give itself entirely without knowing whether it will do good or harm to it. It is a very precious instrument.

It is like a horse of pure breed: if it lets itself be directed, then it will win all the races, everywhere it will come first. If it is untamed, it will trample people and cause havoc and break its own legs or back! It is like that. The one thing to know is to which side it will turn. It loves exceptional things — exceptionally bad or exceptionally good, it loves the exceptional. It does not like ordinary life. It becomes dull, it becomes half inert. And if it is shut up in a corner and told: "Keep quiet there", it will remain there and become more and more like something crumbling away, and finally just like a mummy: there is no more life in it, it is dried up. And one will no longer have the strength to do what one wants to do. One will have fine ideas, excellent intentions, but one won't have the energy to execute them.

So do not wail if you have a powerful vital, but you must have strong reins and hold them quite firmly. Then things go well.

Does depression come from the vital?

Oh, yes. All your troubles, depression, discouragement, disgust, fury, all, all come from the vital. It is that which turns love into hate, it is that which induces the spirit of vengeance, rancour, bad will, the urge to destroy and to harm. It is that which discourages you when things are difficult and not to its liking. And it has an extraordinary capacity for going on strike! When it is not satisfied, it hides in a corner and does not budge. And then you have no more energy, no more strength, you have no courage left. Your will is like… like a withering plant. All resentment, disgust, fury, all despair, grief, anger — all that comes from this gentleman. For it is energy in action.

Therefore, it depends on which side it turns. And I tell you, it has a very strong habit of going on strike. That is its most powerful weapon: "Ah! you are not doing what I want, well, I am not going to move, I shall sham dead." And it does that for the least reason. It has a very bad character; it is very touchy and it is very spiteful — yes, it is very ill-natured. For I believe it is very conscious of its power and it feels clearly that if it gives itself wholly, there is nothing that will resist the momentum of its force. And like all people who have a weight in the balance, the vital also bargains: "I shall give you my energy, but you must do what I want. If you do not give me what I ask for, well, I withdraw my energy." And you will be flat as a pancake. And it is true, it happens like that.

It is difficult to regulate it. Yet naturally, when you have succeeded in taming it, you have something powerful in hand for realisation. It is that which can carry by storm the biggest obstacles. It is that which is capable of turning an idiot into an intelligent person — it alone can do so; for if one yearns passionately for progress, if the vital takes it into its head that one must progress, even the greatest idiot can become intelligent! I have seen this, I am not speaking from hearsay; I have seen it, I have seen people who were dull, stupid, incapable of understanding, who understood nothing — you could go on explaining something to them for months, it would not enter, as though one were speaking to a block of wood — and then all of a sudden their vital was caught in a passion; they wanted simply to please someone or get something, and for that one had to understand, one had to know, it was necessary. Well, they set everything moving, they shook up the sleeping mind, they poured energy into all the corners where there was none; and they understood, they became intelligent. I knew someone who knew nothing practically, understood nothing, and who, when the mind started moving and the passion for progress took possession of him, began to write wonderful things. I have them with me. And when the movement withdrew, when the vital went on strike (for sometimes it went on strike, and withdrew), the person became once again absolutely dull.

Naturally it is very difficult to establish a constant contact between the most external physical consciousness and the psychic consciousness, and oh! the physical consciousness has plenty of goodwill; it is very regular, it tries a great deal, but it is slow and heavy, it takes long, it is difficult to move it. It does not get tired, but it makes no effort; it goes its way, quietly. It can take centuries to put the external consciousness in contact with the psychic. But for some reason or other the vital takes a hand in it. A passion seizes it. It wants this contact (for some reason or other, which is not always a spiritual reason), but it wants this contact. It wants it with all its energy, all its strength, all its passion, all its fervour: in three months the thing is done.

So then, take great care of it. Treat it with great consideration but never submit to it. For it will drag you into all kinds of troublesome and untoward experiments; and if you succeed in convincing it in some way or other, then you will advance with giant strides on the path." (17)

As one can gather from this detailed talk, understanding the vital is central to a consciousness-based approach to defense mechanisms, personality organization, affect dysregulation, mood disorders, grief, tantrums, motivational interviewing, and any type of affect-centered therapy. Today even cognitive-behavior therapy acknowledges the importance of emotion in the treatment process, and thus should really be renamed as cognitive-emotional-behavior therapy.

At the end of this discourse on the vital, the Mother concludes with a hint about her solution, which is to put the mind, the vital, and the body all under the control of the psychic being. That is what she calls the "psychic transformation," and is the necessary precondition to the work on the consciousness of cells that she undertook in the last years of her life, and which we will return to in Chapter 16.

The Soul and Ego in Psychotherapy

There are various ways of conceptualizing the interaction between psychic being and ego in clinical work, and each has its own utility, depending on the context and the clinician's role and practice style. Indeed, much of the writing in transpersonal psychology is about how different clinicians approach this large territory. For example, Cortright has explored this with regards to depth psychotherapy, with many case studies, (18) while Salmon and Maslow have given a detailed account of a client's psychic awakening with reference to a large amount of data from psychology and sociology. (19) The co-author has written about how the hierarchy of ego defenses originally defined by the psychoanalytic tradition can be expanded to include spiritual and psychic processes of ego transformation, and applied this to interpreting CBT and the 12 step program of AA (Alcoholics Anonymous) as well (20). However, for the moment, let us begin by considering how the diagnostic criteria of classificatory systems such as the DSM and ICD do not do justice to human beings as seen from the integral perspective. For example, consider the following case study of an unusual client in Dr. Basu's practice:

> Patient X satisfied perfectly the criteria for schizoid personality disorder. Since his childhood, he always loved to be alone and excelled in mathematics. When he grew up to be a young college student, his social isolation became even more marked, even though he pursued his studies at a premier engineering college. In spite of his ego-syntonic anhedonia, he had a spiritual perspective that was never overtly expressed. He went to Turkey for his post-doctoral studies where, after a year's stay, the changing political scenario with signals of terrorism made him quickly learn how to perform Namaz if confronted by radicals. He also began practicing certain rituals associated with the worship of Krishna which left his parents wondering if there would be an impending psychotic breakdown. Within a few weeks, he reported having receiving intuitive "inner" guidance to abandon his post-doctoral studies and leave Turkey. He boldly declared to his parents that it would not be possible to be in Turkey any longer as it would be infiltrated with radicals. Shortly after his departure, in fact there were wide-spread outburst of radical terrorism which made it very unsafe for foreign students to stay in Turkey. After his return to India, he got a coveted teaching assignment which he pursued successfully.

Of course, schizoid personality disorder is one of the least understood personality disorders and it can be argued that anhedonia would not interfere with a spiritual worldview of a subject. The point to emphasize here is that a pattern of thinking, feeling and acting at the surface personality does not necessarily correlate with the level of development of one's psychic being. In this case, the subject clearly had more psychic development than the limitations of his outer personality would suggest, which lead to him receiving accurate inner guidance to leave Turkey despite the odd manner in which he was behaving, and also allowed him to be a talented and successful teacher.

On the other hand, one of the most studied personality disorders is borderline personality disorder (BPD), which is characterized by a pattern of unstable emotions, impulsivity, and turbulent interpersonal relationships. The name of the disorder is not very patient-friendly, so it is likely to be changed soon to something that focuses on emotional dysregulation. In a brief letter from the 1930s, Sri Aurobindo pegged the essence of this syndrome as being due to an "unstable vital," and he even observed that it appears to be more common in women than men, which mainstream psychology also thought until recent research revealed that men with BPD tend to have more substance abuse and antisocial behaviors so end up in rehabs or jail, while women with BPD tend to have more self-inflicted harm, mood disorders, eating disorders and PTSD, so end up in mental health treatment. (21) Thus, because men tend to express an unstable vital more through substance abuse and aggression than women do, they are less likely to end up in ashrams, which is the setting in which Sri Aurobindo worked:

> "More easily [a loss of balance] occurs in the women than in the men but in some of the latter also. What produces the loss of balance is an inability to control the vital movements by the reason and an instability of the vital itself so that it sways from one feeling to another, one impulse to another without harmony or order." (22)

Remarkably, Sri Aurobindo made these observations in the early 1930s, before Stern coined the term "borderline" in 1938 to describe a group of patients who seemed to fall on the border between psychosis and neurosis. Western psychologists tended to think of this condition as a milder form of psychosis until the 1970s, when they finally came to focus on affect dysregulation as the core of the syndrome, which at the extreme can lead to cognitive distortions that become briefly psychotic. (23) Thus, Sri Aurobindo grasped the essence of affect dysregulation 40 years before Western psychologists did, and it is clear from the following letter that he had practical experience in dealing with some of its manifestations among his disciples. For example, in this discussion of the difficulties of "transforming the vital," he describes cognitive distortions, splitting, and emotional drama, and then goes on to make larger observations about the difficulties of yoga and even mentions parasuicidal behavior:

> "Accustomed as I am to the misunderstanding or misreporting of the Mother's statements, I found that this about her having said that transformation is easy carries the habit to the extreme limit. Needless to say, she did not and could not say anything of the kind and it is astonishing that you should believe she could say anything so absurd and false. I must remind you that I have always insisted on the difficulty of the sadhana. I have never said that to overcome doubt is easy; I have said on the contrary that it was difficult because it was the nature of something in the human physical mind to cling to doubt for its own sake. I have never said that to overcome grief, depression, gloom and suffering was easy; I have said that it was difficult because something in the human vital clings to it and almost needs it as part of the drama of life. So also I have never said that sex, anger, jealousy etc. were easy to overcome; I have said it was difficult because they were ingrained in the human vital, and even if thrown out were always being brought back into it either by its own habit or by the invasion of the general Nature and the resurgence of its own old response. These things I have repeated hundreds of times. Your idea that my difficulties were different from those of human nature is a mental construction or inference without any real basis. If I am ignorant of human difficulties and therefore intolerant of them, how is it that I am so patient with them as you cannot deny that I am? Why for years and years do I go on patiently arguing about your doubts, spending so much of my time, always trying to throw light on your difficulties, to show how things stand, to give reasons for a knowledge gained by living and *indiscutable* expe-

rience? Am I writing these letters every night because I have no understanding and no sympathy with you in your doubts and difficulties? Why do I wait patiently for years for sadhaks to get over their sex difficulties? Why do I tolerate and help and write soothing and encouraging letters to these women who break out and hunger-strike and threaten suicide once a fortnight? Why do we bear all this trouble and *tracas* and *fracas* and resistance and obloquy and harsh criticism from the sadhaks, why were we so patient with men like *X* and *Y* and others, if we had no understanding and no sympathy with the difficulties of human nature? It is because I press always on faith and discourage doubt as a means of approach to the spiritual realisation. What spiritual guide with a respect for truth can do otherwise?" (24)

Today, a variety of competing models of therapy have been developed for affect dysregulation syndrome(s), but almost all of them use some variation of ways to increase the ability of people to correct or balance distorted cognitions, and use cognitive and behavioral skills to regulate distressing emotions. (25) This is *exactly* what Sri Aurobindo meant by stabilizing the vital and using the "reason" to better control vital movements, and he uses reason to correct a cognitive distortion in the letter above. What CBP still has to add to this discussion about vital instability is that patients with affect dysregulation also have psychic beings, and this soul element should also be considered in clinical practice. Following is an example of this from Dr. Basu's practice:

Y, a 29 year old male, met all criteria for borderline personality disorder. In addition, he had a stint of polyandry where along with four other young men, he tried to replicate the way the five Pandava brothers in the Mahabharata co-habited with a single wife, Draupadi. He had experimented with all types of drugs and was himself an erratic genius, composing songs and setting them to tune. He had an aesthetic side and once when he was bent on committing suicide while trekking in the Himalayas, the sight of rhododendron flowers brought him back to his senses. It was very surprising that despite his idiosyncrasies, he could at times sit in deep meditation and once caught a glimpse of an inner light, an experience that overwhelmed him completely. That soul-quality explained why, despite his very unstable vital, he could understand, interpret and translate mystical literature at intervals.

Of note, despite patient Y's severe affect dysregulation and array of unstable relationships, he had somewhat stable transactions with a spiritually oriented therapist. She felt that Y had a very sensitive soul presence, in addition to a very disturbed vital consciousness, which is why he led a disorganized life but also he had some very remarkable talents and qualities. In such cases, therapeutic work on the ego needs to be complemented with an appreciation of the soul-quality in the subject, which should also be supported.

A common source of confusion between psychotherapy and spiritual practice lies in different definitions of the word "ego" in each field. In therapy, the aim is to strengthen the ego by repairing deficits and making unconscious conflicts conscious, whereas in spiritual practice the aim is often described as humility and "not having a big ego." Most of the apparent contradiction between these two approaches is simply a matter of semantics, for what is usually meant by "having a big ego" in common English is actually the ego deficit of narcissistic vulnerability due to insufficient nurturing and mirroring in childhood, as explained in Kohut's self-psychology. Thus, strengthening the ego through empathy-based therapy would actually reduce the narcissistic grandiosity of the "big ego" of common parlance, and thus promote growth towards humility. The co-author has explained how these two different approaches can be integrated in the CBP paradigm through a mature object-relationship with the Divine Consciousness, which is mediated by the psychic being. In this process, the clinical work of facilitating a transcendence of the ego would not be a regression to earlier stages of ego development but would add another source of sustenance — the awareness of the soul or psychic being. (26)

Practical advice about how to develop contact with the psychic being is presented in Chapter 12, along with further discussion of how to understand the relationship between the ego and the psychic being in both treatment and personal growth. For now, the point to emphasize is that CBP views *conscious* efforts to cultivate contact with the psychic being as central to both personal self-development and clinical practice. This work may not go easily or quickly, and it may be a lifetime's work — but it is fruitful work that has lasting value.

The Ego and the Psychic Being in Dementia

In elderly patients with dementia, the brain-based memory functions of the outer being are impaired, resulting in lower self-esteem, and the ego is unable to hold the surface personality together, which can result in a clinically wretched state labelled as "vegetative". However, the deepest soul-imprints are preserved as memory traces in the psychic being and are not affected by outer conditions or diminution of ego-functions. Thus, caregivers need to appreciate that it is not the ego-linked personality but the soul entity of the subject who needs to be addressed. While work with patients with dementia can be difficult and tiring, there is always reason to maintain hope. A deep soul-imprint can sometimes emerge from the depths to strike an unexpected chord, and the embodied psychic being can never be labelled as non-productive or vegetative. It maintains its poise and dignity even amidst adversities, as in the following case studies:

> A writer with cognitive decline found solace when the therapist quoted Milton's "On His Blindness." Milton overcame the existential crisis due to his blindness by identifying with palace sentries. The sentry does not run like a busy executive under the illusion of activity, rather, he just stands still but that is also a God-given role. Likewise, a mere cognitive loss does not rob one's role to serve God. God also needs subjects who serve in silence.

A clinical psychologist used an innovative method to restore the self-esteem of her demented father-in-law, a retired University Professor. She used the family photo album to help him to recognize and relive some of the happiest and proudest moments of his life. She used to remind him how his sacrifices made his children build their careers. He never needed an antidepressant. Later, a strange incident occurred: the Professor was a geneticist but uttered something during his illness which he had never expressed in his pre-morbid stage. He said that Sri Aurobindo had "somatic mutation." On questioning, he did not remember the context in which that term should have been used. However, it was a technically decent way to describe the state of Sri Aurobindo when his physical body remained fresh and without any signs of decomposition for five days after his departure on the 5th of December, 1950. (27)

As the second case above shows, memory is stored in consciousness that uses the brain for expression but is actually independent of the brain. In conducive conditions, a supra-rational faculty like intuition can awaken a dormant memory in the psychic being of a person with dementia. An interesting cultural example to note is that many communists in India have a well-developed spiritual perspective. Many such individuals turned to communism attracted by the gospel of social equality. This was particularly appealing in a country where caste divisions persist (even though decreasing in an age of individualism). Yet, in these people their political faith in communism often remains separate from imbibed spiritual values that may remain dormant behind a veil of atheism. While the façade of atheism is maintained by the ego, the spiritual values are reflected in the soul-essence. At some point in time, the psychic being can come forward and assert its presence. Such a phenomenon can happen on its own, or may follow some disenchantment. In certain cases of cognitive decline, the ego loses its habit of self-gratification paving the way for the deeper soul-element to come forward, adding a touch of sweetness to an otherwise lackluster life. This happened in the following case of a self-professed atheist:

An elderly communist with early cognitive decline was very upset that he was forgetting important things. His therapist told him to invoke the Truth. He asked how to do it. He was told to appeal to his inner Divine. In the Sanatana (perennial) tradition of India, the One Divine is invoked through many names and attributes, so the patient asked his therapist very sweetly how to select his inner Divine. He suddenly remembered that it was Maa Mansha who was his object of adoration during his childhood (Maa Mansha is the Divine Mother in the form where she offers protection from snakes. As many people die of snake-bite in rural Bengal, this aspect of the Divine Mother is quite commonly worshipped in villages). This realization sprang forth and was expressed with such confidence and emphasis that everyone else was surprised. Suddenly, the soul-remembrance took precedence over the ego.

Conclusion

In CBP, the ego is a false albeit temporarily useful construction that has to be replaced by the psychic being, or beyond-ego principle. The ego belongs to Nature or Prakriti, while the psychic being is a poise of the soul or Purusha. The replacement of the ego by the psychic being cannot be done easily and requires a life-long commitment. The core of this conscious discipline entails the psychic movements of aspiration, surrender and rejection as described by Sri Aurobindo. Those who aspire to a personal progress through consciousness should start by delving deep within themselves, in order to come into contact with the psychic being, as described in Chapter 3. Having established this contact, the next step is to witness the workings of the ego from the poise of the psychic being. Kireet Joshi points out that, "The discovery of the power of concentration or contemplation or the power of witnessing of the movements of Prakriti in the state of Purusha consciousness are extraordinary achievements of the yogic science". (28) Joshi also describes that if one wills freedom from subjection to Prakriti,

Prakriti itself collaborates and creates conditions for the rule of the Purusha. Thus, nature or the matrix of the personality facilitates the reign of the soul. (29) Today, many psychotherapies aim to transform problematic aspects of ego functioning using mindfulness and other forms of meditation and energetic work. This transitional zone of ego-transformational processes that starts from the outer being can be fulfilled by finding the psychic being, which is the key to tapping the deepest and highest transformative powers of consciousness.

United were Time's creative mood and tense
To the style and syntax of Identity.
A paean swelled from the lost musing deeps;
An anthem pealed to the triune ecstasies,
A cry of the moments to the Immortal's bliss.

Savitri, *pg. 90*

References

1. CWSA 23-24, pg. 360-361
2. Ibid, pg. 361
3. Agenda II, pg. 294-295
4. CWSA 21-22, pg. 634
5. Ibid, pg. 574-575
6. CWSA 29, pg. 247
7. Ibid, pg. 509
8. CWSA 21-22, pg. 552
9. CWSA 23-24, pg. 358
10. Ibid, pg. 358
11. Ibid,pg. 360
12. Ibid
13. Ibid
14. Ibid
15. Ibid, pg. 357-358
16. Agenda VII, pg. 308-309
17. CWM 05, pg. 253-25
18. Cortright, B: Integral psychology: yoga, growth and opening of heart. Albany: State University of New York Press 2007)

19. Salmon, Don & Maslow, Jan: Yoga Psychology and Transformation of Consciousness – Seeing Through the Eyes of Infinity, Paragon House, US,2007)

20. Miovic, Michael: Integral Yoga Psychology: Clinical Correlations, IJTP,37(1), 2018, pg. 199-225

21. Sansone, R. A., & Sansone, L. A. (2011). Gender patterns in borderline personality disorder. *Innovations in clinical neuroscience*, 8(5), 16–20.

22. CWSA 31, pg. 806

23. National Collaborating Centre for Mental Health (UK). Borderline Personality Disorder: Treatment and Management. Leicester (UK): British Psychological Society; 2009. (NICE Clinical Guidelines, No. 78.) 2, BORDERLINE PERSONALITY DISORDER. Available from: https://www.ncbi.nlm.nih.gov/books/NBK55415/

24. CWSA 31, pp. 198-199

25. Choi-Kain, L. W., Finch, E. F., Masland, S. R., Jenkins, J. A., & Unruh, B. T. (2017). What Works in the Treatment of Borderline Personality Disorder. *Current behavioral neuroscience reports*, 4(1), 21–30. https://doi.org/10.1007/s40473-017-0103-z

26. Miovic, M: Integral Yoga Psychology: Clinical Correlations in Integral Yoga Psychology: Metaphysics & Transformation as Taught by Sri Aurobindo, edited by Debahsish Banerji, Lotus Press, Wisconsin, 2020, pg. 363-402

27. Basu, S: Dementia, Personal Encounters, NAMAH, 19:1, 2011, pg. 25

28. Joshi,Kireet : Yoga Science and Technology of Consciousness in History of Science, Philosophy and Culture in Indian civilization (Gen Ed DP Chattopadhyaya), Vol XI, Part 3, Consciousness, Indian Psychology and Yoga,Ed by Kireet Joshi, Matthijs Cornelissen , Centre For Studies in Civilizations, 2004, pg. 5

29. Ibid, pg. 9

5
Occultism in CBP

Man's house of life holds not the gods alone:
There are occult Shadows, there are tenebrous Powers,
Inhabitants of life's ominous nether rooms,
A shadowy world's stupendous denizens...
Man harbours dangerous forces in his house.
The Titan and the Fury and the Djinn
Lie bound in the subconscient's cavern pit...
The dreadful powers held down within his depths
Become his masters or his ministers;
Enormous they invade his bodily house,
Can act in his acts, infest his thought and life.
Inferno surges into the human air
And touches all with a perverting breath.

Savitri, *pg. 480*

Just as the theory of psychology is incomplete without a meta-physical perspective, the application of psychology to life is also incomplete without appreciating the action of occult forces that are supra-physical. Sri Aurobindo and the Mother use the term "occultism" to refer to this arena of knowledge and action, because the word means "hidden," i.e., not perceptible by the five physical senses or the measuring instruments of material science. Occult-ism deals with forces, beings, and phenomenon that are non-mate-rial in origin, but which can have effects in the physical world or in the psychological system of individuals and even collectives.

One of the most important — and controversial — occult phenomenon in mental health is possession. Often, any mention of the word conjures up images of backwards religious fanatics who reject medical science and try to treat epilepsy only with prayer, or schizophrenia only with exorcism. This is not what we propose here, and as this chapter will show, CBP fully accepts the knowledge of medical science. However, there are occult factors that influence mental and physical health, and this chapter will present an explanatory model that understands the interaction effects among physical and supra-physical factors in illness.

"Possession" has been studied by medical anthropologists, though usually with the connotation that it is a cultural construct, meaning that there are no such things as "spirits" that actually possess people but that there are cultures that believe such things occur. Even well-meaning contemporary work in cultural anthropology that interprets "possession" in a positive light as healing, still falls into this intellectual trap of studiously avoiding the unavoidable problem of worldview. (1) The essential question to ask here is what if supra-physical forces and beings actually exist? While science and academia can conveniently avoid this question, and focus instead on things that can be measured, clinicians may have to confront it directly when they work with clients who believe in or have experienced supra-physical phenomenon. This is where the model of CBP can help. For example, there is a small body of work that takes the phenomenon of possession in its most literal sense, such as the "Spiritist" model of mental illness in Brazil. Derived from the work of Allan Kardec (pseudonym), a 19th century French intellectual, some mental health clinicians in Brazil have adapted the Spiritist perspective without rejecting the biopsychosocial paradigm of psychiatry. In this model of clinical practice, negative influences of disincarnated spirits and the trauma experienced in previous lives are dealt with via séances, passes, prayers and moral guidance. (2) However, while this spiritist approach at least acknowledges the potential existence of occult factors in illness, from the perspective of CBP it would benefit from a deeper look at the types of "entities" involved and their interactions with biopsychosocial mechanisms.

While it is true that there are cases of purported possession that are entirely cultural, it is also true that there are cases of actual occult attack or possession involving supra-physical forces and entities. However, the key is that occult attacks *do not negate the simultaneous reality of biological factors such as seizures or mental illness in possession states*. In a revealing letter written in 1923, Sri Aurobindo advised a concerned father about how to deal with occult influences that had affected his child. The letter is so insightful that it is worth quoting here, to frame the discussion:

> "I think it is best for me to state the case in its worst and not only in its best possible terms because it is necessary that you should know the full truth and have the courage to face it. These cases are not those of a truly physical malady but of an attempt at possession from the vital world; and the fits and other physical symptoms are signs, not of the malady itself, but of the struggle of the natural being against the pressure of the hostile influence. Such a case in a child of this age indicates some kind of accumulation in the physical heredity creating an opportunity or a predisposition of which the vital invasion takes advantage. It is especially the physical consciousness and the physico-vital which contain the germs or materials of this predisposition. The physical being is always changing its constituents and in each period of seven years a complete change is effected. If the symptoms of this predisposition in the nature are detected and a wise influence and training used by the parents to eradicate them and this is done so effectively that in the first seven years no seeds of the malady appear, then usually there is no further danger. If on the contrary they manifest by the seventh year, then the next period of seven years is the critical period and, ordinarily, the case would be decided one way or the other by or before the fourteenth year.
>
> There are normally three possible eventualities. The difficulty in dealing with the case of so young a child is that the mind is not developed and can give no help towards the cure. But as the mind develops in the second seven years it will, if it is not abnormally weak which I think is not the case here, react more and more against the influence. Aided by a good control and influence it may very well succeed in casting out the hostile intrusion and its pressure altogether. In that case the fits and other signs of the physical struggle pass away, the strange moral and vital tendencies fade out of the habits and the child becomes mentally, morally and

physically a healthy normal being.

The second possibility is that the struggle between the natural being and the intruding being may not be decisive in the psychic sense, that is to say, the intruder cannot take full possession but also he cannot be thrown out entirely. In that case anything may happen, a shattered mind and health, the death of the body or a disturbed, divided and permanently abnormal nature.

The third and worst possibility is that the intruding being may succeed and take entire possession. In that case the fits and other violent symptoms will disappear, the child may seem to be physically cured and healthy, but he will be an abnormal and most dangerous being incarnating an evil vital force with all its terrible propensities and gifted with abnormal powers to satisfy them." (3)

Several things are notable in this letter. First, Sri Aurobindo clearly understands the importance of childhood as a critical developmental period, and he even alludes to some of the stages in cognitive development later outlined by Piaget. Second, he makes a careful distinction between occult attacks, which cause transient fits (pseudo-seizures or agitation), and a full possession in which the signs of struggle with the invading entity resolve and a person starts to manifest the "terrible propensities" that in conventional psychology are often described as antisocial personality disorder. Third, Sri Aurobindo specifically cites "physical heredity" as an important predisposing factor for invasion by vital forces. Thus, Sri Aurobindo does not have a naive and simplistic worldview about evil spirits and how to cure them with seances, but a complex understanding about how biological, developmental, cognitive, and occult factors all interact over time to produce a range of possible outcomes.

Returning to what we will call his "interaction model" of possession states, in the 1930s Sri Aurobindo documented a series of astute clinical observations that demonstrate the subtlety of his perceptions and interpretations:

"I don't think — I know it is so [that epilepsy and insanity are due to the influence of evil spirits]. Epilepsy however is not possession — it is an attack or at most a temporary seizure. Insanity always indicates possession. The hereditary conditions create a predisposition. It is not possible for a vital Force or Being to invade or take possession unless there are doors open for it to enter. The door may be a vital consent or affinity or a physical defect in the being.

Insanity is always due to a vital attack, or rather possession although there is often a physical reason as well. Hysteria is due to a pressure from the vital world and there may be momentary possessions also. The same thing cannot be said of ordinary delirium, the cause of which is physical only — except in so far as all illness is an attack of lower forces of Nature, but these lower forces are not vital beings or what we call specifically hostile forces. They are simply performing their role in nature and of course there may be and probably is a being of some kind presiding over each kind of illness — in Bengal they give a special name to some of them and worship them as goddesses to avert the visitation. But as I say these are really Forces, not vital hostiles. As for the interest of vital beings in possessing men — beings of the vital world are not constituted like men — they take a delight in struggle and suffering and disorder — it is their natural atmosphere. They want besides to get the taste of the physical world without being under the obligation of taking on birth and developing the psychic being and evolving towards the Divine. They wish to remain what they are and yet amuse themselves with the physical world and physical body." (4)

Remarkably, Sri Aurobindo made these observations with no formal training in psychology or psychiatry, and at a time when Freud's psychoanalytic model was ascendant, which had no grounding in biology or neuroscience. In the first paragraph above, Sri Aurobindo specifically states that factors such as "hereditary predispositions" and "physical defects" help to create "a door" through which adverse vital forces enter a person and cause temporary or permanent possession states. Today we can describe these "physical defects" in the brain much more accurately than in the 1930s, thanks to MRIs, PET scans, EEGs, and other neuroscience technologies. We also know that abnormalities in neural circuits and functions, which are another sort of "physical defect," are key to the development of conditions such as schizophrenia and bipolar disorder. However, these refinements in scientific knowledge about the brain simply describe in more detail what Sri Aurobindo referred to as the "doors" through which vital forces enter. His basic concept of an interaction effect remains perfectly valid.

The second paragraph further elaborates this thesis, but makes the penetrating observation that the cause of hallucinations in delirium is purely physical — which is exactly what psychiatrists say today, and is why delirium is seen as a medical condition not a mental illness. Still, even if one concedes there is some logic to Sri Aurobindo's position, his views may seem abstract and theoretical. Many readers might still feel that "possession" is an exotic phenomenon that happens only in far off places, like villages in India and tribes in Africa or the Amazon, or in imaginary scenes of satanic possession from the movies. What modern city dweller has ever seen actual possession states in real life?

A good place to start is with two historical examples with which virtually all educated people are already acquainted--Hitler and Stalin. From the early 1930s on, Sri Aurobindo warned that Hitler posed a grave threat to human civilization, and on that basis he supported the Allies during World War II, a stance that was criticized in India where many were hoping that Hitler would topple the British Empire and thus liberate India. In addition to making very rational public comments about the dangerous political folly of hoping for a Nazi victory over the British, Sri Aurobindo and the Mother also made private comments about the fact that Hitler was possessed, and this is what gave him his stunning success early in the war. In the passage below, the Mother describes Hitler's possession states, and explains the occult difference between Hitler and Stalin:

"Was Stalin predestined to be what he was?

Stalin? I am not quite sure that he was a human being…in the sense that I don't think he had a psychic being. Or perhaps he did have one — in all matter, in every atom there is a divine centre — but I mean a conscious psychic being, formed, individualised. I don't think so. I believe it was a direct incarnation of a being of the vital world. And that was the great difference between him and Hitler. Hitler was simply a man, and as a man he was very weak-minded, very sentimental — he had the conscience of a petty workman (some said of a petty shoemaker), in any case of a little workman or a little school-master, something like that, a very small conscience, and extremely sentimental, what is called in French "fleur bleue", very weak.

But he was possessed. He was rather mediocre by nature, very mediocre. He was a medium, a very good medium — the thing took hold of him, besides, during spiritism séances. It was at that moment that he was seized by those fits which were described as epileptic. They were not epileptic: they were attacks of possession. It was thus that he had a kind of power, which however was not very great. But when he wanted to know something from that power, he went away to his castle, and there, in "meditation", there truly he invoked very intensely what he called his "god", his supreme god, who was the Lord of the Nations. And everything seemed to him magnificent. It was a being…it was small — it appeared to him all in silver armour, with a silver helmet and golden plume! It was magnificent! And a light so dazzling that hardly could the eyes see and bear that blaze. Naturally it did not appear physically — Hitler was a medium, he saw. He had a sort of clairvoyance. And it was at such times that he had his fits: he rolled on the ground, he driveled, bit the carpet, it was frightful, the state he was in. The people around him knew it. Well, that being is the "Lord of the Nations." And it is not even the Lord of the Nations in its origin, it is an emanation of the Lord of the Nations, and a very powerful emanation." (5)

Here, the Mother makes an occult distinction between cases of temporary possession by vital entities (Hitler) and cases of direct incarnation of vital beings (Stalin). Note that in this passage she also distinguishes between cases of epilepsy where a brain lesion serves as a gateway for adverse forces to enter (fairly common in clinical practice) and possession in the absence of a brain lesion (not so common). While skeptics and rationalists may smirk at the notion of possession, it should be pointed out that conventional historians still struggle to fully explain the vast scale of Hitler and Stalin's actions, which together account for over 60 million deaths, and many have grudgingly noted the Nazi interest in black magic, although they don't know what to make of it.

A second example of the interaction model of possession states that will be familiar to a wide audience is the controversial topic of aliens and UFOs, which have popped in and out of the news for the last century. Governments and militaries have conducted secret investigations on UFOs, and the U.S. government has recently admitted that UFOs exist — but they have no idea what they are. All they know is that multiple observers have witnessed phenomenon that cannot be explained by any technology known on Earth, and that is all that can be said. In the popular mind, UFOs are inevitably connected with aliens, and there has been a long-standing debate in mental health literature over whether believing in aliens is naïve or delusional. For example, in the 1980s, a spate of people in the United States reported being abducted by aliens and subjected to various experiments in UFOs. In the early 1990s, a Harvard psychiatrist, Dr. John Mack, interviewed some of these subjects using hypnosis and wrote a controversial book concluding that these subjects had, in fact, been abducted by aliens (6). Most of mainstream psychiatry reacted to Dr. Mack's work with condemnation, deeming it unscientific and potentially dangerous in that it could fuel the delusions of patients who need help. More nuanced critics felt that Dr. Mack was well-meaning, but interpreted his work as a failure to manage boundaries appropriately, meaning that he did not adequately separate his sympathy for patients who were suffering from his duty to provide a critical perspective as a professional. They correctly pointed out that Dr. Mack was not alone in grappling with this problem, as other investigators have come to believe in alien abduction, as well, and anthropologists have long struggled with how to balance the need to see a culture through the eyes of its members vs. maintaining a critical perspective. (7)

However, notably absent in all of this debate over aliens and UFOs is any acknowledgment of the fundamental problem of worldview. Both sides continue to assume that *either* aliens are physically real *or* they do not exist. The debate is thus framed as an argument between two different kinds of materialists — those who believe that aliens have physically flown to Earth from other planets light years away, and those who believe they do not physically exist at all. But what if aliens are not actually physical? What if they are non-material? What if aliens and UFOs are "real" but represent an interaction between what are colloquially called "spirit worlds" and our physical reality? Then both sides are partially right.

This is the CBP point of view: aliens and UFOs are real, but not primarily physical. They are entities or beings from subtle planes of consciousness who are either misperceived as being physical because people have no other explanatory model for their experience, or briefly materialize in the physical world. As the Mother and Sri Aurobindo explained, such materializations are possible but cannot last long and thus soon dematerialize. In fact, the Mother explicitly commented on the phenomeon of UFOs in a conversation from October 7, 1964:

> "I don't know if you've heard this, it's something P. told me. She was still in Switzerland, and shortly before she came back here, she had a vision (she was in her home, simply meditating, and she had a vision), and in her vision she saw five big "luminous cigars" going past like this, slowly, one behind the other, in single file. When she woke up, she wondered what

it was....And a few days later (maybe the next day or the day after, I don't know), she read in a newspaper the account of people in southern France (I don't remember in which part) who saw above the sea five "luminous cigars" go by, in single file, exactly the same color as those she had seen. But in their case, they saw it with their physical eyes. So that seems interesting. It was clearly a phenomenon of a subtle physical order (in its origin) or material vital (in its origin), but which manifested physically, and which may very well have come from other planets that are a little more subtle than the earth." (8)

This explains how it is that some people see aliens or UFOs, and yet there is no permanent physical evidence of their existence. From the perspective of CBP, there *are* such things as aliens and UFOs, but it is naïve to think that they physically flew here from half way across the material universe. Rather, aliens and UFOs are a modern mythology in the true sense of the word, meaning they are not "false" but are caused by the very same interaction between spiritual dimensions and the material world that produced other mythologies, such as those of the ancient Greeks, Hindus, Buddhists, Mayans, pagans, Christians, Muslims, Native Americans, Africans, and just about every other culture in the world.

This explanation of aliens and UFOs is not just theoretical. During his residency, the co-author, Dr. Miovic, actually met a patient who had a non-physical experience of alien abduction that demonstrates the validity of the CBP interpretation:

The case involved a Haitian woman with schizoaffective disorder who struggled with periods of suicidal depression. After multiple medication trials and psychotherapy with limited benefit, the patient was so desperate that she decided to go back to Haiti for a voodoo healing. She was actually a member of a Christian Pentecostal church that rejected voodoo practices, but she had been raised in Haiti in a family that practiced voodoo. According to her family tradition, her family was haunted by an African spirit that required propitiation. She had refused to do these rituals on account of her Christian faith, and thus she came to believe that her depression was due to the spirit taking revenge on her. So, she went to Haiti and did a voodoo healing ritual in a graveyard at midnight, which included lying in a coffin in a wedding dress and offering sacrificed chickens to the voodoo spirit. Remarkably, after this ritual she experienced complete remission of all of her symptoms for three months. Unfortunately, when she returned to the United States, she relapsed into psychotic depression with command hallucinations to kill herself. When I saw her in consultation, I had to hospitalize her for safety. After discharge, she spontaneously reported that while in the hospital, a "large, round flying thing" had come over the building and sucked her soul out of her body into the flying ship. While in this ship, strange little beings with black eyes did painful experiments on her, including taking eggs out of her ovaries.

As the patient recounted this vivid experience, I asked no questions other than, "was this experience physical or non-physical?" She repeatedly stated that the experience was *non-physical*, and when the frightening little beings were done, they put her "soul" back into her body in the hospital. Notably, she never used the words "alien" or "UFO," and I never told her about the history of aliens and UFOs in the United States. The topic faded from her memory after a few months, and did not become a lasting source of distress. Over time, she remained much more concerned about the voodoo spirit she felt was still attacking her. Medications helped her depression and command auditory hallucinations to some degree, but never had any impact on her belief in the voodoo spirit. (9)

This case illustrates how Sri Aurobindo's worldview can be useful in clinical practice, that there does not have to be any conflict between biological psychiatry and CBP, and that a patient's worldview can have a real impact on symptomatology. For instance, materialist patients in Europe and the United States may well be overly physicalizing their experiences of aliens and UFOs because they have no other explanatory model available to them. The Haitian woman above was able to translate her subtle experience of aliens and UFOs as being real — but not physical — because she had a non-material worldview. The advantage of CBP is that it allows clinicians to be equally interested in both the latest findings of material science *and* a patient's supra-physical experiences. Currently, mental health clinicians around the world are enjoined to "empathize" with patients, yet the only way to do that with people who have spiritual beliefs and experiences is to acknowledge that their spiritual worldview is right. Empathy requires validating accurate perceptions, and perceptions of supra-physical phenomena can be right.

Types of Occult Influence

There are different types and degrees of occult influence that one can see in clinical practice, and it is important to have a sense of this range and how to respond appropriately to each. The following two cases from Dr. Basu's practice illustrate simple situations that involve an occult influence, but for which no occult intervention is needed. Education, reassurance and standard care usually suffice:

- A 50-year old woman was very upset for over a year after becoming a widow, and reported regularly feeling and smelling an invisible form of her husband. She was even having "coital relations" with this invisible entity.
- A 55-year old woman reported that even ten years after her husband's demise, she was regularly smelling the odour of burnt corpses and funeral grounds. She had no diagnosable psychiatric illness.

In both cases, the subjects did not meet criteria for any major psychiatric illness, and there was no other disruption of their usual daily routines and household functioning. In uncomplicated cases such as these, Dr. Basu typically discusses the occult perspective with the client, and encourages them to make strong mental formations to ward off disharmonious influences. However, there are many cases that are more severe and may require more intensive interventions, including collaborative care that combines psychiatric treatment with occult interventions from a qualified and trusted healer.

In general, there are three important areas where occult intervention is used in many cultures around the world. The first two are addressed in this section, and the third in the next section:

1. Subjective psychological formations that arise in the individual, familial, or socio-cultural matrix
2. Perceived "ill-will" by others towards the subject, particularly when the "others" include persons significant in the subject's life
3. Actual hostile attack, influence, or possession.

The first two types above represent the projections of human mental formations and are addressed below, while the third involves invasion by full-fledged hostile entities and is addressed in the following section.

Subjective Psychological Formations

If one thinks strongly and repeatedly on a particular topic, one can succeed in making a mental formation that becomes an independent occult force. As the Mother explained, "every mental formation is an entity independent of its fashioner, having its own life and tending to realize itself in the mental world". (10) For this reason, the collective mental formations of whole cultures can also create occult mental formations, such as those of the hells, purgatories and paradises imagined in various religions. The Mother explained that these non-physical worlds are just the result of human mental formations, and "have only a very relative significance but with a relativity similar to that of material things here." (11)

However, even though created in imagination and having only a relative significance, such worlds can nevertheless be a source of intense psychological torment and suffering.

On the other hand, just as much as negative formations can cause disharmony, positive formations can be used to restore harmony. This can be done in usual psychotherapeutic settings without the help of occultists, and in fact both positive affirmations and cognitive techniques such as used to create positive "self-talk" in CBT have subtle effects at the level of consciousness that can undo negative mental formations. Similarly, prayers are also positive mental formations whose strength and persistence are built up by emotion and will. As the Mother explained, when one makes a positive formation and then invests it with "emotion, affection, tenderness, love, and an intensity of will, a dynamism, it will have a much greater chance of success". (12) Such a positive formation can be used not only for working on oneself but also to help someone at a distance.

Clinically, the negative effects of subjective psychological formations can present in a variety of ways and degrees. Here is a case of chronic depression where suicidal thoughts nurtured over years became a tormenting formation:

> A lady doctor who had suffered from migraines, chronic depression, and feelings of alienation and meaninglessness for over 15 years, suddenly told Dr. Basu that for the last 3 days she had been visualizing her corpse dangling over her head, and this had become unbearable. Given the extremity of the situation, she was referred for ECT, which alleviated her acute distress. Once she was feeling better, she confessed that unless such a drastic intervention had been done, she would have been driven to commit suicide.

In this case, the patient's nihilistic thoughts repeated over years had built up an organized formation which in turn was "possessing" her.

A second type of case involves psychological formations that arise in a socio-cultural matrix

An 8-year old boy was brought from the fringe areas of a city to the psychiatric clinic for being "possessed" by an entity, because the local faith healer (who usually dealt with "possession" cases) was out of town. The child belonged to a community of low-caste Hindus who earned their living by selling pork. He had stopped attending school without having any fever, which frightened his illiterate parents. On detailed probing, the boy stated that he had become possessed by a "Muslim" ghost in a field near his home. When he sat for the "draw a person" test, he drew a simple male figure; and when he was asked to draw the "Muslim ghost," he drew an almost similar figure. Dr. Basu decided to visit the field where the "ghost" abided. He was surprised to find a huge field in the semi-urban fringes of the city with an abandoned factory, and two rival communities living on either side of the field. On one side was the community of pork-selling Hindus, with a slaughter house for pigs, while on the other side of the field a beef-selling Muslim community with a slaughter house for cows. Not only were the two communities religious rivals, but the main business of each community was dealing with the substance that was taboo for the other. There was no overt conflict between the two communities, but an underlying mutual distrust persisted.

In this case, Dr. Basu did not appreciate the presence of an actual hostile entity that was possessing the boy, and concluded that the field between the two communities acted as a buffer zone where social conflicts converged to make a psychological formation that "possessed" an innocent mind made vulnerable by excessive parental demands for scholastic performance. In fact the boy's house was a simple shed with a crude table for selling pork. The boy's schoolbag and the family ration card (needed to procure subsidized cereals) seemed to be the only valued possessions in the family's make-shift home. Interestingly, the boy represented both himself and the "Muslim ghost" with similar figures. The Muslim community on the opposite side of the field from his home were ultimately derived from the same culture as the Hindus there, for they were originally Hindus who at some point converted to Islam. The boy's drawings thus suggested that despite social conflicts, a cultural commonality also existed between the two communities, and at some level the boy was trying to resolve this. Perhaps working on these communal issues could provide benefits to the mental health of both the boy and the community in the long run.

Perceived Ill-Will by Others

A third type of negative mental formation occurs when a subject strongly feels that someone else has ill-will towards them, particularly when the others include persons significant in the subject's life. While the source of "ill-will" may be wrongly ascribed to an innocent person, as happens in cases of paranoia, it is also a fact that much ill-will and envy does actually exist in various family, social, and cultural settings. From the perspective of CBP, this is why the fear of the "evil eye" cast by a malevolent glare is prevalent in so many traditional cultures around the world, leading to the use of various types of protective talismans. While the use of talismans is mostly superstitious and ineffective — unless prescribed by a capable occultist — the underlying phenomenon of ill-will itself has an occult reality. In many cultures one can hire people to perpetrate "black magic" against enemies, and this sort of ill-will can negatively affect the subject:

> A 15-year old girl presented with marked anxiety just prior to her high school examinations. She revealed that on and off she had been hearing a voice for the last few months, beckoning her to the Ganges River. This was a complaint that did not match with the rest of her clinical profile, which was otherwise healthy and stable. Surprisingly, her father revealed that he, too, had been hearing the same type of voice for the last few months, though he also had no other psychiatric problems.
>
> The psychiatrist was worried, as the family lived on a jute mill on the banks of the Ganges. In India, many folk tales recount incidents in which subjects are beckoned, presumably

by "evil spirits" or "vital entities" to come to the river, where they then drown.

On enquiry, it was found that there was a huge under-current of stress in this affluent family due to property disputes, especially between the girl's father and uncle. It was later discovered that the girl's uncle had commissioned an occultist to use what in common parlance is known as black magic against her father.

In this case, the problem was solved by simply bringing awareness to what was happening, and encouraging the girl and her father to invoke the Highest Truth for protection. The voices stopped, and there was no need to consult an occultist. The family accepted Dr. Basu's suggestion to invoke the Divine, and they felt this intervention was appropriate.

Hostile Attack and Possession

For CBP, it is important to understand that hostile forces and beings (entities) are real and can invade a susceptible individual via the inner or subliminal being. By cutting off the connection between the outer personality and the psychic being (soul), these hostile forces can have a range of negative effects on people, from temporary negative influences to full-blown possession states. Below are a couple of cases from Dr. Basu's practice:

A youngster in his 20s, an ardent devotee of the Lord who had been exclusively pursuing spirituality, complained of being harassed by a hostile, anti-spiritual entity that could take multiple forms to devalue his worth. The harassment was so severe, and the entity seemed to grip his outer personality with such ferocity, that he jumped twice from buildings in suicide attempts. The first time he jumped from a 6-storey building, and five years later from a 3-storey building. Surprisingly, he survived both times. Though he did sustain a spinal injury with resultant complications, he remained

> steadfast in his spiritual faith despite the hostile attacks, which lead to spells of feeling tormented. Psychiatric medications never provided much benefit except sedation and reducing aggressive outbursts.

In this case, there was a clear difference between the patient's psychic being and outer personality, or ego. It was only because of his psychic being that he was able to survive these hostile attacks and maintain faith — but due to weaknesses in his ego, he continued to fall prey to disruptive forces. It takes a long time for the soul to develop to the extent that the psychic being can come forward to replace the ego — and until that time, the outer personality (ego) can continue to face myriad problems. Also, it is worth noting that the psychic being can grow through all life circumstances, including hostile attacks. From the perspective of CBP, what helps in cases such as the above is a combination of external measures needed to mitigate physical harm and suffering, and supportive spiritual measures to encourage patients to continue growing in consciousness and learning how to cultivate contact with their psychic being. There will be many challenges and setbacks along the way, but over the long-term such a strategy at least stands a real chance of being helpful — whereas simply denying the fact of hostile attack and possession will yield no benefit at all.

A second case illustrates how at times subjects can be caught completely unaware of negative forces that grip the ego and lead to catastrophic events:

> A youngster in his early 20s died in a motor bike accident. He was a passenger and his friend who was driving was saved. His father had died two years back leaving him a factory to manage and he had actually gone on the bike for some factory work. Two weeks prior to the incident, his paternal cousin sister, who was also in her 20s, had committed suicide. Two weeks after the bike accident, the victim's maternal uncle in his 50s committed suicide in strange manner. He had no psychiatric problems and was a successful businessman living with his wife, and the couple were happy. On the

fateful day, he came running home from his workplace and shouted at his wife to call the neighbours, because he was going to die so everyone in the vicinity should be summoned. He rushed along proclaiming that his phone would fall off from his hands even if he did not want it — and this actually happened. By the time the neighbours arrived following his wife's frantic calls, he had already hanged himself to death.

Two weeks following this man's death by suicide, the bereaved sisters (the mother of the young man on the bike and the wife of the subject who hung himself were sisters) consulted me over their grief reaction. They were accompanied by their eldest sister, who reported that she was herself dreaming of committing suicide. The elder brother of the three sisters had committed suicide twenty years back.

When Dr. Basu heard this extraordinary sequence of events, apart from feeling shocked and saddened, he recognized the action of hostile forces behind this most improbable chain of events. The girl as well as the man who committed suicide were not biologically related with the subject who had committed suicide twenty years back, or with the lady having suicidal dreams at the present — so a simple genetic explanation of family suicide risk would not suffice. In India, the bonds between family members and their close relatives are very strong, so that one easily identifies with another's misery. Thus, Dr. Basu felt he was dealing with a phenomenon of collective (social) ego — hostile forces were invading this family system via their ego bonds with each other. It is known in the occult tradition that hostile forces can not only cause suicides but can also cause accidents to occur, however, the suicide of the 50-year old gentleman by hanging was really exceptional. While most people commit suicide after isolating themselves, this subject seemed to be dragged by an unseen force to commit the act suddenly and publicly, even though he had no psychiatric, marital, or economic problems. This was another clue as to the operation of hostile forces.

So what did Dr. Basu do? He endeavored to elicit the soul-strength (psychic presence) of the surviving members who had come for consultation. CBP deals with cases of hostile attack and possession by looking at the interaction between the psychic being (soul) and ego (outer personality). Via vulnerabilities in the ego, hostile forces can invade a person and cut off the access to the psychic being. The solution to this problem is to work simultaneously on both fronts: do whatever one can to support a person's spiritual practice and re-establish contact with their psychic being, while at the same time using psychological interventions and psychiatric medications to strengthen ego functioning as it is defined in biopsychosocial model.

Finally, note that hostile influences do not just induce suicidal impulses or psychotic symptoms, they can also incite aggression and violence. Thus, negative occult forces find much expression via people with antisocial personality disorder who lie, exploit and mislead others, lack empathy and conscience, engage in criminal activities, and often perpetrate physical and sexual abuse (addressed in the section on trauma in chapter 17). CBP has much to offer the study of antisocial individuals, also called psychopaths or sociopaths, in terms of the type and degree of hostile forces that they express.

Occult Factors and Suicide

We have already touched on suicide in several of the cases discussed above, but since suicide is such a central concern for psychology and psychiatry, further focus on this topic is warranted.

From the perspective of CBP, one thing to note is that the occult disturbance does not necessarily end with the act of a suicide attempt, or even the fact of a completed suicide. The occult force(s) that caused the suicidal impulses continue to exist in the subtle atmosphere and can exert influences and after-effects on vulnerable subjects. One way these negative occult forces find expression is by lingering in the physical vicinity of where the suicide attempt occurred. Because action gives expression to subtle forces, suicidal actions bring negative occult forces into the subtle physical atmosphere that envelops the physical world, but is not actually material. Thus, if a suicide attempt or completion occurs in a given house, the subtle atmosphere of the place gets infused with negative occult energies, and these can then influence other family members or inhabitants who live in that place, and even visitors can be affected. Likewise for public places, gardens, roads, railway tracks, water-bodies, and other locations where suicide attempts or completions have occurred. (13) This can create suicide "hot spots" that engender many suicide attempts, such as the Golden Gate Bridge in San Francisco did at one point in time. While some of this phenomenon is purely external and conventional (e.g. suicidal people see or read about a place where many suicide attempts have occurred, and decide to go there), one should not be blind to the potential occult factors as well.

Here are some cases from Dr. Basu's practice in which a persisting disturbance of the subtle atmosphere occurred and had consequential after-effects:

A married woman in her mid-twenties suddenly jumped into a pond to commit suicide, but was saved by passing strangers. She had an 8-month old baby, but there was no evidence of post-partum depression prior to the incident. Recently, a ceiling fan has been installed in her room. On enquiry, it turned out that a 12-year old boy (a nephew of her husband) had committed suicide by hanging himself from that same ceiling fan, in a separate house, only a week prior.

A 25-year old woman was continuously hearing a voice directing her to commit suicide, one year after her husband's brother had committed suicide. Another 30-year old woman was being told by a voice to commit suicide for a month after a neighbor committed suicide by hanging in the house just across from her bedroom. In both cases, there were no family histories of depression or any other psychiatric illnesses, and the subjects were completely healthy and happy until they were suddenly affected.

Once, when in the midst of a very busy clinic when he was pressed for time, Dr. Basu acted on an intuition and asked a depressed youngster if there had been a suicide close to his home. Nothing in the history suggested this, but the boy replied that yes, in fact a neighbour had committed suicide by hanging just outside his window a few days back. This had precipitated the boy's depression.

Disturbance of the subtle physical atmosphere by murder and suicide is the reason that many cultures have rituals for "cleansing" the location where such tragedies have transpired. While it is true that there can be imagination and speculation that such occult factors are present when they are not, it is also true that such occult phenomenon do occur. Perhaps the most incontrovertible and chilling proof of this effect are the old Nazi concentration camps preserved in Germany and Poland. The hostile forces were so concentrated there that one can still feel the disturbance in the atmosphere today, some 75 years later. And this is not just the authors' opinion — the dolorous effect of the atmosphere has been documented by countless of visitors over the years.

Another aspect of suicide that benefits from an occult understanding is the phenomenon of "flooding." One of the great practical problems of preventing suicide attempts is that they are so difficult to predict. Despite decades of research that have identified various suicide risk-factors, statistical models that try to use these risk-factors to predict suicide attempts in specific individuals have poor predictive value. One reason is that the string of life events that lead up to a suicide attempt are often not predictable (such as sudden unemployment, break-ups, deaths, and other losses), and another factor is the facilitative role of intoxication with substances (which occultly opens the doors to many negative forces and entities). Together, circumstances and intoxication can precipitate a moment of "flooding," during which the subject is suddenly consumed with an onslaught of cognitions to kill oneself accompanied by intense emotional distress. From the occult perspective, flooding is due to a hostile attack, and hostile forces and entities can also influence life-events leading up to suicide attempt by disturbing the whole atmosphere around a subject. Thus, occult factors are involved in the whole pathway leading up to suicide attempts, and influence psychology, biology, sociology, culture, and even the probability fields that surround the genesis of seemingly random or "freak" accidents and events. To see the reality of these complex interactions among conventional and occult factors, one needs the lens of CBP.

Lastly, a comment on morality and suicide. The semitic religions consider suicide to be a "sin," while Buddhism and Hinduism consider that it engenders negative karma. The Mother several times commented that suicide attempts are an act of cowardice. (14) However, these statements need to be contextualized. She did not believe in religion or conventional morality, and she did not belittle or blame individuals no matter what their difficulties were. She was interested in the transformation of consciousness, and was concerned about the doorway that suicide attempts open for the influx of hostile occult forces and entities. She was a spiritual pragmatist, and from that perspective suicide is useless because one will only be reborn to face the same problem of consciousness again, and she felt it was better to be brave and face life's problems now, rather than to act out of fear and face worse problems later. As Sri Aurobindo observed,

> "Suicide solves nothing — it only brings one back to life with the same difficulties to be faced in worse conditions. If one wishes to escape from life altogether, it can only be by way of by complete inner renunciation and merging oneself in the Silence of the Absolute or by a bhakti that becomes absolute or by a karmayoga that gives up one's own will and desires to the will of the Divine.
>
> I have said also that the Grace *can* at any moment act suddenly, but over that one has no control, because it comes by an incalculable Will which sees things that the mind cannot see. It is precisely the reason why one should never despair, — that and also because no sincere aspiration to the Divine can fail in the end". (15)

Covert Attraction for Hostile Forces

Sri Aurobindo also made the very important observation that completely resolving hostile attacks can take a long time as "these vital beings are very sticky and persistent and are always returning to the attack." (16) Thus, even if an occult intervention is used to free the subject from the invasion of hostile force or entity, they can relapse repeatedly. The cure can be made rapid if the subject, even at a young age, develops a will in the mind to change,

> "for that will take away the ground of the hostile influence. It is because something in him (*the subject*) is amused and takes pleasure in the force which comes with the influence that these things are able to recur and continue. This element…calls the invading presence back even when it has been centrally rejected". (17)

The Mother also commented on how people can call back the hostile influence, leading to relapse. The cause for this can be simple amusement or pleasure in the experience, as Sri Aurobindo mentions here, or narcissistic or histrionic traits as the Mother mentions below. These ego-based problems can certainly be addressed in therapy, and the issue applies to both children and adults. The Mother explains this mixture of occult and ego-based dynamics lucidly in the following talk:

> "You have something in you which attracts this force; take, for example (it is one of the most frequent things), the force of depression, that kind of attack of a wave of depression that falls upon you: you lose confidence, you lose hope, you have the feeling you will never be able to do anything, you are cast down. It means there is in your vital being something which is naturally egoistic, surely a little vain, which needs encouragement to remain in a good state. So it is like a little signal for those forces which intimates to them: "You can come, the door is open." But there is another part in the being that was watching when these forces arrived; instead of allowing them

to enter, the part which sees clearly, which knows, which has power, which resists, says: "No, I do not want that, it is not true, I do not want it", and sends them back. But you have not necessarily been cured of the little thing within you which permitted them to come. You must go very deep within, work within you persistently to be able to efface all possibility of calling. And so long as you have not completely effaced it, the attack will recur almost unexpectedly. You push it back — it is like a ball you throw against the wall, back it returns; you push it back once again and again it returns — until the moment there is no longer anything to attract it. Then it does not return again.

Therefore, the most important thing to do when you are attacked by an adverse force, is to say to yourself: "Yes, the force comes from outside and the attack is there, but there must certainly be a correspondence in my nature, otherwise it could not have attacked me. Well, I am going to look and find within me what allows this force to come and I am going to send it back or transform it or put the light of consciousness upon it so that it may be converted, or drive it away so that it remains no longer within me...." There is a way, you see? When the force comes, the adverse force, when it attacks, the part which corresponds rushes out to meet it, it goes forward. A kind of meeting takes place. If at that time, instead of being altogether overwhelmed or taken by surprise and off your guard, you observe very closely what it was within you that vibrated (it makes the sound tat, tat, tat: another thing has entered), then you can catch it. At that moment, you catch it and say to it: "Get out with your friends, I don't want you any longer!" You send away the two together, the part that attracted and the thing it attracted; they are sent away and you are absolutely clear.

For that, you must be very vigilant and have a little courage, in the sense that at times you have to grip it hard and then pull it out — it hurts a little — and then you throw it out along with the forces you send away. After that, it is finished. And so long as this is not done, it comes back and back again;

and then if one is not in oneself sufficiently courageous or vigilant or persevering, the fourth or fifth time one falls flat and says: "That's too much, I have had enough!" So the force installs itself, contented, satisfied with its work; and then you can see it laughing, it enjoys itself immensely, it got what it wanted. Now to send it back again means a very considerable work. But if you follow the other method, if you look closely this way: "Well, I am going to catch the thing that has allowed it to come", you see somewhere within you something rising, wriggling, coming up in response to the evil force which is approaching. That is the moment to seize it and throw it out with all the rest.

But when we throw it out, it does not die. Then it can go elsewhere once more, for it remains in the world.

Exactly. It remains in the world and it will surely go else-where — until it meets someone who has sufficient spiritual and occult power to dissolve it, and that is very difficult.... One must be very strong, possess a very great knowledge and power to dissolve a movement that has (this can be said at least) its reason for existence in the world — I do not say it is legitimate, but still it has its reason for existence. There are things which can be dissolved; but if somewhere in the world it exists in someone, he can reconstitute it. It is the same thing when people are attacked by small beings of the vital world, hostile beings who attack them, install themselves in their atmosphere, trying to possess them, that is, enter into them and use their body and all the rest. These beings — it is very difficult for the individual to get rid of them: that needs a very, very hard yoga. But one who has the knowledge and the power and who sees them can very well get them out of the atmosphere and destroy them. But if one who is at-tacked keeps within himself this little affinity which allowed the thing to enter, then he will recall it. I have had several examples of the kind, several.

I had the example of a person who was three-fourths pos-sessed and at the moment manifested a kind of power, a force that was not very good, but all the same it gave the impression of a force, a power, a capacity. Only he recognised that it was bad and was for evil, and prayed to be relieved of it. The opportunity comes: the being shows itself separately from the person it possesses, it can be seized, pulled out and dissolved. Then the one who had been possessed suddenly feels that he is becoming as commonplace as anybody else. That feeling of power he had is now lost and he feels he is becoming quite ordinary and says: "I have no special faculties, I have no special value, I have no special capacity, I am quite an ordinary person and less than ordinary, of a sickening commonness!" Now what does he do? He prays to have his possession back again. And so a few days later, I find him as possessed as ever.

Well, here it is truly not worth the trouble. One has only to leave them to their fate. This has happened many a time. In such people, you know, it is a kind of vanity which generally opens the door to those forces; they wished to be big, powerful, to play an important role, to be somebody; that attracts the force and so they become like that, possessed. The thing is taken away from them: all their remarkable capacity disappears at the same time and their self-satisfied vanity as well. They have the feeling they have become something quite ordinary and a tiny little thing within them says: "Oh! it was better before...." For one that is destroyed, there are always ten ready to come in. That's how it is, it is a strange task!" (18)

Thus, far from being naive spiritualists who did not understand psychology, Sri Aurobindo and the Mother had a sophisticated understanding of how occult factors interact with the ego-based dynamics of the outer being. This understanding includes a role for physical factors in illness (heredity, brain lesions, biology), psychological factors (depression, narcissism, histrionic traits, even antisocial personality disorder), cultural factors, and occult forces and beings.

Occult Influences in Children

Occult influences in children are underestimated and ill-understood, though it may be necessary to detect and counter such effects in formative years so as to prevent permanent suffering later in life. In India, Dr. Basu has found cases of children who were not traumatized or abused, but who suffered negative occult influences via from visits to cremation and funeral grounds at too early an age (before cognitive capacities flower), usually to attend the last rites of grandparents. Again, it is not that every child under such circumstances will suffer — only vulnerable individuals are affected, which can lead to chronic psychiatric problems later in life.

Precautions to ward off hostile influences depend on whether the child has developed cognitive faculties or not. If the cognitive repertoire is not fully developed, as is the case before seven years of age, the mind cannot help or be helped in the therapeutic process. Sri Aurobindo suggested two remedies for mitigating occult influences in children. The first and easiest is hypnotherapy, although:

> "it must be applied by someone who is not himself under the influence of evil powers, as some hypnotists are. For that obviously will make matters worse. Moreover, it must be done by someone who has the proper training and knows thoroughly what he is about, for a mistake might be disastrous". (19)

The second way to cure would be the spiritual power and influence of a sufficiently conscious healer or spiritual teacher, especially augmented by "certain psycho-spiritual means" (this is in obvious reference to occult-spiritual techniques). However, Sri Aurobindo opined that it is rare to find the person with the right knowledge. He explained that the "spiritual influence by itself can do it but the working is likely to be slow". (20) An augmentation by occult-spiritual techniques would be more efficacious but this would need a practitioner with yogic qualities such as having quiet will, confidence and calmness; being both fearless and yet detached; and being unshaken by resistance and undiscouraged by the manifestations of the illness.

Occult Effects of Standard Treatments

Finally, it is important to consider how to approach occult phenomenon such as hostile attack and possession in clinical work environments that do not accept the reality of supra-physical forces. There are two components to this: first, understanding how and why standard treatment within the current biopsychosocial model is itself a sort of occult intervention; and second, how humor can be used to address the cultural taboo against possession.

To begin with, remember Sri Aurobindo's interaction model of possession: physical factors are real gateways through which adverse forces can enter a person, and these physical factors can be addressed with the medical model. Thus, many occult influences can be blocked unknowingly, yet effectively, by clinicians who prescribe psychiatric and anticonvulsant medications, and CBP sees a great value in doing so. Also, just as ill-will can have a negative occult influence on people (as described previously), so too can the goodwill of the mainstream medical and mental health systems have positive healing effects, some of which effects are in fact non-local. Medical ethics and standard-of-care treatment are nothing if not an extended cultural exercise in creating a sustained and positive mental formation. The huge amount of global work, cooperation, compassion, and intellectual discipline that went into the building of this biopsychosocial model from the dawn of civilization until today, is itself a powerful occult force for the good. A case from the co-author's experience as psychiatry resident in the United States nicely illustrates this point:

> The case involved a man with schizophrenia who was suffering extremely violent paranoid delusions and needed to be placed in a locked cell for several months. I went in to interview him one day and was struck by the dark, demonic force that clouded his consciousness. Chills ran down my

spine, fear gripped my heart, and I felt like fleeing the room. I had no doubt that I was in the presence of an evil force that had possessed the man. The next day I rotated onto another clinical service and had no further contact with the patient until a year later, when I happened to meet him again at an outpatient day treatment program. At that point he was on clozapine (a powerful antipsychotic medication) and was participating in a day hospital program that employed highly skilled social workers, psychiatrists, nurses and support staff. I was surprised to find that the formerly possessed man had become one of the most tender and gentle patients I had ever seen. The darkness in his aura was mostly gone, pushed far into the background as a potential that could return but was now effectively held in check, and the man had a lovely psychic sweetness about him though his cognitive capacity remained quite confused due to chronic schizophrenia.

Since this man did not receive any occult intervention that his team was aware of, I concluded that the positive consciousness of the mental health system itself had repelled the hostile attack on him. That is, the goodwill of the staff who cared for him, the science involved in making and managing his medication, and the humanistic values of the society that supported his treatment, were altogether unpalatable to the hostile being that wished to destroy him. So the demon withdrew, perhaps to wait for a lapse in treatment to attack again, or to go in search of some other place where the practice of medical ethics and knowledge was less robust. (21)

Thus, it must be emphasized that CBP views medical science and standard-of-care treatment as absolutely essential to dealing with negative occult forces. In fact, the suggestion by some proponents of complementary medicine that standard treatment is dangerous — is itself dangerous, and reflects an attempt by hostile forces to undermine Reason. CBP makes a careful distinction between infra-rational vital movements (fear, superstition, irrational subjectivity, etc.) and supra-rational intuition. The aim in CBP is to set Reason as the minimum consensus level of healthcare discourse, and then to build upwards beyond that with the integration of true spirituality and intuition into mental health theory and practice.

Once one understands this first step of applying the standard biopsychosocial model to treating occult forces, one can then weave in the second step, which is dealing with the cultural taboo against possession among clinicians and/or patients. A recent case from Dr. Miovic's work at a community medical hospital in the United States illustrates one way in which this can be done:

> A 62-year old woman was admitted to the Neurology service for work up of possible seizures. She was having repetitive spells of blurting out suicidal statements such as "Kill me now, kill me now!", "Stab a knife through my heart!" and "Die, die, die, die!!" During these spells she would make frightening faces and sometimes swear or yell. After the episode passed, 5-10 minutes later she would recall having felt anxious or distressed, but showed no evidence of depression or suicidal thinking. EEG, brain imaging, and CSF studies were all normal, so the neurologist concluded the presentation must be psychiatric. She astutely wondered if the problem might be tics of Tourette's disorder.
>
> When Dr. Miovic saw the patient, he agreed that it looked like an unusual presentation of Tourette's syndrome. However, he also observed that the episodes looked like mini-possession states. A negative occult consciousness could be felt coming through the patient during these episodes, but she was otherwise very peaceful and pleasant in between the spells. Because neither the patient nor clinicians in this situation believed in supra-physical forces, Dr. Miovic dealt with the situation using humor — he made some joking comments about medieval medicine and that "If I didn't know better, I'd say this woman is possessed." The nurses and doctors laughed and agreed that it did look like mini-possession states. The patient was given risperidone 0.5 mg twice per day, which completely suppressed the episodes. Both the patient and the clinicians were relieved, and felt satisfied to

know she had Tourette's syndrome and not some hocus-pocus medieval possession state. However, in private Dr. Miovic concluded she had both.

Conclusion

CBP uses an interaction model in dealing with occult phenomenon such as hostile attack and possession. In this model, medications, psychotherapy, and other biopsychosocial interventions are all important in dealing with the physical and psychological gateways through which adverse supra-physical forces can enter people. Spiritual and/or supra-physical approaches to healing can be integrated according to patient and clinician comfort level, and we shall return to this topic in Chapter 12. However, note that CBP recommends against an infra-rational approach to occultism in which practitioners try to counter one lower occult force by leveraging another lower force. This method is potentially dangerous to both the subject and the occultist. Psychiatrically unstable subjects (especially those suffering from psychosis, depression and personality disorders) can decompensate when subjected to such "occult correction" by countering one hostile entity with another. A safer and more useful method is to take a more spiritual approach in which one invokes higher forces of Consciousness, and allows these to establish a sense of harmony, peace and equilibrium. Recognizing the occult action of hostile forces and beings requires intuitive development on the part of the clinician, and one should only venture into this realm of practice if one has a strong faith in the Divine, an absence of fear regarding these forces, and a sort of detachment so that one does not get sucked into the drama off which these forces feed.

Finally, note that because occultism leads to a sort of objective knowledge — that is, objective in the sense of depending on the skill rather than the intentions of the user of this knowledge — it can be misused. Occultism can be used to harm or heal, and its lowest applications are compassed by the term "black magic." Not surprisingly then, it has developed a bad reputation and it is due to these negative applications that many spiritual traditions avoid occultism altogether. However, to avoid occult knowledge completely is to throw out the proverbial baby with the bath water. Scientific knowledge, too, can be misused and applied to unethical ends, but we do not therefore stop the development of all material science. Rather, we develop a culture of ethical standards to guide the appropriate use of scientific knowledge — and the same has to be done with occultism. In fact, this chapter is part of developing such a culture. As the Mother emphasized:

"Occult knowledge without spiritual discipline is a dangerous instrument, for the one who uses it as for others, if it falls into impure hands. Spiritual knowledge without occult science lacks precision and certainty in its objective results; it is all-powerful only in the subjective world. The two, when combined in inner or outer action, are irresistible and are fit instruments for the manifestation of the supramental power". (22)

And as he sang the demons wept with joy
Forseeing the end of their long dreadful task
And the defeat for which they hoped in vain,
And glad release from their self-chosen doom
And return into the One from whom they came

Savitri, *pg. 417*

References

1. Seligman, R. Possessing Spirits and Healing Selves: Embodiment and Transformation in an Afro-Brazilian Religion. Palgrave MacMillan series on Culture, Mind and Society, 2014.

2. Moreira-Almeida, Alexander & Lotufo Neto, Francisco: Spiritual views of Mental Disorders in Brazil, Transcultural Psychiatry, Vo.42(4), 2005:570-595

3. CWSA 36, pg. 374-375

4. CWSA 31, pg. 805-806

5. CWM 5, pg. 377-378

6. Mark, John E: Abduction: Human Encounters with Aliens, Scribner, New York,1994

7. Eghigian, G. "The Psychiatrist, the Aliens, and 'Going Native.'" *Psychiatric Times*. 2014; 31:11.

8. Agenda V, pg. 222

9. Miovic, M: Integral Yoga Psychology: Clinical Correlations, International Journal of Transpersonal Studies, 31(1), 2018, pp.199-225

10. CWM 8, pg. 253

11. Ibid, pg. 217

12. CWM 8, pg. 253

13. Basu, S: Aftermath of Suicide – a consciousness perspective. Namah, The Journal of Integral Health, 26:1, 2018, pg. 38

14. CWM 7, pg. 23

15. CWSA 35, pg. 620

16. CWSA 36, pg. 376

17. Ibid.

18. CWM 5, pg. 93-96

19. CWSA 36, pg. 375

20. Ibid, pg. 376

21. Op. cit. Integral Yoga Psychology: Clinical Correlations

22. CWM 12, pg. 91-92

6

Individual and Collective Growth

One soul's ambition lifted up the race

Savitri, *pg. 44*

Thus far we have been focusing on individual psychology. However, the individual exists within a collectivity or social matrix, and hence this dimension also needs to be considered from the consciousness perspective. In mainstream psychology, this social dimension has been approached through several schools of thought, including Erickson's model of development across the lifespan, which studied how individuals learn over time to work, maintain mature relationships, and achieve generativity towards others. It has also been approached through social psychology, which has studied how an individual's thoughts and behaviors can be altered (often manipulated) by social interactions; and in a larger sense by sociology and anthropology, which have studied the influence on human behavior of things such as class, caste, gender, economic factors, religious affiliation, political orientation, culture, etc. All of this work has focused mostly on what the Mother and Sri Aurobindo called the outer being, and on the dynamics of the ego within this social matrix. Relatively little work has been done on the interaction between the inner being and the social matrix. Religious education is mostly an outer process that does not address this inner dimension of growth, and to the degree that more truly spiritual attempts were made to address the social matrix of development, these were generally small and focused on a limited number of adults who had dedicated themselves to a spiritual quest (e.g., ashrams, sangams, hermitages for nuns and monks, and other such small groups).

One of the major contributions that Sri Aurobindo and the Mother made to CBP was to articulate that psycho-spiritual development should and could embrace a social dimension. Sri

Aurobindo explained some of the theoretical aspects of this in *The Human Cycle,* which addresses the quest for a spiritualized society that would be global in scope while yet retaining the unique spiritual essence of each country and culture in the world. He began to experiment with the practical aspects of what he called "collective yoga" by founding the Sri Aurobindo Ashram, in Pondicherry, in 1926. However, it was the Mother who oversaw the day-to-day operations of the Ashram and interacted constantly with members of this community, and in this leadership role she brought forth pioneering advances in spiritual practice.

In the 1930s, the Sri Aurobindo Ashram was a small community of adult disciples, most of whom had come from various parts of India, but a few of whom had come from Europe and the United States. Over time, friends and family members of these original disciples learned about the work of Sri Aurobindo and the Mother, and wanted to have more contact with the Ashram, which was done via brief visits. In 1943, in response to the threat of a potential Japanese invasion of north-east India, family members of ashram inmates wanted a safe place to raise their children. The Mother accepted this request, and founded the Ashram school. It was major innovation. Up until that moment, for the prior 3,000 years or more, ashrams and Buddhist sangams had always given more focus on teaching grown-ups. With the founding of the Ashram school, the Mother suddenly extended the scope of yoga to include children.

During the 1950s, the Mother poured much energy into developing the Ashram school, including teaching French and participating in sports activities (she was a fairly good tennis player). She built a gym, swimming pool, and sports grounds, and encouraged students to participate in a wide range of sports and creative activities. She used a "free progress" philosophy that allowed each student to choose the subjects that interested them, and progress at the pace the student wished. She did not believe in mandated curricula, grades, and teaching to achieve test scores. She felt that the real role of education was to help a student find his or her psychic being, and to help the soul organize and express itself in life in whatever way the psychic being was inclined. As part of this work, she gave evening talks on integral yoga to a mixed audience of adults and younger students. She spoke in French, to help students learn the language, and also used the venue to answer a wide range of questions and give practical advice. These extemporaneous talks, translated from French, express Sri Aurobindo's ideas in accessible language and often with vivid illustrations from her own life, or from well-known historical events.

The Mother observed that many children have a sort of innate or pre-abstract spiritual sensibility, and that this spontaneous inner opening usually fades as people "grow up." Her explanation for this phenomenon was simple yet profound: children have souls, yet usually lose contact with their souls as they age and place more emphasis on mental development. This view of development fits with the universal human perception that children have an innocent sort of wisdom that adults lose, and yet mainstream models of psychology completely overlook this aspect of development. According to current psychology, adults are mature and children are immature, and adults are in every way more developed than children. The genius of the Mother was to point out this "normal" view of development is wrong — adults are more developed than children in some ways, but often less developed in others. We all know and feel this, and yet there were no words to describe this phenomenon until the Mother expressed it.

It is in this context of commitment to the growth of the psychic being in humans of all ages, that one must appreciate the Mother's talk to the Ashram students on January 8, 1951. She starts with some choice words on the ills of religion and standard methods of education, shows that she thoroughly understands the modern concept of cultural relativity, and then she goes on to articulate her philosophy of psychic education:

> "There is another quality which must be cultivated in a child from a very young age: that is the feeling of uneasiness, of a moral disbalance which it feels when it has done certain things, not because it has been told not to do them, not because it fears punishment, but spontaneously. For example, a child who hurts its comrade through mischief, if it is in

its normal, natural state, will experience uneasiness, a grief deep in its being, because what it has done is contrary to its inner truth.

For in spite of all teachings, in spite of all that thought can think, there is something in the depths which has a feeling of a perfection, a greatness, a truth, and is painfully contradicted by all the movements opposing this truth. If a child has not been spoilt by its milieu, by deplorable examples around it, that is, if it is in the normal state, spontaneously, without its being told anything, it will feel an uneasiness when it has done something against the truth of its being. And it is exactly upon this that later its effort for progress must be founded.

For, if you want to find one teaching, one doctrine upon which to base your progress, you will never find anything — or, to be more exact, you will find something else, for in accordance with the climate, the age, the civilization, the teaching given is quite conflicting. When one person says, "This is good", another will say, "No, this is bad", and with the same logic, the same persuasive force. Consequently, it is not upon this that one can build. Religion has always tried to establish a dogma, and it will tell you that if you conform to the dogma you are in the truth and if you don't you are in the falsehood. But all this has never led to anything and has only created confusion.

There is only one true guide, that is the inner guide, who does not pass through the mental consciousness.

Naturally, if a child gets a disastrous education, it will try ever harder to extinguish within itself this little true thing, and sometimes it succeeds so well that it loses all contact with it, and also the power of distinguishing between good and evil. That is why I insist upon this, and I say that from their infancy children must be taught that there is an inner reality — within themselves, within the earth, within the universe — and that they, the earth and the universe exist only as a function of this truth, and that if it did not exist the child would not last, even the short time that it does, and that everything would dissolve even as it comes into being. And because this is the real basis of the universe, naturally it is this which will triumph; and all that opposes this cannot endure as long as this does, because it is That, the eternal thing which is at the base of the universe.

It is not a question, of course, of giving a child philosophical explanations, but he could very well be given the feeling of this kind of inner comfort, of satisfaction, and sometimes, of an intense joy when he obeys this little very silent thing within him which will prevent him from doing what is contrary to it. It is on an experience of this kind that teaching may be based. The child must be given the impression that nothing can endure if he does not have within himself this true satisfaction which alone is permanent.

Can a child become conscious of this inner truth like an adult?

For a child this is very clear, for it is a perception without any complications of word or thought — there is that which puts him at ease and that which makes him uneasy (it is not necessarily joy or sorrow which come only when the thing is very intense). And all this is much clearer in the child than in an adult, for the latter has always a mind which works and clouds his perception of the truth.

To give a child theories is absolutely useless, for as soon as his mind awakes he will find a thousand reasons for contradicting your theories, and he will be right.

This little true thing in the child is the divine Presence in the psychic — it is also there in plants and animals. In plants it is not conscious, in animals it begins to be conscious, and in children it is very conscious. I have known children who were much more conscious of their psychic being at the age of five than at fourteen, and at fourteen than at twenty-five; and above all, from the moment they go to school where they undergo that kind of intensive mental training which draws their attention to the intellectual part of their being, they lose almost always and almost completely this contact with their psychic being.

If only you were an experienced observer, if you could tell what goes on in a person, simply by looking into his eyes!…It is said the eyes are the mirror of the soul; that is a popular way of speaking but if the eyes do not express to you the psychic, it is because it is very far behind, veiled by many things. Look carefully, then, into the eyes of little children, and you will see a kind of light — some describe it as candid — but so true, so true, which looks at the world with wonder. Well, this sense of wonder, it is the wonder of the psychic which sees the truth but does not understand much about the world, for it is too far from it. Children have this but as they learn more, become more intelligent, more educated, this is effaced, and you see all sorts of things in their eyes: thoughts, desires, passions, wickedness — but this kind of little flame, so pure, is no longer there. And you may be sure it is the mind that has got in there, and the psychic has gone very far behind". (1)

This simple insight — that too much mental development obscures contact with the soul — has enormous implications for psychology. Most of human life such as it is currently structured is aimed at developing people's minds from a very young age, teaching them to use the mind to solve life's problems, and then rewarding them economically and with social status for having used the mind to do something in the world. And yet Sri Aurobindo commented succinctly that the mind had indeed gone bankrupt! Sri Aurobindo and the Mother observed that the mind does not definitively solve any problems in human life — rather, it converts one type of problem into another type. Thus, the miseries of pre-industrial life (high infant mortality, food scarcity, oppressive monarchies, poor medical care, etc.) have been converted into the post-industrial problems of overpopulation, resource depletion, climate change, urban dystopias, multi-drug resistant organisms, the threat of global nuclear war, and increasingly polarized and paralyzed democratic states. Yes, good things have happened along the way — but bad things never go away, and every social or technological fix leads sooner or later to unanticipated negative consequences that create new, larger and more complex problems than people had previously imagined were possible.

The Mother's public-health solution to all these ills is psychic education: create a social matrix from cradle to grave, the goal of which is to help people find and maintain contact with the psychic being, and to express the psychic being in life and action across the lifespan. That, in short, is what she was doing in the Ashram and the Ashram's school. In 1954, she wrote a short statement about her visionary plan, entitled "A Dream." As you can see, while being optimistic about the future, she was a realist about the limitations of the world (and her own ashram) such as it is at the moment:

"There should be somewhere on earth a place which no nation could claim as its own, where all human beings of goodwill who have a sincere aspiration could live freely as citizens of the world and obey one single authority, that of the supreme truth; a place of peace, concord and harmony where all the fighting instincts of man would be used exclusively to conquer the causes of his sufferings and miseries, to surmount his weaknesses and ignorance, to triumph over his limitations and incapacities; a place where the needs of the spirit and the concern for progress would take precedence over the satisfaction of desires and passions, the search for pleasure and material enjoyment. In this place, children would be able to grow and develop integrally without losing contact with their souls; education would be given not for passing examinations or obtaining certificates and posts but to enrich existing faculties and bring forth new ones. In this place, titles and positions would be replaced by opportunities to serve and organise; the bodily needs of each one would be equally provided for, and intellectual, moral and spiritual superiority would be expressed in the general organisation not by an increase in the pleasures and powers of life but by increased duties and responsibilities. Beauty in all its artistic forms, painting, sculpture, music, literature, would be equally accessible to all; the ability to share in the joy it brings would be limited only by the capacities of each one and not by social or financial position. For in this ideal place money would no longer be the sovereign lord; individual worth would have a far greater importance than that of material wealth and social standing. There, work would not be a way to earn one's living but a way to express oneself and to develop one's capacities and possibilities while being of service to the community as a whole, which, for its own part, would provide for each individual's subsistence and sphere of action. In short, it would be a place where human relationships, which are normally based almost exclusively on competition and strife, would be replaced by relationships of emulation in doing well, of collaboration and real brotherhood.

The earth is certainly not ready to realise such an ideal, for mankind does not yet possess sufficient knowledge to understand and adopt it nor the conscious force that is indispensable in order to execute it; that is why I call it a dream. And yet this dream is in the course of becoming a reality; that is what we are striving for in Sri Aurobindo's Ashram, on a very small scale, in proportion to our limited means.

The realisation is certainly far from perfect, but it is progressive; little by little we are advancing towards our goal which we hope we may one day be able to present to the world as a practical and effective way to emerge from the present chaos, to be born into a new life that is more harmonious and true". (2)

Auroville

In 1968, the Mother advanced her work in the communal aspects of the evolution of consciousness by founding Auroville. Located just north of Pondicherry, it is an international community dedicated to the growth of consciousness according to the principles outlined in her statement above. At this point, Auroville has over 3300 permanent residents who hail from countries around the globe, and many thousands more who visit every year to participate in some way in this collective experiment. UNESCO has passed five resolutions in support of Auroville, and its existence and development is protected by the government of India. Thanks to the internet, today it is easy to find information Auroville's remarkable history and current activities at www.auroville.org.

Sensitive to the fact that the Sri Aurobindo Ashram follows the traditional Indian pattern of being a small community dedicated to its "gurus," which may not appeal to some people, the Mother founded Auroville with a broader aim in mind. She intended that the community would ultimately grow to about 50,000 residents, and she specifically said that residents were *not* expected to view Sri Aurobindo and the Mother as "gurus" or spiritual teachers (indeed, some residents of Auroville have very little knowledge of their writings). She specifically stated that there should be no religions in Auroville, and that she wanted it to be a place where people from around the world would come to seek human unity and experiment with a wide range of inner and outer ways to grow in consciousness. Her charter for Auroville expresses her vision of the place and the ideals she wished Aurovillians to pursue:

> (a) "Auroville belongs to nobody in particular. Auroville belongs to humanity as a whole. But, to live in Auroville, one must be a willing servitor of the divine consciousness.
> (b) "Auroville will be the place of an unending education, of constant progress, and a youth that never ages.
> (c) "Auroville wants to be the bridge between the past and the future. Taking advantage of all discoveries from without and from within, Auroville will boldly spring towards future realisations.
> (d) "Auroville will be a site of material and spiritual researches for a living embodiment of an actual human unity".(3)

The Mother further elaborated these points in her comments on what it means to be a "true Aurovilian":

> 1. "The first necessity is the inner discovery in order to know

what one truly is behind social, moral, cultural, racial and hereditary appearances.

At the centre there is a being free, vast and knowing, who awaits our discovery and who ought to become the active centre of our being and our life in Auroville. The fulfilment of one's desires bars the way to the inner discovery which can only be achieved in the peace and transparency of perfect disinterestedness.

2. One lives in Auroville in order to be free from moral and social conventions; but this freedom must not be a new slavery to the ego, to its desires and ambitions.

3. The Aurovilian should lose the sense of personal possession. For our passage in the material world, what is indispensable to our life and to our action is put at our disposal according to the place we must occupy. The more we are consciously in contact with our inner being, the more are the exact means given to us.

4. Work, even manual work, is something indispensable for the inner discovery. If one does not work, if one does not put his consciousness into matter, the latter will never develop To let the consciousness organise a bit of matter by means of one's body is very good. To establish order around oneself helps to bring order within oneself. One should organise one's life not according to outer and artificial rules, but according to an organised inner consciousness, for if one lets life go on without subjecting it to the control of the higher consciousness, it becomes fickle and inexpressive. It is to waste one's time in the sense that matter remains without any conscious utilisation.

5. The whole earth must prepare itself for the adent of the new species, and Auroville wants to work consciously to hasten this advent.

6. Little by little it will be revealed to us what this new species must be, and meanwhile, the best course is to consecrate oneself entirely to the Divine".(4)

Mental Illness in the Sri Aurobindo Community

With such high ideals expressed by Sri Aurobindo and the Mother, it is only natural to ask: yes, but what about the reality? What about the actual people who constitute the Ashram and Auroville? Are they any different from people in other faith communities?

At this point, the Sri Aurobindo community encompasses not only the residents of the Ashram and Auroville, but over 10,000 people in India and around the world who study the teachings of Sri Aurobindo and the Mother and visit the Ashram and/or Auroville as they are able. Most of the people in this diaspora live in India, but there are several thousand disseminated around the globe in Europe, the United States, Australia, South America, and other parts of Asia. While there is no epidemiological data on members of this community, it is the general impression of the author(s) that people in this community are about the same as people elsewhere. There are the same rates of medical illnesses and mental health problems, in roughly the same frequency distributions as anywhere else. People use the same mix of medical treatments, complementary/alternative treatments, and psychiatric treatments. Members of the community take antidepressants, anxiolytics, mood stabilizers, antipsychotics, and have undergone inpatient psychiatric treatment and ECT. Also, the community has had the same sorts of internal debates and schisms as happen in any religious or spiritual community, and Auroville went through a very difficult social phase in the 1970s that has been documented. In short, there is no reason to assert that members of this community are "better" or "more healthy" than people elsewhere.

However, the Sri Aurobindo community does have one lesson to share with the world, which is that a person can have *both* mental health problems *and* a real spiritual life, including experiences of the psychic being. All too often this topic is approached as an either/or proposition, when life is more complex. The core understanding of CBP is that people have both an inner and outer being, a soul and an ego-structure, and thus many permutations of inner and outer constellations are possible. Members of the community know this by first-hand experience with friends and family, but due to privacy concerns little of this can be shared publicly. However, there was one member of the community (now deceased) who was such an example of this complexity, and who was so open about it, that his case can be shared (personal communication):

> Patient A was an American man who became a resident of the Sri Aurobindo Ashram in the early 1950s. As a child had been abused by his father and was emotionally unstable. He was very dramatic and flamboyant, and believed himself to the reincarnation of Alexander the Great. His list of diagnoses included: severe ADHD, PTSD, episodes of dissociation, a mood disorder with bipolar features (cyclothymia vs. bipolar II), hypochondriasis, somatization disorder, polysubstance abuse (both prescription and non-prescription), a mix of both electrical and pseudo-seizures, many features of temporal lobe epilepsy, schizotypal personality, severe histrionic personality disorder, narcissistic personality disorder, and spells of borderline paranoia and ego fragmentation. He was completely amoral with respect to social conventions, and lied liberally to bureaucracies in pursuit of his goals (e.g., malingering), but he did not have antisocial personality disorder in the interpersonal sphere, as he had great empathy for individuals and abhorred cruelty. He had a highly disorganized thought process with non-pressured logorrhea and a slowly tangential stream of associations that would jump from topic to topic but have recurrent themes and permutations, sort of like listening to jazz. In addition to all this, patient A was deeply attached to his biological mother, and had Freud met the man he would have diagnosed an obvious Oedipus complex.
>
> Despite patient A's florid psychopathology, he had a rich and real spiritual life. He was raised in the Unitarian tradition of Emerson and Thoreau, and from a young age was drawn to the Gods and Goddesses of ancient Greece. Around 1950, he studied Buddhism in Sri Lanka, where he

heard celestial sounds and music during meditation, and experienced the rising of the *kundalini* power leading to a state of yogic bliss. He then took up study of "white" Tantra under the tutelage of Panditji in Rameswaran (one of India's foremost tantrics at the time), and rapidly excelled at this, having frequent experiences of the Gods and Goddesses in both their Indian and Greek forms. With the permission of the Mother, he continued this discipline after he made the Sri Aurobindo Ashram his permanent home, and at times wandered about India having other notable spiritual contacts and experiences. For instance, he had a powerful vision of Ramana Maharshi while visiting Arunachala, met Ananda Moi Ma multiple times (he considered her to be an incarnation of Hera, the queen of the Greek pantheon), and was told by Papa Ram Das that he would "attain to yogic realization — but not until the end of your life." Patient A was able to do astral projection (or what the Mother calls "exteriorization"), but true to his outrageous nature he used this yogic gift only to play tricks on people, which he found amusing. He was highly intuitive, and on many occasions demonstrated spontaneous paranormal abilities including telepathy and precognition. The Mother once described him as both extremely intuitive and extremely unstable.

To contain patient A, the Mother gave him an island to live on just south of Pondicherry, and encouraged him visit the Ashram only 4-5 times per year, which he interpreted as 4-5 times per week. She also gave him a personal attendant, as he was too disorganized to make breakfast or get dressed in the morning. With help from Ashram workers, patient A built a small home and statues to the various Greek deities, and set about doing Tantric pujas to the Gods. Initially these were simple meditations with mantras and yantras (sacred symbols in geometrical patterns), but over time patient A's dramatic nature demanded a grander display. He put local musicians in a barge and had them circumnavigate his island as he set off fireworks to the Gods and offered libations of wine. He spent much time in local bars sourcing the wine, and he became well known to the police who often brought him home at night passed out in bullock cart. Eventually, in a great synthesis of sentiment, spirituality, and symptomatology, patient A brought his own biological mother to live with him on the island. The Mother of the Ashram received her warmly and said "I'm glad you've come, you know, he needs two mothers." Being practical, she also gave the brave woman an air conditioner, to endure the ferociously hot summers.

Although patient A was unruly, the Mother humored him, and he made many friends in the Ashram. He had an irrepressible sense of *joie de vivre* and when he as in good spirits his aura was full of light and he radiated a psychic presence. He was capable of great magnanimity and affection, and he was deeply devoted to the Mother. In the 1950s, he put on songs and dances for her at Ashram performances, and she commented that no one else made her laugh the way he did. Until her health declined, the Mother paid a personal visit to patient A on his island every year on his birthday, a unique ritual she did for no other resident of the Ashram. When asked why she tolerated patient A's excesses, the Mother answered that he had one of the oldest psychic beings in the world and very few souls had taken as many births as he had. To this day people in the Ashram remember patient A fondly and tell stories of him with a smile on their faces.

Over the course of his long life, patient A travelled widely and sought extensive psychiatric care in India, Europe, and the United States. He tried all classes of psychiatric medications with limited benefit, and abused benzodiazepines, barbituates, and stimulants whenever they were given to him. Antipsychotics had no effect on his thought process or spiritual visions, but low doses of risperidone helped a bit as "ego glue" for his affect dysregulation. Subjectively, he always felt carbamazepine helped stabilize his moods and seizure activity to some degree, which would fit with his neurological and psychiatric profile.

In the 1990s, patient A developed basal cell cancer of the face, and returned to the United States for plastic surgery. In between episodes of medical and psychiatric care in the Veteran's Administration system (he had served briefly in the Navy during WWII but was discharged with a diagnosis of "anxiety due to missing his mother"), patient A spent the next 15 years wandering around southern Mexico worshiping the Mayan Gods in Palenque. Eventually his health declined and he entered a VA nursing home. In the last year of his life (2014-2015), patient A experienced the consciousness of the cells in his body, thus vindicating the Mother's patience and persistence with him.

Now, there are many angles from which one could analyze the case of patient A. For instance, Freud would have found evidence for his theory that patient A's frequent experiences of the famous "oceanic feeling" were due to regression to pre-Oedipal fusion states given his lifelong dependence on not one but two mothers. On the other hand, Jung would have found equal confirmation for his theory of archetypes, as patient A's vivid experiences of various Gods and Goddesses, coupled with spells of grandeur and ego-inflation, made his subconscious process a riot of ancient mythologies. Transpersonal psychologists would have found many instances of real paranormal phenomenon and trans-egoic states, as well as possibly some "spiritual emergencies," while neuropsychiatrists would have had reason to believe that some of patient A's symptoms and experiences were due to neurophysiological causes. In short, patient A was a walking, talking textbook of psychiatry.

However, from the perspective of CBP, a critical perspective to include is the important role the Sri Aurobindo community played in patient A's life. He was untreatable in the conventional sense of the biopsychosocial model, and had he lived most of his adult life in the United States, he would have been seen by society as a failure. He never worked, and the combination of his florid symptomatology and eccentric spiritual practices earned him nothing but the stigma of mental illness in the United States. However, in the Ashram culture his external "failures" were seen within the context of his internal gifts and accomplishments. He had real friends both in the Ashram and in the Sri Aurobindo diaspora around the world, and he was valued for his psychic development and devotion to the Mother. Wherever he went in Europe and North America, he always found people with "good hearts" who helped him in whatever way they could, and he was always in contact with at least one person from the Sri Aurobindo community. This communal seeing of the soul in him had an enormous positive impact on the course of patient A's life. One could posit other psychological interpretations of his role in the Ashram community, such as playing the court "jester" or allowing for vicarious enjoyment of his disregard for rules, but these partially true theories do not capture the whole truth. The fullest truth is that patient A had a highly developed psychic being and was engaged in a very difficult work of transformation that can only be understood within the worldview of CBP. Together with the Mother and the community she developed, patient A achieved something truly extraordinary: he demonstrated that not even mental illness need disqualify a person from realizing the heights and depths of yogic consciousness.

It was perhaps with patient A in mind that the Mother commented on her vision of the Supramental world described in the last chapter:

"But our conceptions of Good and Evil are so ridiculous! Our ideas of what is near to the Divine or far from the Divine are so absurd! The experience of the other day [February 3] was quite a revelation to me, and I came out of it utterly changed.... When I came back, I was at first struck by the futility of life here; our petty conceptions seem so comical, so laughable ... We say that certain people are mad, but their madness is perhaps a great wisdom from the supramental point of view, and their behavior is perhaps very near the truth of things – I am not speaking of the obscure insane who have had some brain disorder, but of many other incomprehensible mad people, the luminous mad: they have wanted to leap across the border too quickly, and the rest did not follow." (5)

From these comments it is clear that the Mother understood the relativism of all values expressed in intellectual terms by postmodern thought, and that there are cases of mental illness due solely to brain dysfunction. However, here she also revealed an understanding of another phenomenon — the "luminous mad" of people such as patient A whose inner beings are progressing more rapidly than their outer beings.

Growth Through Adversity

The most difficult question in religion and spirituality is why is there pain and suffering in the world? If there is a Supreme Being, why does It allow horrible things to happen, atrocities such as violence and rape and oppression and starvation and child abuse? As applied to the sphere of psychology, this question most often gets translated into some version of "why do bad things happen to good people?" In healthcare, the most common and uncomplicated presentation of this problem is terminal illness, so we will start here and then work up to more complex situations.

Integrating complementary and spiritual approaches to healing into medical practice is certainly positive, but at some point in life we will all develop terminal health problems that no treatment can fix. How to approach such situations? The following case study about a professor in India illustrates this point:

He was a bachelor in his early sixties and lived with his sister and her husband. By a strange coincidence, the Professor and his brother-in-law both developed cancer six months apart. First it was his brother-in-law who developed nasopharyngeal carcinoma, and then the Professor was diagnosed with a malignant lymphoma. However, despite these sad developments, the Professor retained his calm and serenity. In a typical day, he would undergo his chemotherapy session and once it was over he would proceed to visit his brother-in-law in an adjacent hospital, consoling and praying for him. His spiritual activities continued unabated and he radiated a sense of joy, peace and wholeness. Whoever came into contact with him felt enriched by his presence. When his brother-in-law passed away, he supervised the last rites and helped to console his sister. Before he himself passed away, his associates could feel that he was preparing for a graceful exit. He demonstrated how a personality integrated around the soul could bear through a fatal illness. Before his death he was cheerful, poised and at peace.

In this case, the Professor was clearly in contact with his psychic being and that made all the difference in how he faced family tragedy and terminal illness. It also had a positive impact on the people around him, which illustrates how individual and collective growth can be connected. Contact with the psychic being imparts a sense of wholeness, integrality, peace and joy — even in adverse situations. Thus, from the perspective of consciousness, "integral health" cannot just be an eclectic combination of diverse therapies but must be founded upon a growth out of the ego and into the consciousness of the psychic being.

Once one grasps that it is possible to live in the psychic consciousness even in the midst of adversity, the path is then open to face adversity from an integral perspective. Sri Aurobindo and the Mother have commented on this issue both from the theoretical and practical perspectives, and explained that adversity exists because it still helps the evolution of consciousness on earth at this point in time, but could disappear in the future if it becomes unnecessary for progress. Theoretically, the framework for an answer depends upon metaphysics, because the question often carries behind it an unstated assumption of an extra-cosmic creator who stands outside the universe it created and callously watches human beings suffer and die with detached indifference. But as Sri Aurobindo explained, the Divine did not create the universe as an object separate from itself — It *became* and continuously *becomes* the universe and is the very stuff of matter. What people call "God" therefore experiences all human pain and suffering on a scale of intimate intensity that no human consciousness can fathom. This is the mystical truth behind Christ on the Cross and it poses another set of mysteries to the human intelligence, but not that of an extra-cosmic Creator who engineered a heartless world and then abandoned it. For a nuanced discussion of this complex issue from an Aurobindonian perspective, please see the talk by Dr. Alok Pandey, a psychiatrist, on YouTube. (6)

Practically speaking, adverse experiences are a challenge that stimulate the search for solutions. In the moment of pain and loss it can seem that no solution could ever be possible, but over time individuals and collectives in fact grow in consciousness and master life's problems. This is not to say that growth in consciousness is easy, for indeed it can be very hard, but at root the fact of growth through adversity is common wisdom. After all, what self-reflective person has not gone through a painful experience at one point in life, that later lead to growth of character? We have all had losses and setbacks that stimulated us to search for a deeper direction in life, taught us a valuable lesson, or stimulated us to persevere and grow in some way. Many people have spoken about how their experience of adversity lead to an increased capacity to empathize with others and motivation to make the world a better place. Today, psychologists are writing about "post-traumatic resiliency" and how certain individuals have been able to grow through life-threatening experiences such as cancer and violence. Sri Aurobindo and the Mother's perspective on growth through adversity simply extends this common wisdom into the realm of subtle perceptions and mastery of the hidden forces of life. Some of these issues are illustrated in the following case of a young man who was stimulated to grow by the death of a friend to suicide:

A bright youngster who was an idealist, and had a flair for creative writing, became disenchanted with the hypocritical side of intellectual litterateurs he adored. He started to abuse cannabis in search of what he called "a zero feeling," and he decided to take a job as a school teacher in a remote village where he thought he would be able to impart high values to children coming from impoverished backgrounds. He had an artist friend who drew the picture of a classical

Chinese dragon surrendering at the feet of Mother Goddess. This imagery was so significant to him that it inspired him to pursue spirituality and surrender his "dragon desires" to the Supreme. At this juncture, his artist friend committed suicide. This sudden shock changed his quality of introspection into a deeper existential search for the meaning of life. He discovered that there were two types of zero-experience. The first was the zero of the nadir — the zero of the Inconscience full of darkness. He understood that his foray into drug abuse led him to the zero of darkness. But he also experientially perceived another zero that was full of light — the zero of the zenith, the zero of the Superconscience which is effulgent and glorious and gives meaning to life. This zero was the great Void which the mystics extolled. He worked through these introspective insights, and this process helped him not only to come out of his drug abuse but also aided in his personal growth centered around the psychic being, or soul. It is worth noting that the subject's creative activities aided his introspective quest.

In the terms of CBP, some adversity in life is due to the influence of the Inconscient (described in Chapter 18), while some is due to the action of negative occult forces (described in Chapter 5). As Sri Aurobindo explained about the latter, the influence of hostile forces prompts human beings to seek for a higher consciousness so as to overcome the adversity:

"The hostile forces have a certain self-chosen function: it is to test the condition of the individual, of the work, of the earth itself and their readiness for the spiritual descent and fulfilment. At every step of the journey, they are there attacking furiously, criticising, suggesting, imposing despondency or inciting to revolt, raising unbelief, amassing difficulties. No doubt, they put a very exaggerated interpretation on the rights given them by their function, making mountains even out of what seems to us a mole-hill. A little trifling false step or mistake and they appear on the road and clap a whole

Himalaya as a barrier across it. But this opposition has been permitted from of old not merely as a test or ordeal, but as a compulsion on us to seek a greater strength, a more perfect self-knowledge, an intenser purity and force of aspiration, a faith that nothing can crush, a more powerful descent of the Divine Grace." (7)

And again:

"If one knows how to profit by experience, even the Hostile Forces and their attacks can be useful — although of course that does not mean that the attacks should be invited. What they do is to press with all their force upon some weak point of our nature and if we are vigilant, we can see and throw away that weakness. Only the attack method of these Forces is too violent and upheaving and endangers the good things in one also, faith and peace etc. — so one has to be careful to keep these against all attacks." (8)

Thus, if approached in the right way, one can use all circumstances in life — even very hard ones — as opportunities to look within, develop faith, and grow in consciousness. Of course, the key is to correctly figure out what "the right way" means in to each person in each situation. Sri Aurobindo and the Mother did *not* recommend victim blaming or blind acquiescence to sociopathic behavior, and one should not distort their common sense advice to mean that abused children are responsible for their abuse, that victims of rape "invited" it due to their state of consciousness, that Africans were responsible for slavery, that Jews deserved the Holocaust, and that indigenous Americans needed to grow through genocide. No, everything about their lives shows that Sri Aurobindo and the Mother took progressive social stances and were not passive in the face of injustice. Rather, what Sri Aurobindo and the Mother recommend is that people use life's circumstances as opportunities to find their souls and bring the psychic being forward to meet life's challenges.

Naturally this spiritual practice needs to be understood in

a nuanced and context-dependent fashion that is individualized to each person in each circumstance. For instance, in some situations negative life experiences are opportunities to observe the errors of one's ego and learn humility, patience, and empathy; or how to see life through the perspective of another person, gender class, race, culture, religion, or ideology. In other circumstances, the psychic guidance may lead one to speak out against falsehood or ignorance, stand up for one's rights, fight against injustice, or even go to war. There is no fixed rule in these matters; it is for each soul to discover what it has to do inwardly or outwardly in each situation in order to grow. However, Sri Aurobindo and the Mother are confident that each person can find inner guidance and strength to face life's problems by searching deep within their souls — even in extremely difficult circumstances. For example, in the case of one person with paralysis who was not improving through the efforts of a gifted healer, the Mother commented, "for everyone, what happens is the best thing to lead his individuality towards the goal — the goal of consciousness – and if he has faith, the action takes place in an even more precise way, and, we might say, even more rapidly. So in this case, it would mean that his paralysis helps him go faster towards his goal." (9) Of course, in a different circumstance with a different soul, the outcome might have been just the opposite, with a resolution of the paralysis.

At a social level, Sri Aurobindo and the Mother pointed out that all of the violence, ignorance, and injustice we see in the world are the product of the human mind and human nature such as they are currently constituted. As a result, there is no form of government or social engineering that can permanently "fix" the world, because that world is the manifestation of our own consciousness. This is why every technology and social movement that human beings propose as a solution to life's problems, over time generates unintended negative consequences that become new problems. The only definitive solution to this unending cycle of the mind converting one kind of problem into another kind of problem, is to rise above the mind. As Sri Aurobindo and the Mother explained, both individuals and collectives can evolve to a higher and deeper level of consciousness. In the pursuit of this goal, what we might call mystical activism is every bit as important as social activism, because consciousness is a unitary field and therefore by changing oneself one is in fact changing the world. Ultimately, there is no essential difference between inside and outside, for it is all a single, continuous field of Consciousness. This is why, in CBP, the individual and collective evolution of consciousness are inextricably linked.

Lo, all these beings in this wonderful world!
Let us give joy to all, for joy is ours.
For not ourselves alone our spirits came
Out of the veil of the Unmanifest…
To lead man's soul towards truth and God we are born,
To draw the chequered scheme of mortal life
Into some semblance of the Immortal's plan,
To shape it closer to an image of God,
A little nearer to the Idea divine.

Savitri, *pg. 720*

References

1. CWM 04, pg. 24-27
2. CWM 12, pg. 93-94
3. CWM 13, pg. 193-194
4. Ibid, pg. 207-208
5. Agenda 1, pg. 144-145
6. See Dr. Alok Pandey on YouTube, at https://www.youtube.com/watch?v=zXrnpldKYCcWSA
7. CWSA 31, pg. 758
8. Ibid, pg. 761
9. Agenda X, pg. 154

7

Deeper and Higher Orders of Cognition

Truths they could find and hold but not the one Truth:
The Highest was to them unknowable.
By knowing too much they missed the whole to be known:
The fathomless heart of the world was left unguessed
And the Transcendent kept its secrecy.

Savitri, *pg. 271*

The study of cognition is central to any theory of psychology, indeed, one could say that every school of psychology has added some dimension to what can be cognized. Until now, the term "cognition" has been used with different connotations and within divergent branches of psychology that rarely communicate with each other. Thus, cognition has the association of being restricted to computational models of neural processing in cognitive psychology, to positive or negative "self-talk" in cognitive-behavior therapy, to non-local capacities in parapsychology, etc. And often the term "cognition" is used loosely across the branches to refer to functions such as memory, attention, and problem-solving that are felt to be "mental" in the sense of not emotional or transpersonal. However, if we take a fresh and unbiased look at the word "cognition," it becomes apparent that the term is actually broad and all-encompassing. Wikipedia defines cognitive psychology as the study of mental processes such as "attention, language use, memory, perception, problem solving, creativity, and thinking." Thus cognition includes domains such as perception, creativity, and thinking that are very much part of transpersonal and spiritual experiences.

For what is a spiritual or mystical experience if not a cognitive event? If the materialist is content to study hallucinations as part of cognitive psychology, then by what logic would we deem spiritual and transpersonal experiences not to be cognitive events? The answer to this puzzle is that, in fact, cognition is the lynchpin that holds together the diverse branches of psychology, including parapsychology and transpersonal psychology. This fact becomes critical when we start to elaborate the consciousness-based model of psychology implicit in Sri Aurobindo's thought. Sri Aurobindo made a detailed study of cognition, highlighting different domains, types, and levels of cognition. He studies cognition at different levels of the being as well as along different planes of consciousness. He started by examining the "surface cognition" from a consciousness perspective and identified ways in which we try to understand three things:

1. the world outside us and its objects and happenings,
2. our inner movements , and
3. one's inmost self (psychic being)

Sri Aurobindo described a "fourfold order of knowledge" or "four cognitive methods of Nature" available to the "surface cognition" that pertains to the outer and surface being, which is studied as "personality" in modern psychology:

1. Sensory perception ("wholly separative knowledge by indirect contact"),
2. Reason ("knowledge by separative direct contact"),
3. Non-judgmental (Witness) attitude ("knowledge by intimate direct contact"), and
4. Identification ("knowledge by identity"). (1)

Cognition through Sensory Perception

The attempt of the surface being to take cognizance of all that is outside is based on the assumption that everything outside (the world, its objects and happenings) is "separate" from oneself. The endeavour to understand entities separate from oneself starts with our sensory perception. The senses cannot give information of the world with a sort of directness and intimacy — rather it gives an impressionistic view (like the impression that the sun moves around the earth or the perceptible blueness of the sky) which might not stand the trial of a deeper cognitive appraisal. In fact, one cannot perceive the essential reality of objects outside oneself, one only meets with figures, images and representations of them. Hence the impression of the senses has to be supplemented with inputs from reason, memory, intelligence, intuition, etc.

> "Even so our knowledge of the world we live in is narrow and imperfect, our interpretations of its significances doubtful: imagination, speculation, reflection, impartial weighing and reasoning, inference, measurement, testing, a further correction and amplification of sense-evidence by Science, - all this apparatus had to be called in to complete the incompleteness. After all that the result still remains a half-certain, half-dubious accumulation of acquired indirect knowledge, a mass of significant images and ideative representations, abstract thought-counters, hypotheses, theories, generalisations, but also with all that a mass of doubts and a never-ending debate and inquiry. Power has come with knowledge, but our imperfection of knowledge leaves us without any idea of the true use of the power, even of the aim towards which our utilisation of knowledge and power should be turned and made effective." (2)

Rishabhchand points out that this inherent deficiency of such type of knowledge gives a certain plausibility to the theory of Phenomenalism and also was the starting point of the radical change Kant's mind underwent in regard to the unknowability of the Things-in-themselves. (3) It is interesting that modern scientists now agree that the awareness of the world is actually a construct of the mind and the sensory qualities of objects perceived as well as notions of time and space exist only relative to our human consciousness. This logic has been applied to explain that the way scientists illustrate how the universe evolved from the Big Bang may be misleading because there was no human mind at that point to construct such imagery. Therefore the knowledge acquired by the surface being of the world around us through sensory perception is a limited knowledge "enveloped and invaded by ignorance, and to a very large extent, by reason of its limitation, itself a kind of ignorance, at best a mixed knowledge-ignorance". (4) Sri Aurobindo named this type of knowledge as indirect (because it is mediated by senses) and separative (because of the gulf between the knower and the known).

Cognition through Reason

Sensory information is our first gateway to knowledge. However, the senses have their errors and limitations. The mystic can develop the faculty of direct cognizance without the aid of sense organs or develop inner, subtle senses or even can endeavour to transform one's senses — but these are capacities not available ordinarily. Even if they were available, knowledge would still need another foundation to work upon. This foundation is provided by Reason. The boundaries, limitations and errors of sensory perception have to be supplemented by Reason.

Sri Aurobindo described, "Reason using the intelligent will for the ordering of the inner and the outer life is undoubtedly the highest developed faculty of man at his present point of evolution". (5) Ordinarily however, human beings do not utilize the full potentialities of reason. A great part of the ordinary mentality confines the potentialities of reason to "the circle of our sensible experience, admits its law as the final truth and concerns itself only with the study of phenomenon, that is to say, with the appearances of things in their relations, processes and utilities". (6) It is because of the "mixed action" of reason due to its dependence on the senses that we find scientists with exceptionally rational minds trying to explain phenomena like consciousness, creativity, aesthetics, mystical experiences solely on the basis of mechanistic terms (viz. in terms of physics, chemistry, computer analogies, genetics, molecular biology, etc).

Reason is also capable of a "purer" action when it can directly judge a phenomenon independent of sensible experience, or else it can use the sensible experience as a starting-point but leave it far behind, "so far that the result may seem the direct contrary of that which our sensible experience wishes to dictate to us."… "To correct the errors of the sense-mind by the use of reason is one of the most valuable powers developed by man and the chief cause of his superiority among terrestrial beings". (7)

The superiority of reason over the other faculties of human beings is that it exists for the sake of knowledge. It can detach itself from activity and pursue knowledge in a disinterested way. It can analyze the processes underlying any phenomenon and disengage its principles.

> "Reason is science, it is conscious art, it is invention. It is observation and can seize and arrange truths of facts; it is speculation and can extricate and forecast truth of potentiality. It is the idea and its fulfillment, the ideal and its bringing to fruition. It can look through the immediate appearance and unveil the hidden truths behind it. It is the servant and yet the master of all utilities; and it can, putting away all utilities, seek disinterestedly Truth for its own sake and by finding it reveal a whole world of new possible utilities. Therefore it is the sovereign power by which man has become possessed of himself, student and master of his own forces, the godhead on which the other godheads in him have leaned for help in their ascent; it has been the Prometheus of the mythical parable, the helper, instructor, elevating friend, civiliser of mankind." (8)

It is interesting to study the way reason acts as a harbinger of progress. Sri Aurobindo explains that reason acts through the symbol of "idea" which has first to be conceived and then made applicable in life by constantly comparing the idea with "facts" in the world of material reality. Indeed, reason has to continuously inter-relate ideas and facts to build coherent logical systems.

> "It has to be always questioning facts so that it may find the ideas by which they can be more and more adequately explained, ordered and managed, and it has always to be ques-

tioning ideas in order, first, to see whether they square with actual facts and secondly, whether there are not new facts to suit which they must be modified or enlarged or which can be evolved out of them. For reason lives not only in actual facts, but in possibilities, not only in realized truths, but in ideal truths; and the ideal truth once seen, the impulse of the idealizing intelligence is to see too whether it cannot be turned into a fact, cannot be immediately or rapidly realized in life. It is by this inherent characteristic that the age of reason must always be an age of progress." (9)

In spite of the great utility of reason, Sri Aurobindo opined that the rational person is not the highest expression of humanity, nor is the rational society the highest possible expression of the human being's collective life. There are two great difficulties with reason: 1) its constant creation of opposing points of view, and 2) the fact that the roots of life are both infra and supra-rational.

The power of sustaining opposite views

Reason can always counter a thesis by a brilliantly analytical antithesis and can produce multiple eclectic combinations.

"It can in its nature be used and has always been used to justify any idea, theory of life, system of society or government, ideal of individual or collective action to which the will of man attaches itself for the moment or through the centuries. ...It can place itself with equal effectivity at the service of utilitarianism, economism, hedonism, aestheticism, sensualism, ethicism, idealism or any other essential need or activity of man and build around it a philosophy, a political and social system, a theory of conduct and life. Ask it not to lean to one idea alone, but to make an eclectic combination or a synthetic harmony and it will satisfy you; only, there being any number of possible combinations or harmonies, it will equally well justify the one or the other and set up or throw down any one of them according as the spirit in man is attracted to or withdraws from it." (10) In fact, reason's "inconstancy, its divisibility against itself, its power of sustaining opposite views are the whole secret of its value." (11)

This ability of reason to produce with equal vigour different and contradictory views on the same subject shows that reason cannot grasp all truth in its embrace because truth is too infinite for it, still it grasps something of the truth which we immediately need and "its insufficiency does not detract from the value of its work, but is rather the measure of its value." (12) Sri Aurobindo pointed out that it is not possible for human beings to grasp the whole truth of his being at once. Instead, we move towards truth through a succession of experiences that help in self-enlargement. "The first business of reason then is to justify and enlighten to him his various experiences and to give him faith and conviction in holding on to his self-enlargings." (13) In the movement towards self-enlargement, man finds that the theories, hypotheses, concepts and ideas forwarded by the rational mind at a certain point lose its value after some time, get petrified, limited and lifeless. This phenomenon brings in the "saving faculty of doubt" (14) leading to a revolt against existing systems. Whatever had been built gets destroyed, new experiments are made and larger potentialities and possibilities are brought into play justifying the ancient saying — the old order changeth giving place to new. Thus, the very limitation of reason resulting from its divisibility against itself has this advantage that it ushers in progress.

> "By this double action of the intelligence, affirming and imposing what it has seen and again in due season questioning what has been accomplished in order to make a new affirmation, fixing a rule and order and liberating from rule and order, the progress of the race is assured, however uncertain may seem its steps and stages." (15)

> "For so man moves towards the infinity of the Truth by the experience of its variety; so his reason helps him to build,

change, destroy what he has built and prepare a new construction, in a word, to progress, grow, enlarge himself in his self-knowledge and world-knowledge and their works." (16)

The Infra-rational and Supra-rational Roots of Life

Reason cannot embrace the totality of life because it deals with the finite and has no measure for the infinite. Indeed, a purely rational human life would be too mechanical to survive. This is because the root-powers of human life have their irrational and supra-rational sources. (17) On one hand, human beings continue to be subject to the tyranny of needs, desires, prejudices, cultural taboos, habitual thinking and dogmatic ideas – "the irrationality of human existence".(18) As such, the human being misuses reason and freedom to enforce one's opinions not only on others but "even at the expense of or, as it is euphemistically put, in competition with the life of others."(19) On the other hand, despite being partially controlled by reason, certain elements of our existence viz. life, imagination, emotion, the ethical and the aesthetic need seek an independence from the formulas and systems imposed by reason and seem to move, if not consciously, even vaguely towards some greater godhead than reason. (20)

The advantages and disadvantages of the rational intellect find their most complete expression in the application of science. While science has allowed for a "rationalistic and altruistic humanitarianism," it has also ushered in a culture of consumerism, vulgarism and aggression. Some thinkers consider this kind of abject materialism to be the result of the divorce of religion and idealism from the modern rational intellect. Sri Aurobindo did not subscribe to this over-simplified view. Instead, he ascribed this phenomenon to the imperfection of reason itself:

"The truth is that upon which we are now insisting, that reason is in its nature an imperfect light with a large but still restricted mission and that once it applies itself to life and action it becomes subject to what it studies and the servant and counsellor of the forces in whose obscure and ill-understood struggle it intervenes." (21)

Because of the inherent limitations of reason, Sri Aurobindo called cognition based on reason as knowledge by separative direct contact (22): 'separative', because there is still a separation of the knower from the known and "direct", because we do not have to depend on the physical senses.

Cognition through Non-judgmental (Witness) Attitude

There is a less separative, more intimate way of knowing our own movements where the gap between the knower and the known is further narrowed. This is the type of cognizing we experience when in our subjective consciousness, some element of awareness by identity enters so that:

> "we can project ourselves with a certain identification into these movements....this can happen in the case of an uprush of wrath which swallows us up so that for the moment our whole consciousness seems to be a wave of anger: other passions, love, grief, joy have the same power to seize and occupy us; thought also absorbs and occupies, we lose sight of the thinker and become the thought and the thinking." (23)

However, if we are completely overwhelmed, swayed and swept away by our own psychological movements like anger or joy, we cannot simultaneously cognize these movements. We can do so only if we can, in a double movement, develop a sort of detachment - a sort of a witness attitude that observes and controls our movements with which simultaneously, we are partially identified. This detached witness part of ourselves is different from reason because it is more unbiased and non-judgmental. If we do not have this power of detachment, we cannot attain mastery over our own psychological movements. This is why mindfulness meditation techniques often cultivate the witness attitude to aid in personal growth and provide therapeutic benefits.

> "Thus we have a double knowledge of the subjective movement: there is an intimate knowledge, by identity, of its stuff and its force of action, more intimate then we could have by any entirely separative and objective knowledge such as we get of things outside us, things that are to us altogether not-self; there is at the same time a Knowledge by detached observation, detached but with a power of direct contact, which frees us from engrossment by the Nature-energy and enables us to relate the movement to the rest of our own existence and world existence." (24)

However, it is comparatively easy to practice detachment when we observe our own passions, desires or life-impulses but it is more difficult to do so when we attempt to observe our own thoughts:

> "In thought separation of the thinker and the thinking is more difficult. The thinker is plunged and lost in the thought or carried in the thought current, identified with it; it is not usually at the time of or in the very act of thinking that he can observe or review his thoughts, -- he has to do that in retrospect and with the aid of memory or by a critical pause of corrective judgment before he proceeds further : but still a simultaneity of thinking and conscious direction of the mind's action can be achieved partially when the thought does not engross, entirely when the thinker acquires the faculty of stepping back into the mental self and standing apart there from the mental energy. Instead of being absorbed in the thought with at most a vague feeling of the process of thinking, we can see the process by a mental vision, watch our thoughts in their origination and movement and, partly by a silent insight, partly by a process of thought upon thought, judge and evaluate them. But whatever the kind of identification, it is to be noted that the knowledge of our internal movements is of a double nature, separation and direct contact: for even when we detach ourselves, this close contact is

maintained; our knowledge is always based on a direct touch, on a cognition by direct awareness carrying in it a certain element of identity."(25)

Thus, Sri Aurobindo labeled this type of knowledge as knowledge by intimate direct contact.

Cognition through Identity

A still deeper type of knowledge is the Vedantic way of knowledge by identity. In its purest form, this type of knowledge is available at a deeper level of consciousness, identifies the knower and the known, and produces basic concepts that arise spontaneously in the surface cognition . Because of this, one can conceptualize "I exist", "I am", even at the level of the surface cognition though not with the authenticity with which at a deeper level of consciousness the mystic exclaims, "I am He", "Thou art that", "this self is the Brahman". The rationale of the conviction carried by knowledge by identity lies in the mystical revelation that there already is a "pre -existent inner awareness and knowledge" (26) which is unravelled more spontaneously through knowledge by identity, and less consciously by the other methods of superficial cognition. The truth behind this knowledge by identity is that existence is one, Being is one, consciousness is one and when one goes down to the all-pervading bedrock of consciousness, one can become united with anything and everything that it contains; the depth and range of this identification depending upon the development and power of the subject's own consciousness and the capacity to transcend one's ego. The less the dominance of the ego in the subject, the greater is the possibility of union with the world and with the Supreme Reality of which the world is a manifestation in terms of its multiplicity. (27)

In fact, knowledge by identity is "the original and fundamental way of knowing, native to the occult self in things."(28) As Sri Aurobindo and many others have noted, the lives of mystics reveal significant instances of knowledge by identity:

"When Christ says, "I and my Father in Heaven are one," it is his inmost consciousness identifying itself with the infinite Consciousness of the Supreme that expresses the spiritual oneness, and not his philosophic mind or even his intuitive intellect…..Once, when a man was treading over a lawn, Sri Ramakrishna felt in himself the pain of the trampled grass, and shrieked out in agony." (29)

It is worth noting that some sort of direct knowledge which appears to be a type of intuition is found in the infra-rational levels of the hierarchy of consciousness. This is what has been studied as "instinct" in animals. Sri Aurobindo pointed out that, "instinct in the animal acts with great power within certain limits, for a certain end, yet finds itself helpless outside those limits." (30) This instinct belongs to the species and is imparted at birth to individual members. In the animal, the instinct is automatically correct as a rule because, unlike man, the surface consciousness does not usually have the capacity to interfere with its automatic, mechanical action. With an evolutionary ascension from the infra-rational to the rational stage of the hierarchy of consciousness, the range and capacity for error increases. The instinct that is automatic in the animal is deprived of its intuitive character in the mental man "by being taken up and materialised and by that change becomes less sure, though more assisted, when not replaced, by the plastic power of adaptation of things and self-adaptation proper to the intelligence." (31)

With the emergence of mind in life, there is an expansion in the repertoire of consciousness but there is also an increase in the range and capacity of error. If the surface consciousness of man were always receptive to the action of intuition, the intervention of error would not have been possible. "But this could not be, because the hold of the Inconscience on the matter, the surface substance, in which mind and life have to express themselves, makes the surface consciousness obscure and unresponsive to the light within." (32) As a result, even if intuition comes, it gets garbed and disguised with a mental coating and cannot have full play. "There are intuitions of actuality, of possibility, of the determining truths behind things, but all are mistaken by the mind for each other. A great confusion of half-grasped material and an experimental building with it, a representation or mental structure of the figure of self and things rigid and yet chaotic, half formed and arranged, half jumbled, half true, half erroneous, but always imperfect, is the character of human knowledge." (33)

Thus, in the animal intuition is manifest as a mechanical instinct with a limited scope of action, while in man intuition stands veiled behind our mental operations which dilute and obstruct its flow. By an extension of psychological experience, mystics and seers have developed the faculty of intuition to such an extent that it gives knowledge of existence by an identity of the self (or essence of the individual) with the essence of all that exists. "It is on this possibility that Indian Vedanta has based itself. It has sought through knowledge of the Self the knowledge of the universe." (34) Ancient Vedanta, with the help of Intuition, formulated through a knowledge of Identity the three great declarations of the Upanishads, "I am He", "Thou art that, O Swetaketu", "All this is the Brahman; this Self is the Brahman".

Case Study

One of the best examples of cognition by identity is that of Sri Ramana Maharashi, who at age 16 spontaneously attained attained *moksha*, or realization of the Self. We have his own recorded statement of the event, and the remainder of his exceptional life was so well documented by multiple observers that there can be little doubt as to the veracity of his spiritual awakening:

"It was about six weeks before I left Madura for good that a great change in my life took place. It was quite sudden. I was sitting in a room on the first floor of my uncle's house. I seldom had any sickness and on that day there was nothing wrong with my health, but a sudden, violent fear of death overtook me. There was nothing in my state of health to account for it; and I did not try to account for it or to find out whether there was any reason for the fear. I just felt, 'I am going to die,' and began thinking what to do about it. It did not occur to me to consult a doctor or my elders or friends. I felt that I had to solve the problem myself, then and there.

The shock of the fear of death drove my mind inwards and I said to myself mentally, without actually framing the words: 'Now death has come; what does it mean? What is it that is dying? This body dies.' And I at once dramatized the occurrence of death. I lay with my limbs stretched out stiff as though rigor mortis had set in and imitated a corpse so as to give greater reality to the enquiry. I held my breath and kept my lips tightly closed so that no sound could escape, so that neither the word 'I' or any other word could be uttered, 'Well then,' I said to myself, 'this body is dead. It will be carried stiff to the burning ground and there burnt and reduced to ashes. But with the death of this body am I dead? Is the body 'I'? It is silent and inert but I feel the full force of my personality and even the voice of the 'I' within me, apart from it. So I am Spirit transcending the body. The body dies but the Spirit that transcends it cannot be touched by death. This means I am the deathless Spirit.' All this was not dull thought; it flashed through me vividly as living truth which I perceived directly, almost without thought-process. 'I' was something very real, the only real thing about my present state, and all the conscious activity connected with my body was centred on that 'I'. From that moment onwards the 'I' or Self focused attention on itself by a powerful fascination. Fear of death had vanished once and for all. Absorption in the Self continued unbroken from that time on. Other thoughts might come and go like the various notes of music, but the 'I' continued like the fundamental sruti note that underlies and blends with all the other notes. Whether the body was engaged in talking, reading, or anything else, I was still centred on 'I'. Previous to that crisis I had no clear perception of my Self and was not consciously attracted to it. I felt no perceptible or direct interest in it, much less any inclination to dwell permanently in it." (35)

The historical record shows that Ramana Maharshi was socially well-adjusted as a child, came from a stable family with orthodox Hindu values, and had no particular developmental challenges or concerns. Thus, there is not explanation for this extraordinary psychospiritual experience other than the eternal truth of Vedanta.

Subliminal Cognition

In spite of the different types of surface cognition, we still know very little of ourselves, for as Sri Aurobindo points out:

> "It is quite evident that we know ourselves with only a superficial knowledge, - the sources of our consciousness and thought are a mystery; the true nature of our mind, emotions, sensations is a mystery; our cause of being and our end of being, the significance of our life and its activities are a mystery : this could not be if we had a real self-knowledge and a real world-knowledge". (36)

Our main barrier to "self-knowledge" and "world knowledge" is the "ego-centric individualization" which denies us access to the inner depths of our being and also shuts out all that is not centered around the ego as "non-self". However the ego is only a provisional device - a representative and instrumental formation of the spirit within in physical nature:

> "Our self-ignorance and our world-ignorance can only grow towards integral self-knowledge and integral world-knowledge in proportion as our limited ego and its half-blind consciousness open to a greater inner existence and consciousness and a true self-being and become aware too of the not-self outside it also as self, — on one side a Nature constituent of our own nature, on the other an Existence which is a boundless continuation of our own self-being. Our being has to break the walls of ego-consciousness which it has created, it has to extend itself beyond its body and inhabit the

body of the universe. In place of its knowledge by indirect contact, or in addition to it, it must arrive at a knowledge by direct contact and proceed to a knowledge by identity. Its limited finite of self has to become a boundless finite and an infinite." (37)

Therefore we have to explore how a cognitive process emerges in the depths our consciousness – a domain accessed usually by mystics and yogis but now ready to be probed by a new psychology. Sri Aurobindo explained that in order to cognize the depths of consciousness, one has to break the barriers of ego-consciousness and be capable of what he calls "subliminal cognition". (38) The subliminal cognition should not be confused with the witness consciousness for it is an unique plane with which one has to identify by traversing the surface cognition. Sri Aurobindo used the term "subliminal" to describe a distinct inner or subliminal being that stands behind the surface personality of mind, life, and body. It has certain important features:

1. It has an inner mind, an inner vital (the repertoire of our energy, dynamism, vitality, emotions) and inner physical. The inner mind can directly know things by supra-rational faculties and has a memory that holds both an active and involved past as well as a future that is ready to evolve. The inner vital can hold the life-energy free from the habitual clutches of the body and mind. The inner (subtle) physical has subtle senses that lead mystics and yogis to have "visions", hear "inner voices" and feel "auras".

2. The inner being is the meeting ground of the individual and universal or cosmic consciousness. Thus through the subliminal, there can be "a direct contact of consciousness with other consciousness or with objects" by a "revealing intimation or a self — communicating impact of thoughts, feelings, forces. It is by these means that the inner being achieves an immediate, intimate and accurate spontaneous knowledge of persons, of objects...." (39); and "it is possible to become directly aware of the thoughts and feelings around us, to feel their impact, to see their movements; to read a mind and a heart becomes less difficult, a less uncertain

venture".(40) The subliminal not only is in communication with inter-personal forces around us, it is also in communion with impersonal forces around us viz. the physical forces which science studies. However the cosmic consciousness with which the subliminal cognition is in contact also contains giant forces of cosmic ignorance and falsehood which can distort knowledge. Hence, the subliminal cognition is bound to be a mixture of knowledge and ignorance.

3. The subliminal or inner being cannot be organized around the ego but needs the support of a beyond-ego principle, or psychic being (evolving soul).

In spite of this novel cognitive capacity, the subliminal cognition is not complete. Sri Aurobindo warned that as the subliminal cognition is a mixture of knowledge and ignorance, it is capable of erroneous as well as of true perception, "since it works not by knowledge by identity, but by a knowledge through direct contact and this is also a separative knowledge, through more intimate even in separation than anything that is commanded by our surface nature." (41) Moreover, as the subliminal is still a movement of knowledge-ignorance, it has a greater knowledge but also the possibility of a greater self-affirming ignorance. It is in contact not only with greater becomings and powers of knowledge but also with greater becomings and powers of ignorance. Sri Aurobindo pointed out that we can surpass the limitation of the subliminal by going still deeper behind it to the psychic being, which is the true source of individual identity.

Following is a case study that illustrates why understanding various types of subliminal cognition is important for clinical practice. It is about a man who had an experience in an inner plane of consciousness during sleep that he was unable to integrate:

A 50 year old male carpenter presented with chronic anxiety and obsessive ruminations. He had been taking psychiatric medication (SSRIs) for many years, which gave him only temporary relief. He traced his insecurities to a dream he had when 12 years old, and which he still remembered vividly. In the dream, he had soared up into the sky with his hand grasped by a certain Hindu god (one of the demigods or lesser gods of the Indian tradition). When they had flown high into the sky, the god suddenly released his grasp and the boy fell headlong onto the earth. The primal insecurity of this dream has remained with him throughout his life.

This dream cannot be understood using any sort of Freudian approach to interpretation, for it is about inner and higher planes of consciousness that actually exist. In this case, the man's dream experience reveals a fear of, or apprehension about, the vast domains of consciousness that lie above the rational mind. Thus, people can suffer from rejection of the subliminal and the super-conscious just as much as they can suffer from repression of the subconscious.

The Chakra System

An important part of the subliminal being is the chakra system of classical yoga. From the perspective of CBP, the opening of the chakras actually involves the activation of different planes of consciousness in the subliminal being, as each plane is connected to the outer being via a chakra. Because the chakras serve as subtle organs of perception, reception and transmission that connect the individual consciousness to universal forces in the cosmic consciousness, it is appropriate to study the chakras from the angle of cognition.

To begin with, one of the most important innovations Sri Aurobindo brought to yoga was the discovery of a new way to open the chakras. Instead of trying to raise the Kundalini power from the root chakra upwards, he allowed the Higher Consciousness from above (felt over the head) to descend into the subtle body and open the chakras from top to bottom. This inverse process is safer than the classical method of raising the Kundalini because the inherent wisdom of the higher consciousness will pause the process if a chakra is not ready to open, and wait for the right time and circumstances. On the other hand, using the mental will to raise the Kundalini from below is risky, because doing so can lead to premature openings that destabilize the system, which in transpersonal psychology has been described as causing cases of "spiritual emergencies." In Sri Aurobindo's words:

> "There is [in Integral Yoga] no willed opening of the chakras, they open of themselves by the descent of the Force. In the Tantrik discipline they open from down upwards, the Muladhara first — in our Yoga, they open from up downward. But the ascent of the force from the Muladhara does take place....
>
> In the Tantra the centres are opened and Kundalini is awakened by a special process, its action of ascent is felt through the spine. Here it is the pressure of the Force from above that awakens it and opens the centres. There is an ascension of the consciousness going up till it joins the higher consciousness above. This repeats itself (sometimes a descent also is felt) until all the centres are open and the consciousness rises above the body. At a later stage it remains above and widens out into the cosmic consciousness and the universal Self. This is a usual course, but sometimes the process is more rapid and there is a sudden and definite opening above." (42)

Sri Aurobindo listed the chakras as follows, and explained that they exist in the subtle body, not in the physical body:

> "The centres or Chakras are seven in number —
> (1) The thousand-petalled lotus on the top of the head.
> (2) In the middle of the forehead — the Ajna Chakra — (will, vision, dynamic thought).
> (3) Throat centre — externalising mind.
> (4) Heart-lotus — emotional centre. The psychic is behind it.
> (5) Navel — higher vital (proper).
> (6) Below navel — lower vital.
> (7) Muladhara — physical.
> All these centres are in the middle of the body; they are sup-

posed to be attached to the spinal cord; but in fact all these things are in the subtle body, *suksma deha*, though one has the feeling of their activities as if in the physical body when the consciousness is awake." (43)

He further elaborated how the chakras are described in classical yoga, followed by their psycho-spiritual functions in his system of yoga. Note that here "lotuses" refers to the chakras:

"The colours of the lotuses and the numbers of petals are respectively, from bottom to top: — (1) the Muladhara or physical consciousness centre, four petals, red; (2) the abdominal centre, six petals, deeper purple red; (3) the navel centre, ten petals, violet; (4) the heart centre, twelve petals, golden pink; (5) the throat centre, sixteen petals, grey; (6) the forehead centre between the eyebrows, two petals, white; (7) the thousand- petalled lotus above the head, blue with gold light around. The functions are, according to our Yoga, (1) commanding the physical consciousness and the subconscient; (2) commanding the small vital movements, the little greeds, lusts, desires, the small sense-movements; (3) commanding the larger life-forces and the passions and larger desire-movements; (4) commanding the higher emotional being with the psychic deep behind it; (5) commanding expression and all externalisation of the mind-movements and mental forces; (6) commanding thought, will, vision; (7) commanding the higher thinking mind and the illumined mind and opening upwards to the intuition and overmind. The seventh is sometimes confused with the brain, but that is an error — the brain is only a channel of communication situated between the thousand-petalled and the forehead centre. The former is sometimes called the void centre, *sunya*, either because it is not in the body, but in the apparent void above or because rising above the head one enters first into the silence of the self or spiritual being."(44)

There have been attempts to locate neurophysiological correlates of chakras, for instance, some have speculated that the seven chakras correspond to seven main nerve ganglia emanating from the spinal column. Sri Aurobindo noted that there are certain centres in the physical body with which the chakras correspond, yet he was emphatic that these physical sites are not the chakras proper, as the chakras exist in the subtle body. (45) He also explained that there are no chakras in the subconscious:

> "There is no subconscient centre…the subconscient is too vague to have a centre. It has a level — below the feet as the superconscient is above, but from there it can surge up anywhere". (46)

Likewise, there are no chakras in the superconscious realms, where the consciousness is no longer embodied and there is no Kundalini Shakti:

> "There is no Kundalini Shakti above the head. Above the head is the universal or Divine Consciousness and Force. The Kundalini is the latent power asleep in the chakras." (47)

Finally, note that the psychic being has no chakra. Many people experience it as existing deep behind the heart chakra in some inmost dimension of consciousness, but it can come forward and infuse the chakras with its pure presence and power, and place the chakras under its guiding control. As Sri Aurobindo explained,

> "the Power from above has in its descent to open all the centres (including the lowest centre) and to bring out the psychic being; for until that is done there is likely to be much difficulty and struggle of the lower consciousness obstructing, mixing with or even refusing the Divine Action from above. If the psychic being is once active this struggle and these difficulties can be greatly minimized." (48)

Dr. Basu has presented Sri Aurobindo's approach to the chakras in courses on personality development for corporate teams, and participants have found the concept of working on the subliminal planes of consciousness to be more appealing than the classical approach. In fact, highlighting the inner planes of consciousness was more approachable for all sections of the audience, regardless of diverse belief-systems, than the classical model of raising the kundalini force through the chakras.

Clinically, Sri Aurobindo's model of how the chakras connect to various planes of consciousness is useful because it leads to a consciousness-based framework that allows us to interpret how *all* treatment modalities also act upon these same planes of consciousness. For example, in his book on *Integral Health* (49), Dr. Basu has explained that the pharmacological agents of modern medicine work primarily at the physical plane of consciousness. Homeopathy, flower essences and acupuncture seem to work at the vital plane, which corresponds to the chakras of the chest and abdomen (the *higher* and *central vital*, respectively) and the pelvis (*lower vital*). Techniques such as progressive relaxation and bio-feedback work at the level of the *physical mind*, corresponding to the throat chakra. Certain psychotherapies act at the level of the vital mind involved in dynamism and emotional turbulence, cor-responding to heart and navel chakras. Hypnosis acts on the sense mind at the level of the inner being, while techniques such as reiki, pranic therapy and prayer act by strengthening the vital-physical, which is a sort of subtle force-field or envelope projected around the body. The planes and parts of the being, and their connection to treatment, are explored further in Part II of this book.

> *The inner planes uncovered their crystal doors...*
> *A vision came of higher realms than ours,*
> *A consciousness of brighter fields and skies...*
>
> Savitri, *pg. 28*

References

1. CWSA 21-22, pg. 543-544
2. Ibid, pg. 548-549
3. Rishabchand. The Integral Yoga of Sri Aurobindo, SABDA,

Pondicerry, 2nd Ed,1959, pg. 354

4. CWSA 21-22, pg. 549
5. CWSA 25, pg. 102
6. CWSA 21-22, pg. 66
7. Ibid, pg. 67
8. CWSA 25, pg. 104-105
9. Ibid, pg. 194-195
10. Ibid, pg. 121
11. Ibid, pg. 122
12. Ibid
13. Ibid
14. Ibid, pg. 115
15. Ibid
16. Ibid, pg. 122
17. Ibid, pg. 123
18. Ibid, pg. 107
19. Ibid, pg. 197
20. Ibid, pg. 105
21. Ibid, pg. 120-121
22. CWSA 21-22,, pg. 544
23. Ibid
24. Ibid, pg. 545
25. Ibid, pg. 546
26. Ibid, pg. 544
27. Op.cit Rishabchand pg. 350-351
28. CWSA 21-22, pg. 543
29. Op.cit Rishabchand pg. 355-356
30. CWSA 25, pg. 106
31. CWSA 21-22, pg. 637
32. Ibid, pg. 638
33. Ibid, pg. 641
34. Ibid, pg. 71
35. Maharshi, Ramana: Death Experience, www.sriramanama-harshi.org
36. CWSA 21-22, pg. 549
37. Ibid, pg. 551
38. Ibid, pg. 559
39. Ibid, pg. 556
40. Ibid, pg. 557-558
41. Ibid, pg. 559

42. CWSA 29, pg. 460-461

43. CWSA 28, pg. 229

44. Ibid, pg. 230-231

45. CWSA 10-11, pg. 1388

46. CWSA 28, pg. 244

47. CWSA 29, pg., 461

48. Ibid, pg. 307

49. Basu,S : Integral Health, 2nd Edition, SAIIIHR, Pondicerry, 2011, pg. 88-92

8

Supra-Rational Cognition

Savitri, pg. 705

People often speak of "intuition" as though it were just one thing, but in fact it is a vast and varied phenomenon. As we saw in the last chapter, there are inner or subliminal planes of consciousness from which one may derive intuitions either while asleep or awake, and in this chapter we will consider the many higher planes of consciousness from which one may derive supra-rational intuitions. Sri Aurobindo made a detailed study of what we loosely call "intuition," and this is important to understand both for personal self-development and clinical work.

For example, many people are interested in astrology, which is an intuitive discipline that has been developed in a number of cultures. In India, it is common for patients to seek the advice of an astrologer while also taking psychiatric medications and/or attending therapy sessions. In terms of CBP, the main problem with any intuitive discipline is that intuitive insights can get diluted at the level of ordinary cognition. Intuition belongs to an overhead plane of consciousness that lies above our usual thinking mind, and when intuitive revelations descend to the level of the mind, they usually get mixed up with ordinary thoughts, emotions, and wishes. As a result, if some intuitive predictions are exceptionally brilliant, others can turn out to be miserably wrong. And as Sri Aurobindo constantly emphasized, the highest spiritual consciousness overpasses astrology and can annul it. Nothing is fixed and final. There is a Divine Grace that can change fate, dissolve Karma, and create a new destiny for any soul at any time. The Supermind is all-powerful, and the intimate relationship between the psychic being (evolving soul) and the Supreme consciousness is a mystery of consciousness that astrology cannot fathom. (1)

Also, it is important to understand that clinicians can be culturally conditioned either for or against astrology, and both biases need attention. Following is a case example of how Dr. Basu's cultural bias towards astrology lead him to ignore a subtle intuition that needed immediate attention:

> An artist who was well known for his instantaneous sketches of human faces, which were widely displayed at exhibitions and fairs, had been under treatment for detoxification from alcohol. He was also an intuitive astrologer who could read faces, and several times he predicted certain things about me that actually came to pass. He had low self-esteem about his baldness, for which he always wore a wig. One day, he came to my clinic and spent a lot of time singing nostalgic songs. He asked my wife, who had formerly done some counseling sessions with him, to lend her voice to his songs, and she agreed. He told me repeatedly that he would be proud to die at my hands. My wife and I did not make much of these comments. We assumed that due to his astrological skills, if there were any negative occult influences at work, he had taken steps to ward them off. Sadly, the next day he died suddenly from a massive heart attack.

In retrospect, Dr. Basu realized that he had missed certain suggestions of impending death that were revealed through this man's statements and choice of nostalgic songs. Dr. Basu actually had a fleeting thought that this patient might be singing his "swan-song," but he unfortunately ignored this brief intuition as he assumed the man's skill in astrology would protect him. We start on this cautionary note because the phenomenon of intuition is complex and many-sided, and CBP does not approach it in a simplistic and naïve fashion.

First, let us review where psychology stands today on the issue of intuition. There is an interesting debate as to whether "intuition" should be considered as an extra-rational, ESP-like ability or a natural part of an information processing system. Simon proposes that if intuition has to do with making a correct judgment without conscious awareness of the process behind it, then such capacity is a common ingredient in everyday, cognitive functioning. (2) For instance, a skilled chess-player can make a sudden, unplanned move without knowing why and often it can turn out to be a correct move. Such an intuitive execution is based on two things: 1) a well-organized knowledge base, and 2) a corresponding elaborate discrimination net that makes for quick and accurate judgments. This means that a repertoire of extensive experience facilitates the phenomenon of intuition. Even our capacity to recognize a friend in a crowded street depends on one's considerable experience with a large number of "friends".

Another intuitive ability that has come under investigation is the phenomenon of "incubation". This is said to occur when the individual sets a problem aside for a while and may even do something unrelated to the problem, and then later the correct solution suddenly springs up. Factors like unconscious processes that go on in the interval, stress reduction, selective forgetting have been proposed as explanations. A purely rational, information processing explanation can be expanded to cover the phenomenon of incubation. However, experiments in controlled settings have proved difficult to account for what actually happens during incubation. Sri Aurobindo was well aware of how psychologists view intuition and in 1916 he wrote:

> "It is even thought by the intellectualists that the intuition itself is nothing more than this rapid process in which the whole action of the logical mind is swiftly done or perhaps half-consciously or subconsciously done, not deliberately worked out in its reasoned method. In its nature, however, this proceeding is quite different from the intuition and it is not necessarily a truth-movement. The power of its leap may end in a stumble, its swiftness may betray, its certainty is too often a confident error." (3)

Still, even science is beginning to acknowledge instances of intuition that seem to point towards supra-rational sources of knowledge that go beyond the reach of an individual's past experience. For example, certain scientific discoveries have been made on the basis of intuitive experiences that need a more satisfactory explanation than simple information processing. A classic example of this is the discovery of the benzene ring, which was inspired from a dream-vision of a coiled snake eating its own tail. Here, the experimenter was certainly trying out many models for the structure of benzene, and these trials and errors were stored in his repertoire of experience. However, the dream-vision of the snake cannot be satisfactorily explained as part of information-processing and past experience, and in the terms of CBP came from a plane of consciousness above the reasoning mind. Frances E. Vaughn, psychologist and author of *Awakening Intuition* suggests:

> "At any given moment one is conscious of only a small portion of what one knows. Intuition allows one to draw on that vast storehouse of unconscious knowledge that includes not only everything that one has experienced or learned, either consciously or subliminally, but also the infinite reservoir of the collective or universal unconscious, in which individual separateness and ego-boundaries are transcended."(4)

That reservoir of collective knowledge may contain things not experienced before by the subject. If so, then the knowledge-base of an individual does not allow for information processing to account for an intuitive idea — unless we accept that the individual knowledge-base can get connected to an universal knowledge-base. For example, even in the midst of our current age of rationality and evidence-based medicine, sometimes an experienced doctor can intuitively decide the correct intervention even before the laboratory test results arrive, or even before the evidence exists. One remarkable instance of this is the heart specialist, Dr. Mimi Guernari, who could not stop the a patient's bleeding on the operating table. She suddenly had the intuitive idea of using gel foam, an idea that came out of blue and actually saved the patient's life. (5) This practice later became evidence-based standard of care.

This leads us to another interesting area, which is the phenomenon of "medical intuitives". The term was coined by neuro-surgeon, Dr. Norman Shealy, to describe intuitive individuals who could visualize and diagnose patients without using medical tests or scans. He studied such medical intuitives and found that one of them, Caroline Myss, was 93% accurate (6). Dr. Shealy's book covers just a small range of the number of individuals in the world who have such intuitive capacities, at least within a certain sphere of action. However, while impressive in its moments of success, medical intuition can also have its errors and falls. This admixture of success and failure can be understandably confusing in the best of circumstances, and in the worst can lead some individuals to re-ject science completely, leading to disinformation, fraud, and pre-ventable death. One recent example of this is "anti-vaxxers" who are against vaccines not based on data or veridical intuition, but based on infra-rational conspiracy theories deriving from overval-ued wrong ideas or even frank delusions. It is these dangerous ex-tremes that make some doctors wary of the term "intuition," which can become a code-word that means anti-science.

Nevertheless, the solution to complexity is not blind rejec-tion of either spirituality or science, but to find an approach to consciousness that can successfully embrace the valid insights of both. This is what Sri Aurobindo does in his nuanced study of the varieties of intuitive experience:

"Our mind stands between a superconscience and an in-conscience and receives from both these opposite powers: it stands between an occult subliminal existence and an out-ward cosmic phenomenon; it receives inspirations, intuitions, imaginations, impulsions to knowledge and action, figures of subjective realities or possibilities from the unknown inner source; it receives the figures of realised actualities and their suggestions of further possibility from the observed cosmic phenomenon. What it receives are truths essential, possible or actual; it starts from the realised actualities of the physical universe and it brings out from them in its subjective action the unrealised possibilities which they contain or suggest or to which it can arrive by proceeding from them as a starting-point: it selects some out of these possibilities for a subjective action and plays with imagined on inwardly constructed forms of them; it chooses others for objectivisation and attempts to realise them. But it receives inspirations also from above and within, from invisible sources and not only from the impacts of the visible cosmic phenomenon; it sees truths other than those suggested by the actual physicality around it, and here too it plays subjectively with transmitted or constructed forms of these truths or it selects for objectivisation, attempts to realise." (7)

This passage is unique in that it acknowledges both Simon's view of intuitive experiences arising at one plane from an already existing knowledge-base and sorting nets, as also Vaughan's view of intuitions arising from an ego-transcending, universal wisdom-base which must have a different origin at some other plane of consciousness. In fact, Sri Aurobindo dealt with intuitive experiences in several different ways. He classified intuitive experiences that come from sources higher than the mind in a graded way, and he also described how intuition at the level of present organization of consciousness in human beings gets influenced by reason, emotions (vital) and senses resulting in a mixed action. This is relevant to understanding intuition from the psychological angle.

The Higher Orders of Cognition

Sri Aurobindo and the Mother described supra-rational levels of cognition which are connected with various non-material planes of consciousness. The Mother explained that this paradigm begins with a sort of map of consciousness that describes the gradation of these occult worlds:

"The occult world is a gradation of regions, one could perhaps say, of more and more ethereal or subtle regions, anyway, those farther and farther removed in their nature from the physical materiality we ordinarily see. And each of these domains is a world in itself, having its forms and inhabited by beings with a density, one might say, analogous to that of the domain in which they live. Just as in the physical world we are of the same materiality as the physical world, so in the vital world, in the mental world, in the overmind world and in the supramental world — and in many others, infinite others – there are beings which have a form whose substance is similar to the one of that world. This means that if you are able to enter consciously into that world with the part of your being which corresponds to that domain, you can move there quite objectively, as in the material world". (8)

Sri Aurobindo often referred to the planes of consciousness that stand above the reasoning mind in the occult hierarchy as "the overhead planes," because subjectively they are often felt to be associated with the crown chakra and the region above the head. In the following letter, he described these high-order cognitive matrices in greater detail, and gave each gradation a name:

"The Self governs the diversity of its creation by its unity on all the planes from the Higher Mind upwards, for there some realisation or vision of the One Truth or the Universal is the natural frame and basis of the whole consciousness. But the higher one rises upward, the more the spiritual view changes, the power of consciousness changes, the Light becomes ever more intense and potent. The essential static realisation of Infinity and Eternity and the Timeless One remains the same, but the vision of the workings of the One becomes ever wider and is attended with a greater instrumentality of Force and a more comprehensive grasp of what has to be known and done. All possible forms and constructions of things become more and more visible, more perfectly put in their proper place, more luminously utilisable. A clear spacious thought-knowledge in the Higher Mind becomes a mass of illuminations in the Illumined Mind and heightens into direct intimate vision on the Intuition level. But the Intuition sees in flashes and combines through a constant play of light

— through a chain or coordinated harmony of revelations, inspirations, intuitions, swift discriminations. The Overmind sees calmly, steadily, in great masses and deep and large extensions of space and time and relation, globally, in wholes; it has the universal touch not only in spirit but in its manner. It creates and acts in the same way — for the Overmind is the world of the great Gods, the divine Creators. But each Godhead creates in his own way; he sees all but that all is seen from his own divine viewpoint. There is not the absolute supramental harmony and certitude. These are some of the differences. I speak of these planes in themselves — for when they act in the human consciousness, they are necessarily much diminished in their working, for they have to work with and depend on the human instrumentation or man's smaller seeking mental intelligence, his passionate turbid vital and mental, his cabined and narrow physical intellect – their workings get badly mixed up with these inferior modes of consciousness and their diluted light of ignorance. Only when these lower impotencies are quieted can those higher powers get a fuller force and reveal more of their original luminous character." (9)

Thus, Sri Aurobindo names and describes higher orders of cognition related to supra-physical planes of consciousness, which are summarized below. Sri Aurobindo notes that experientially these planes of consciousness, or levels of cognitive organization, are associated with the crown chakra of Indian yoga — except for the last one, the Overmind, which is felt to pour down from above the head. While experiences of these higher planes of consciousness are still rare in the general population, knowing that such transpersonal development is possible is important for the ongoing self-development of anyone who is interested in transformative spirituality. It can also be useful for clinicians who are doing transpersonal work and want to help clients sort out from which plane of consciousness and inspiration or experience may derive. In a broad sense, it is impossible to do a differential diagnosis of psycho-spiritual experience unless one knows the full range of what is actually possible.

The Higher Mind

The Higher Mind is capable of mass-ideation where an automatic and spontaneous outpouring of masses of knowledge is experientially perceived. Knowledge here is not culled from premises and data. The relation between idea and idea is not established by deductive logic but is pre-existent. The idea is invested with a dynamic energy to become a composite idea-force. This is the domain of the thinker where thought should be powerful for communication through language and for knowledge to be objectivized from its abstract connotations. While the ordinary cognitive field needs to deconstruct existing constructs to accommodate new constructs, the Higher Mind structures go on expanding. There is a greater totality of Truth known but still a totality capable of infinite enlargement.

One example of the Higher Mind at work that most people will recognize are Jefferson's famous lines from the American Declaration of Independence:

> "When in the Course of human events, it becomes necessary for one people to dissolve the political bands which have connected them with another, and to assume among the powers of the earth, the separate and equal station to which the Laws of Nature and of Nature's God entitle them, a decent respect to the opinions of mankind requires that they should declare the causes which impel them to the separation.

> We hold these truths to be self-evident, that all men are created equal, that they are endowed by their Creator with certain inalienable Rights, that among these are Life, Liberty and the pursuit of Happiness. — That to secure these rights, Governments are instituted among Men, deriving their just powers from the consent of the governed, — That whenever any Form of Government becomes destructive of these ends, it is the Right of the People to alter or to abolish it, and to

institute new Government, laying its foundation on such principles and organizing its powers in such form, as to them shall seem most likely to effect their Safety and Happiness." (10)

While Jefferson the man certainly had flaws, including the fact that he owned slaves, from the perspective of CBP this just illustrates how inspiration from a higher plane of consciousness gets diluted by the ordinary action of lower planes. Despite Jefferson's many errors, there is nevertheless a sweep of vision in this passage, a swift grasping of the relationships among multiple issues in human life, that expresses the wholistic thinking of the Higher Mind. This writing is at once a poetic, philosophical, and political statement that weaves together many lines of thought into a unified vision of the whole. Note how quickly the thought moves across topics from the relationship between God and Nature, to the flow of human history, to theology and human rights, to the structure of government, to the relationship between the individual and the collective. Also, note how Jefferson specifically states that the truths he is expressing are "self-evident," that is, not arrived at by logic or experiment but seen instantly as a mass of spontaneous knowledge. It is precisely because of the higher inspiration in these two paragraphs that so many people have been inspired by it — and that democratic nations have worked for centuries to achieve the ideals that Jefferson himself did not live up to.

The Illumined Mind

The Illumined Mind represents a cognitive matrix where Truth flashes as a revelatory ideograph. Classically it is the domain of the mystic's mind to whom the body of Truth is revealed as an illumined vision, albeit with ardour and ecstasy but without any need of verbal representation through language. While language is one of the key components to understand the usual cognitive process, the Illumined Mind is a cognitive field that can operate through inner vision without linguistic representation. No wonder, mystics throughout the world have similar realizations irrespective of a wide difference in culture and language. The energy or force implicit in the matrix of the Illumined Mind is more powerful than that of the Higher Mind with an integrating effect on the senses, feelings and thought; and is accompanied by a luminosity and descent of peace.

These qualities and characteristics of the Illumined Mind are illustrated in the following vignette of mystical experienc. In his classic treatise on mysticism from 1911, Underhill narrated how the Revelations of Angela of Foligno described the "formless vision" and its complement, the "formless word". A sudden illuminated vision of the Divine Presence gave her a clarity that surpassed the functionings of the physical senses. It was a vision more clear than the physical seeing of a person by a person. Therefore it was surmised that the illumined vision was a vision of the soul:

> "For the eyes of the soul behold a plenitude of which I cannot speak: a plenitude which is not bodily but spiritual, of which I can say nothing. And the soul rejoices in that sight with an ineffable joy….And the soul can behold nothing else…This beholding, whereby the soul can behold no other thing, is so profound that it grieves me that I can say nothing of it. It is not a thing which can be touched or imagined, for it is ineffable." (11)

In fact, the combination of "the plenitude of the vision" and the accompanying "ineffable joy" gave the certitude of the Divine Presence. Underhill quotes Recejac to re-affirm the validity of such illuminative knowledge:

> "The whole consciousness is flooded with lights to unknown depths, under the gaze of love, from which nothing escapes. In this stage, intensity of vision and sureness of judgment are equal: and the things which the seer brings back with him when he returns to common life are not merely physical impressions, or the separate knowledge of 'science' or 'poetry'. They are rather truths which embrace the world, life and conduct: in a word, the whole consciousness". (12)

The Intuitive Mind

The plane of Intuition is a yet higher cognitive matrix characterized as a direct outleap of a superior light; an edge of a far-off light from a very high Supramental source. It is represented through truth-remembrance or truth-conveyance, truth-touch, truth-hearing; as revelations, as flashes or blazes breaking through ignorance and nescience though it has got every chance to be distorted and misrepresented when it reaches the ordinary mind unless the subject develops the power of a higher judgment and discrimination that places things in their proper perspectives. The pure light and power of intuition brings a greater integrality and perfection but stops short at the level of the Inconscience that it cannot altogether penetrate and transform.

It is through intuition that Ayurvedic seers discovered that *Rawalfia Serpentina* is the correct pharmacological treatment for the hallucinations of schizophrenia. It works by depleting dopamine, and its efficacy was not surpassed until dopamine blocking agents (chlorpromazine) were synthesized in the late 1950s. It is also through intuition that Rig Vedic seers described three types of "fire" — Jada Agni (ordinary fire), Vaidutya Agni (electric fire) and Saurya Agni (solar or nuclear fire), prompting Sri Aurobindo to comment in 1926, "Science has only entered upon the first and second of these fires. The fact that the atom is like the solar system could lead it to the knowledge of the third." (13) It was only in 1939 that energy release from nuclear fission was experimentally confirmed, thus validating Einstein's paper from 1905 that had put forward the equivalence between mass and energy.

For psychology and psychiatry, one of the most striking intuitive insights in the ancient Indian tradition of Tantra was the discrimination between what was called the right-handed path of knowledge and the left-handed path of action. This discrimination was used not only to design unique mystical disciplines but also in associating different mudras in classical dance with different attributes. Sri Aurobindo elaborated in 1909:

> "The faculties of the right hand are comprehensive, creative and synthetic; the faculties of the left hand critical and

analytic. To the right hand belong Judgment, Imagination, Memory, Observation; to the left hand Comparison and Reasoning. The critical faculties distinguish, compare, classify, generalize, deduce, infer, and conclude; they are the component parts of the logical reason. The right-hand faculties comprehend, command, judge in their own right, grasp, hold and manipulate. The right-hand mind is the master of the knowledge, the left-hand its servant. The left hand touches only the body of knowledge, the right hand penetrates its soul. The left-hand limits itself to ascertained truth, the right-hand grasps that which is still elusive or unascertained. Both are essential to the completeness of the human reason." (14)

In this passage, the term "right hand" denotes the right hemisphere of the brain, while the "left hand" means the left hemisphere. It was only in the later part of 20th century that neuroscience elaborated what Tantra knew long back, namely, that different cognitive functions are lateralized to the left and right hemispheres of the brain: "It seems that the mode of operation of the brain's left hemisphere is linear: it processes information sequentially, one bit after another, in an ordered way....In sharp contrast, the right hemisphere is specialized for simultaneous processing: that is, it operates in a more holistic, relational way." (15)

There is another group of intuitive experiences where knowledge is communicated to individuals in such a way that it can be used to construct religions, philosophies, and codes of conduct. The most striking fact about this order of knowledge is that it carries a power, a force that enables it to survive the vicissitudes of time and history. For example, this type of knowledge was communicated to individuals such as Moses, Prophet Mohammed, and Guru Nanak, and transpersonal psychology has shown that such revelations cannot be carelessly equated with the psychopathology of schizophrenia. Finally, there is a yet higher class of intuitive spiritual experiences where individuals have mighty enlightenments from very high planes of consciousness - e.g., Christ's vision of a kingdom of Heaven on Earth, the Buddha's realization of Nirvana, or Ramana Maharshi's realization of the Self. It is impossible to judge such intuitive experiences without the help of Sri Aurobindo's model of CBP.

As always, Sri Aurobindo was careful to describe the limitations of intuition and how it gets diluted in the operations of the normal human mentality. First, he notes that at the level of the mind, Intuition acts by flashes, point by point, not as a whole:

> "it is still occasional, partial, fragmentary and of an intermittent character. It casts a sudden light, it makes a luminous suggestion or it throws out a solitary brilliant clue or scatters a small number of isolated or related intuitions, lustrous discriminations, inspirations or revelations, and it leaves the reason, will, mental sense or intelligence to do what each can or pleases with this seed of succour that has come to them from the depths or the heights of our being." (16)

One mistake people can make is to equate Intuition with any rapid process in which the whole action of the logical mind is swiftly done or perhaps half-consciously or subconsciously done, without being worked out by reason. Such a movement may lead to errors, and Sri Aurobindo explained that this is quite different from true Intuition. The true Intuition carries its own guarantee of truth and is never contradicted by experience:

> "the intuition may be verified by the reason or the sense-perception afterwards, but its truth does not depend on that verification, it is assured by an automatic self-evidence. If the reason depending on its inferences contradicts the greater light, it will be found in the end on ampler knowledge that the intuitional conclusion was correct and that the more plausible rational and inferential conclusion was an error. For the true intuition proceeds from the self-existent truth of things and is secured by that self-existent truth and not by any indirect, derivatory or dependent method of arriving at knowledge".(17)

In light of the above, Sri Aurobindo was cautious not to equate his concept of true Intuition with the Sanskrit term *buddhi*, as the latter does not differentiate Intuition from Intellect. Also, Sri Aurobindo explained that at the level of the habitual workings of the mind, Intuition usually gets mixed up with ordinary mental stuff, leading to cognitive errors, misinterpretations, deviations and distortions. Usually, the intuitive insights are either ignored so that they do not have time to settle and extend their full powers for illumination, or else they are exaggerated out of context "to the exclusion of the larger truth that the more consistent use of the intuitive faculty might have given." (18) Moreover, there are certain thought movements that seem like intuitions ("seeming intuitions") on all levels of the being which do not qualify as intuitions but are rather "communications" that are variable in nature. (19) Some of such "communications" are actually pseudo-intuitions which imitate intuitions but originate at levels of consciousness lower than the mind.

For instance, many such imitative pseudo-intuitions originate at the vital plane, which is the repertoire of drives, passions, and emotions. Some of these can originate from an unillumined, dark and dangerous source. (20) The faculty of sensory perception can also influence the phenomenon of intuition in two ways. Based on the information processing networks and already existing knowledge-base, a swift retrieval mimicking a true intuition can occur and at times may be factually correct. Or else a true intuitive movement can get distorted by the immature inputs from the information processing network. Further down in the scale of evolution, the archetype of intuition is represented as instinct in animals, and acts through information-processing mediated by senses, minus the input from Reason that is available to human beings.

Case study

A case study of how mixed intuitive phenomenon can be is that of Joao Teixeira de Faria of Brazil, who came to be known as "John of God." He was a gifted medium who was credited with many spectacular healings achieved through the use of intuitive capacities coupled with the ability to transmit "spiritual energies." Subjects who had positive experiences described opening to and receiving healing supra-physical energies from many entities (beings) residing in higher planes of consciousness. Thus, many individuals testified as to having had bona fide healings with John of God, and the authors of this book personally know of several such cases that were veridical. However, over time many victims came forth with reports of sexual abuse and other forms of exploitation, and these have also been confirmed. So how do we explain such glaring contradictions? This is difficult for psychology to do, impossible for science, but simple for CBP: because there are many planes of consciousness, and many admixtures thereof, a whole range of mixed phenomenon are possible. In the case of John of God, there was a mixture of everything — placebo effects, veridical intuitions and healings, and vital falsehood and abuses of power all at the same time, or in a changing proportion over time. Consciousness is too complex to be reduced to simple either/or statements. However, the authors hasten to add that such theoretical comments need to be clearly distinguished from standards of practice. Practically, CBP holds that medical ethics need to be maintained, and that boundary violations and abuses of power need to be prosecuted to the full extent of the law. Reason is the minimum acceptable level for standards of truth in the collective process, and the goal of CBP is to raise the bar of Truth not fall below it. If a healer or spiritual teacher can stay above the level of Reason, all is well and should proceed; if they fall below into vital falsehoods and abuses of power, then it is time to stop them.

The Overmind

The Overmind is the plane of consciousness at which there is a shift from an individual to a global cognitive matrix. This global cognitive field cannot be accessed unless there is an effacement of the ego. The Overmind is in fact a superconscient cosmic mind which is the origin of the primal ideas implicit with force or energy that proceed to manifest the multiplicity in creation though at the same time aware of the underlying unity so as not to reflect chaos or confusion. It holds multiple complementary and contradictory ideas at origin; knowledge rushes in from all sides and one can see objects from all points of view and each thing from all points. At the level of the ordinary functioning of the mind, the harmony characteristic of global cognition or Overmind is lost as each idea has the right of independent self-assertion. Inspirations from the Overmind have inaugurated most of the world's major religions, spawned immortal moments of literature and art and music, revealed breakthroughs in science and technology, and created the mythologies and cultural developments that have driven the evolution of civilization. The Overmind is a massive and pluripotent Creator of forms and forces that disregards the normal distinctions of the reasoning mind. In the following passage, Sri Aurobindo compares and contrasts the characteristics of overmental cognition with that of the ordinary mind or reasoning intelligence:

> "If we would understand the difference of this global Overmind Consciousness from our separative and only imperfectly synthetic mental consciousness, we may come near to it if we compare the strictly mental with what would be an overmental view of activities in our material universe. To the Overmind, for example, all religions would be true as developments of the one eternal religion, all philosophies would be valid each in its own field as a statement of its own universe-view from its own angle, all political theories with their practice would be the legitimate working out of an Idea Force with its right to application and practical development in the play of the energies of Nature. In our separative consciousness, imperfectly visited by glimpses of catholicity and universality, these things exist as opposites; each claims to be the truth and taxes the others with error and falsehood, each feels impelled to refute or destroy the others in order that itself alone may be the Truth and live: at best, each must claim to be superior, admit all others only as inferior truth-expres-

sions. An overmental Intelligence would refuse to entertain this conception or this drift to exclusiveness for a moment; it would allow all to live as necessary to the whole or put each in its place in the whole or assign to each its field of realisation or of endeavour. This is because in us consciousness has come down completely into the divisions of the Ignorance; Truth is no longer either an Infinite or a cosmic whole with many possible formulations, but a rigid affirmation holding any other affirmation to be false because different from itself and entrenched in other limits. Our mental consciousness can indeed arrive in its cognition at a considerable approach towards a total comprehensiveness and catholicity, but to organize that in action and life seems to be beyond its power. Evolutionary Mind, manifest in individuals or collectivities, throws up a multiplicity of divergent view-points, divergent lines of action and lets them work themselves out side by side or in collision or in a certain intermixture; it can make selective harmonies, but it cannot arrive at the harmonic control of a true totality....An Overmind world would be a world of harmony; the world of Ignorance in which we live is a world of disharmony and struggle." (21)

As Sri Aurobindo describes it here, the Overmind is a global cognition characterized by true Wholeness — it sees the Whole and the truth of each perspective within the Whole at the same instant, and does not set one idea or mental viewpoint against another as an opposition or contradiction. Specifically, he notes that in the Overmind all religions, philosophies and political systems are true, and all aspects of individual and collective life exist in harmony. He also describes how our current level of mental consciousness is just the opposite and characterized by division, conflict, contradiction, disharmony and struggle. Thus, a truly "whole-person" approach to health and psychology would aspire not just to a system of Reason enlightened with synthetic moments of Intuition, but to the true wholeness of a fully overmental view of life and the world.

In Western thought, something similar to Overmind has

been studied as the "Noosphere," denoting the unified field of consciousness described by sages of all cultures and all times. The term "Noosphere" was jointly coined by the French philosopher Edouard Le Roy, the Jesuit paleontologist Pierre Teilhard de Chardin, and the Russian geochemist Vladimir Vernardsky in Paris in 1926. (22) Though parallels are often drawn between the Noosphere and Overmind, the formulation of the Noosphere falls short of Sri Aurobindo's description of the Supermind. Sri Aurobindo experienced the descent of the Overmind into the physical consciousness in 1926. In the same year, South African philosopher Jan Smuts published one of the first expositions of holistic philosophy in his book *Holism and Human Evolution*, where life and evolution are defined in terms of the synthesis of whole systems rather than analysis of minute parts. Also in the same year, a few days before he passed away on November 3, the French psycho-mathematician Charles Henry published a monograph titled *The Post-Mortem Survival of Consciousness*, which visualizes a transcendence of consciousness into a greater whole. (23)

According to Sri Aurobindo and the Mother, the Overmind is the world of the Gods and Goddesses. Many cultures have religions have referred to a number of Gods and Goddesses, and some of these traditions are still living as in India, while others are defunct as in Greece. Today, these traditions are often called "mythology," which has the connotation of being not quite true. At the best, mythology is viewed as fulfilling the important psychological function of making meaning of life via narration, while at the worst it is viewed as being nothing more than quaint old stories told by pre-scientific people. In contrast, Sri Aurobindo views mythology as a repository of valid perceptions of supra-physical planes of consciousness that actually exist:

> "There are no planes of manifestation without forms — for without form creation or manifestation cannot be complete. But the supraphysical planes are not bound to the forms like the physical. The forms there are expressive, not determinative. What is important on the vital plane is the force or feeling and the form expresses it. A vital being has a characteristic

form but he can vary it or mask his true form under others. What is primary on the mental plane is the perception, the idea, the mental significance and the form expresses that and these mental forms too can vary — there can be many forms expressing an idea in different ways or on different sides of the idea. Form exists but it is more plastic and variable than in physical nature.

As to the Gods, man can build forms which they will accept; but these forms too are inspired into man's mind from the planes to which the God belongs. All creation has the two sides, the formed and the formless; the Gods too are formless and yet have forms, but a Godhead can take many forms, here Maheshwari, there Pallas Athene. Maheshwari herself has many forms in her lesser manifestations, Durga, Uma, Parvati, Chandi etc. The Gods are not limited to human forms — man also has not always seen them in human forms only". (24)

"The Overmind is the world of the Gods and the Gods are not merely Powers, but have Forms also". (25)

Practically, this means that the current Hindus worship many of *the same* Gods and Goddesses as the ancient Greeks, only these beings have appeared in different forms in different times and places. From the perspective of the Overmind, these mythologies and religions are not as different as people usually take them to be. By extension of this principle, the Mayan Chac, the Greek Poseidon, and the Hindu Varuna are not three different Gods imagined by three different storytelling cultures, but one God expressed in different forms in three cultures with correct perceptions of a single overmental being. The same can be said of many other Gods and Goddesses, and indeed yoga has a fascinating knowledge about the occult correspondences among the various mythologies of the world. Far from being useless speculations buried in esoteric books read only by people with schizotypal traits who engage in mistaken magical thinking, this knowledge has very real relevance to the study of psychology, religion, and culture.

Cosmic Consciousness

The term "cosmic consciousness" has been used in many ways in Western thought and transpersonal psychology, but Sri Aurobindo gives it a specific sense that has a place in his metaphysical system. As a global cognitive field, the Overmind is the basis of total cosmic consciousness. However, in Aurobindonian terms the cosmic consciousness itself is represented at many levels — for it includes all of the planes of consciousness from the Overmind down to the Subconscient and the terrestrial Inconscience (see Table 1). Thus, the Overmind represents the upper range of cosmic consciousness, albeit the plane of consciousness from which the cosmic consciousness (in a movement of diffusion) as well as the individual consciousness (in a movement of concentration) manifest. For that reason, Sri Aurobindo also called the Overmind the "superconscient cosmic Mind". (26) The cosmic mind ordinarily is perceived in the poise of ignorance and should be differentiated from the "superconscient cosmic Mind" or Overmind.

Table 1. The Planes of Consciousness

    Sachchidananda
    Supermind
    Mind
      Overmind
      Intuitive mind
      Illumined mind
      Higher mind
      Reason
      Infra-rational levels of mind
    Life
      Higher vital
      Middle vital
      Lower vital
    Physical
      Levels of organizations of Matter
    Subconscient
    Inconscient

There are two important distinctions between the Overmind and the ordinary cosmic or universal mind in ignorance:

1. In the ordinary usage of the term, the cosmic or universal mind holds multiple contradictory and complementary ideas together and is in communion with the inner being of the individual. It is through this route that the universal rhythms of art, music, poetry enter the individual and are responsible for creative activity. The universal mind also holds what Jung refers to as the collective unconscious. The Overmind, on the other hand, holds multiple contradictory and complementary ideas at their origin. In the Overmind cognition, knowledge rushes upon from all sides and one can see objects from all points of view and each thing from all points. Thus the cosmic consciousness is represented not merely in its static aspect but also in its dynamic, reality. It is the expression of something above.

2. The cosmic consciousness at the level of the universal mind in ignorance is not immune to the play of a magnified ego or the vaster attacks of the hostile forces for they too are part of the cosmic consciousness. The cosmic consciousness at the level of the Overmind, however, is marked by an effacement of the centralizing ego-sense , or as Sri Aurobindo said, "a wide cosmic perception and feeling of a boundless universal self and movement replaces it: many motions that were formerly egocentric may still continue, but they occur as currents or ripples in the cosmic wideness." (27)

In terms of individual psychology, Sri Aurobindo gave a very vivid description of what it is like to live in the cosmic consciousness as experienced in the Overmind. This is one of those passages from the annals of human experience that ought to become canonical in transpersonal psychology:

"Thought, for the most part, no longer seems to originate individually in the body or the person but manifests from above or comes in upon the cosmic mind-waves: all inner individual sight or intelligence of things is now a revelation or illumination of what is seen or comprehended, but the source of the revelation is not in one's separate self but in the universal knowledge; the feelings, emotions, sensations are similarly felt as waves from the same cosmic immensity breaking upon the subtle and gross body and responded to in kind by the individual centre of the universality; for the body is only a small support or even less, a point of relation, for the action of a vast cosmic instrumentation. In this boundless largeness, not only the separate ego but all sense of individuality, even of a subordinated or instrumental individuality, may entirely disappear; the cosmic existence, the cosmic consciousness, the cosmic delight, the play of the cosmic forces are alone left: if the delight or the centre of Force is felt in what was the personal mind, life or body, it is not with a sense of personality but as a field of manifestation, and this sense of the delight or of the action of Force is not confined to the person or the body but can be felt at all points in an unlimited consciousness of unity which pervades everywhere." (28)

Evidently, to live in such a state of awareness would be to radically transform psychology such as it is currently understood. Nevertheless, Sri Aurobindo was not satisfied that this overmental cosmic cognition should be the final step in the evolution of consciousness. He and the Mother worked to attain a fully Supramental status of consciousness, which could be described as integral cognition. As they explained, the Supermind is too powerful to act directly on the mental cognitive field and the darkness of the Inconscience would not be able to bear the direct impact of its Truth and Light and Force. Thus, the Overmind functions as an intermediary medium between the Supermind and the Ignorance. In Sri Aurobindo's words, it acts "as a protective double, a screen of dissimilar similarity", a luminous "corona", a "delegate" through which the Supermind can indirectly influence the Ignorance because the latter cannot directly take the impact of the supreme Light. (29) As an intermediary, it stands between the integral unity of the Supramental Knowledge and the multiplicity of creation which lapses into Ignorance as consciousness descends from the Overmind into matter and the Inconscience. The Overmind can:

> "transform in each man it touched the whole conscious being, inner and outer, personal and universally impersonal, into its own stuff and impose that upon the Ignorance illumining it into cosmic truth and knowledge. But a basis of Nescience would remain". (30)

Thus, the Overmind can neither offer security against the downward pull of the Inconscience, nor can it dynamise the Transcendence into manifestation and action on Earth. Moreover, the Overmind deals with different possibilities and each possibility can be worked out to its extreme in a loose relation with the terrestrial manifestation. But what is needed is a yet higher cognitive field, the Supermind, where the principle of unity can take all diversities into itself and control them as parts of the unity, rather than allowing the diversities to fulfill themselves independently as the Overmind does. Nevertheless, though limited in its ultimate powers and possibilities, the Overmind is an important step in the evolution of consciousness, and its characteristics must be replicated in the individual consciousness as part of the evolution.

The Supermind, on the other hand, is a supra-cognitive field that holds the pre-programmed essence of the whole manifestation and antedates even the global cognitive field. The Supermind alone has the power to triumph over the resistance of the Inconscience. Sri Aurobindo explained that if the Supermind principle manifests in the earth-consciousness, human beings could be transformed, leading to the emergence of gnostic beings or supermen.

> "When the Supermind will descend, there will take place a radical transformation of all existence, material, vital and mental. Evolution does not, of course, stop with the emergence of the Supermind, for above the Supermind there are the still higher principles of Bliss, Consciousness-Force and Pure Being, but when the Supermind emerges, there is a radical change in the character of evolution, for henceforth it will

be through knowledge and not through ignorance. As a result of this radical change human beings will be transformed into gnostic beings or beings who have shed all ignorance and are illumined by the light of knowledge". (31)

Messengers from our subliminal greatnesses,
Guests from the cavern of the secret soul.
Into dim spiritual somnolence they break
Or shed wide wonder on our waking self,
Ideas that haunt us with their radiant tread,
Dreams that are hints of unborn Reality...

Savitri, *pg. 500*

References

1. Basu, S: Apropos astrology and health, Namah, The Journal of Integral Health, 25:4, 2018, pg. 4

2. Simon: Reasons in Human Affairs, Oxford. Basil Blackwell 1983, quoted by Geir Kaufmani in Creative Management, edited by Jane Henry, Sage Publications,UK,1991, pg. 126-127)

3. CWSA 23-24, pg. 478

4. Vaughn, Francis E: Anchor Books, 1979, quoted by Weston H. Agor, in op.cit. Creative Management, pg. 165

5. Houston, Muiris: Medical Matters: Doctor's Intuition –is it a real thing?; www.irishtimes.com, 31stJan, 2017

6. Myss,Caroline and Shealy,C.Norman: The Creation of Health- The Emotional,Psychological and Spiritual responses that promote Health and Healing,Harmony,USA, 1998

7. CWSA 21-22, pg. 449

8. CWM 8, pg. 216

9. CWSA 30, pg. 404-405

10. Jefferson, Thomas - The American Declaration of Independence, July 4th, 1776

11. Underhill, Evelyn: Mysticism, Dutton, New York, 1981 paperback edition, pg. 282

12. Ibid. pg. 262

13. Sri Aurobindo: Quoted by Satprem in The Adventure of Consciousness, Sri Aurobindo Ashram, Pondicherry, 1968, pg. 323

14. CWSA 01, pg. 387

15. Mintzberg Henry in op. cit Creative Management, pg. 59

16. CWSA 23-24, pg. 801

17. Ibid, pg. 479

18. Ibid, pg. 802

19. CWSA 21-22, pg. 982

20. Ibid

21. Ibid, pg. 298-299

22. Noosphere II Research Paper, Galactic Research Institute, Foundation for the Law of Time,2004;

www.lawoftime.org

23. Ibid

24. CWSA 28, pg. 457

25. Ibid

26. CWSA 21-22, pg. 292

27. Ibid, pg. 985

28. Ibid, pg. 985-986

29. Ibid, pg. 293

30. Ibid, pg. 988

31. Maitra, SK: An Introduction to the Philosophy of Sri Aurobindo, Sri Aurobindo Ashram,Pondicherry, 2nd Ed, 1965, pg. 56

9

The Supermind (Integral Cognition)

The Truth supreme, vast and impersonal
Fits faultlessly the hour and circumstance,
Its substance a pure gold ever the same
But shaped into vessels for the spirit's use,
Its gold becomes the wine jar and the vase.

Savitri, *pg. 662-663*

Though psychological thought was implicit in the Vedic and Upanishadic hymns in India, and was explicitly expressed by ancient Greek thinkers, historically it was difficult to conceive that psychology, which studies the individual as a unit in the multiplicity, can be a gateway to spirituality separate from religion. This was because both in the East as well as in the West, the metaphysical reconciliation of the One (the Absolute) and the Many (the manifestation) had not yet been worked out. Either the One was seen as always unrelated to the Many, or the Many were seen as subordinate and ephemeral or unreal while the One was the only Reality. Or else the One and the Many were always simultaneously existent as two different Realities or different poises of the same Reality. Indian tradition considered that the Many were derived from the One, or to put it more succinctly, by the Will and Consciousness of the One and could thus resolve back into the One. This was realized by seers in principle, but the transition of the One into the Many was traditionally described by the term Maya, which had a pejorative connotation as meaning illusory and therefore unreal. However, Swami Vivekananda pointed out that Maya was a descriptive and not an explanatory term, a mere statement of facts that did not reveal the actual mechanisms involved. (1)

For the first time in history, Sri Aurobindo's approach to metaphysics in *The Life Divine* solved this problem by explaining how the One becomes the Many via involution, and how the Many return to the One via evolution. This also creates a new approach to cosmology that explains how pure Consciousness (the absolute Sachcchidananda) creates or becomes Matter. The key turning point of this process is the Supermind, which is a plane of consciousness that had never been explicitly identified and characterized until the advent of Sri Aurobindo. As he describes it, the Supermind mediates between the One and the Many; it is the creative matrix that in its unitary poise holds the pre-programmed essence of multiplicity. This metaphysical approach has major implications for psychology. Instead of annihilating the mind, it opens up a trajectory of progressively evolving supra-rational cognitive matrices that could culminate in the "integral cognition" of the Supramental Consciousness. The Supermind thus becomes the harbinger of a new consciousness-based psychology that can serve as a gateway to transformative spirituality.

Sri Aurobindo makes a careful and important distinction between the Overmind and the Supermind. As Sri Aurobindo defines the term:

"I mean by the supermind a power, a level, an organisation of consciousness which is not only above the human mind, but above all that can be called mind,--another higher and wider essence and energy of consciousness altogether. Mind is that which seeks after truth of any kind or of all kinds within its range, labours to know it, attempts to direct and utilize it. But by supermind I mean a divine awareness which inherently possesses truth, knows it by its own intrinsic identity with it and puts it into action or effect spontaneously by its own sovereign power without any need of endeavour or labour. Mind even though it seeks after knowledge and can sometimes grasp its figure or touch its shadow, is a product of the cosmic Inconscient or of a Half-Conscience-Ignorance; supermind is an eternal Truth-consciousness, a divine Knowledge self-maintained for ever and luminous in its own right beyond all Ignorance". (2)

Sri Aurobindo further explains that the evolution of consciousness from the poise of Mind to that of the Supermind signifies not merely a substitution by some higher instrument of thought and knowledge, but a complete "conversion" of the whole consciousness. It is not only the thought but the will and sense and feeling which are transformed:

> "The supermind knows most completely and securely not by thought but by identity, by a pure awareness of the self-truth of things in the self and by the self…Thought is only one means of partially manifesting and presenting what is hidden in this greater self-existent knowledge….The supramental knowledge or experience by identity carries in it as a result or as a secondary part of itself a supramental vision that needs the support of no image, can concretise what is to the mind abstract and has the character of sight though its object may be the invisible truth of that which has form or the truth of the formless." (3)

For Sri Aurobindo and the Mother, the Supermind was not an abstract, philosophical idea but a vivid experiential reality. Their yoga of transformation delved into supramentalizing the physical senses and the very cells of the body. While Sri Aurobindo left only hints about this process in his poems and writings, the Mother was more explicit and recorded a detailed account in the *Agenda*, which is a series of conversations recorded over more than a decade. For example, the following passage describes the beginning of supramental vision:

> "….And it is a different quality of vision, a vision… (how can I explain it?) as if light were shining from within things instead of shining on them: it isn't a reflected light. It isn't luminous, it isn't like a candle, for instance, or a lamp, not that, but instead of being lit by a projected light, things have their own light, which doesn't radiate….
>
> ….For instance, I noticed this while washing early in the morning: I go into the bathroom before turning the light

on, because I turn it on from inside; but I see just as clearly as when the light is on! It makes no difference. And then everything was as if behind a kind of veil. Then I turned my attention (or rather my attention was drawn) and I said to myself, "But all this is becoming so lackluster, it's completely uninteresting!" And I started thinking (not thinking, but becoming aware of one thing or another), and suddenly, I saw that phenomenon of a bottle in the cupboard becoming so clear, so... with an inner life *(gesture as if the bottle lit up from inside)*. "Oh!" I said – the next minute, it was over.
But I seemed to be told, "Yes, you can. You no longer see this way, but you can see that way; you no longer see the ordinary way, but you can see..." *(inward gesture)*. I have been left with enough vision to be able to move around freely, but this is clearly the preparation for a vision through the inner light rather than projected light. And it is...oh, it's warm, living, intense – and of such precision! You see everything at the same time, not only the color and shape, but the character of the vibration: in a liquid, the character of its vibration – it's marvelous. Only, it lasts a moment, it's like promises that come and tell you (like when you make a promise to someone to comfort him and give him heart), "It will be like this." Very well. *(Mother laughs)* In how many centuries, I don't know!"(4)

What the Mother describes here is not visual deterioration due to a cataract or other ophthalmological problem, but the beginning of supramental physical vision: objects are seen as being lit from within, accompanied by a simultaneous perception of their vibration of consciousness. Thus, the Supermind consciousness is a bona fide cognitive field, which includes both the global and the individual cognitive fields while yet surpassing them. Note also that Sri Aurobindo and the Mother were realistic about how long a supramental transformation of human beings into the next step of the evolution of consciousness on Earth — on the order of centuries at the least, and quite possibly much longer. They often cautioned people not to romanticize their mystical experiences, and not to imagine that intuitive experiences are supramental when they are almost always not. At this point in time, it is too early to give examples of the Supermind from daily life or world cultures, so we will only give some general indications and discourage fanciful speculation.

Sri Aurobindo describes the Supermind as marked by the following five unique characteristics: integrality, unity, Truth-consciousness, creativity, and transformative capacity. Thus, the ultimate outcome of a supramental evolution on Earth would be the emergence of a new type of life-form that they called the *gnostic being*. This would not be a magnified human being but a transformed being in evolutionary terms. Idealists have always dreamt of superior human beings with emphasis on one or other attribute at the cost of other attributes. Sri Aurobindo visualized the gnostic being as manifesting an integral consciousness wherein all attributes are harmonized. Chaudhuri explains,

> "The Christian emphasis on Love, the Nietzschean emphasis on Power, and the Greek emphasis on Knowledge, represent but complementary fragments of truth. A harmonious blending of these elements of ultimate reality would be required in order to obtain a full-orbed vision of Supermanhood." (5)

Note that such a Supramental being would be different from what Professor Alexander considered the insinuation of angelic beings with empirical qualities through a process discontinuous with the evolutionary trajectory (6). Also, the gnostic being would be different from what until now has been considered as a Divine Incarnation, or Avatar, such as Jesus Christ, Gautama Buddha, Sri Ramakrishna, etc. In the Aurobindonian paradigm, the Avatar comes to lead the evolutionary journey at critical turning points of civilizational history, while the gnostic being is essentially a product or a flowering of the evolutionary process per se. (7)

For Sri Aurobindo and the Mother, the ultimate outcome of evolution will be the emergence of a new type of body endowed with physical properties that to us would seem supernatural. The

Mother opined that the present masculine and feminine principles constitute an arrangement of convenience maintained by Nature for the purpose of procreation — but that the Supramental being will be sexless and fuse the masculine and feminine principles together in a single body, as is intuited in the ancient Indian symbol of Ardhanariswara (where Shakti is inseparable from Shiva). She described her experience of a vision she had of it, "it was the trunk that was quite different from the chest down to the waist; neither man nor woman. And it was pretty…A very pretty form."(8) This future body will have other features such as extraordinary strength and flexibility, lightness, plasticity, adaptability under all conditions, and luminosity that vibrates at a cellular level. (9) Sri Aurobindo described that in this future body, the organs would be subtle of a very different character, more as "forms of dynamism or plastic transmitters" (10) rather than the gross material organs we have today. He also envisaged that the future body will replace the usual process of procreation by the evolution of "new means of a supraphysical kind" for "a voluntary creation of bodies for souls that seek to enter the earth-life". (11)

While to current thinking these propositions seem highly speculative, already there are several social developments that point towards the emergence of new ways for souls taking birth to be raised and gain life experience. These include the rise in adoptions, the development of IVF babies, and the emergence of transgender and gender-fluid individuals. Also, although the increase in divorce and breakdown of the conventional family unit in the last 50 years has been distressing for many, for some it has opened up the possibility of a different type of family — a collectivity based on soul-kinship spread out in space and time. This is why the Mother once remarked that the breakdown of the family "was, and is, still an indispensable movement to bring humanity to a higher and broader realization". (12) When asked if children can thrive in alternative arrangements that do not involve biological parents and family, she observed with great open-mindedness:

"Here also both things must be equally admitted and prac-

ticed. There are many cases in which it would be a blessing for the baby to be separated from his parents.
A minimum of rules.
A maximum of freedom.
All possibilities must have equal scope for manifestation, then humanity will progress more rapidly." (13)

Significantly, Sri Aurobindo also foresaw that the development of spiritual-occult means of procreation would be preceded by a physical science that would "find physical means for passing beyond the ordinary instrumentation or procedure of Nature in this matter of propagation or the renewal of the physical life-force in human or animal beings." (14) He wrote these words in 1950, before the discovery of DNA — and history has born out his predictions. The first report of biochemical pregnancy came in 1953, followed by a series of experiments culminating in the birth of the first IVF babies in the United Kingdom, in July of 1978, and in Calcutta in October of 1978. In July, 1996, scientists at the Roslin Institute in Scotland successfully cloned the first mammal from a somatic cell using the process of nuclear transfer. This sheep, named Dolly, was cloned from the cell of the mammary gland, thus proving that a cell taken from outside the reproductive organs can recreate a whole individual. Finally, in February of 2015, UK lawmakers approved the creation of IVF babies with DNA from three parents. While more scientific developments in genetic engineering and reproduction are no doubt on the way, already in 1950 Sri Aurobindo had looked passed that into an even more futuristic future in which:

> "the resort to occult means and the intervention of subtle-physical processes, if it could be made possible, would be a greater way which could avoid the limitations, degradations, incompleteness and heavy imperfection of the means and results solely available to the law of material force." (15)

In short, the current scientific approach to physics and biology uses the reason mind to probe the forces of matter and life in matter, while Sri Aurobindo and the Mother aimed at something else — the emergence of a new and higher level of consciousness, the Supermind, which will have a more direct and radically transformative action on matter and life in matter than Mind can do.

Other Approaches to the Supermind

Sri Aurobindo's formulation of the Supermind can be compared and contrasted with that of other thinkers whose work deals with the future of evolution on Earth. First, it must be pointed out that there is a line of dystopian materialist thinking that foresees a technologically altered future but without any fundamental growth in consciousness. For instance, recently Yuval Noah Harari has discussed how *Homo sapiens* can soon break its biologically determined limits with technologies of "intelligent design," such as genetic engineering, engineering of inorganic life, and/or cyborg engineering which would produce beings with combinations of organic and non-organic parts. Harari also speculates that through genetic manipulation, the pre-Homo sapiens species, such as Neanderthals, might be resurrected and scientists could bring down the curtain on *Homo sapiens*. (16) These and many other material scenarios are possible, and no doubt there will be experimentation with a range of technologies to modify and "enhance" the current human being.

However, the problem with this materialist line of thought is that it assumes Mind is the highest possible type of consciousness, and then concludes that the magnification of mental powers to the greatest possible degree must be the outcome for evolution. By these standards, dinosaurs should still dominate the Earth because of their enormous physical size and vital ferocity, and even lions and tigers today should still dominate human beings because they can beat us in a fight. But that is not what happened: evolution brought forth a new principle of consciousness, Mind, which completely surpassed the possibilities of physical strength and vital power. Similarly, what if Mind is dethroned by a new principle of consciousness, Supermind, which operates in entirely new ways?

Then the future of human beings may not be slavery to robots and cyborgs of gargantuan AI capabilities, but rather something more mundane and humbling — we may just become beloved pets to vastly more conscious and loving supramental beings, like cats and dogs are to us now. Or will they keep us in zoos for public safety and come watch us on Sundays? That is another possibility, unless we can learn to tame our wild minds and aggressive behaviors.

So much for dystopian materialistic visions of the future that miss the consciousness of matter. On the more hopeful and consciousness-based side, there are a few thinkers and traditions that bear reviewing, the geographically Western and the so-called "Western." The most important of these are the various indigenous American traditions of spirituality, which are geographically Western in that they arose in the Western hemisphere of the Earth. It is a significant fact that virtually *all* indigenous American cultures from past to present have regarded the Earth as a sacred being who is conscious. This has lead to an Earth-centric spirituality that is best characterized not as a thought-system but rather as a body of intuitions about the consciousness of the Earth. The authors are not qualified to expound upon these traditions, so rather than misrepresenting them we will simply express our appreciation for the correct perception that the Earth is a conscious being, and look forward to a future in which this previously marginalized spiritual orientation will take a leading role in world culture.

The second line of thinking that is consonant with the proposition of a supramental evolution on Earth are so-called "Western" ideas that actually arose in the Eastern hemisphere of the Earth. The most luminous of these was Christ's allusion to a "kingdom of Heaven on Earth." Christ did not elaborate on this, but Sri Aurobindo commented that the parable of the fall of man in the Hebrew Genesis hints at how the involutionary "fall" into Mind is to be redeemed by an evolutionary emergence into Supermind:

> "That fall is his deviation…into a dividing consciousness which brings with it all the train of the dualities, life and death, good and evil, joy and pain, completeness and want,

the fruit of a divided being. This is the fruit which Adam and Eve, Purusha and Prakriti, the soul tempted by Nature, have eaten. The redemption comes by the recovery of the universal in the individual and of the spiritual term in the physical consciousness".(17)

In the 20th century, two European thinkers took up the topic of such an evolution of consciousness on Earth, one from the Christian perspective (Teilhard de Chardin) and one from the secular, post-modern perspective (Gilles Deleuze).

Teilhard de Chardin

Teilhard de Chardin (1881-1955) was a paleontologist and Catholic priest who tried to unite his personal religious conviction with science by positing the Omega Point as the Divine Milieu where the spirit of the Cosmic Christ becomes fully manifested in the universe, so that all human beings are united with each other and with Christ-Consciousness.(18) Teilhard de Chardin's Omega Point, which has often been compared with Sri Aurobindo's Supermind, represents the culmination of the law of complexification executed through a non-mechanical psychic force or "radial energy" so that evolution converges to an "end-point" or Omega. Science often muses on the doomsday but Teilhard boldly states:

"All pessimistic representations of the earth's last days – whether in terms of cosmic catastrophe, biological disruptions or simply arrested growth or senility – have this in common: that they take the characteristics and conditions of our individual and elemental ends and extend them without correction to life as a whole. Accident, disease and decrepitude spell the death of men; and therefore the same applies to mankind. But have we any right to generalize in this simple way?… In its present state, the world would be unintelligible and the presence in it of reflection would be incomprehensible, unless we supposed there to be a secret complicity between the infinite and the infinitesimal to warm, nourish and sustain to the very end – by dint of chance, contingencies and the exercise of free choice – the consciousness that has emerged between the two. It is upon this complicity that we must depend. Man is irreplaceable. Therefore, however improbable it might seem, he must reach the goal, not necessarily, doubtless, but infallibly." (19)

Thus, Teilhard de Chardin asserts emphatically that to deny man (i.e., human beings in contemporary language) his aspired goal would be a denial of the Intelligence that sustains the consciousness between the Infinite and the infinitesimal in a matrix where man is irreplaceable and his fulfilment inevitable. Frank Tipler took up the idea Omega Point and described it as denoting the ultimate fate of the universe as required by the law of physics, and later equated this state with a Christian heaven where humans achieve omnipotence so that the past personalities can be re-lived, synonymous to the rising of the dead. (20) While one might be skeptical and wonder if Truth needs to be modeled exclusively in Jesuit terms, it is also worth noting that nomenclatures hardly matter in the higher realms of Consciousness, where the same experience may be described in different ways — if at all words suffice to do justice to the experience.

Note that while the Omega Point is the goal or end result of Chardin's evolutionary cosmology, the Supermind in Sri Aurobindo's paradigm is simultaneously the culmination (Omega) as well as the initiating creative principle (Alpha) in the manifestation. Chardin's Omega Point is Transcendent in the sense that it is outside the framework where universe arises, and it is by the attraction of the Omega Point that the universe moves towards it through progressively higher forms of complexity, consciousness and personality. In Sri Aurobindo's scheme of things, the Supramental Reality is simultaneously Transcendent, Universal (Cosmic) and Individual, and hence implicit at all levels of Consciousness, manifest or unmanifest, Personal or Impersonal. If evolution moves to the highest goal through increasing complexity, it has been preceded by an equally complex involutionary movement through which the Supermind principle progressively condensed itself to be finally veiled in the Inconscience, moving through non-evolutionary typal worlds.

Furthermore, Tipler's notion of the Omega Point as a Transcendent zone analogous to the Christian heaven, where past personalities can be relived like the resurrection of the departed to achieve omnipotence, is in sharp contrast to Sri Aurobindo's concept of the Supermind manifesting on the Earth itself, in the matrix of material life and resulting in not a resurrection of the dead but in a transformation of the living leading to the appearance of an entirely new race of Gnostic Beings. The Supramental manifestation as envisaged by Sri Aurobindo is not an aggrandizement of the human being to support omnipotence, rather it can support the pursuit of immortality in some sense or the other. The immortality that once had been an aspiration of the Vedic Rishis has to be realized in different denouements today. The immortality of the soul was always known in the Indian tradition, and the capacity of willed death had been achieved by yogis, but the pursuit of the Supramental Consciousness opens new pathways, such as the possibility of immortality of the human species through the appearance of progressively higher species along an evolutionary trajectory.

Gilles Deleuze

It is significant how a secular post-modernist, Gilles Deleuze (1925-1995), came quite close to Sri Aurobindo's concept of the Supermind, albeit with a different terminology. Deleuze described a sort of virtual body, a "body without organs" (corps sans organes) referring to the deeper reality underlying well-formed wholes constructed from fully functioning parts. The making of such a body implies a transformation characterized by an extension of the experiencing capacities to be aware of the virtual field of intensities, ideas and feelings which constitute the differences of the actual world. (21) In an excellent overview, Banerji studies the convergences of Sri Aurobindo's thought with that of Deleuze:

1) Instead of considering individual beings as autonomous, Deleuze views the collective reality of each type of being as a life on a "fold" of pure immanence. Subject and cosmos exist integrally in each other. Human beings possess critical and creative subjectivity and can "deterritorialize" the fixity of relations to make a "body without organs". (22) One is reminded of the future body in the Aurobindonian paradigm where material organs would become "forms of dynamism or plastic transmitters rather than what we know as organs." (23)

2) Deleuze, contemplating on the future humanity, develops the idea of the "superfold" – the fractal ground natural to super-man which facilitates a creativity capable of an "unlimited finite" As Banerji comments:

> "It implies that every fine point in space and "moment" of time is a creative actualization of infinity. Superfold is the cosmic medium, potent with such a possibility and super-man is the individualized subjectivity which can express this capacity as its native mode of existence…Deleuze's superfold can well be thought of as close or analogous to an immanent version of Sri Aurobindo's supermind, the medium which holds unity and infinity as its conscious properties every-where and is the nexus between the infinite and the finite in its absolute immanence. So too, the relation between super-fold and superman in Deleuze is analogous to the relation between supermind and superman in Sri Aurobindo, in that the latter term in each doublet represents the subject with interiority, proper to the being and full creative expression of the capacities of the first term." (24)

In Aurobindonian terms, each Individual Self or Jivatman can be ordinarily conceived to represent a "fold" (in Deleuzian terms) of cosmic consciousness. This is why the Jivatman is a singular yet plural entity, plural because of the multiplicity of "folds", singu-lar because each fold exists in the same cosmic matrix. What De-leuze considered as "deterritoralisation" is represented here in the capacity of the human being to evolve further to a higher poise. In a higher poise, the Individual Self represents a "superfold" of the higher echelons of cosmic consciousness in the regions of the Overmind, and higher planes surpassing the Overmind, to manifest a progressive array of Gnostic Beings.

Banerji describes other points of convergence between the thought of Deleuze and Sri Aurobindo's theory of practice:

> "Deleuze's Plane of Consistency is defined in terms not far from Sri Aurobindo's Supermind, an absolute consciousness characterized by irreducible and radical univocity and infinity….Deleuze's call to experimentation is seconded by the personalization of practice based on the emergence of consciousness by Sri Aurobindo; Deleuze's "scale of intensities" can be seen as synonymous with the conversion of all experience to forms of bliss in Sri Aurobindo." (25)

Relevance to Psychology: Integral Cognition and Psychedelics

To return from what may sound more like philosophical speculation than psychology, let us now try to connect the Supermind and integral cognition to some example from contemporary life with which people may be familiar. This can be done with a case study of the Mother's extraordinary experience with LSD, documented in the *Agenda*. In a remarkable conversation from May 18, 1966, the Mother discussed an Italian visitor to the Ashram who wrote to her about his experiences with LSD. (26)

She commented on its effects both in terms of yoga (planes of consciousness), and from a psychological standpoint in that she understands the reality of the subconscious and grasps that LSD "trips" can serve as a sort of Rorschach test (Rorschach is a projective psychological test). But this was not the end of the story. About a year later, right before the Summer of Love unfolded in San Francisco, the Mother returned to the topic of LSD in the most extraordinary way. On April 12, 1967, she decided to undertake a radical experiment — to experience LSD using only the power of consciousness, that is, to experience the drug without physically ingesting it. By the power of consciousness alone, she identified her awareness with the substance of LSD and underwent a veridical "acid trip" without physically ingesting the drug. Here is her own description of the experience:

> "It was an avalanche, a stampede of forms, sounds, colors, even odors, which imposed themselves with a reality and intensity — I had never known that before, never…And I saw it was a magnified faculty of sensation – inordinately magnified…Because the equilibrium between all the faculties of the being had been disrupted. The natural equilibrium which makes things balance each other, harmonize and organize spontaneously into a coherent whole with a conscious experience, was shattered – shattered to the benefit of the faculty of sensation. Naturally, that faculty of sensation was terribly multiplied (or aggravated, I might say) and even imposed itself brutally. And I saw that something had upset the equilibrium. Something that had the power to upset the equilibrium of the being – to insist on one point to the detriment of all others…The effect is the dislocation of the being's equilibrium." (27)

Two aspects of the Mother's experience bear emphasizing. First, that she had the full sensory effects of LSD without actually taking any of the substance. Second, that while having these psychedelic effects, at the same time she was able to observe the experience from higher planes of consciousness and note the relationship between the magnified sensations and the other planes and parts of consciousness. *This is what is meant by supramental or integral cognition — the ability to identify consciousness with the inner essence of a thing and to see it from all angles simultaneously.* While a skeptic might argue that perhaps the Mother physically consumed LSD, it seems highly improbable that an 89 year old woman sitting in India, whose whole life demonstrated a complete disinterest in drugs and alcohol, would suddenly decide to take LSD, especially as she had no need of it to achieve transpersonal states of awareness. We are thus left with the conclusion that her self-report is valid, and it demonstrates that there is virtually no limit to the power of a supramental or integral cognition.

Furthermore, the Mother's experiential analysis of her own LSD experience is supported by recent scientific findings on how psychedelics affect the brain. Until now, scientists believed that psychedelic effects are related to increase in brain activity, such as via activating serotonin receptors, especially the 2A subtype (5-HT2A), although it is uncertain why such activation produces psychedelic effects. However, in a recent reversal of stance, new evidence suggests that psychedelics such as LSD may open the "doors of perception" by inhibiting parts of the brain. Drs. Carhart-Harris and Nutt carried out brain-mapping experiments on 30 psychedelic users through functional magnetic resonance imaging (fMRI) and found that psychedelics reduced neuronal activities in brain regions (such as the medial prefrontal cortex and anterior cingulate cortex) which are involved in emotional regulation, cognitive processing and introspection. It seems that psychedelics reduce activity in specific "hub" regions, diminishing their ability to co-ordinate activity in downstream regions of the brain. In other words, the brain regions responsible for constraining consciousness within the narrow boundaries of the normal waking state are inhibited. The end result is an expansion of various parts of brain activity but at the cost of a disharmony in the whole due to reduction of certain core brain activities. (28) Thus, the Mother's description of the psychedelic experience as arising from the dislocation of the being's equilibrium and exaggeration of one point to the detriment of others is reflected in this new evidence that psychedelics shift the fulcrum upon which brain activity balances. (29)

Now, it has been postulated that psychedelics can have thera- peutic value in situational contexts and provide valuable clues to explain the workings of the mind. Due to the alteration in the brain's functioning caused by psychedelics, the negative patterns of cognition and neural activity caused by depression and addiction may weaken, producing therapeutic effects. Cortright explains how psychedelics such as LSD, mescaline and psilocybin can act as non-specific awareness amplifiers that enable consciousness to expand. There can be a refinement of sensory perception, the perceptual worlds of sight and sound may reveal novel experiences, the aesthetic sense can be heightened, creativity may bloom, experiences of clairvoyance may occur, perception of auras and energy-fields may become possible, and seeing spirits together with celestial quasi-mystic experiences of the soul with its light, love, joy and peace have been reported. (30) Cortright also sums up the seminal work of Stanislav Grof, the world's leading psychedelic researcher:

> "Grof maps out three realms of consciousness revealed by psychedelics. The first realm he describes as the sensory barrier and the personal unconscious. Here the psychedelic effect is to open the senses and to increase a person's access to the personal unconscious.
>
> 'The second realm Grof calls the perinatal realm, and it relates to the birth process. His observations have led him to conclude that there are four basic perinatal matrices, each one corresponding to a different stage of birth and each providing an organizing schema for related psychological material.
>
> The third major realm Grof calls the transpersonal realm. This is the area of spiritual experiences. Grof notes that a connection seems to exist through the perinatal realm, as if birth provides a kind of doorway to the spiritual.
>
> Grof's map has found wide acceptance as a thorough explanation of the phenomena encountered in altered state work. Although he has attempted to apply this map to consciousness in general, this wider application is problematic and has not been greeted with such enthusiasm."(31)

CBP accepts the fact of clinical instances where subjects using controlled doses of psychedelics with therapeutic intent have experienced positive effects, while simultaneously acknowledging that clinical experience also shows that excessive use can turn into abuse and a disruption in functioning. The Mother clearly described the dangers of psychedelic misuse, and transpersonal psychologists have reached the same conclusion, namely, that psychedelic abuse can bypass working on one's ego and its defenses. In real spiritual work, nothing durable can be achieved without dealing with the ego and conquering it for the sake of the psychic being. As Cortright points out, new and positive self-structures cannot be built and sustained through psychedelic experiences. (32)

Again, note that this last statement does not contradict the many anecdotal reports of tribal cultures which use natural psychedelics in a spiritual and therapeutic way during rituals (such as psilocybin or peyote used by the Native American Church), or the emerging clinical evidence that psychedelics and psychedelic-assisted psychotherapy may offer promising new treatments for PTSD, depression, and cancer-related anxiety. In fact, in her comments on LSD from April 15, 1967, the Mother specifically stated that hallucinogens could have both harmful and therapeutic effects, and she recommended that they should be studied as part of a scientific discipline and administered with appropriate safeguards and supervision. Unfortunately, after the U.S. outlawed research on psychedelics in 1970, her advice was not followed and it has only been recently, after a lapse of decades, that clinical research is finally following the advice she gave from the very beginning. (33, 34)

Conclusion

While it is still far too soon to speculate about the evolution of supramental beings on Earth, the work of Sri Aurobindo and the Mother shows that it is perfectly reasonable to believe that such an evolution is possible. In Part 1 of this book, we have explored the planes of consciousness above the reasoning mind that offer a pathway for consciousness to evolve from its current level of mental organization towards a fully supramental or integral cognition. The Supermind-principle can only manifest if the evolution of consciousness is comprehensively followed so that the mental consciousness is gradually outgrown and surpassed. Along this trajectory of a progressive transformation of consciousness, human nature will change not once but many times and in many ways. To keep pace with this growth, psychology will also have to evolve and undergo many reappraisals as the powers and potentials of consciousness become manifested more widely in the evolutionary process. The concept of cognition itself will undergo a radical change as higher ranges of mind manifest. The knowledge of the unitary basis of Reality, which is not ordinarily available to the mind, will gradually reveal itself in an increasingly broader way, finally culminating in an integral synthesis of Knowledge and Will so that the Will becomes luminous and Knowledge becomes effective. Thus, our present approach to psychology must be kept sufficiently flexible to accommodate the greater psychology of tomorrow that is pressing to emerge.

Finally, as this work of evolution proceeds, it will become increasingly evident that a purely psychological transformation of the cognitive capacities is necessary but not sufficient. An exalted psychological transformation that changes the mind into a principle of light, the life-force into a power of purity, and which shifts control of the nature from the ego to the soul, is a critical preparatory movement but it will be constantly challenged and resisted by the subconscious and Inconscient. The body with its animal origin and atavistic traits, the Inconscience that supports the reign of ignorance and imperfection, the personality with its desires and idiosyncrasies, and the unexpected occult forces in the cosmic ignorance will all seek to retard and obstruct the higher parts of the nature. Therefore, as Sri Aurobindo emphasized, "A transformation of the body must be the condition for a total transformation of the nature." (35) This implies that along with other considerations, a transformational psychology must also include a comprehensive mastery over the body-consciousness. Indeed, the Mother's experiential foray into the realms of consciousness that span from the cellular consciousness to the Supermind provides the basic framework for this psychology of the future.

The Spirit shall look out through Matter's gaze
And Matter shall reveal the Spirit's face.
Then man and superman shall be at one
And all the earth become a single life...

Savitri, pg. 709

References

1. Vivekananda, Swami: Complete Works, Mayavati Memorial Edition, Advaita Ashram, Kolkata, 16th Ed, 1989, Vol. 11,97

2. CWSA 12, pg. 259-260

3. CWSA: 23-24, pg. 831-833

4. Agenda VI, pg. 111-113

5. Chaudhuri, Haridas: Sri Aurobindo – The Prophet of Life Divine Sri Aurobindo Ashram, 1960, pg. 125

6. Ibid,pg. 134-135

7. Ibid, pg. 143

8. CWM 11, pg. 302

9. CWM 03, pg. 175-176

10. CWSA 13, pg. 555

11. Ibid, pg. 548

12. CWM 14, pg. 292

13. Ibid, pg. 293

14. CWSA 13, pg. 548

15. Ibid

16. Harari, Yuval Noah: Sapiens-A Brief History of Humankind, Vintage,London, 2011

17. CWSA 21-22, pg. 56

18. iksc.org/PhilosophiesEvolution_R.Kleinman3,pdf;pg. 234

19. Chardin, Teilhard de: The Phenomenon of Man, Harper & Ross, New York,1975 Ed, pg. 275-276

20. Tipler, Frank: The Physics of Immortality, Doubleday, 1994

21. Banerji, Debashish: Seven Quartets of Becoming. A Transformationa Yoga Psychology Based on the Diaries of Sri Aurobindo, Na-

landa International, USA & D.K Printworld (P) Ltd, India, 2012, pg. 19

22. Ibid, pg. 20

23. CWSA 13, pg. 555

24. Op. cit. Seven Quartets of Becoming, pg. 21-22

25. Ibid, pg. 23

26. Agenda VII, pg. 112-115

27. Agenda VIII, pg. 105-106

28. Halberstadt Adam, Geyer Mark: Do Psychedelics Expand the Mind by Reducing Brain Activity? www.scientificamerican.com/article, May15, 2012

29. McStravic Alan, redOrbit.com — Your Universe Online: Researchers Work to Understand How Psychedelics Affect the Brain, www.rawstory.com. July 4, 2014

30. Cortright Brant: Psychotherapy and Spirit, Theory and Practice in Transpersonal Psychotherapy, SUNY Press, 1997, pg. 184-185

31. Ibid,pg. 186-187

32. Ibid, pg. 202

33. Reiff CM, Richman EE, Nemeroff CB, et al. Psychedelics and Psychedelic-Assisted Psychotherapy. Am J Psychiatry. 2020;177(5):391-410. doi:10.1176/appi.ajp.2019.19010035

34. Agenda VIII, pp. 107-108

35. CWSA 13, pg. 537

PART 2

GROWTH AND TREATMENT

10
The Structure of the Being

An architect hewing out self's living rock,
Phenomenon built Reality's summer-house
On the beaches of the sea of Infinity.

Savitri, *pg. 329*

Thus far, we have approached Sri Aurobindo and the Mother's complex world-view one step at a time, with many cases studies and cultural examples to help readers connect what they already know to the new perspective of CBP. However, we have now reached the point where we must present their whole model of consciousness as a complete unit, because this model is needed to understand the CBPs orientation towards growth and treatment presented in Chapters 11-17. The "map" of consciousness presented in this chapter is a sort of spiritual anatomy of awareness that describes the various planes of consciousness and parts of the being that together constitute what Sri Aurobindo refers to as the "structure of the being." This structure can be used as a framework for both personal growth and for clinical work. It is impossible to say that one part of this framework is relevant for personal self-development while the other is for clinical use, because of the complexity of each individual human being. It is *not* the case that the clinician is or has to be "more developed" within this framework while the client is "less developed," because the reality is that the client may well be more developed along certain lines and dimensions than the clinician, while less so in others. For example, the case of patient A in Chapter 6 gave the example of a person who had a more developed psychic being than just about every clinician he met, but who had a plethora of symptoms in the vital and mental planes of consciousness for which contact with less psychically developed clinicians was at times helpful. Thus, in CBP both the client and the clinician are seen as growing in consciousness across the lifespan, and the life-span and the question is rather what could be clinically helpful for the client while they continue their self-development both in and outside of the treatment setting. On the other hand, the clinician should attend to their own continued growth in consciousness, both as a clinician and outside of the clinical setting.

According to Sri Aurobindo and the Mother, consciousness is simultaneously a pluri-dimensional and integral reality. It is essentially the same throughout but variable in status, condition and operation. (1) In this paradigm, the individual entity who is a particular formation of consciousness can be studied along two main perspectives: 1) along a vertical hierarchy which ranges from the "superconscious" to the "subconscious" and down into the "inconscience"(See Table 1); and 2) along a horizontal perspective that views the individual as a series of concentric rings or sheaths of consciousness arranged as the outer being, inner being and inmost being, respectively. As Sri Aurobindo notes, these two axes of consciousness are discernible as "two systems simultaneously active in the organization of the being and its parts". (2)

The Vertical System

The vertical system extends from the Inconscience to the Superconscious resembling "an ascension and descent, like a flight of steps, a series of superimposed planes with the Supermind-Overmind as the crucial nodus of the transition beyond the human into the Divine."(3) It is important to note that "In all the series of the planes or grades of consciousness there is nowhere any real gulf, always there are connecting gradations and one can ascend from step to step." (4) [Table 1, 1A]

The superconscious is the source of higher inspirations which impels human beings to exceed their limitations. While the subconscious supports our ordinary nature, the superconscious supports our spiritual possibilities and nature. The "inconscience" is not an absence of consciousness but the nethermost level where consciousness is fully involved and suppressed and from which evolution starts with the manifestation of matter.

In the vertical system, each plane of consciousness between the Inconscient and the Supermind is a whole world or universe of existence with forces and beings proper to that plane. The physical plane of consciousness is the vast material universe we perceive with our physical senses, and which science studies in great detail, from the mysteries of subatomic matter to the vast expanses of galaxies that constitute the material universe. However, there are equally valid universes (or multiverses) as well — subtle physical planes, vital planes, mental planes, and the planes of spiritual mind and Supermind reviewed in Chapters 7-9. What Sri Aurobindo and the Mother call "the Creation" or "the Manifestation" is thus a series of stacked universes that range from the Inconscient to the Supermind in an infinitely graded series of planes of consciousness. Beyond the Supermind is the unmanifest Reality or Sachchidananda which has been described as the triune supernal (Existence-Consciousness-Bliss). Evidently, this vast vision of creation makes the material universe as seen by Science a rather small thing.

Table 1. The Individual: Vertical Perspective

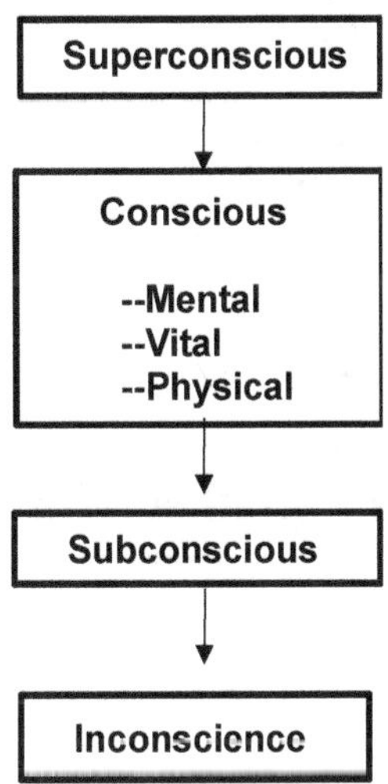

Table 1A

Gradations of the Superconscious

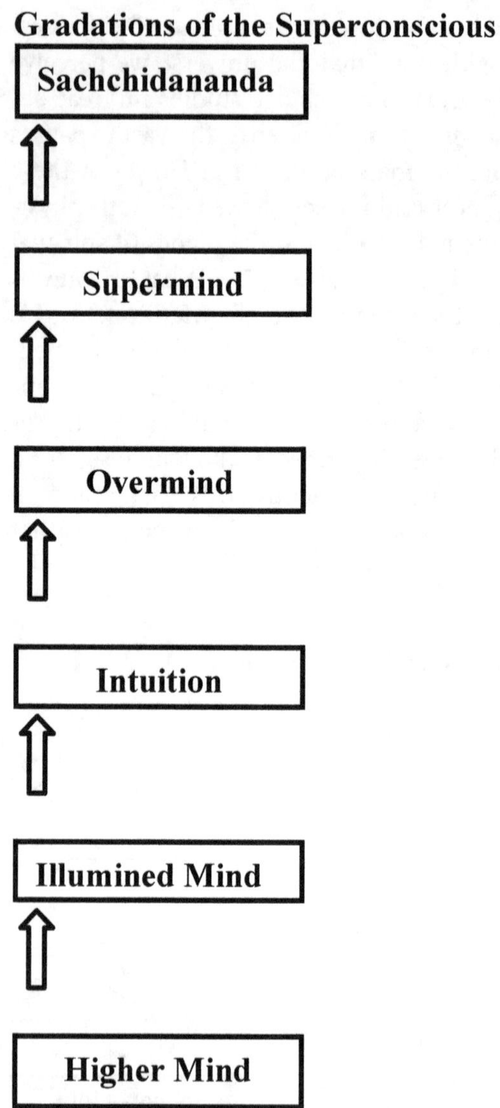

The Concentric System

The concentric system co-exists with the vertical system and is composed of a series of rings or sheaths of consciousness, with the psychic being at the centre. Firstly, there is the outer being which is the ego-bound surface personality, and this exists in the physical plane of consciousness of the vertical system. Secondly, there is an inner being, which exists in the non-physical planes of consciousness in the vertical system, has a subtle-physical, an inner vital and an inner mind behind the outer personality; it extends below to the Inconscience which at one point merges with the terrestrial Inconscience, while it soars above to the Superconscious ranges. This inner being accounts for many instances of intuitive vision, clairvoyance, revelatory guidance, meditative experiences, and healing energies, as well as a body-consciousness that acts independently of the mental will. These capacities of consciousness were always known to spiritual and mystical traditions from cultures around the world, but Sri Aurobindo organized this large range of phenomenon into a sort of structure and hierarchy that he called the inner being or subliminal personality. This subliminal personality is non-physical and thus cannot be supported by the ego; it needs a deeper source of support, which is the third part of the concentric system — the inmost being or psychic being. As previously explained, this psychic being is an evolving soul that is put forward by unevolving Self or the Central Being that stands above or outside the manifestation.

The Outer Being (Surface Personality)

The "outer being," or what is known as "personality" in psychology "is a composition of Nature" (5) and is made up of the physical, vital and mental planes of consciousness intermingled with each other and projected into the physical plane of consciousness. Sri Aurobindo described this outer being as "a partly stable, partly unstable selective determination of habitual, yet developing experiences" that arise in a sort of "*disorderly order*". (6) The outer being is centered in the ego, which is not the real self but an instrumentation of Nature by which it has developed a sense of limited and separate individual being in mind, life and body. As Sri Aurobindo explains, through self-identification of the soul with the ego, Nature "induces the soul to consent to this action and accept these habitual limiting conditions." (7) The ego successfully substitutes the truth of the universalized individuality by a separative individuality.

While the physical consciousness of the outer being has inputs from the non-material planes of consciousness (such as the vital and the mental planes), these are generally so intermingled with each other that it is difficult to appreciate their separate characteristics unless a person has developed some awareness of their inner being. Also, through a growth in consciousness (yoga) it is possible to become aware that the physical body has a consciousness of its own that is proper to its limbs, organs, glands, tissues, and cells. This body-consciousness is unique for each individual and can be developed.

The phenomenon of intermingling of various planes of consciousness in the outer being produces combinations with unique attributes. Some important combinations are:

(a) **The Physical Mind** is that part or poise of the mind that is enmeshed in the physical schemata, relies on sensory feedback and:

"goes on repeating the past customary thoughts and movements or at the most adds to them such further mechanical reactions to things and reflexes as are in the round of life. The true physical mind is the receiving and externalising intelligence which has two functions – first, to work upon external things and give them a mental order with a way of practically dealing with them and, secondly, to be the channel of materialising and putting into effect whatever the thinking and dynamic mind sends down to it for the purpose." (8)

The lowest range of the physical mind is a sort of "mechanical mind", "whose nature is to go on turning around in a circle on the thoughts that come into it". (9) As Sri Aurobindo explained:

> "The mechanical mind is a sort of engine — whatever comes to it it puts into the machine and goes on turning it round and round no matter what it is." (10)

> "This is part of the physical mind and you should not be disturbed or alarmed by its rising up, but see what it is and quiet it down or get control of its movements." (11)

> The Mother also described the **cellular mind,** which is the most unconscious part of the physical mind. This cellular mind exists in animals and has a faint beginning in plants but the physical mind proper really begins to exist in the human being. (12)

(b) **The Vital Mind** is that poise of the mind which is enmeshed in the repertoire of emotions, passions, drives and dynamism. Sri Aurobindo noted that this vital mind:

> "lives by imagination, thoughts of desire, will to act and enjoy from its own impulse and this is able to seize on the reason itself and make it its auxiliary and its justifying counsel and supplier of pleas and excuses". (13)

The vital mind is the source of defense mechanisms classically described in psychoanalysis. Sri Aurobindo elaborates:

> "the function of this mind is not to think and reason, to perceive, consider and find out or value things, for that is the function of the thinking mind proper....but to plan or dream or imagine what can be done. It makes formations for the future which the will can try to carry out if opportunity and circumstances become favourable or even it can work to make them favourable. In men of action this faculty is

prominent and a leader of their nature; great men of action always have it in a very high measure. But even if one is not a man of action or practical realisation or if circumstances are not favourable or one can do only small and ordinary things, this vital mind is there. It acts in them on a small scale, or if it needs some sense of largeness, what it does very often is to plan in the void knowing that it cannot realize its plans or else to imagine big things, stories, adventures, great doings in which oneself is the hero or the creator." (14)

Thus the "vital will" is an impulse or force first and a thought afterwards, in contrast to the "mental will" which is a thought first that acts through a will. (15)

(c) **The Vital Physical** is that part of the physical consciousness which is modulated by the vital to resonate to its own wavelength, infusing the physical to shift from its mode of inertia to the buoyancy of life-energy. In the process, it has to link the physical, which is material, with the life-energy that is not material. This link is consolidated through neuro-physiological substrates, enabling vital movements to have physical expressions. That is how pure vital movements like love, hatred, anger or jealousy can be expressed through physical means, and how clinical states like anxiety, phobia or depression can have physical connotations.

The Inner Being (Subliminal Personality)

There is an inner dimension of consciousness behind the outer being or surface personality, but which is not really the soul-principle, and this is called the inner being or subliminal personality. Components of this inner dimension have been explored by various spiritual and mystical traditions in different times and cultures, but usually in different ways. Thus, some were interested in accessing the inner energy that is in communion with the universal energy, some in exploring the subtle senses or the subtle body, some in seeking a bliss without any extrinsic motivation, and some in developing supra-rational faculties such as intuition or revelation. Sri Aurobindo's contribution to this large but scattered body of traditional knowledge was to describe the existence of an organized and coherent "inner being" or "subliminal personality" to which all these various inner experiences could be meaningfully related. His yogic conception of the inner or subliminal being is different from the Western idea of the subconscious. As Sri Aurobindo explained, inner or subliminal being stands behind the surface personality and consists of an inner mental, inner vital and inner subtle-physical entity (16):

The inner mind can directly know things by supra-rational faculties like intuition. Unlike the ordinary memory which knows the past in fragments and has no inkling of the future, this mind has a memory which holds an active and involved past as well as a future that is ready to evolve .

The inner vital can hold the life-energy free from the habitual clutches of the body and mind, and can utilize the body for dynamic action by making the will of the mind effective. It can also work on the organs of the body and make their actions more supple and subtle. The inner vital is in dynamic communion with the universal energy.

The inner or subtle-physical has inner or subtle senses: "a subliminal sight, touch, hearing; but these subtle senses are rather channels of the inner being's direct consciousness of things than its informants: the subliminal is not dependent on its senses for its knowledge, they only give a form to its direct experience of objects; they do not, so much as in waking mind, convey forms of objects for the mind's documentation or as the starting-point or basis for an indirect constructive experience." (17). These subtle senses lead mystics and yogis to have "visions", hear "inner voices" and feel "auras". Sri Aurobindo described that the inner being:

"is much larger in its potentialities, more plastic, more powerful, more capable of a manifold knowledge and dynamism than our surface mind, life or body; especially, it is capable of a direct communication with the universal forces, movements, objects of the cosmos, a direct feeling and opening to them, a direct action on them and even a widening of itself beyond the limits of the personal mind, the personal life, the body, so that it feels itself more and more a universal being no longer limited by the existing walls of our too narrow mental, vital, physical existence. This widening can extend itself to a complete entry into the consciousness of cosmic Mind, into unity with the universal Life, even into a oneness with universal Matter". (18)

The inner being and the outer being are not water-tight compartments, as each plane of consciousness in the outer being is actually a surface projection of the corresponding plane in the inner being. Thus:

> "What we call our mind is only an outer mind, a surface mental action, instrumental for the partial expression of a larger mind behind of which we are not ordinarily aware and can only know by going inside ourselves. So too what we know of the vital in us is only the outer vital, a surface activity partially expressing a larger secret vital which we can only know by going within. Equally, what we call our physical being is only a visible projection of a greater and subtler invisible physical consciousness which is much more complex, much more aware, much wider in its receptiveness, much more open and plastic and free." (19)

In CBP, it is important to differentiate the subliminal or inner being from the subconscious. The task is made difficult as the subliminal itself descends into a subconscious below, as much as it opens to a superconscious above. As Sri Aurobindo noted, "Part of it is subconscient, lower than our waking consciousness; part of it is on a level with it but behind and much larger than it; part is above and superconscient to us." (20) Nevertheless, the subliminal is not to be equated with the subconscious. Sri Aurobindo emphasized that the subconscious only records "impressions" of what goes on in the outer being. These impressions are rather vague and they can surge up to the outer being in two ways: 1) they can come up "in dreams in an incoherent jumble distorted altogether"; or 2) they can come up in the waking state as habitual ruminations, as "mechanical recurrence or repetition of the same suggestions, impulses (subconscient vital) or sensations." (21)

In contrast, the subliminal or inner being has a clarity that surpasses the outer being. It has a clearer memory and can retain exact images (22) that can be revealed if one has intuitive access to the inner being, unlike usual memory that is retrieved in the conscious mind with the application of will. Sri Aurobindo observes: "Also the memory can be lost or defaced, so that one remembers wrongly or forgets altogether, but that is still an imperfect action of the conscious mind, not an action of the subconscious." (23) The memory in the outer mind may be affected due to senility, disease and trauma affecting the mind and brain, but the subliminal memory remains intact though it needs the outer being for its expression in life. Indeed, without the subliminal, we would not retain a clear memory for the subconscious keeps only vague and inchoate impressions. When the subliminal comes up in dreams, it has a more veridical message, it can be intuitive, it can convey premonitions and is distinctly different from the incoherent dreams originating in the subconscious. Sri Aurobindo explained all of this further in a letter,

> "Exact images are retained by the subliminal memory. All that is subliminal is described by ordinary psychology as subconscient; but in our psychology that cannot be done, for the consciousness that held them is as precise and far wider and fuller than our waking or surface consciousness, so how can it be called subconscient? Conscious memory is that which can bring up at any moment we like the memory of a thing, it is under our control. Subliminal memory can hold all things, even those which the mind cannot understand, e.g. if you hear somebody talking Hebrew, the subliminal memory can

hold that and bring it up accurately in some abnormal state, e.g. the hypnotic. Subconscient memory is a memory of impressions; when they come up as in dream, either the result is something incoherent or fancifully rearranged or it is only the essence of the thing, its psychological deposit that comes up, e.g. sex, fear, some particular libido as the psychoanalysts call it, but the expression given to the latter need not be the same as memory would give, -- it may repeat the same forms if it gets hold of the mechanical mind in the physical to help its expression, but also it may be quite different from anything in real life." (24)

The inner being is thus active when the outer being is inactive during sleep, which allows the occurrence of subliminal dreams. However, sleep is an active physiological state. It would be interesting to speculate if the inner being can continue to be active while the outer being is inactive in a pathological state. In reversible cases of unconsciousness or coma, even during the phases of physiological inarousal, the inner being can be active and traverse hitherto untrodden ranges of consciousness. Sri Aurobindo explained of such phenomena:

"What has really happened is that the surface mind-force has been withdrawn into the subconscious mind and the surface life-force into sub-active life and either the whole man has lapsed into the subconscious existence or else he has withdrawn his outer life into the subconscious while his inner being has been lifted into the superconscient." (25)

This would be the basis for NDE (Near Death Experiences) reported by subjects who have survived comatose states or OBE (Out of Body Experiences) in subjects during anesthesia.

The Chakra System
Sri Aurobindo and the Mother were well aware of the chakras, or centers of consciousness, of classical yoga. They explained that

the chakras are located in the inner being and "belong organically to the subtle body" (26) and act as channels of communication between the inner and outer beings (27). As the inner being extends to the cosmic consciousness, the chakras also act as channels between the individual and the cosmic consciousness. In a sense, the chakra system serves as a link between the vertical and concentric systems of consciousness (see below), because they are located in the inner being yet open inwardly to the planes of consciousness encompassed in the vertical system. Further details about Sri Aurobindo's innovative approach to the chakra system have already been described in Chapter 7, in the section on Subliminal Cognition.

The Inmost Being

The inner being is supported by the inmost being. The inmost being, or true being , is represented by the true mental being at the mental plane (*manomaya purusha*), the true vital being (*pranamaya purusha*) at the vital plane, the true physical being (*annamaya purusha*) at the physical plane and supporting all these is the psychic being (*chaitya purusha*). The inmost being is represented in each part of the being in the poise most appropriate to that part, but it is the centrally poised psychic being that acts as "the capital of the system." (28) The inmost being represents an evolving projection of the unevolving Self or Purusha, and is distinguished from the Prakriti or Nature which comprises of the outer being as well as the inner (subliminal) being.

The Psychic Being

In Sri Aurobindo's parlance, the real individuality emerges when the ego is replaced by the psychic being or soul element. One then starts living at a deeper level of consciousness and experiences a sense of wholeness, integrality, peace, unity, collaboration and unalloyed Joy. (See Table 2) One can refer back "all the initiation of our action to this secret intuitive Self and Spirit, the ever-present Godhead within us, and replacing by its influences the initiations of our personal and mental nature to get back from the inferior external thought and action to another, internal and intuitive, of a highly spiritualized character." (29) In fact, the psychic being "is the builder of the inner life, it is that which manifests in the outer nature the order and rule of the Divine Will." (30)

The sense of individuality imparted by the ego gives the impression that one has cut off one from others and exists in isolation from the rest of the world, and that one can only be united with others through external means, such as social bonding and cultural ties. The psychic being, on the other hand, creates a sense of individuality that is both unique and simultaneously in continuity with the universal consciousness. Thus, the psychic being never feels cut off or isolated from others or the world. It is a special mode of expression "objectifying the one universal consciousness". (31) Usually people are not aware of the presence of the psychic being as it is poised in the deeper recesses of consciousness and veiled by our outer personality. If one is conscious of it, the process of transformation, "instead of a slow labour extending through centuries, can be pressed into one life or even a few years."(32)

The psychic being is a projection of what Indian yoga refers to as the Jivatman, which is the unevolving Self or Central Being that stands above the manifested being. The Jivatman is superior to birth and death and is the eternal true being of the individual. The psychic being is the Jivatman in its evolving form while the ego is only a dark shadow of this true integrating principle. The psychic being grows through life experiences from birth to birth. If it comes forward, it governs the instincts and can transform the nature. Usually, one is ruled by the outer personality of the physical, vital and mental consciousness held loosely together by the ego and desire. Ordinarily, we are not aware of the psychic being except at certain moments of life when it influences us strongly and we spontaneously feel an inner happiness, wholeness, joy and goodwill. This state is not dependent on outer conditions and may even appear in unfavourable conditions. Such a psychic consciousness is free from psychological disturbances and helps one build up an integrated personality. It is also free from the subconscient and egocentric disturbances. The realization of the psychic being brings "Bhakti, self giving, surrender, turning of all the movements Godward, discrimination and choice of all that belongs to the Divine Truth, Good, Beauty, rejection of all that is false, evil, ugly, discordant, union through love and sympathy with all existence, openness to the Truth of the Self and the Divine."(33) The realization of the Jivatman brings "silence, freedom, wideness, mastery, purity, a sense of universality in the individual as one centre of this divine universality". (34)

The psychic being expresses Truth and rejects falsehood through a higher order of intuitive discrimination that is different from the voice of conscience ordinarily construed to arise from morality. Since it is a projection of the unevolving Self, the psychic being does not carry the burden of the Inconscience and hence can spontaneously manifest a higher intuitive vision that arises from Superconscient realms. The ordinary voice of conscience arises from the conflict between codes of conduct, whose resolution through ethical values can check human egoism and its follies up to a certain extent. The intuitive discrimination of the psychic being can only be operative if the ego has been surpassed. When The Mother was asked why Sri Aurobindo did not consider the voice of the ordinary conscience to represent the voice of the soul, she explained:

"The voice of the ordinary conscience is an ethical voice, a moral voice which distinguishes between good and evil, encourages us to do good and forbids us to do evil. This voice is very useful in ordinary life, until one is able to become conscious of one's psychic being and allow oneself to be entirely guided by it – in other words, to rise above ordinary humanity, free oneself from all egoism and become a conscious instrument of the Divine Will. The soul itself, being a portion of the Divine, is above all moral and ethical notions; it bathes in the Divine Light and manifests it, but it can truly govern the whole being only when the ego has been dissolved." (35)

The Jivatman (Central Being)

The Jivatman is not a pure isolated "I". It is the unborn and unevolving status of the soul that is outside the manifestation but is at the same time the origin of manifestation. In Sri Aurobindo's words,

> "The word "I" always comes with an under-suggestion of ego, of separativeness, but there is no separativeness in this self-vision, for the individual here is a spiritual living centre of action for the One and feels no separation from all that is the One."(36)

The Mother explained that the Jivatman represents "a unity which is not a uniformity". (37) In its poise of unity, it is identified with the Divine that is Infinite, Absolute and all-pervading. In another poise, it is identified in the multiplicity where the truth of each being is an individual truth even though it is identified with the Divine. In its unitary poise, the Jivatman is actually a representation of the Divine oneness and hence is the same for everybody. In the multiplicity, it supports the individual truth of being which is unique for each individual and hence appears to be particular for every individual. The Jivatman is therefore simultaneously a singular and a pluralistic entity justifying the concept of the multiple Divine. In the poise of the One Divine, the Jivatman is surpassed by the transcendent Self, the Atman, immutable and eternal, above all manifestation. When the One Divine manifests in the multiplicity to become the multiple Divine, it presides over the manifestation through the poise of the Jivatman.

Table 2. The Individual: The Perspective of Beings

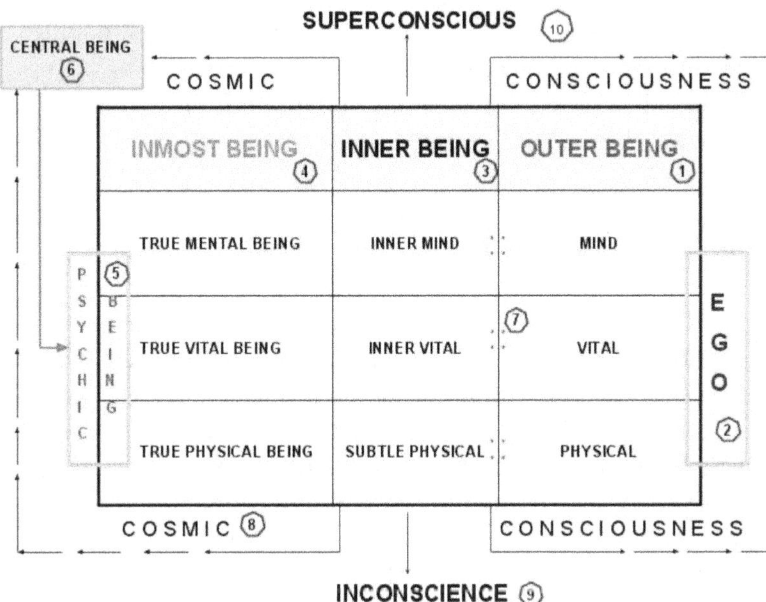

1. The Outer Being is known as "Personality" in psychology.

2. The ego is a formation of the outer being and is known as the "self" in psychology.

3. The Inner Being (subliminal personality) stands behind the outer being, sinks to the Inconscience, arises to the Superconscious and is connected with the Cosmic Consciousness.

4. The Inmost Being represents the different poises of the Self in the manifestation.

5. The Psychic Being, is a projection of the Jivatman. It is the soul element in evolution. It is the central poise of the Inmost Being.

6. The Central Being or the Jivatman is the poise of the Self above the manifestation.

7. The channels of communication between the Inner Being and Outer Being are the Chakras which are primarily located in the Inner Being. Can be activated by arousing the Kundalini from

below or by the Force of Transformation from above.

8. The Cosmic Consciousness is connected with the individual through the Inner Being.

9. The Inconscience is not only a psychological but also a vital and physical Inconscience.

10. The Superconscious can descend into the being which is needed in the saga of Transformation.

The Link between the Vertical and Concentric System

The vertical system spans from the Inconscience to the Superconscious through a series of planes of consciousness that culminates in the Supermind, which is the creative knowledge-will-power of the Infinite. The concentric system includes ranges of a vast subliminal inner being, culminating in contact with the psychic being, which is an evolutionary projection of the non-evolving Central Being (Jivatman). [Table 2]. In Sri Aurobindo's system of yoga, the psychic being must come forward and link together and take command of the vertical and concentric systems of consciousness *before* there can be an ascension upwards towards the Supermind. In the process, the planes of consciousness contacted via the chakras are automatically activated by the higher, transforming forces regardless of whether the seeker is aware of this or not. As Chaudhuri explains, "Inspired by the ideal of divine transformation of the lower nature, Purnayoga (*Integral Yoga of Sri Aurobindo*) concentrates not so much upon the awakening of the Kundalini as upon the coming to the front of the Psychic Being." (38) The psychic being guides the descent of the transforming forces and the ascent of the evolutionary consciousness:

> "First, there must be a conversion inwards, a going within to find the inmost psychic being and bring it out to the front, disclosing at the same time the inner mind, inner vital, inner physical parts of the nature. Next, there must be an ascension, a series of conversions upwards and a turning down to convert the lower parts. When one has made the inward con-

version, one psychicises the whole nature so as to make the divine change."(39)

Thus, an individual who has integrated the myriad strands of the being, the diverse planes of the personality around the psychic being, is ready to ascend the rising tiers of consciousness. However, it is important to remember that the ascension upwards has to be done by the whole being integrated around the psychic being, not by the psychic being alone:

> "It is the whole consciousness, mental, vital, physical also, that has to rise and join the higher consciousness and, once the joining is made, the higher has to descend into them. The psychic is behind all that and supports it." (40)

Sri Aurobindo explained that the psychic being is not in initial contact with the Supramental plane but

> "Once the connection between the supramental and the human consciousness is made, it is the psychic being that gives *the readiest response* — more ready than the mind, the vital or the physical. It may be added that it is also a purer response; the mind, vital and physical can allow other things to mix with their reception of the supramental influence and spoil its truth. The psychic is pure in its response and allows no such mixture. The supramental change can take place only if the psychic is awake and is made the chief support of the descending supramental power." (41)

The Environmental Consciousness

In between the individual and the cosmic consciousness, Sri Aurobindo described a secret circumconscient or environmental consciousness. However, this environmental consciousness is not the consciousness of a collectivity, it is essentially an individual phenomenon. (42) Sri Aurobindo elaborated:

"Everyone carries around him an environmental consciousness or atmosphere through which he is in relation with others or with the universal forces. It is through this that these forces or the thoughts or feelings of others enter…

"Yet all the time the universal forces are pouring into him without his knowing it. He is aware only of thoughts, feeling etc. that rise to the surface and these he takes for his own. Really they come from outside in mind waves, vital waves, waves of feeling and sensation etc. which take particular forms in him and rise to the surface after they have got inside.

"But they do not get into his body at once. He carries about with him an environmental consciousness (called by the Theosophists the aura) into which they first enter. If you can become conscious of this environmental self of yours, then you can catch the thought, passion, suggestion or force of illness, or whatever it may be, before it enters and prevent it from entering into you. If things in you are thrown out, they often do not go altogether but take refuge in this environmental atmosphere and from there try to get in again or they go to a distance outside but linger on the outskirts or even perhaps far off, waiting till they get an opportunity to attempt entrance.

"It [the environmental consciousness] can become silent when there is the wideness. One can become conscious of it and deal with what passes through it. A man without it would be without contact with the rest of the world."(43)

Despite being the meeting ground of the individual and the outer world, the environmental consciousness, or "circumconscient" as he sometimes calls it, is fundamentally an individual phenomenon. Nonetheless, it is "not wholly our formed and realized self but ourself plus the external world-nature"; (44) and is perceived as an individual aura by Theosophists, parapsychologists and energy-field therapists (like Reiki practitioners, Pranic healers). The real world outside that is of relevance to the individual in the psychological perspective is the Cosmic Consciousness.

The Cosmic Consciousness

Yoga understands reality through three different experiential poises: Transcendent, Universal (or Cosmic) and Individual. The individual is a particular formation constructed from a selection of forces and movements of the universal mental, the universal vital and the universal physical Nature. However, the ordinary individual who knows the world only by the outer mind and senses has a limited knowledge of cosmic forces and does not know the technique of universalisation. When the consciousness subtilizes sufficiently, the individual can expand the range of experience so as to perceive the essence of objects and events in a much more direct way that is not revealed to the senses and reason. The stage is then set for the next step — an universalisation of consciousness by surpassing the ego to come

> "in direct contact with an immense range of things in the world, then to contain them as it were,-- as it is said to see the world in oneself, — and to be in a way identified with it. To see all things in the self and the self in all things — to be aware of one being everywhere, aware directly of the different planes, their forces, their beings — that is universalisation."(45)

As Sri Aurobindo explained further:

> "The cosmic consciousness is that in which the limits of ego, personal mind and body disappear and one becomes aware of a cosmic vastness which is or filled by a cosmic Spirit and aware also of the direct play of cosmic forces, universal mind forces, universal life forces, universal energies of Matter, universal Overmind forces. But one does not become aware of all these together; the opening of the cosmic consciousness is usually progressive. It is not that the ego, the body, the personal mind disappear, but one feels them as only a small part of oneself. One begins to feel others too as part of oneself or varied repetitions of oneself, the same self modified by Nature in other bodies or, at the least, as living in the larger universal

self which is henceforth one's own greater reality. All things in fact begin to change their value and appearance; one's whole experience of the world is radically different from that of those who are shut up in their personal selves. One begins to know things by a different kind of experience, more direct, not depending on the external mind and the senses. It is not that the possibility of error disappears, for that cannot be so long as mind of any kind is one's instrument for transcribing knowledge, but there is a new, vast and deep way of experiencing, seeing, knowing, contacting things; and the confines of knowledge can be rolled back to an almost immeasurable degree."(46)

The individual thinks oneself to be a separate being but truly speaking, most of what one is comes in from the cosmic consciousness. In Sri Aurobindo's terminology, there is "a wall of separative ignorance" (47) between the individual and the cosmic consciousness. Once this wall or barrier breaks down, the individual becomes aware of the cosmic Self, of the consciousness of the cosmic Nature and of the forces playing in it. "The cosmic consciousness is that of the universe, of the cosmic Spirit and cosmic Nature with all the beings and forces within it. All that is as much conscious as a whole as the individual separately is, though in a different way. The consciousness of the individual is part of this, but a part feeling itself as a separate being". (48)

The cosmic consciousness is connected with the subliminal or inner being, and through the inner being the cosmic consciousness can influence the outer being. Though only a little of the cosmic consciousness escapes through the inner being via centres of inner consciousness (the chakras) into the outer life of human beings, that little is the best part of ourselves and is responsible for art, philosophy, ideals and high aspirations.(49) The universal rhythms of music and love, the universal appeal of virtues, the universal ground of knowledge, the universal source of strength, the universal fountain of creativity, the universal call of the Divine — all enter our lives from the cosmic consciousness through our subliminal being. However, it is important to note that there are equally great negative forces in the cosmic consciousness, great anti-divine forces, great hostile powers, great Satanic influences, huge forces of destruction, annihilation, greed, lust and ill-will. In psychological language, one could say there is a great stream of world-libido that originates in the cosmic consciousness and can also get expressed in human life. As Sri Aurobindo cautioned,

> "The things one has to be on guard against in the cosmic consciousness are the play of a magnified ego, the vaster attacks of the hostile forces –for they too are part of the cosmic consciousness — and the attempt of the cosmic Illusion (Ignorance, Avidya) to prevent the growth of the soul into the cosmic Truth. These are things that one has to learn from experience; mental teaching or explanation is quite insufficient. To enter safely into the cosmic consciousness and to pass safely through it, it is necessary to have a strong central unegoistic sincerity and to have the psychic being, with its divination of truth and unfaltering orientation towards the Divine, already in front in the nature".(50)

The Dimension of Impersonality
Modern psychology studies the being in terms of the "personal-

Table 3 . The dimensions of the Being

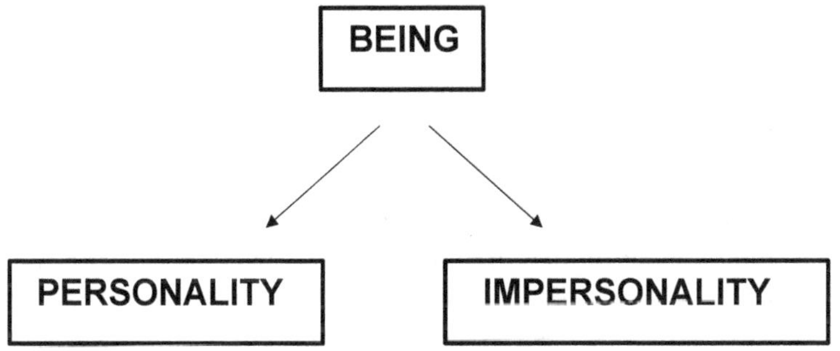

ity". In yogic parlance, there is also the dimension of impersonal-ity [Table 3]. The impersonal dimension expresses itself at different levels of consciousness with different connotations. There are three important levels to be understood:

1. As the individual disentangles from the ego and comes into contact with the inner or subliminal being, one begins to experience a vast impersonality supporting the ego-bound surface movements of the outer personality. A base of silence, peace and stability supports the dynamism that is needed to balance the turbulences of the outside life. Strength does not depend merely on activity, it also emanates from silence. Dynamism without a base of stability can give rise to stress-linked problems and is actually responsible for the classical workaoholic Type A personality who is more prone to ischemic heart disease. An inner poise of peace, silence and stability can be cultivated through yogic techniques of personal growth.

2. As the individual progresses further in the dimension of ego-transcendence one enters the cosmic consciousness. Time is no more experienced in a linear way, one recognizes the simultaneity of all events at any moment. Space expands and one's individual space coalesces with other spaces, while a particular point can be perceived as the "giant point" (51), omnipotent and omnipresent. Great spiritual figures like the Buddha acted from this poise of impersonality and history is witness to the enormous magnitude of their work. Impersonality thus is complemented by the movement of universality. As Sri Aurobindo commented: "Impersonality is the first character of cosmic self; universality, non-limitation by the single or limiting point of view, is the character of cosmic perception and knowledge: this tendency is therefore a widening, however rudimentary, of these restricted mind areas towards cosmicity, towards a quality which is the very character of the higher mental planes,--towards that supercon-scient cosmic Mind which, we have suggested, must in the nature of things be the original mind-action of which ours is

only a derivative and inferior process."(52)

3. As one comes into experiential contact with the soul-principle in the poise of the Central Being or Jivatman that upholds the manifestation, one experiences the consciousness of eternity through the poise of timelessness and spacelessness. This is the basic impersonality that sustains the manifestation, itself immutable, but creating mutable space and time-bound personalities by interaction with cosmic Nature. The Jivatman projects an evolutionary mode within the manifestation that grows into a soul-personality or psychic being, of which the ego is only a dark shadow. Thus the Jivatman potentially holds simultaneously the dimensions of personality and impersonality. The Jivatman rises into transcendence, it feels its "oneness with the universal' but also at the same time its "central separateness as a portion of the Divine". (53)

In terms of practical psychology, the dimension of impersonality makes the self felt as a universalised individual who is "the same in essence as others, extended everywhere from each being but centered here. Of course centre is a way of speaking, because no physical centre is usually felt – only all the actions take place around the individual."(54) The impersonality is experienced as being "everywhere without form or limitation in any place or time". (55)

Uniqueness of Sri Aurobindo's Paradigm

The structure of the being as explained by Sri Aurobindo and the Mother has certain unique characteristics:

First, it is in consonance with the perennial wisdom that all existence is one but with a constantly active principle of variation and individuation. The corollary that follows is that there is a "general individuality of Man which the totality of mankind represents in its full play of oneness and variety" and within that general individuality, there are innumerable variations supporting a particular individuation of the indefinable Reality. (56) Thus, the being has a dimension of personality that has psychological, social and cultural components, as well as a dimension of impersonality that transcends all other perspectives. Such a comprehensive paradigm allows for diverse theories of personality each to have a valid place and purpose within the whole.

Second, the structure of the being allows the transforming forces to descend and transmute the lower nature. Sri Aurobindo explained that the higher powers descend at first into the mind, which is more subtle and supple and receptive to these spiritual influences than are the turbulent vital and the inert physical consciousness. Indeed, he commented that it would actually be risky if the higher powers attempted to transform the emotional or vital being before the mind was changed, (57) and that even the mind needs to be transformed slowly "for the mind-centres are not a region isolated from the rest of the being; the mind-action is penetrated by the action of the vital and the physical parts, and in those parts themselves are lower formations of mind, a vital mind, a physical mind, and these have to be changed before there can be an entire transformation of the mental being." (58)

Third, the multi-faceted complexity of the being as described by Sri Aurobindo provides an unique opportunity for "the power of consciousness to live in more than one status at a time". (59) Note that this is different from the clinical condition of dissociative identity disorder (formerly called multiple personality disorder), which is characterized each personality or "part" acting out at a different time, and with the total personality exhibiting at least some degree of dysfunction. In contrast, what Sri Aurobindo describes is a higher level of functioning in which a person can simultaneously live at many levels and planes, and also integrate all of these different planes of consciousness and parts of the being around the psychic being.

Lastly, Sri Aurobindo and the Mother see the being not as a static or a finished product, but rather as an always evolving work in progress that grows along the trajectory of an ascending consciousness towards an as yet unrealized supramental summit. For this to be possible, the structure of the being has to be both flexible and dynamic so as to hold the parts which have already evolved, the parts that are in the process of being further evolved, and the possibilities that are yet to evolve. In this worldview, psychology is not only a description of the current capacities and functioning of human consciousness, but also an evolutionary preparation for the supra-human capacities and functioning of the Supramental Consciousness that has yet to evolve on Earth.

The architecture of the Infinite
Discovered here its inward-musing shapes
Captured into wide breaths of soaring stone....
Savitri, *pg. 360-361*

References

1. CWSA 28, pg. 17
2. Ibid, pg. 84
3. Ibid
4. Ibid
5. CWSA 23-24, pg. 633
6. Ibid, pg. 639
7. Ibid, pg. 632
8. CWSA 28, pg. 183
9. Ibid, pg. 207-208
10. Ibid, pg. 207
11. Ibid, pg. 208
12. Agenda VI, pg. 230
13. CWSA 28, pg. 175
14. Ibid, pg. 179-180
15. Evening Talks, pg. 406
16. CWSA 21-22, pg. 442
17. Ibid
18. Ibid, pg. 290
19. CWSA 28, pg. 204
20. Ibid
21. Ibid, pg. 224
22. Ibid, pg. 223

23. Ibid, pg. 224

24. Ibid, pg. 223-224

25. CWSA 21-22, pg. 193

26. CWSA 28, pg. 231

27. CWSA 30, pg. 325

28. CWSA 23-24, pg. 804

29. Ibid

30. CWM 3, pg. 62

31. Ibid, pg. 63

32. Ibid

33. CWSA 28, pg. 106-107

34. Ibid, pg. 106

35. CWM 16, pg. 248

36. CWSA 28, pg. 73

37. CWM 7, pg. 224

38. Chaudhuri, Haridas :Sri Aurobindo—The Prophet of Life Divine, Sri Aurobindo Ashram, Pondicherry, 2nd Ed, 1960, pg. 93

39. CWSA 28, pg. 84

40. Ibid, pg. 118

41. Ibid, pg. 102 (footnote)

42. Ibid, pg. 213

43. Ibid, pg. 213-214

44. CWSA 21-22, pg. 995

45. CWSA 30, pg. 273

46. Ibid, pg. 271-272

47. Ibid, pg. 269

48. Ibid

49. Ibid, pg. 325

50. Ibid, pg. 272

51. CWSA 33-34, pg. 24

52. CWSA 21-22, pg. 289

53. CWSA 28, pg. 55

54. Ibid, pg. 31

55. Ibid, pg. 11

56. CWSA 12, pg. 314

57. CWSA 21-22, pg. 993

58. Ibid

59. Ibid, pg. 994

11
Disharmonies in Consciousness

For with pain and labour all creation comes.
This earth is full of the anguish of the gods...
The spirit is doomed to pain till man is free.
Savitri, pg. 444

There are many ways to understand the genesis of clinical problems. In fact, it is already standard practice to understand any clinical presentation from multiple angles — psychodynamic, cognitive-behavioral, genetic, neuro-biological, family-systems, socio-economic, cultural, etc. CBP accepts each of these perspectives as valid within its own sphere but complements and completes them by embedding them all within a larger consciousness perspective. And just as diagnosis and case formulation are considered to guide treatment in the standard biopsychosocial model, CBP also has its own formulation of psychopathology based on its consciousness paradigm. This chapter explains CBP's ultimate diagnosis of the various causes of psychopathology, which it traces to six potential levels of disharmony in consciousness, as well as the gap between Consciousness and Force that is inherent to human nature. This is the most abstract chapter in the book, but it is needed to give the conceptual foundation for the consciousness-based clinical work described in Chapters 12-18. In CBP, all of the symptoms and behaviors that are currently labelled as "psychopathology" are simply manifestations of disharmonies in consciousness.

Formulation: from Dissonance to Harmony

From the perspective of CBP, the genesis of psychological and psychiatric problems can be traced to two general forms of impurity in consciousness that affect all human beings, and several different types or levels of disharmony in consciousness that can affect individuals in more specific ways. The two general forms of "impurity" are due to the fact that human beings are transitional, meaning we are not the end of evolution but rather an evolutionary step in a gradation of consciousness that will eventually surpass the current human mentality. (1) These two general problems are:

(a) That evolution begins with Matter as its base, but the "material universe begins from an apparent inconscience." (2) What Sri Aurobindo and the Mother call the Inconscience holds the essence of whatever is scheduled to evolve in the future as an involved or dormant potentiality. Functionally, this Inconscience is the source of all negativity and resistance to the unitary truth of Consciousness, and as such is the primal origin of all ignorance, falsehood, limitation, and division. The Inconscience imparts a separative quality to the process of individuation, and thus creates an ego that is a temporary binding factor for the emerging individuality, and this ego becomes a fulcrum for separative ignorance. Thus, all human beings are born with a defect that derives from the ordeal of our evolutionary past. As Sri Aurobindo noted, "this defect is a radically wrong and ignorant form given to the proper action of each part of our instrumental being." (3)

(b) As evolution progresses, higher planes of consciousness manifest that surpass the limitations of the preceding planes. In the process, the limitations of the preceding planes partially dilute and negate the potentials of the higher planes, which results in a sort of disharmony. Thus, the inertia of the material plane dilutes the flow of life-energy, while both the material inertia and the turbulence of life-energy partially hinder to the concentrated functioning of the mind. Sri Aurobindo writes that this impurity:

"is born of the successive process of an evolution, where life emerges in and depends on body, mind emerges in and depends on life in the body, supermind emerges in and lends itself to instead of governing mind, soul itself is apparent only as a circumstance of the bodily life of the mental being and veils up the spirit in the lower imperfections. This second defect of our nature is caused by this dependence of the higher on the lower parts; it is an immixture of functions by which the impure working of the lower instrument gets into the characteristic action of the higher function and gives to it an added imperfection of embarrassment, wrong direction and confusion." (4)

It is due to this defect that a denial of the influence of the Superconscious by the mental or vital parts of the being can lead to imperfection in personality development, which can at times cause psychological or psychiatric symptoms.

In addition to these two primary sources of psychological disturbance, there are the practical levels of disharmony that can result in psychopathology for given individuals. These levels or types of disharmony are summarized in Table 1, and further explained below.

Table 1.

LEVELS OF DISHARMONY

Level 1: At Outer Being
Level 2: Subconscious & Inconscient Forces
Level 3: Mismatch between Outer & Inner Beings
Level 4: Intermediate Zone
Level 5: Disruptive Cosmic Forces
Level 6: Forceful pulling of Superconscient forces

The first level of the disharmonies causing psychopathology originate due to the discordances among the various intertwined planes of consciousness in the outer being or due to recalcitrant points within any plane. The ego being skewed in its action is unable to manifest harmony in the outer being.

The second level of disturbances occurs when forces from the Inconscience and the Subconscious invade the outer being after traversing the inner being. Whatever is rejected from consciousness sinks into the subconscious and from there it finally sinks into the Inconscience, from which it can resurge to produce psychopathology. However, the Inconscience described by Sri Aurobindo surpasses the psychological unconscious of Freud, it is simultaneously a vital and a material inconscience. As such it not only causes psychopathology from resurgence of repressed materials, it is also responsible for relapse of illnesses and chronicity of psychosomatic disorders as well as for transmission of hereditary characteristics.

The third level of disturbances originate from the mismatch between the inner being and the outer being at various points. The inner being proper is not supported by the ego but by the psychic being, which is a soul-element or Truth-principle and hence psychopathology per se does not originate in the inner being or in the psychic being. However, in subjects practicing spirituality, the inner being can progress at a faster pace than the outer being, and the outer being's failure to keep pace with the inner growth may result in disharmony that precipitates pathology, even in advanced mystics and yogis. As Sri Aurobindo commented, during spiritual growth a long stage may come:

> "in which the inner being is sufficiently transformed but the outer is still involved in a mixed and difficult movement of imperfect change. This disparity repeats itself at each step of the ascent; for in each change the inner being follows more readily, the outer limps after, reluctant or else incompetent in spite of its aspiration and desire: this necessitates a constantly repeated labour of assumption, adaptation, orientation, a labour reproduced in new terms always but always the same in principle." (5)

The fourth level of disharmonies occur in the intermediate zone between the outer being and the inner being, which represents a confused passage of half-truths that subjects may encounter when they get out of the personal consciousness and open into the cosmic consciousness--but without transcending the ordinary mind.

It is a zone where one can become prone to delusions, perceptual disorders, and other psychopathological forces that do not primarily emerge from the Inconscience. Thus embarking on a spiritual discipline does not automatically guarantee a freedom from disharmony and resultant psychopathology.

The fifth level of disharmonies occur when disruptive Cosmic Forces enter through the inner being and cut off the psychic being from the rest of the being (Chapter 5). Negative and disruptive forces can invade from the realm of Cosmic Consciousness, enter the individual through the connection between the inner being and cosmic consciousness, and succeed in blocking the influence of the soul-principle (psychic being) on the rest of the being. This is the genesis of occult "possession" from the CBP perspective and can give rise to psychopathology by its own merit. Such occult forces can invade a subject's consciousness at an unsuspecting moment, and this can even happen to subjects who have a fair amount of spiritual development. For, as Sri Aurobindo explains,

> "But even when the outer and the inner nature of the individual arc unified in a harmonized spiritual consciousness, that still more external but occult part of him in which his being mixes with the being of the outside world and through which the outside world invades his consciousness remains a field of imperfection. There is necessarily a commerce here between disparate influences: the inner spiritual influence is met by quite opposite influences strong in their control of the present world-order; the new spiritual consciousness has to bear the shock of the dominant and established unspiritualised powers of the Ignorance. This creates a difficulty which is of capital importance in all stages of the spiritual evolution and its urge towards a change of the nature." (6)

Thus, disruptive occult influences can invade with equal strength an ordinary subject, an intellectually refined person or a spiritually developed person, and produce psychopathology.

The sixth level of disharmonies occur when a Power or Force from the Superconscious realms is suddenly drawn into an unprepared and improperly balanced structure of the being.

Also, it is worth emphasizing that since CBP accepts the reality of matter, physics, chemistry, genetics, cellular biology, and all other fields of material and medical science, it is also understood that all subjects who are biologically susceptible to, or constitutionally prone to psychological and psychiatric dysfunction may be at risk of developing psychopathology by disharmonies arising at any level of consciousness. CBP does not pose an "either/or" conflict between spiritual and material worldviews, but rather sees an evolving interaction among all of the planes of consciousness manifested in matter.

Consciousness and Force

Finally, another way that CBP explains the etiology of psychopathology is via the hiatus or gap between knowledge and will-power which is a basic phenomenon of creation. Sri Aurobindo explains that the hiatus is not there at two extreme ends of the cosmic phenomenon. At the highest level of spiritual experience, Consciousness and Force are inseparably linked in the Superconscious. At the material level of creation, there is a dormant form of knowledge implicit within mass and energy, but this knowledge acts within a limited sphere. Thus, electrons "know" that they have to go on automatically rotating in their orbits, and at a higher stage of evolution, in insects and animals, instincts further express a type of knowledge. Thus, the bee knows how to build its hive and the ant knows how to organize a colony — but this instinctual knowledge is confined within certain immediately practical limits. At the level of the human mind, in contrast, the potential sphere of knowledge becomes vastly larger — but knowledge and will-power also become de-linked, which can create chaos and disharmony in both individuals and collectives. The evolutionary work of the human being is to re-link Knowledge and Will (Force) together along a growing trajectory of consciousness, culminating in the perfect harmony of consciousness and force implicit in the Supermind. However, until that evolution is complete, the problem human beings face is that in our current physical constitution, the hiatus between Consciousness and Force is maintained by an inertia arises from the Inconscience and resists the transmuting effects of the higher planes of consciousness. Thus, we generally lack the concentration of Consciousness-Force needed to ward off suffering and pain. As Sri Aurobindo explained,

> "all pain and suffering are the result of an insufficient consciousness-force in the surface being which makes it unable to deal rightly with self and Nature or unable to assimilate and to harmonise itself with the contacts of the universal Energy; they would not exist if in us there was an integral presence of the luminous Consciousness and the divine Force of an integral Being". (7)

An appreciation of the functioning of Consciousness-Force at different planes of consciousness offers a wide variety of creative approaches to treatment, addressed in the next chapter. In terms of formulating the etiology of various types of psychopathology, Table 2 summarizes how the mismatch or dissonance between Consciousness and Force gets expressed at each major plane of consciousness (physical, vital, mental) or part of the being (ego). The general solution to these discords is to integrate these planes of consciousness and parts of the being around the psychic being, which has an inherent harmony between consciousness and force. Actually, the harmonization itself takes place in the inner or subliminal being, which is supported by the inherent harmony of the psychic being.

Psychological Risks of Spiritual Practice

Because CBP recognizes a wide range of potential etiologies of disharmonies in consciousness, it has a realistic appreciation of the risks of spiritual practice, as there are situations in which spiritual and mystical experiences can lead to psychopathology. Transpersonal psychology has described some such adverse effects under the rubric of 'spiritual emergency'. As Cortright notes:

> "Spiritual emergency, which is one of the best examples of how transpersonal psychotherapy is a synthesis of psychology and spirituality, refers to how the self becomes disorganized and overwhelmed by an infusion of spiritual energies or new realms of experience which it is not yet able to integrate…The concept of spiritual emergency is important for three main reasons. For one it brings into view a range of human experience that was formerly unseen or misinterpreted by traditional psychology. Second, it is clinically useful in proposing a diagnosis and treatment for a set of psychological symptoms. Third, and perhaps most important although least commented upon, it poses a major challenge to the dominant, biologically based psychiatric paradigm." (8)

In CBP, it is understood that the symptoms exhibited during disturbances in spiritual pursuit can arise from different levels of consciousness, in accordance with the development of the subject's psyche. It must be remembered that there are some striking simi-

Table 2. Dissonance between Consciousness and Force: Consequences at different planes

Physical Plane	Inertia
Vital Plane	Desire, Emotional turbulence
Mental Plane	Cognition-Volition discord
Ego	Nodal point of dissonance

larities between mystical and psychotic experiences. Thus, what we call hallucinations in the case of schizophrenics appear to be outwardly similar to the revelations reported by exceptional spiritual personalities like Moses, Prophet Mohammed, Guru Nanak and the great rishis. It might be argued that the mystical revelation has an integrative effect while the schizophrenic hallucination is disruptive in its symbolism. However, it may also be the case that the inner being of the mystic is receptive to higher intuitive influences while the inner senses of the schizophrenic get hooked to negative and destabilizing energies in the cosmic consciousness. Or else, the experiences of the inner senses may not be assimilated in the consciousness of the subject. As Cortright elucidates, even certain mystics who have valid mystical experiences may not be able to assimilate such inner experiences in behaviourally or emotionally adaptive ways. "Hearing other's thoughts or seeing subtle beings can be difficult to integrate. As ordinary self/other boundaries dissolve, it can feel like the self is falling apart." (9) This would result in hallucinations or delusions in mystics akin to schizophrenia or psychosis. It is significant that such hallucinations may not be associated with paranoia, as if they are hallucinations of "higher order" (10) implying a sort of "regression in the service of transcendence" or RIST. (11) Cortright differentiates between usual schizophrenic experiences and those that occur during spiritual pursuit with RIST characteristics: "Schizophrenics have little insight into their process, whereas those experiencing RIST have profound insights….Schizophrenia disrupts reality testing and cognition, but a person experiencing RIST maintains the capacity for abstract thinking. Even when hallucinations occur in RIST, they are of a higher order, and though they might advise, they never command." (12) If so, the line between the psychotic and mystical experiences has to be cautiously drawn.

The phenomenon of delusions in spiritual states that bear psychiatric connotations are also interesting. Western literature has documented that such delusions very often have mythological themes. The eight major mythological themes described in the West revolve around themes of death, rebirth, journey on a mission, spirit encounters, cosmic conflict, magical powers of parapsychological paradigm, the rapid change in the New Age, and the recurrent and eulogized theme of Divine Union. (13) However, in the CBP paradigm, one important cause of delusions in spiritual aspirants would be pseudo-intuitions or the effects of intuitive ideas getting diluted at the level of the mind in such a way that distorted ideas acquire a legitimacy. Even if not suffering from any delusions or mental illness, a spiritual aspirant may exaggerate overvalued ideas to such an extent as to formulate dogmatic and fundamentalist concepts that lead to cult phenomenon.

Following is a list of how CBP understands other situations in which spiritual practices can produce psychopathology:

1. The physical, vital and mental planes of consciousness mediated by the ego as a fulcrum are intermingled in the outer being (surface personality) to such an extent that they cannot be differentiated. Any forceful attempt to differentiate the planes at the outer level may result in a skewed dissociation and mismatched disharmony that can lead to any type of pathology or psychopathology. This is why differentiation leading to dissociation has been identified as a cause of spiritual pathology in transpersonal terminology. It is only in the inner being or subliminal personality that true differentiation of the different planes can be attempted — not for dissociation but for integration around the psychic being.

The fact that a disharmony and dissociation between the different planes of consciousness can give rise to psychopathology is also represented in Wilber's concept of structural imbalance, where symptoms like free-floating anxiety and somatization occur due to improper use of spiritual techniques. (14) However, there is an important difference with the CBP paradigm which recognizes that at the level of the outer being, a structural imbalance automatically exists regardless of whether spiritual practices have been properly or improperly followed. It is only at the level of the inner being or subliminal personality that the harmony can be initiated as the ego does not retain its hold there, while the crux of structural balance is achieved with the integration around the psychic being.

2. Closely linked to the structural imbalance resulting from disharmony between the planes of consciousness in the outer being, is the pathology arising from the skewed nature of the ego's

functioning. In CBP, the ego is a temporary variable balancing the discordant parts of the outer being and it is necessarily biased towards one or the other component. The ego can get magnified by desire arising from the mind or vital to produce a host of physical and psychiatric illnesses, and it can get distorted or deformed as in personality disorders. The ego can also succumb to the grip of disruptive cosmic forces, as Jung recognized in the phenomenon of ego inflation, where the infusion of spiritual energies can be co-opted by the ego, resulting in grandiosity and narcissistic inflation. (15) Wilber in his description of psychic inflation explains how universal-transpersonal (cosmic) energies can get exclusively linked to the individual ego causing extreme imbalance. (16) In traditional spirituality, the ego was dispensed with so that only egolessness could be a criterion for perfection. In CBP, the aim is neither to annul nor aggrandize the ego, but to replace it via the emergence of the psychic being.

Unless the ego is surrendered and substituted with a deeper soul-principle, the spiritual transformation cannot proceed and may even end up with psychopathology in vulnerable aspirants. As Sri Aurobindo explained to an aspirant facing unforeseen obstacles in his spiritual pursuit:

> "There is in a very fundamental part of your nature a strong formation of ego-individuality which has mixed in your spiritual aspiration a clinging element of your pride and spiritual ambition and is supported by a long-formed habit of leadership, self-confident activity and self-reliance. This formation has never consented to be broken up in order to give place to something more true and divine." (17)

He then explains that as a result, the spiritual Force invoked either falls into inertia (tamas) or gets swept up in disruptive outbursts (rajasic gusts). (18) Either of these consequences can have pathological ramifications. The inertia may lead to a depressive episode or schizophrenic withdrawal. The disruptive outbursts may be overtly psychotic or resemble impulse control disorder.

3. Sometimes, a forceful and overenthusiastic pulling of high-

er spiritual forces without having first established peace, harmony and balance in one's system can precipitate problems that range from psychogenic headache, allergies and functional gastrointestinal problems, to more severe physical illness (cardiac ailments), anxiety, depression, mania and even psychosis. This is why the Mother emphatically warned aspirants not to "pull" forces. (19) It is difficult to practice spirituality with a high achievement motivation that inflates the ego. The aspirant has to cultivate infinite patience and the habit of surrender of what one is and what one does to the Supreme Truth. Any hurry or impatience can be counter-productive. Wilber takes a cue from Sri Aurobindo's thought to describe how such a problem (Wilber named it "Yogic illness") occurs when a great intensity of higher and subtle energies can overload the "lower circuits". (20)

4. In mystics and yogis, serious spiritual practice for many years can result in a state where the inner being progresses quickly while the outer being cannot follow suit as it is tied up with the world of gross forms, desires and habits. The resultant mismatch may lead to serious physical illnesses or psychiatric problems. Even if illness does not occur, the inner being may be so engrossed in the higher, unitive consciousness that the mystic may lose touch with physical reality to such an extent that he or she temporarily needs care-giving from others. For example, Cortright points out that Ramana Maharshi had such a profound absorption in Samadhi in the initial phase of his Self-realization, which in the West might have led to psychiatric intervention to bring him back to so-called "reality." (21)

The Mother lucidly explained how the transforming power of Yoga is operative only to a certain degree in the body as the receptivity in the body is limited whereas the mind can be more receptive and change and progress swiftly:

> "But rapid progress in one part of the being which is not
> followed by an equivalent progress in other parts produces
> a disharmony in the nature, a dislocation somewhere; and

wherever or whenever this dislocation occurs, it can translate itself into an illness. The nature of the illness depends upon the nature of the dislocation. One kind of disharmony affects the mind and the disturbances it produces may lead even as far as insanity; another kind affects the body and may show itself as fever or prickly heat or any other greater or minor disorder." (22)

Thus, the disharmonies arising from the mind are more likely to be caused by being overwhelmed with a rapid march of forces that cannot be balanced by other parts of the being, while disharmonies in the body are more likely to be due to resistance or inertia or inability to keep pace with the progress.

5. A serious difficulty can arise when, after a meaningful experiential contact with the soul, one loses the touch and feels dry and abandoned resulting in a state of despondency, despair or depression. In the West, this has been named as the "dark night of the soul." (23) In the Eastern tradition, one very often retains one's faith in the Divine Compassion, and yet such states of despondency are not unexpected. As Sri Aurobindo poetically put it: "To this world's Inconscient Power Thou hast given the right/ To oppose the shining passage of my soul". (24) This indicates that working through the Inconscience may become necessary for an individual, whether one likes it or not. However, he has also cautioned how a giant force of Falsehood emerging from the Inconscience like a "cowled fifth columnist" can confront the saga of the soul in such a way as any introspection or healing touch can become challenging and one has to seek redemption from the Divine Grace that is beyond the purview of therapy.

6. A particular form of depression has been described in spiritual aspirants who overemphasize the metaphysical value of suffering — as, for instance, in certain forms of Buddhism where seekers can be overwhelmed with depression in the initial stages of awareness training. Wilber named this state "pseudo-duksha" and he postulated it to be "the result of residual existential, psychoneurotic, or, more often, residual contamination of the psychic fulcrum of development". (25) However, in the CBP paradigm, a sud-

den opening to the cosmic consciousness can make anyone, even a genuine and mentally stable spiritual aspirant, vulnerable to giant energies of cosmic suffering if the subject has not developed the art of constructing an occult defense. As an extension of this logic, psychiatrists and psychotherapists working with the dark side of human nature who are not trained in the art of occult defense may succumb to negative energies set loose by clients, or they can be overwhelmed by cosmic energies of suffering and falsehood.

7. The awakening of the latent and coiled Kundalini force by gradually opening the chakras from below upwards is fraught with its own risks. An activation of the lower chakras can generate lot of physical and libidinal energies and in the absence of a proper guide, the energy may get stuck at any plane and produce psycho-pathological states. That is how Tantra lost its way and came to be identified with sexual gymnastics. Wilber clumps the disorders linked with misdirected awakening of Kundalini and erratic activation of other Pranic (inner vital) energies as Pranic disorders (26), and advocated guided supervision. As previously noted (see Chapters 7 & 10), Sri Aurobindo and the Mother recommended a different approach to dealing with the Kundalini, whereby the chakras are opened from above downwards by a descending force of the higher Consciousness. This superconscious Force is not latent and asleep at the base of the chakras, but rather is felt to reside above the being in a wide and awakened poise, and descends from the overhead planes of consciousness down into the whole system. The essential movement here is one of an inner opening and surrender to this higher Consciousness, and allowing it to do its work in its own way. (27) This process does not follow any set mental rule or procedure, for it is a force of higher Knowledge and Power (Shakti) that sees the unique needs and structure of each individual. This higher Consciousness can work on the chakras in any order, opening and developing each when the time is right and in the way that is needed, and it simultaneously stabilizes the poise of the psychic being. Such an innovative approach does not lead one astray and is free from the dangers associated with the traditional awakening of the Kundalini from below upwards.

8. A number of psychopathological states can arise from

contact with what Sri Aurobindo called the "intermediates zones." These zones of consciousness, which he also described as "zones of lesser coherence", exist in the "No-man's land" between the subliminal or inner being and the surface personality (outer being). Significantly, "the confusion of these intermediate zones has no kinship to the Inconscience." (28) Thus, these are zones of consciousness where one may be prone to confusion leading to delusional and perceptual disorders though the confusion there is not necessarily derived from the Inconscience.

> "The intermediate zone means simply a confused condition or passage in which one is getting out of the personal consciousness and opening into the cosmic (cosmic Mind, cosmic vital, cosmic physical, something perhaps of the cosmic higher Mind) without having yet transcended the human mind levels. One is not in possession of or direct contact with the divine Truth *on its own levels*, but one can receive something from them, even from the Overmind, indirectly. Only, as one is still immersed in the cosmic Ignorance, all that comes from above can be mixed, perverted, taken hold of for their purposes by lower, even by hostile Powers." (29)

Sri Aurobindo described how the intermediate zone can cause psychopathology in spiritual aspirants:

> "For this intermediate zone is a region of half-truths – and that by itself would not matter, for there is no complete truth below the Supermind; but the half-truth here is often so partial or else ambiguous in its application that it leaves a wide field for confusion, delusion and error. The sadhak thinks that he is no longer in the old small consciousness at all, because he feels in contact with something larger or more powerful, and yet the old consciousness is still there, not really abolished. He feels the control or influence of some Power, Being or Force greater than himself, aspires to be its instrument and thinks he has got rid of ego; but this delusion of egolessness often covers an exaggerated ego. Ideas seize upon

him and drive his mind which are only partially true and by overconfident misapplication are turned into falsehoods; this vitiates the movements of the consciousness and opens the door to delusion. Suggestions are made, sometimes of a romantic character, which flatter the importance of the sadhak or are agreeable to his wishes and he accepts them without examination or discriminating control. Even what is true, is so exalted or extended beyond its true pitch and limit and measure that it becomes the parent of error. This is a zone which many sadhaks have to cross, in which many wander for a long time and out of which a great many never emerge. Especially if their sadhana is mainly in the mental and vital, they have to meet here many difficulties and much danger; only those who follow scrupulously a strict guidance or have the psychic being prominent in their nature pass easily as if on a sure and clearly marked road across this intermediate region. A central sincerity, a fundamental humility also save from much danger and trouble. One can then pass quickly beyond into a clearer Light where if still there is much mixture, incertitude and struggle, yet the orientation is towards the cosmic Truth and not to a half-illumined prolongation of Maya and Ignorance." (30)

For example, apropos a 60 year-old subject who developed psychiatric problems when he started to practice yoga after reading Sri Aurobindo's books, Sri Aurobindo commented in a letter dated 21st April, 1937:

"The condition... was a breakdown, not a state of siddhi (realization). He passed out of the normal mental consciousness into a contact with some intermediate zone of consciousness (not the spiritual) where one can be subjected to all sorts of voices, suggestions, ideas, so-called aspirations which are not genuine....The sadhak (spiritual aspirant) can avoid entering into this zone – if he enters, he has to look with indifference on all these things and observe them without lending any credence, by so doing he can safely pass into the true spiritual light. If he takes them all as true or real without discrimination, he is likely to land himself in a great mental confusion and, if there is in addition a lesion or weakness of the brain – the latter is quite possible in one who has been subject to apoplexy – it may have serious consequences and even lead to a disturbance of the reason. If there is ambition, or other motive of the kind mixed up in the spiritual seeking, it may lead to a fall in the Yoga and the growth of an exaggerated egoism or megalomania…once there has been an upset of this kind the wisest course is discontinuance." (31)

Note, again, how Sri Aurobindo specifically mentions the interaction between non-material forces and biology in this passage, highlighting how a "lesion or weakness in the brain" can exacerbate problems that originate in the intermediate zone. Today, our understanding of the details of neuroscience is much more developed than when Sri Aurobindo wrote these words, but his understanding of an interaction effect remains beyond current models of psychiatry and psychology. In another case, an overzealous spiritual endeavour led to a "coarse kind of violence" where Sri Aurobindo felt that a physical mind which is either organically weak or lacks an optimal finesse, can be easily vulnerable to the "charlatanism of the vital being but would not by itself amount to madness, though it may sometimes seem to go very near it." (32)

Sri Aurobindo was also very particular that the concepts of passivity, indifference and self-surrender must not be championed at the expense of discriminatory choice and self-control, for this could make one vulnerable not merely to lower universal forces but to hostile influences from the vital worlds. (33) Such a phenomenon could manifest not only in an individual without proper guidance (34) but also in a group meditation where subjects at different levels of immaturity could create a very mixed milieu, especially if there was no one in the circle who had the occult capacity to protect the group. (35) As he noted:

"It is by creating fear through terrible forms and menaces

that the hostile beings prevent the Sadhaka (spiritual aspirant) from crossing over the threshold between the physical and vital world and it is also by creating fear and alarm that they are able to break in on the vital being of the body. Courage and unalterable confidence are the first necessity of the Sadhaka." (36)

Thus, the practice of spirituality *per se* does not automatically lead to psychological well-being, and it can be fraught with its own risks that lie outside the biopsychosocial model and require a new paradigm for understanding, which is what CBP provides.

Thy spirit's fate is a battle and ceaseless march
Against invisible opponent Powers,
A passage from Matter into timeless self.

Savitri, pg. 458

References:

1. CWSA 23-24, pg. 645
2. Ibid, pg. 630
3. Ibid, pg. 645
4. Ibid, pg. 645-646
5. CWSA21-22, pg. 994
6. Ibid, pg. 994-995
7. Ibid, pg. 622
8. Cortright, B: Psychotherapy and Spirit, SUNY, New York, 1997, pg. 156-157
9. Ibid, pg. 165
10. Nelson, J: Healing the Split, Tarcher: Los Angeles, 1990
11. Washburn, M: Transpersonal Psychology in a Psychoanalytic Perspective. Suny Press, Albany, NY, 1994
12. Op. cit. Psychotherapy and Spirit, pg. 172
13. Ibid, pg. 171
14. Wilber, Ken: The Collected Works of Ken Wilber, Vol.4, Shambala, Boston and London, 1999, pg. 129

15. Op. cit. Psychotherapy and Spirit, pg. 69-70
16. Op. cit. The Collected Works of Ken Wilber, pg. 128
17. CWSA 36, pg. 367
18. Ibid, pg. 368
19. CWM 03, pg. 87
20. Op. cit. The Collected Works of Ken Wilber, pg. 130
21. Op.cit. Psychotherapy and Spirit, pg. 163
22. CWM 03, pg. 86
23. Op.cit. The Collected Works of Ken Wilber,pg. 129
24. CWSA 02, pg. 614
25. Op.cit. The Collected Works of Ken Wilber, pg. 129
26. Ibid, pg. 129-130
27. CWSA 32, pg. 192
28. CWSA 21-22, pg. 580
29. CWSA 30, pg. 295
30. Ibid, pg. 299-300
31. CWSA 35, pg. 397-398
32. CWSA 36, pg. 347
33. Ibid, pg. 338-339
34. Ibid, pg. 335
35. Ibid, pg. 339-400
36. Ibid, pg. 340

12

The Superconscious

A Truth in which negation had no place...

Savitri, *pg. 555*

Sri Aurobindo and the Mother use the term "superconscious" to describe the domain of consciousness poised beyond the ordinary cognitive field and accessible by the inner being. It extends upwards to the supra-rational planes and also deep within to the soul-space of the psychic being. Thus, the territory of consciousness-based phenomenon that are superconscious, or appear so to the mental/vital consciousness of the outer being, is potentially large. Clinically, the pursuit of the Superconscious matters because it is the very raison d'être for transpersonal psychology in general, and CBP in particular. Following is a case that demonstrates why this area matters:

> K, a young housewife, suddenly started suffering from giddiness. Investigations were done and her right ear was operated upon. Still her attacks of vertigo persisted. To make matters worse, these spells were accompanied by a feeling of depression, meaninglessness and a desire to run away from her household work. She felt that life was futile. Neither her giddiness nor her depression responded to antidepressants. On detailed probing, it was found that she had been developing a strong spiritual urge for some years. She had an intense desire to start meditative practices. However, she kept rationalizing that she was too mediocre for spirituality. The conflict between her aspiration for spiritual growth and her self-doubts and reluctance to heed her inner calling, seemed to have precipitated her giddiness and depression. She was counselled to follow her inner urge and ignore her doubts and self-criticisms. She started meditating and the giddiness

and depression were relieved, without medications.

Thus, patients can suffer not only from repression of the subconscious, but also from suppression or avoidance of the superconscious. Practically, as one searches for and tries to apply the superconscious to the purpose of healing, CBP can be used in two ways: either as the primary interpretive framework for all of healthcare for those who wish to adopt this worldview, or as a secondary framework to stimulate reflection in those who wish work from within some other therapeutic paradigm. For example, psychodynamic clinicians could think about the psychic being's impulse towards growth and conflict-free influence on ego functioning (see next section), while Jungians could enrich their study of the collective unconscious by exploring the inner or subliminal being and how this connects to the cosmic consciousness. Humanistic, existential, and gestalt approaches to therapy could all find new layers of depth and meaning by taking up cues from the integral and evolutionary perspective of CBP, especially its growth orientation. Cognitive therapists could start to engage seriously with intuition and higher forms of cognition, while behaviorists could supplement relaxation techniques with exercises that help widen the consciousness. (1) Those interested in biology and neuroscience have much to glean from the Mother's exploration of the consciousness of cells, and vice versa the ongoing developments in medical science are inherently fascinating to practitioners of integral yoga who are interested in matter and the transformation of the body.

Also, practitioners of various forms of complementary therapies could find important keys in CBP's study of the planes and parts of the being. For instance, the subtle nature of the vital force or plane of consciousness might be the reason why homeopathic drugs remain potent in high dilutions where theoretically no molecules should remain. As Sri Aurobindo commented, "Sometimes the infinitesimal is more powerful than the mass; it approaches more and more the subtle state and from the physical goes into a dynamic or vital state and acts vitally." (2) Likewise, acupuncture may activate the energy of the vital plane in a different way. The "vital-physical or nervous envelope" (3) that surrounds the physical body acts as a protective force-field, may be glimpsed as an "aura" by Kirlian photography, and can be strengthened with faith, prayer and meditation. This vital physical aura may also be the zone of therapeutic action for Pranic Therapy, Reiki and magnetic healing. The mental plane of consciousness is involved in many psycho-therapeutic techniques, and relaxation therapies, biofeedback and other stress-reduction techniques may all have beneficial effects on what Sri Aurobindo calls the physical mind (further addressed below). Hypnosis can affect the "subliminal sense-mind" (4), and finally all of these varied forms of mind-body therapies could potentially be deepened and extended to tap what Sri Aurobindo calls the central Pranic Force or Shakti. This is the fountain-head of all the energy systems in the mental-vital-physical complex which is the outer being, and ultimately this Pranic Shakti can be placed under the guidance of the psychic being.

However one chooses to use CBP for personal growth and/or clinical treatment, it is important to remember that growth is not a linear process defined by the mind and carried out according to a so-called treatment plan. Rather, growth is a process that is fundamentally intuitive and experiential, and through which consciousness explores its own potentials and grows into mastery of its own inherent powers. That being said, since as a species we are still very mental beings, there is a utility to organizing possibilities for both self-development and treatment into a format the mind may find useful. We do this in Chapters 12 to 18 with reference to the various planes of consciousness, starting from the Superconscious and descending to the Inconscience. The planes of consciousness are presented in this descending order because Sri Aurobindo and the Mother recommend that one should first make firm contact with the Psychic Being and spiritual planes of consciousness, and then use these to gradually transform the outer being from top to bottom, in descending order from the Mind through the Vital, into the Physical and then the Subconscious.

Contacting the Psychic Being

Sri Aurobindo and the Mother recommended that the central practice of both personal growth and treatment should be to develop increasing contact with one's psychic being. As noted in Chapter 7, the psychic being does not have its own chakra but rather exists in a dimension unto itself. When people are "searching" for the psychic contact, they often first feel it deep behind the heart chakra (higher vital), as a spark or light or feeling of inexplicable joy that lives deep inside. However, the more the psychic being comes forward and takes command of the outer being, the more one feels it to be large and all-enveloping. For in fact the psychic being carries the chakras and the outer nature within itself, not vice versa. The Mother clarified some of these points of confusion in the following talk:

"You must remember that the inner beings are not in the third dimension. If you open up your body you will find only the viscera of the body which are in the third dimension. The inner beings are in another dimension, and when I say that some men do not have their psychic being with them, I do not mean that it is not at the centre of their being, but that their outer consciousness is so small, so limited, so obscure that it is not able to keep a contact, not only conscious but intimate, with the psychic being which extends beyond it in every way; it is so much higher and deeper than the other outer consciousness that there is no relation either of quality or of nature between them. Religions say that you have a divine spark in you –it is well they call it a "spark", for it is so small indeed that it can be placed anywhere in the body without difficulty. But it does not mean that it is in the body: it is within the consciousness in another dimension, and there are beings who are in contact with it, others who haven't. But if you come to the divine Presence in the atom, the image is easier to understand, for there you touch so infinitesimal a domain that you are on the borderline where you can no longer distinguish between two, three, four or five dimensions. If you study modern physics you will understand what I mean. The movements constituting an atom are, in the matter of size, so imperceptible that they cannot be understood with our three-dimensional understanding, the more so as they follow laws which elude completely this three-dimensional idea. So if you take refuge there, you may say that the divine spark is at the centre of each atom and you won't be far from the truth; but I was not speaking of the divine spark, I was speaking of the being, the psychic consciousness which is another thing. The psychic being is an entity which has a form; it is organized around a central consciousness and, having a form it has a dimension, but a dimension of another kind than the third dimension of outer consciousness." (5)

The Mother also described many meditations or visualizations that people can use to contact the psychic being, according to their different needs and turns of nature. Huppes has organized these in a practical way in her workbook on *Psychic Education,* which gives several introspective methods to come in contact with the psychic being. (6) Here are some exercises she quotes from the Mother's talks:

1) To the question of how to get the experience of the psychic being, the Mother answered:

"To go within yourself, that is the first step.

And then, once you have succeeded in going within yourself deeply enough to feel the reality of that which is within, to widen yourself progressively, systematically, to become as vast as the universe and lose the sense of limitation.

These are the first two preparatory movements. And these two things must be done in the greatest possible calm, peace and tranquillity. This peace, this tranquillity brings about silence in the mind and stillness in the vital.

This effort, this attempt must be renewed very regularly, persistently. And after a certain lapse of time, which may be longer or shorter, you begin to perceive a reality that is different from the reality perceived in the ordinary, external consciousness.

Naturally, by the action of Grace, the veil may be suddenly rent from within, and at once you can enter the true truth; but even when that happens, in order to obtain the full value and full effect of the experience, you must maintain yourself in a state of inner receptivity, and to do that, it is indispensable for you to go within each day." (7)

2) For those who can make strong visual formations, the Mother recommends the following technique:

"To sit in meditation before a closed door, as though it were a heavy door of bronze — and one sits in front of it with the will that it may open — and to pass to the other side; and so the whole concentration, the whole aspiration is gathered into a beam and pushes, pushes, pushes against this door, and pushes more and more with an increasing energy until all of a sudden it bursts open and one enters. It makes a very powerful impression. And so one is as though plunged into the light and then one has the full enjoyment of a sudden and radical change of consciousness, with an illumination that captures one entirely, and the feeling that one is becoming another person. And this is a very concrete and powerful way of entering into contact with one's psychic being". (8)

3) For those who are more conceptual, the Mother suggests the following meditation:

"You must find the key.

Or you sit down in front of the door until you have found the word, the idea or the force which opens it –as in the *Arabian Nights* tales.

It is not a joke, it is very serious. You must sit down in front of the door and then concentrate until you have found the key or the word or the power to open it.

If one doesn't try, it doesn't open by itself. Perhaps after thousands of years, but you want to do it immediately, you must sit down *obstinately* before the door until you have found the means. It may be a key, it may be a word, it may be a force, it may be anything at all, and you remain there before the door until it opens.

And you do not think of anything else.

Only of the door". (9)

Of course, these exercises are only suggestions, for ultimately individuals have to find the way that works for them. Now, while the first effort of yoga is to develop and then maintain contact the psychic being, the second is to apply the power of the psychic being to change the daily functioning of the outer ego structure. This is a willed process that relies upon what Sri Aurobindo described as three psychic "movements" through which the psychic being acts to transform the outer mental, vital, and physical consciousness. He named these psychic movements as "aspiration, surrender and rejection," and for clinical purposes these must be distinguished from defense mechanisms, because they do not avoid, distort, displace, or disguise painful or negative mental/vital content in any way. Rather, psychic movements face such negative content *directly* and aim to transform it. In the following passage, Sri Aurobindo defined the yogic sense of these words:

> "The personal effort required is a triple labour of aspiration, rejection and surrender, —
>
> an aspiration vigilant, constant, unceasing — the mind's will, the heart's seeking, the assent of the vital being, the will to open and make plastic the physical consciousness and nature;
>
> rejection of the movements of the lower nature — rejection of the mind's ideas, opinions, preferences, habits, constructions, so that the true knowledge may find free room in a silent mind, — rejection of the vital nature's desires, demands, cravings, sensations, passions, selfishness, pride, arrogance, lust, greed, jealousy, envy, hostility to the Truth, so

that the true power and joy may pour from above into a calm, large, strong and consecrated vital being, — rejection of the physical nature's stupidity, doubt, disbelief, obscurity, obstinacy, pettiness, laziness, unwillingness to change, tamas, so that the true stability of Light, Power, Ananda may establish itself in a body growing always more divine;

surrender of oneself and all one is and has and every plane of the consciousness and every movement to the Divine and the Shakti." (10)

Evidently, to practice aspiration, surrender and rejection in the way Sri Aurobindo defines these terms is a tall order. Nevertheless, this discipline of consciousness stands behind much of human achievement in all fields of life, even if done in only a small and imperfect way, and the essence of integral yoga is to constantly and consciously seek to improve one's practice of these psychic movements. With regards to psychology, it bears noting that the famous 12 steps of addiction treatment map directly to aspiration, surrender, and rejection, as listed in Table 1. While it is true that most people who participate in 12-step treatments do so from a mental/ vital consciousness and do not have conscious contact with their psychic beings — it is also true that the 12 steps were inspired by an intuition of spiritual truth, and the authors have met individuals whose psychic beings saved them with the help of 12-step programs. (See Table 1)

Table 1: The 12 Steps of Alcoholics Anonymous

Aspiration

1. We admitted we were powerless over alcohol — that our lives had become unmanageable.

2. Came to believe that a Power greater than ourselves could restore us to sanity.

Surrender

3. Made a decision to turn our will and our lives over to the care of *God as we understood Him.*

4. Made a searching and fearless moral inventory of ourselves.

5. Admitted to God, ourselves, and to another human being the exact nature of our wrongs.

6. Were entirely ready to have God remove all these defects of character.

7. Humbly asked Him to remove our shortcomings.

Rejection

8. Made a list of all persons we had harmed, and became willing to make amends to them all.

9. Made direct amends to such people wherever possible, except when to do so would injure them or others.

10. Continued to take personal inventory and when we were wrong promptly admitted it.

Aspiration, Surrender and Rejection

11. Sought through prayer and meditation to improve our conscious contact with God as we understood Him, praying only for knowledge of His will for us and the power to carry it out.

12. Having had a spiritual awakening as the result of these steps, we tried to carry this message to alcoholics, and to practice these principles in all our affairs. (11)

Also, in clinical practice clients often use the functions of what psychodynamic theory calls the "observing ego" to witness, go into, and understand problematic aspects of thought, emotion and behavior. This can and does lead to positive changes in ego functioning, and the process can be deepened and extended to include ego transformation. For example, in contemporary psychotherapy much work is now done with mindfulness, meditation, mind-body therapies, and even subtle energetic techniques. While such work usually starts in the outer mental and vital consciousness, it can be deepened to include the inner being — and if pursued deeply enough, it can lead to people receiving intimations or even clear influences from their psychic beings. Thus, for practical purposes, the co-author has proposed that the standard hierarchy of ego functioning should be extended to include processes of ego

transformation with two levels of action: 1) therapeutic movements of the observing ego that lead to curative insight; and 2) the
psychic movements of aspiration, surrender and rejection. (See
Table 2)

Table 2. Hierarchy of Ego Functioning

I. Ego defense mechanisms (adapted from DSM-V and Vaillant,
1993)

Psychotic
Delusional projection
Denial
Distortion

Immature
Projection
Fantasy
Hypochondriasis
Passive aggression
Acting out
Dissociation

Intermediate (Neurotic)
Displacement
Isolation/Intellectualization
Repression
Reaction formation

Mature
Altruism
Sublimation
Suppression
Anticipation
Humor

II. Ego transformational processes

Therapeutic movements
Observing ego
(e.g. witnessing, going into, understanding)

Psychic (soul) movements
Aspiration
Surrender
Rejection (12)

Finally, since developing sound judgment and will-power are important in CBP — and are executive elements of the psychic movement of rejection — following are two practices to help with willpower:

1. In conventional practice, concentrating on the centre or chakra between the eyebrows strengthens the will. However if a concomitant replacement of the ego by the deeper soul-principle (psychic being) is not effectuated, an isolated development of will-power can make one egoistic and arrogant. Thus, a less risky and yet still integral approach is to invoke the Divine Will to take up the individual will and subjugate it to its workings. Instead of concentrating to increase the individual will-power, one expands the space between the brows to link oneself with the Cosmic Will and the Transcendent Will. Thus, instead of the movement of a somewhat forceful concentration in the brow centre, one expands and surrenders to the Divine Will to become an instrument for its workings.

2. Another powerful exercise that increases will power, links one with deeper energies, and demonstrates the power of subtle senses (which need subtle-energy for execution) is as follows: The subject is guided to a relaxed state, and is then told to imagine a piece of white paper where a pen writes his or her name. One has to hold the name to see it at one go. This is difficult as letters have a habit of running away. Once

the name has been consolidated in imagination, the therapist asks the subject to fill the empty space on the white paper with as many flowers as one can. One is then told to pluck one flower and touch its parts very softly and delicately. One is also asked to carefully touch the thorns in the stem if there are any. Finally, the subject is told to take a deep breath and smell the flower if the flower has a fragrance. One then puts the flower back to the place from where it was plucked and sits in a relaxed state.

This last exercise is modified from a standard psychosynthetic technique, and can be creatively adapted in many ways. Surprisingly, most subjects can actually smell the fragrance. When this exercise is coupled with breath-work and widening of consciousness, one can have some access to the deeper energies for rejuvenating oneself. Note that an extra benefit can be obtained by conveying the psychological significance of the flower, as described by the Mother. (13)

Opening to the Shakti

Another central practice in CBP is to open to a "Force" over the head that descends into the whole system and guides the opening of the chakras in its own time and sequence, as noted in Chapter 14. Sri Aurobindo uses the word "Force" in his letters on yoga, because it is the English translation of the Sansrkit term *Shakti*. This Shakti has many levels or layers of formulation and action, and one of Sri Aurobindo's great contributions to psycho-spiritual practice was to describe how to open to this Force from above downwards, rather than vice versa. From the perspective of CBP, many spiritual and subtle-energy practices converge inwardly in that they can open and connect one to what Sri Aurobindo called the Pranic Shakti. He elaborated the characteristics and potentialities of the Pranic Shakti as follows:

First, the Universal Energy (Shakti) that pervades the worlds is represented in the inner or subliminal being of the individual as specialized formulation, the Pranic Shakti. All the energy-systems operating in the surface personality of the individual are derivations of the central Pranic Shakti. The Pranic Shakti:

> "supports and fills the body and supplies all the physical and vital activities, -- for the physical energy is only a modified form of this force, -- and supplies and sustains too from below all our mental action. This force we feel in ourselves also, but we can feel it too around us and above, one with the same energy in us, and can draw it in and down to aggrandise our normal action or call upon and get it to pour into us." (14)

Second, the Pranic Shakti can be harnessed for its therapeutic potentials:

> "This pranic force we can use we can use for any of the activities of life, body or mind with a far greater or effective power than any that we command in our present operations, limited as they are by the physical formula. The use of the pranic power liberates us from that limitation to the extent of our ability to use it in place of the body-bound energy. It can be used so to direct the prana (life-energy) as to manage more powerfully or to rectify any bodily state or action, as to heal illness or to get rid of fatigue, and to liberate an enormous amount of mental exertion and play of will or knowledge... The pranic Shakti can be directed not only upon ourselves, but effectively towards others or on things or happenings for whatever purposes the will dictates." (15)

Third, the Pranic Shakti can be activated not only through physical techniques of yoga practices but also by psychological measures as well as through consciousness-based spiritual approaches:

> "The exercises of Pranayama are the familiar mechanical means of freeing and getting control of the pranic energy. They heighten too and set free the psychic, mental and spiritual energies which ordinarily depend for their opportunity

of action on the pranic force. But the same thing can be done by mental will and practice or by an increasing opening of ourselves to a higher spiritual power of the Shakti." (16)

Thus both behavioural and psychotherapeutic techniques can be creatively designed to tap the potentials of the Pranic Shakti. Fourth, the universal Shakti is represented in the individual not only by the Pranic Shakti at the level of the subliminal or inner being but also at a higher plane of consciousness by:

"a pure mental energy which is a higher formulation of the Shakti." (17) This higher mental energy is not available ordinarily in its purity as it is too mixed up with the pranic energy; it has to be cultivated through a consciousness paradigm of psychological growth which leads to a poise "above the physical mind." (18) This higher mental energy "can be made to act upon the pranic energy and can impose upon it the influence, colour, shape, character, direction of our ideas, our knowledge, our more enlightened volition and thus more effectively bring our life and vital being into harmony with our higher powers of being, ideals and spiritual aspirations." (19)

The higher mental energy surpassing the Pranic Shakti is itself surpassed by yet higher superconscient powers of the Spirit:

"And we are aware soon of a far higher power of the Spirit and its Shakti concealed or above, superconscient to mind or partially acting through the mind, of which all this is an inferior derivation." (20)

Thus, if the cultivation of the Pranic Shakti brings harmony into living systems and displays therapeutic benefits, the tapping of the higher ranges of the Shakti leads one along the trajectory of a growth in consciousness.

> *A power is in thee thou knowest not;*
> *Thou art a vessel of the imprisoned spark.*
>
> Savitri, *pg. 453*

References

1. Basu,S: The Synthesis of Eastern and Western psychological paradigms in the Light of Sri Aurobindo.Indian Journal of Social Psychiatry, Vol.11(1),1995,pg 35-39

2. Evening Talks, pg. 208

3. CWSA 28, pg. 205

4. CWSA 23-24, pg. 651

5. CWM 04, pp. 139-140

6. Huppes, Neeltje: Psychic Education – a workbook, based on the writings of Sri Aurobindo and The Mother, Sri Aurobindo Education Society, New Delhi, 2001.

7. CWM 10, pg. 19-20

8. CWM 07, pg. 268

9. CWM 08, pg. 144

10. CWSA 32, pg. 6

11. Miovic, Mi-chael: Integral Yoga Psychology: Clinical Correlations, IJTP,37(1), 2018, pg. 199-225

12. Miovic, M: Integral Yoga Psychology: Clinical Correlations in Integral Yoga Psychology: Metaphysics & Transformation as Taught by Sri Aurobindo, edited by Debahsish Banerji, Lotus Press, Wisconsin, 2020, pg. 363-402.

13. The Mother: Flowers and their Messages, Sri Aurobindo Ashram, Pondicherry, 4th Ed, 1992

14. CWSA 23-24, pg,755

15. Ibid, pg. 755-756

16. Ibid, pg. 756

17. Ibid

18. Ibid, pg, 757

19. Ibid, pg. 756-757

20. Ibid, pg. 757

13
Dreams and Visions

Vision and dream were fables spoken by truth
Or symbols more veridical than fact,
Or were truths enforced by supernatural seals.

Savitri, pg. 30

CBP has much to offer the study of dreams and visions. In yogic terms, during sleep the inner consciousness lets go of the egocentric awareness of the outer being and is free to range through other realms. Dreaming is thus an important gateway to the other levels of reality beyond the physical reality perceived by our outer senses, and Sri Aurobindo spoke of the correspondence between dreams and outer life as follows:

> "It is a mistake to think that we live physically only, with the outer mind and life. We are all the time living and acting on other planes of consciousness, meeting others there and acting upon them, and what we do and feel and think there, the forces we gather, the results we prepare have an incalculable importance and effect, unknown to us upon our outer life. Not all of it comes through, and what comes through takes another form in the physical – though sometimes there is an exact correspondence; but this little is at the basis of our outward existence. All that we become and do and bear in the physical life is prepared behind the veil within us. It is therefore of immense importance for a Yoga which aims at the transformation of life to grow conscious of what goes on within these domains, to be master there and be able to feel, know and deal with the secret forces that determine our destiny and our internal and external growth or decline". (1)

Because dreams can arise from many different planes of consciousness and parts of the being, in CBP the same symbol can have different meanings at different planes of consciousness, and at different points in time. Thus, a dream symbol has to be interpreted in consonance with the poise of the dreamer in the hierarchy or holarchy of consciousness. For instance, the energy symbolized by the snake is usually considered to be libidinal in conventional dream-interpretation. In CBP the snake can symbolize such vital forces, but under certain mental conditions it can also symbolize mental ill-will (2), while at yet higher planes of consciousness snakes can represent some luminous or divine energy (3), or even the serpentine power (kundalini) of universal evolution. (4) Here is an example of this from the author's clinical practice:

> A 25 year old single woman who held a post-graduate degree in Yoga presented with a dysthymic mood, which she related to the inconveniences she faced due to her uterine fibroids. She had an obsessive personality and her reaction to her fibroids appeared exaggerated. It was difficult for her to go beyond the clutches of the physical mind. She had a marked anger against her mother, on whom she said she was too psychologically dependent. She was not fully comfortable talking about her relationship with a man, which she kept downplaying. She revealed that on and off she dreamt of snakes, especially green snakes and that she had, in her own words, a "perverse attraction" to snakes. She simultaneously detested snakes and felt attracted to them. Obviously, these snakes represented both libidinal energy at the vital-physical and forces of ill-will that disturbed her mental equilibrium. She was told that as a yoga expert, she should desist from awakening the Kundalini power from below upwards, as she would be unable to handle the forces that were unleashed. Instead, it would be safer to open herself to the Transcendent Shakti and allow it to work in her system. She immediately resisted this suggestion, as she said she could not differentiate between the Transcendent Shakti and her biological mother, whom she both loved and detested. This resistance proved that the snakes she dreamt also signified mental ill-will. She had to be counseled to differentiate her biological mother

from the Transcendent Force.

However, snakes can symbolize other things as well, and this is just one example. Here is a second case of dream symbolism interpreted from the perspective of CBP:

An 18 year old boy who was studying in an European medical school was brought to his hometown in India after he was found to be skipping classes and not responding to phone calls from home for over two months.

On clinical examination, he complained of extreme lethargy bordering on depression, with evening exacerbations. He was not sure if he could continue his medical career or if he should shift to some other discipline like engineering. Though he was studying in a foreign country, he did not seem to suffer from any type of culture shock. He felt no relief on coming home. He had a difficult family background with marked parental discord and a somewhat hostile attitude on the part of his elder brother, who was suffering from a clinical profile of obsession and paranoia and rarely moved from his rooms. His mother was an atheist and was always bubbling with energy, as compared to the listlessness and lethargy of both her sons. His father was an intellectual with a spiritual inclination and was a technocrat of repute, but took queer decisions at times that disrupted family bonding.

During an interactive session, the youngster revealed to the therapist a dream he had never shared with his family. When he was barely 10 years old, and in his fifth standard at school, he dreamt of being trapped by unseen forces. He finally managed to escape and board a car but the car got stuck! He felt like he was trapped in the crossroads. The dream was so vivid that he always remembered it and now when his life was really stuck at crossroads, he felt that the dream had come true.

Shortly after his dream, a series of unfavourable life events began to unroll. His maternal uncle, with whom he was closely associated, had an unnatural death, probably murdered. He himself had recovered from caries spine. There were huge disputes about ancestral properties. His father had such severe differences with his mother that he would shortly be out of the home for few years. His elder brother bore the full brunt of parental discord and he started showing behavioral problems that finally resulted in the clinical picture of obsession, pain syndrome and paranoia.

Now, normally a psychotherapist working with such a youngster would naturally focus on resolving complexes arising from parental discord, sibling rivalry, the brother's illness behavior and his predicament in an foreign culture. However, a therapeutic intervention could also be done in a different way through dream-work. The client himself gave prime importance to the childhood dream, and the dream had indeed contained a message and a warning: it was as if it was ordained that he would be trapped in the crossroads of life one day. Thus, a psychotherapist working with the CBP perspective could take the opportunity to draw up a counselling programme based on dream-work. The therapeutic programme is based on the premise that any disharmony, even an illness, offers an opportunity for a progress in consciousness. In this case, the fact that the car got stuck in crossroads was a warning of a situation in life where escape would be denied. However, the dream also contained a hidden message: the car symbolized movement, and movement means progress. If one could not move mechanically, one could still move through consciousness. This was the opportunity given to the dreamer, a reason why he was stuck not in a closed room but in a car. If one could learn the technique of progressing through matrices of consciousness and force, knowledge and will-power, the car would become the vehicle of progress. Thus, instead of focusing on the past, the therapist-client duo could focus on the future and the growth of the psychic being. Instead of focusing on the dynamics of the unconscious, they could focus on the dynamics of progress.

These two cases suggest the wide range of ways in which dream symbols can be approached in CBP, and many more are possible as well. Indeed, in a revealing conversation the Mother explained how variable the dream symbols can be:

"Basically, to tell the truth, everyone has his own symbolism. And for myself, I have seen that it depended on the periods in my life, on the activities, on the degree of development. There are things I see again now in which I see another meaning, which was behind the meaning I had seen.
It's very interesting, but it belongs entirely to the domain of relativity.

It's very mental.

I remember, for instance, there was a time when I used to see people in the form of animals!...It was the indication of the type of nature they belonged to. And I remember, when I was still in France, having one day seen (I was sitting in a large room) hosts of small animals coming, especially rabbits, cats, dogs, all kinds of animals, birds; they kept coming and coming, all of them onto my knees! And there were hosts and hosts of them...And there suddenly entered the room a big tiger, which rushed at them all and vrff! sent them scurrying off in all directions! But the animals were people...and the tiger, too, was someone.

It's amusing.

But now I see that there are superimposed depths: you have one symbolism, then deeper, there's another symbolism. And ultimately, all form is a symbol. All forms: our form [the human form] is a symbol — not a very brilliant one, I admit!" (5)

Elaborating further on the difficulty of interpreting dreams, the Mother stated:

"They are more difficult to interpret, since each person has his own world of dream-imagery peculiar to himself. Of course, there are dreams that do not signify much, those that are connected with the most superficial and physical layer of consciousness, those that are the result of stray thoughts, random impressions, mechanical reactions or reflex activities. These have no regular or organized form and shape and meaning; they are hardly remembered and leave almost no trace in the consciousness. But even dreams that have a somewhat deeper origin are still obscure, since they are peculiarly personal, in this sense that they depend for their make-up almost entirely upon the experience and idiosyncrasies of the individual. Visions also are made up of symbols that do not necessarily obtain universal currency. The symbols vary according to race and tradition and religion. One symbol may be peculiarly Christian, another peculiarly Hindu, a third may be common to all the East and a fourth only to the West. Dreams, on the other hand, are exclusively personal; they depend upon everyday occurrences and impressions. It is exceedingly difficult for one man to explain or interpret another's dream. Each man is like a closed circle to every other man. But everyone can study for himself his own dreams, unravel them and find out their meaning". (6)

As the Mother explains here, dream content can come from many different planes of consciousness, and sometimes it may be more useful to simply identify the plane of consciousness involved than to try to unravel the complexities of specific symbols and imagery. For example, dreams from the subconscious can be used as sort of personal barometer for psychological growth; they point out the sources of our fears and insecurities, lapses and defects; they point out the fallacy of taking what has been achieved in waking life for granted, by showing that what has been "done" can be "undone" at any moment; and they reinforce "how obstinately the subconscious retains what has been settled and done within the upper layers of the consciousness." As such, dreams from the subconscious "enable us to pursue things to their obscure roots…and excise them." (7)

The physical mind is a plane of the mental consciousness that deals with sensory schemata as divorced from the influence of the will and reason, and dissociated from the intellectual faculty. As such, dreams originating from the physical mind reprint the chaotic state of the physical world as we perceive it. The physical world per se is not chaotic, but our sensory perception of it is chaotic because senses give us an impressionistic view that may be more phenomenal than real (like the sensory information that the sun rotates around the world which is phenomenally correct but in reality incorrect). Sri Aurobindo wrote,

> "The dreams of the physical mind are an incoherent jumble made up partly of responses to vague touches from the physical world round which the lower mind-faculties disconnected from the will and reason, the buddhi, weave a web of wandering phantasy, partly of disordered associations from the brain-memory, partly of reflections from the soul travelling on the mental plane, reflections which are, ordinarily, received without intelligence or co-ordination, wildly distorted in the reception and mixed up confusedly with the other dream-elements, with brain-memories and fantastic responses to any sensory touch from the physical world". (8)

Dreams of the vital plane ordinarily transcript the turbulences of the vital mind, whose formations can try to influence the mind (though one can work upon them to nullify this influence). However, the inner vital being can enter the vital worlds, can impart a sensation of floating in the air, (9) and can activate adverse forces to invade the mind with disturbing dreams. Moreover, as the vital plane is the repository of contradictory emotions, vital dreams can contain both pleasant and unpleasant experiences together. (10) As the vital plane is closest to the physical consciousness, dreams of the vital plane are vividly remembered. (11) Usually, in dreams of the vital plane,

> "the figures of the physical life take another form and meaning and the consciousness that lives and acts among them is not the outer physical consciousness but some inner vital part of the being." (12)

Very often, dreams on the vital plane are "merely formations, thoughts or feelings put into shape"; thoughts that not only belong to the subject "but those of others also or things floating in the atmosphere." (13) At times the dreams of the vital plane are:

"formations of the obscure lower-vital consciousness; they are made up of its desires, instincts and subconscious memories, all jumbled together to weave an incoherent dream-scene and dream-story and, in this case, used by some vital Desire-Force of that plane…They have no other value…than to show you vividly what is there in your lower vital nature, whether awake on the surface or lying in wait in the subconscient parts. The only thing to do with them is to turn the Light upon those parts and call on the Divine Power to expunge them from nature. It is perfectly easy for this Desire-Force or for the subliminal part of the mind to create images of anyone it pleases or to reproduce the voice and make him or her speak or act in any way convenient to it". (14)

The inner or subliminal being of developed subjects can get connected with the cosmic consciousness and dreams emanating from there are akin to universal recorders, carrying messages from collective suggestions, universal archetypal symbolizations, universal rhythms of arts and music as well as signals of universal catastrophes. It requires great knowledge, tact and discrimination to interpret these dreams. They often point out universal obstacles to be crossed as well as universal ideals to be pursued. It is a dream from the cosmic consciousness that led to the unraveling of the collective unconscious by Jung. Jung's collective unconscious is a part of the cosmic consciousness which is in continuity with the individual consciousness. The cosmic consciousness per se is, however, much vaster than Jung's concept of the collective unconscious; it extends to supra-physical worlds that contain non-evolutionary beings as well. Dream formations can arise from such forces and beings which:

"need not become true in the physical world, but they may still have effects on the physical if they are framed with that purpose or that tendency and, if they are allowed, they may realize their events or their meaning – for they are most often symbolic or schematic – in the inner or the outer life". (15)

Finally, there are dreams originating from higher intuitive ranges of consciousness to which we can gain access through our subliminal or inner being. These dreams are of a different quality: they are not chaotic, fragmentary or obscure. Instead, such dreams are veridical, clear, and have no ambiguity. They often transmit creative ideas and actually such dreams have led to great scientific discoveries (as the dream-symbol of a snake eating its own tail gave the idea of the benzene ring). They have also led to great works of creativity as well as significant metaphysical theories. Often such intuitive dreams have saved life and also carried remedies for cure of illness. At times, they have carried divine messages, too. Intuitive dreams often carry premonitions that actually happen in the future,

> "dreams that are fulfilled immediately…and premonitory dreams that are fulfilled over varying lengths of time. And according to their position in time, these dreams are seen on various planes". (16)

However, one must have a highly developed consciousness to get the full significance of intuitive dreams. If one is not trained at intuitive discrimination, one may miss the significance or dilute the meaning with subconscious elaborations. One can also have premonitions of all important psychological events that are to take place in waking hours.

Visions

Visions are different from dreams and are understood in CBP as experiential revelations perceived by the inner or subliminal senses in the inner or subtle-physical, though their origin may be at different supra-physical planes of consciousness. In other words, a vision is a direct perception from a supraphysical plane of consciousness — like seeing something with one's physical eyes, only in the case of vision the eyes and the vision are supraphysical. Subjects can visualize lights or subtle beings, hear mantras or church-bells, and have other experiences of clairvoyance and clairaudience. One can have visions in the waking state, during meditation and in trance states. One can also have visions during dream-states. In the transformational yoga of Sri Aurobindo, the descent of light and power from the superconscient ranges is often accompanied by supra-physical visions and revelations. The symbolic value of such visions is different from that of the Jungian archetypes. Jung constructed archetypes from dream experiences found recurring in myths, while Sri Aurobindo explained visions as yogic experiences which are independent of myths, though at times these can be corroborated with myths. (17) As he explained,

> "This faculty of sensing supra-physical things internally or externalizing them, so to speak, so that they become visible, audible, sensible to the outward eye, ear, even touch, just as are gross physical objects, this power or gift is not a freak or an abnormality; it is a universal faculty present in all human beings, but latent in most, in some rarely or intermittently active, occurring as if by accident in others, frequent or normally active in a few. But just as anyone can, with some training, learn science and do things which would have seemed miracles to his forefathers, so almost anyone, if he wants, can with a little concentration and training develop the faculty of supraphysical vision". (18)

> "Further, vision is of value because it is often a first key to inner planes of one's own being or one's own consciousness as distinguished from worlds or planes of the cosmic consciousness". (19)

The inner vision "does not come as easily to intellectuals as it does to men with a strong life-power or the emotional and the imaginative. It is true that the field of vision, like every other field of activity of the human mind, is a mixed world and there is in it not only truth but much half-truth and error. It is also true that for the rash and unwary to enter into it may bring confusion and misleading inspiration and false voices…One must look at this field calmly and with discrimination, but to shut the gates and reject this or other supra-physical experiences is to limit oneself and arrest the inner development".(20)

Visions are not hallucinations and do not represent psychosis. The supra-physical contains a hierarchy of planes, and visions can be generated from a wide array of such planes : "they come from the subtle physical, the vital, the mental, the psychic or from planes above the Mind. (21) S.P. Singh has given an insightful elaboration on three classes of visions described by Sri Aurobindo, and different these from Jungian archetypes:

"Subtle-physical visions are related to events of the gross physical world. They are visions particularly in the sense of reflecting future events of the gross world through the subtle body. They are not obstructed by the spatial barrier either. That is why distant objects and events are reflected in the form of vision in the inner being of the individual. These visions are related with subtle causal form of events and objects which is universal at this stage and lies awaiting concretization in the future. This viewpoint may very well explain the element of futurity in Jungian visions and archetypes". (22)

Actually, whatever manifests in the physical has antecedents in the subtle-physical. Such antecedents can be glimpsed through visions even before the actual physical manifestation.

"The second class of Aurobindonian visions is related with the vital world which is called the "intermediate zone". Beings of this zone pose various problems…They assume the role of the teacher or guide. They may also disguise themselves as gods or goddesses. This is what we find also in some of the Jungian archetypes. They also appear as divine or demoniac beings. Thus the Jungian gods are not real gods. They are only beings of the "intermediate zone" appearing as gods in disguise". (23)

And finally,

> "Sri Aurobindo associates the third class of visions with the mental world. This world has cosmic Mind for its substance in the same way as our visible world has Matter or the vital world has Life for its substance. As the mental world is formed by way of descent of the supramental towards the world of Matter, it naturally tends to get its fulfilment through participation in the affairs of our world. As our (individual) mind is derived from the world of (cosmic) Mind, the latter seeks the participation through its derivative. Thus, when the (individual) mind gets cleared of the clouds of physicality and vitality, it becomes receptive to impacts, visions and beings of the world of (cosmic) Mind. It is these beings that have been regarded as gods and goddesses in the Vedas". (24)

In other words, non-evolutionary formations in the world of cosmic Mind can be perceived as gods and goddesses in visions. At planes below the cosmic Mind, these beings could be perceived in modified forms or as constellation of forces at the level of ordinary mental functioning and Singh suggests that Jungian archetypes of "mandala" and "mother" may represent such reconstitutions. (25) Also, gods and goddesses in the cosmic Mind can appear in a plethora of forms and have been perceived in many cultural traditions. Thus, one may have visions of them not only in Vedic or later Hindu forms, but in the form of Greek, Mayan, Buddhist, and other cultural traditions. The Mother noted,

> "To what you see you give the form of that what you expect to see….You have the vision of one in India whom you call the Divine Mother, the Catholics say it is the Virgin Mary, and the Japanese call it Kwannon, the Goddess of Mercy, and others would give other names. It is the same Force, the same Power, but the images made of it are different in different faiths". (26)

Finally, it is important to understand that having visions does not necessarily indicate spiritual progress, as this ability rather reveals the depths and ranges of one's subliminal consciousness. Sri Aurobindo explained,

"Visions do not come from the spiritual plane... What comes from the spiritual plane are experiences of the Divine, e.g. the experience of Self everywhere, of the Divine in all, etc. (27) Moreover, "vision in dream is more difficult to distinguish from a vivid dream-experience, but one gets to feel the difference". (28)

Visions can also be false in the sense that they can represent mere thoughts or images remembered by the mind and not reflect anything other than imaginative mental formations. The Mother further added that it requires a great clarity of intellect to interpret a particular vision:

"It is only those that can go beyond beliefs and faiths and myths and traditions who are able to say what it really is; but these are few, very few. You must be free from every mental construction, you must divest yourself of all that is merely local or temporal, before you can know what you have seen". (29)

The universe is an endless masquerade:
For nothing here is utterly what it seems;
It is a dream-fact vision of a truth
Which but for the dream would not be wholly true...

Savitri, *pg. 61*

References

1. CWSA 30, pg. 217-218
2. Agenda VI, pg. 124
3. CWSA 30, pg. 170
4. Agenda VI, pg. 124-125

5. Ibid, pg. 125

6. CWM 3, pg. 14

7. CWSA 31, pg.. 459

8. CWSA 23-24, pg. 521-522

9. CWSA 31, pg. 461

10. Ibid, pg. 467

11. Ibid, pg. 460

12. Ibid, pg. 462

13. Ibid, pg. 466

14. Ibid, pg. 466-467

15. Ibid, pg. 457

16. CWM 10, pg. 123

17. Singh SP: Sri Aurobindo and Jung, Madhucchandas Publications, Aligarh,1986, pg. 76

18. CWSA 30, pg. 89

19. Ibid, pg. 92

20. Ibid, pg. 95

21. Ibid, pg. 87

22. Op. cit. Sri Aurobindo and Jung, pg. 73

23. Ibid, pg. 73-74

24. Ibid, pg. 74

25. Ibid

26. CWM 3, pg. 18

27. CWSA 30, pg. 87-88

28. Ibid, pg. 101

29. CWM 3, pg. 17

14
The Mental Consciousness

"O Savitri, from thy hidden soul we come.
We are the messengers, the occult gods
Who help man's drab and heavy ignorant lives
To wake to beauty and the wonder of things
Touching them with glory and divinity:
In evil we light the deathless flame of good
And hold the torch of knowledge on ignorant roads;
We are thy will and all men's will towards Light."

Savitri, pg. 501

What we call the mind represents a consciousness that is basically non-local though it needs the brain for its expression. The mind is represented through different strata of consciousness. As previously explained, Sri Aurobindo and the Mother described an interfusion of consciousness-force among the chakras, leading to the physical, vital, and mental planes of consciousness influencing each other. Thus, the *physical mind* is the stratum of the mental consciousness that is enmeshed in sensory schemata. The *vital mind* is that stratum which modulates emotions, passions and dynamism. The *mind proper* is the realm of ideas and reason, of cognition and imagination. It is the mind that plans and designs, works out strategies and projects its workings into the future. It is the mind that creates and manifests. It produces the rationalist, the logician, the thinker, the artist, the atheist, the agonistic, the believer, the conformist, the moralist as well as the rebel, the anarchist, the dissenter, the revolutionary. If it produces the scientist and mathematician, it also produces the poet, the philosopher and the musician. Indeed, it is the mind proper that makes the human being the most unique of all created forms in the earthly manifestation.

Willpower at the level of the mind proper is different from willpower operating at the level of the vital mind. As Sri

Aurobindo explained,

> "The vital mind is an impulse first and thought afterwards. It is, you can say, force first and thought afterwards. For instance, desire — if deprived of the element of "desire" — is an impulse or force going out or trying to realize itself. While mental will is the will connected with thought. It is primarily a thought-force. Every thought has its will." (1)

It is very natural therefore that deficiencies, disruptions, deviations and distortions of the mental functioning can lead to psychopathologies that can have repercussions in multiple areas of life. For a full flowering of mental abilities, a systematic education is needed, and the knowledge base required for this is contained in sum cultural knowledge evolved by human beings around the globe and across time. Thus, in order for the mind to develop its full potential, a truly global culture is needed.

One of the most important limitations of ordinary mental functioning is the preferential importance given to certain ideas to the exclusion of ideas that carry opposite significance. The individual mind normally prefers ideas that are in consonance with one's culture, temperament, education, belief-system and upbringing. This preference allows the mind to continuously raise counter-arguments, draws the mind to debate and to construct anti-thesis to counter thesis but fails to effectuate synthesis. Ideational preferences can lead to prejudices, biases and faulty judgment.

In some instances, the preferential importance to a set of ideas may be so driven by passion at the expense of reason that the result is a world-view centered on exclusivism and overvalued ideas. Such idiosyncratic overvalued ideas may not be considered to be completely psychopathological or indices of psychiatric illness, or they may be construed as lying on the borderline between normality and abnormality. However, such overvalued ideas can have dramatic and sometimes dangerous repercussions in social life. Overvalued ideas can dominate religion, shape politics, fashion cults, impose wrong theories in any field (even in science), and lead to fanaticism and fundamentalism. All such exclusive mental idea fall short of the integrative view which is required to perfect mental functioning. The Mother explained that the New Consciousness must surpass exclusivism:

> "The bankruptcy of religions was because they were divided – they wanted you to follow one religion to the exclusion of all others. And all human knowledge has gone bankrupt because it was exclusive…The step forward humanity must take immediately is a definitive cure of exclusivism." (2)

In some instances, overvalued ideas may get exaggerated and distorted to the point of producing delusions, which may or may not be associated with passions and emotions. An overvalued idea results from a purportedly logical extension of one's idiosyncratic way of thinking, while the subject yet remains rooted in reality and in consonance with the subject's socio-cultural and educational milieu. In contrast, a delusion is an aberrant occurrence in which the subject loses contact with reality and is not in consonance with one's education and socio-cultural background. A delusion may be entirely irrational, impervious to logical correction, and may even turn out to be bizarre, macabre or sinister, and have horrendous ramifications. However, such usual views of delusion are descriptive but not explanatory, and the significance of the irrationality characteristic of delusion remains unexplored. Perhaps at the level of the ordinary mental functioning, this answer may always remain elusive — both because thoughts invade us from outside, and because we are not trained to pursue non-linear thinking. Presumably, the possibility of delusional thinking would be reduced if people were taught from an early age to develop non-linear thinking, in which the rational mind is surpassed to reach what Sri Aurobindo called the Higher Mind (Chapter 8), which is capable of mass ideation and which can simultaneously hold contradictory and complementary ideas without chaos and confusion. With the rise in radicalization of youth by fundamentalist zealots, mental health has to widen its scope. A program in personal growth that leads to a developing of the faculties of the Higher Mind can allow the equal appreciation of contradictory ideas. Children could be trained to think simultaneously with alternative ideas of the same topic. A sort of lateral thinking is now acknowledged to enhance creativity but something more is needed. One has to train oneself to be unbiased towards one's own alternative set of ideas. This would make them capable of unbiased thinking and would counter exclusivism and improve the mental health of the community at large. True, this cannot be conducted en masse, but even if selective minds are addressed, the message would spread.

Another important limitation of mental functioning is the chasm between knowledge and will. In ordinary mental life, knowledge is not integrated with will. A person may be very knowledgeable but might not have the will to manifest the knowledge in reality so that ideas remain utopian and the personality remains bookish. Likewise, a person may have an indefatigable will that is not backed by an optimal knowledge base. In fact, the gap between knowledge and will has resulted in inappropriate handling of many social, political and administrative issues affecting public life. At the psychological level, the rift between knowledge and will is demonstrated when a sensible person cannot control his or her anger (as in intermittent explosive disorder), or when a depressed intellectual cannot muster enough motivation to do productive work.

However, the most important limitation of the current consensus understanding of mental functioning is our failure to appreciate the yogic insight that the mind does not produce thoughts or manufacture ideas, but rather acts as a receiving and transmitting station. The great value of meditation is that it can help people to develop a witnessing consciousness from which the mind can be observed and its true nature and function discovered.

Disturbances of the Physical Mind

Clinically, disturbances of the physical mind (which is enmeshed in sensory schemata) are often demonstrated in obsessive spectrum disorders, while disturbances of the vital mind (which modulates mood, emotions and dynamism) are evident in mood disorders. Following is a case involving the physical mind:

A 20 year old young man suffered from compulsive masturbation, which pre-occupied him throughout the day. In addition to this, he had a calendar memory for the last six years since he started to masturbate. Ask him any date of any year within the last six years, and he can vividly recall the number of times he masturbated that day. It is now recognized that such a personal mental calendar is an automatic and obsessive process and difficult to explain based on neurobiology. As such cases are usually very difficult to treat, an understanding in terms of consciousness can provide clues to help guide treatment.

In terms of consciousness, both OCD (Obsessive compulsive disorder) and calendar memory can be traced to the physical mind. It is that part of the mind which is enmeshed in sensory schemata and is thus at the lowest end of the mind-range. It ruminates on habitual and trivial thoughts that are usually related to life's ordinary pre-occupations, and it has a nethermost part that Sri Aurobindo called the mechanical mind, which automatically repeats content like a machine. Typically, the physical mind deals with primitive behaviours and not with intellectual stuff. The physical mind is that part of the mind-range closest to the Inconscience.

The repetitive and habitual patterns of the physical mind arise de novo as an intrinsic property of the physical mind and cannot be explained by the psychoanalytic theory of resurgence of repressed material. CBP recognizes the resurgence of repressed materials but such repressions represent material usually rejected from planes of consciousness above the physical mind. The habitual patterns of the physical mind can be better explained by the principle of automaticity, which is now used to explain most of the operations of executive dysfunction in ADHD. Note that this principle of automaticity has to be differentiated from the phenomenon of pathological automatism where acts are performed involuntarily in an unconscious manner, as in somnambulism or temporal lobe epilepsy (or even hypoglycemia). These latter phenomenon demonstrate an episodic time-span of automatic behaviour which is invariably brief and followed by normal behaviour. In contrast, the principle of automaticity is exhibited in conscious states and not as episodic patterns but as chronic, persistent, repetitive and often pervasive patterns. It is only in the beginning of 21st century that the principle of automaticity is being recognized in psychology as an alternative explanation for habitual behaviours that cannot be adequately explained by resurgence of repressed material, though Sri Aurobindo dwelt on it a century ago and explained how evolution began with a blind "automatism of Matter" resulting in a obscure harmony of a limited type of existence and action (3).

It is also interesting to note that OCD is now no longer being explained in psychoanalytic terms. Instead, the principle of automaticity is being traced to brain circuits regulating primitive aspects of behavior (such as aggression, sexuality, bodily excretions), to neuro transmitters and to gene mutations. It is true that in a subset of OCD subjects, stress and traumatic events are present in the background, but it might be that they are not prime causative factors, rather, OCD subjects may be more vulnerable to these influences. Moreover, OCD subjects do not appreciably respond to psychoanalysis or depth psychotherapy, but do better with CBT, medications, and in extreme cases, psychosurgery. From the consciousness perspective, all of these treatments are closer to the physical plane of consciousness than depth psychotherapy, which touches more on the vital.

Note that in OCD there is an ideational as well as an action component, whereas in other obsessive spectrum disorders like trichotillomania, and in most of other habit disorders like tics or torticollis, there is no ideational component but only mechanically recurrent habitual movements which are even more refractory to behavioural interventions. These disorders arise from the mechanical mind, which is the lowest level of the physical mind.

Finally, there are a host of other significant problems associated with the physical mind which do not manifest as OCD spectrum disorders. One troublesome attribute of the physical mind is that it exhibits slow arousal, unlike the emotional mind or intellectual mind that can respond quickly to stimulation. The phenomenon of slow arousal leads to dysfunctional attempts to "wake up" the consciousness with coarse forms of stimulation, such as sadism and masochism (4). This is also the reason why subjects who are idle and lazy need to be stimulated with strong, spicy foods, and cinematic scenes of violence or pornography. At the extreme, this is why certain individuals engage in physical or sexual violence in real life, or commit serial murders — it is all an attempt to stimulate the drowse of the physical mind. The physical consciousness is also marked by passivity resulting in chronicity of ailments and the state of "helplessness". Thus "helplessness" that manifests in a perceived absence of control over the outcome of a situation arises not only as a "learned behaviour" in the terms in which Seligman and his colleagues described but also as an intrinsic property of physical consciousness marked by inertia.

In terms of treatment, any type of physical exercise is the first CBP step in overcoming the inertia of the physical consciousness. However, since the mind can go on ruminating (mechanically repeating thoughts) even during exercise, for such cases it may be more helpful to engage in exercises that require the mind and body to work together, such as table tennis, lawn tennis, squash, golf, martial arts, etc.

Psychotherapeutic Interventions at the Mental Plane

The individual mind is like a station that receives, records and transmits ideas in consonance with its temperament, culture, education, upbringing, preferences, indoctrination and milieu. Consequently, psychotherapeutic techniques at the mental plane are multiple and varied and it is difficult to conceive of a tailor-made technique that would be suitable for all types of minds. Even where a technique is suitable, it is doubtful how long can it survive the onslaught of time and the change of cultures. Reality necessitates acknowledgement of multiple psychotherapeutic techniques that serve a variegated array of mind-sets, are sensitive to cultural epochs, and are relevant during a particular time-period.

Nonetheless, one mental exercise that has been shown to be helpful in virtually all times and places is to develop what Sri Aurobindo called a "silent mind." This is done through meditation, prayer, or similar methods. Silencing the mind does not signify a demeaning of the practice of thinking or a lapse into nihilism, rather it means to silence the trivial, repetitive, habitual thoughts with which one is usually pre-occupied. This helps not only to rise above the thoughts that ordinarily preoccupy the mind and waste time, but has two other advantages as well. Firstly, it helps to prepare the subject for a descent of peace from the overhead planes of consciousness (or for an emergence of peace from the psychic being). Secondly, silencing the mind creates a favourable space for the efflorescence of higher intuitive and creative thoughts. (5)

Here are several exercises to help silence the mind and prepare it to receive intuitive to influences from the psychic being and/or overhead planes of consciousness.

1. An initial imagery would be to consider the mind as an empty and quiet house that is locked. Thoughts like visitors come to the house and as they cannot enter a locked house, they have to encircle the house and gradually fade away. When the image of this empty house of the mind is consolidated, the subject is told to visualize a white column of peace and silence descending, entering the house of the mind by piercing its roof and filling it up. Practicing this exercise at intervals facilitates not only the settlement of peace and quietude but also an opening to supra-rational influences. The mind can then benefit from both cognitive and mindfulness techniques.

2. The second exercise is based on the premise that the mind is not the brain but utilizes the brain for its expression. The subject is told to imagine that the mind has been physically lifted from the brain so that the centre of thinking has been shifted upward. Next, one has to imagine that the mind has spread out like a vast ethereal surface or an endless expansion of water. At the third stage, one has to imagine that from very high above, creative thoughts descend on the surface of the expanded mind like droplets of shining light or rainbows and get absorbed. If performed at intervals, the subject can

become receptive to intuitive inspirations.

3. A third exercise which has been commonly practiced in India is the cultivation of the witness-attitude. One draws back from the surface mind to a poise behind oneself, and watches the stream of thoughts that come, exaggerate themselves and finding no support fades away. This is a powerful exercise to practice detachment in a non-judgmental way. One can then extend the movement of detachment at the planes of emotion and the body.

Finally, the Mother has given another a fourth exercise to deal with the ruminations of the physical mind. One needs to write down the ruminating thoughts on a piece of paper and then tear the paper into pieces while willing not to invite the thoughts back again. (6)

Case Examples

The silent mind is needed not only for the client but also for the therapist.

The author once experienced this in a vivid way on a busy summer day with temperature soaring to nearly 40 degrees centigrade. He was running a rural clinic where clients had to be quickly examined due to the large volume. To do justice to his clients in short time, he silenced his mind to look for intuitive cues. When confronted with a new Muslim client from a low socio-economic background, he intuitively told him to get rid of his anti-social habits. The client, who had not spoken a word, was taken aback. His cousin went on to reveal that the client was known for his anti-social deeds and was reported to have been involved in a series of murderous acts. A few weeks later, the author was informed that immediately after this brief clinical encounter, the client had suddenly abandoned his anti-social activities and had taken the life of a wondering mendicant (fakir). Five years later, he was still roaming as a fakir. Thus, a moment of intuitive inspiration received through a silent mind had changed the course of a patient's life.

One powerful way to deal with non-psychotic clients who voluntarily consult for anger management or impulse control problems is to train them to cultivate the witness attitude. If the client finds it difficult to adopt the witness-attitude, one alternative would be to use a psychodrama technique where the client plays a role opposite to one's character, like placating an angry subject. After that it usually becomes easier for the client to adapt the witness attitude.

The therapist himself or herself must also integrate the parts of the being around one's psychic center, and/or have a poise in the Higher Mind. This entails a lifelong endeavour, which is why it is better for the integral psychotherapist to start working from the surface personality of the client and only shift to working with the inner being when the therapist has reached a sufficient degree of spiritual development.

On the other hand, sometimes it is the client not the clinician who has the moment of intuition. A good clinician will recognize this and seize on the inspiration, as in the following case:

A Muslim woman with bipolar disorder had been taking mood stabilizers and seeing a therapist for three decades. Sadly, one of her three sons, a 21 year old post-graduate student in engineering, left his studies to join a fundamentalist group, much to the dismay of his family. He changed his dress and hairstyle to resemble a Taliban type look. He went along with his group and despite fervent appeals from his family, he refused to come back to the mainstream. After three years of this, one day he suddenly returned home. His mother had always nursed a hope that if her son returned, she would take him to the author who could try to persuade him to return back to mainstream.

It was the time of Durga Puja, which is the biggest Hindu

festival in Bengal. The Muslim woman brought her son to the clinic, and unexpectedly asked her therapist, who was Hindu, to give her some fruits which had been offered to the Goddess. Her son, who was a Muslim fundamentalist, was taken aback but could not protest as the therapist had been treating his mother for three decades and was revered by the family. Her mother relished the fruits and explained to her son that a fruit was a fruit by its own right, and did not carry the stamp of any religion. This intuitive utterance suddenly changed the milieu in such a way that the therapist took the chance to counsel the youngster to return to mainstream and join professional life, while keeping his faith and his world-view. His mother was visibly happy.

That night the Muslim woman had a stroke and died. In retrospect, the therapist understood that the woman's intuitive utterance in clinic had been her parting gift to her son, a statement from her soul that changed the dynamics of the family. For in fact her son did return to the mainstream and eventually gave up his fundamentalist pursuits.

Finally, in some cases it can be helpful to give exercises to develop a better balance between the cognitive functions of the left and right hemispheres of the brain, which support the operations of different mental faculties. The non-linear, non-verbal, creative and aesthetic faculties of the right brain have to be synergized with the linear, verbal, analytical and logical faculties of the left brain. Dr. Surya, one of the doyens of Indian psychiatry, lucidly explained that the synergism between the left and right brain activities is most profoundly expressed in the classical Indian symbolism of Ardhanariswara, "the male and female element in the same unity, who in the full harmony of their love give birth to Kumara, the eternal youth, the herald of the Divine Forces." (7) Clinically, left and right brain function can be assessed through neuropsychology testing and review of social and academic functioning. However, the co-author has noticed that in some cases it can be seen instantly on facial exam: some patients who are having trouble with left brain function will have decreased expression and responsiveness on the right side of the face, while those with deficits in right brain function will have decreased responsiveness on the left side of the face. Indeed, fascinating insights can be gleaned by looking at photographs of clients and comparing the expression of the right to the left side of the face, as the two sides sometimes express very different traits.

Following is a case study of right vs left brain asymmetry:

A 12 year old girl from a semi-urban setting was brought for consultation for an adjustment disorder with marked hostility towards her mother for reasons unknown to the latter. She lacked concentration in studies, except mathematics where she excelled. She was extremely irritable and had an intense revulsion towards her pubertal changes. She detested her menstrual periods, which had started a year prior, leading to her despising of her own femininity. Both her parents were school teachers, her father of mathematics and her mother of biology. She had a younger sister with whom she had intense sibling rivalry.

During the mental state examination, she confessed that a neighbouring lady had, for the last four years, been telling her that she was actually a step-child and not a "real child" of her mother. For unclear reasons, the girl had believed this story but never revealed it to anyone lest she be an object for ridicule.

On inquiry, the girl's mother recalled that this neighbour had once been a colleague at the school where she taught. The neighbour had developed hostility to the mother after the latter was promoted to the rank of a senior teacher in preference to her. Evidently, the neighbor had then taken revenge by brainwashing the daughter to believe that she was a step-child and that all the affection shown to her by her mother was a show. The girl was thus plunged into a severe identity crisis, and her misery peaked after menarche.

Unfortunately, the girl refused to comply with counselling sessions. The therapist faced a difficult situation, as it was hard to understand how an intelligent girl with a talent for mathematics could be so easily hoodwinked by her neighbor? Why did not she have an iota of doubt that this proposition could be untrue? It was at this moment of impasse in the treatment that an interesting side of the girl's character surfaced. An analysis of her school records showed that all along she had fared well in science subjects, especially in mathematics, while she always performed poorly in literature and arts. The girl was coached by her parents at home. Her father was a wizard in mathematics and under his influence, her mathematical ability blossomed more than her literary ability. Her parents had also ignored literature as they thought that someone who excelled in mathematics would automatically cross the hurdles of literature. The "scientific" mind-set was supposed to be more pragmatic.

It was decided to handle this girl's problems mainly on the basis of lateralization of brain function and not through usual counselling techniques. Clearly, her educational programmes were biased towards left hemispheric analytic and sequential processing, at the cost of the non-verbal and holistic processing of the right hemisphere. This was evident in the girl's case as she could solve mathematical problems and was at ease in the world of figures and symbols, but she could not write imaginative essays or spin stories of fantasy. She could sing well but never knew that the cultivation of music was as important as solving mathematical problems. It was hypothesized that as a result of deficits in right hemisphere development, she could not intuitively differentiate between her mother's real feelings and her neighbour's cooked up story, nor learn to adapt to the changing narrative of her life and body as she entered puberty.

Along with her parents, the girl was instructed on the importance of developing right hemispheric functions, and she was given an educational programme to develop the faculties she lacked. Special learning techniques were used to enhance her creative flair in the domain of humanities. She was also encouraged to develop her musical aptitude. Her parents actively helped her and her mental state improved considerably within six months. She accepted her pubescence and understood the necessity to develop herself holistically without rejecting her femininity. With time, her therapist was able to convince her that she mistakenly believed in the story cooked-up by her neighbor. (8)

Finally, there is a whole realm of therapeutic interventions that revolves around not the smaller cognitions usually addressed in CBT, but the larger cognitions or master ideas that people use to organize their lives. Such guiding ideas can be touched on in any type of therapy, but certainly have been well described in existential therapy. Following is a case of how a young artist adjusted his over-arching idea about aesthetics and changed the course of his life:

> A young man in his early twenties was a student of Fine Arts. He was greatly inspired by his teacher, a legendary artist who was famous for a series of paintings depicting the state of famine-stricken victims. The youngster modeled his own art after his teacher and devoted his energy to drawing emaciated human figures, desolate and forlorn in the midst of hunger and poverty. At that time, his university campus was full of heroin abuse, and he also fell for it. He became dependent on heroin and within a year, he lost his appetite and withdrew from social contacts while continuing to draw emaciated figures. He was intellectually satisfied with himself as he thought that his aesthetic sense served to show the face of reality which the elite evade. However, heroin abuse made him emaciated and sickly-appearing, and he became identified, both psychologically and physically, with the figures he drew. He knew it was unethical to abuse heroin on the campus, especially as he was draining his family's funds, but decided that ethics could be sacrificed for showcasing stark reality.
>
> His family, who were cultured and liberal, were not so much concerned with ethical issues as they were with his deteriorating health. They sent him for detoxification. His mother was an idealist, a litterateur and at the same time

a deeply spiritual person with firm conviction in a higher Truth. He had a supportive girl friend who was open-minded and also had a strong belief in spirituality. His father had a liberal mindset and never interfered with his children. Due to this background of culture and spirituality, the young man had a finesse which allowed him to accept his therapist without any qualms, though there was the customary periodic ambivalence about treatment.

The therapist in this case noted that the patient had a palpable psychic (soul) quality of sweetness and harmony behind his conflict-ridden surface personality. This made it easier for the therapist to introduce a counter-balancing aesthetic idea: he explained to the young man that if ugliness was a reality, beauty was also a reality. The Bliss or Ananda in creation was the greater reality and a deviation from it was unfortunate and needed to be studied so that one could get back to the wavelength of Bliss again. Could he not draw the pictures depicting the Beauty to which the world must move?

The young man's psychic being made him receptive, and he accepted this suggestion even thought the therapist was not an artist. The patient started to depict more beautiful themes, and as he did so the rest of his life became reorganized in a positive way. He recovered from his spell of substance abuse, completed his university course, married, and got settled as an artist.

A greater truth than earth's shall roof-in earth
And shed its sunlight on the roads of mind;
A power infallible shall lead the thought,
A seeing Puissance govern life and act,
In earthly hearts kindle the Immortal's fire.
A soul shall wake in the Inconscient's house;
The mind shall be God-vision's tabernacle,
The body intuition's instrument,
And life a channel for God's visible power.
Savitri, pg. 707

References

1. Evening Talks, pg. 406

2. Agenda XI, pg. 22-24

3. CWSA 21-22, pg. 962

4.Basu,S: Integral Health,SAIIIHR, Pondicherry, 2nd Ed, 2011, pg. 28-29

5. Basu,S: The Silent Mind, Namah-The Journal of Integral Health,Vol.22, No.4, 2015, p.46

6. CWM 15, pg. 309-310

7. Surya, N.C: Aham (Personal Autonomy), Private manuscript in Sri Aurobindo Ashram, pg.78

8. Basu, Sharmila: Case Study, Namah-The Journal of Integral Health, Vol.3, No.2, 1996, pg. 63

15
The Vital Consciousness

This too the supreme Diplomat can use,
He makes our fall a means of greater rise.

Savitri, *pg. 34*

Sri Aurobindo used the term "vital" as a noun to designate the plane of life-energy and dynamism, which is the basis for all of our conflicting emotions, passions, ambitions, and repulsions. Love and hatred, joy and sorrow, sacrifice and revenge, excitement and depression, possessiveness and jealousy, compassion and cruelty, attraction and repulsion, craving and disgust all exist together in this turbulent zone of life energies. The vital holds our energy, dynamism, desires, egoistic pursuits, libido and primary instinctual drives, our life-instinct as well as death-instinct. In Sri Aurobindo's words, the vital:

> "is a thing of desires, impulses, force-pushes, emotions, sensations, seekings after life-fulfilment, possession and enjoyment; these are its functions and its nature; -- it is that part of us which seeks after life and its movements for their own sake and it does not want to leave hold of them if they bring it suffering as well as or more than pleasure; it is even capable of luxuriating in tears and suffering as part of the drama of life". (1)

The vital plane of consciousness is also the source of our creative force, without which the creative idea cannot materialize. Creative geniuses tend to have a strong vital energy, which is why they can be both intensely productive and innovative, and yet at the same time unstable. For example, psychologists have long been intrigued with the personality of Vincent Van Gogh. The famous artist has been diagnosed as suffering from one disease or another, ranging from schizophrenia, bipolar disorder, and epilepsy to acute intermittent porphyria and Meniere's disease. However, a symposium of 30 international medical experts in September, 2016, weighed all available evidence and concluded that nothing definitive can be pronounced about his medical status except that the diagnosis in his last years was probably more prosaic. But whatever the diagnosis, from the perspective of CBP there is no doubt that Van Gogh had a strong vital, and was both creative and unstable. Like him, many other great artists, actors, musicians, writers, and other cultural icons have had strong vital natures that imbued their personalities with both creative dynamism and turbulent excesses and character flaws.

Because the vital is marked by turbulent passions, what is commonly called "love" cannot guarantee permanence in relationships. The vital by its very character is a repository of conflicting moods, emotions and passions which cannot be placed under moral or rational control, because the vital at times tries to subjugate the reason to justify its impulses. As Sri Aurobindo noted, the vital is not concerned with "self-knowledge" but with "self-justification and assertion" on one hand, and on the other hand with "self-depreciation and a morbid and exaggerated self-criticism". (2) This last observation is very penetrating. Everyone can notice the vital grandiosity of characters such as former President Donald Trump, but it can be harder to discern the morbid vital of religious leaders and moralists who cloak their vital energies in a veil of false humility. Sri Aurobindo also commented that vital represents frequently:

> "A mixture of the charlatan and mountebank, the poser and actor; it is constantly taking up a role and playing it to itself and to others as its public. An organized self-deception is thus added to an organized self-ignorance". (3)

Sri Aurobindo's concept of the vital is larger than that of the Freudian Id, although it encompasses the characteristics of the Id. The vital is thus the domain from where defense mechanisms arise. The concept of defense mechanisms are implicit in the Aurobindonian paradigm, but they are understood within a larger evolutionary context:

> "The vital started in its evolution with obedience to impulse and no reason — as for strategy, the only strategy it understands is some tactics by which it can compass its desires. It does not like the voice of knowledge and wisdom – but curiously enough by the necessity which has grown up in man of justifying action by reason, the vital mind has developed a strategy of its own which is to get the reason to find out reasons for justifying its own feelings and impulses". (4)

This passage clearly implies the existence of the "unconscious" in the psycho-analytic sense, and describes the defense mechanism of rationalization. (5) Dalal also explained how perception and cognition are strongly influenced by the feelings and impulses of the vital resulting in the defense mechanism of projection. (6) One can also use the concept of the vital to understand why mood disorders can manifest either through depression or through manic excitement, and why children who have not yet been able to cognize depression can express their anguish through aggression (7).

Sri Aurobindo explained that the vital plane of consciousness has some general attributes that can cause psychological distress and disharmony, as well as more specific characteristics of various layers or sub-levels of the vital that can cause clinical problems. Some of the general problems of the vital are desire, impatience, fear, and anger.

The vital is characterized by desire. Desire per se is a motivator in life, it "is at once the motive of our actions, our lever of accomplishment and the bane of our existence." (8) Without a modicum of desire, one is not motivated to struggle to achieve any goal. Yet an excess of desire leads to a plethora of personality attributes that might be socially disconcerting or psychologically disturbing. On the other hand, a voluntary suppression or unconscious repression of desire without any experiential contact with a higher or deeper consciousness can lead to neurotic conditions or psychosomatic diseases. It is thus that Buddha considered desire to arise from ignorance. If an indulgence in desire gives sensual pleasure, mental satisfaction or egoistic boost, a conscious control over desire (without suppression or repression) leads to a greater joy and bliss, a sense of fulfilment and a glimpse of the ego-transcending consciousness. Following is a case that illustrates the nature of vital desire:

> M, a middle-aged, self-made man walked into a city clinic one day to know how to die. Why? He had struggled all his life and achieved whatever he wanted. There was nothing more to want now. He was born into a poor family but he had amassed a lot of wealth. His parents were sparsely educated but he himself had completed his post-graduate studies. His father was a clerk while he was a bureaucrat. In his childhood he was teased and bullied due to his short stature and weak physique which he compensated later by extensive gymnastic work. Unlike his unstable childhood marked by parental discord, M led a stable family life. His children were being properly educated and his wife had no discontent. He had thus achieved whatever he desired. There was nothing more to achieve in his life-time and he had only one desire left — to die! (9)

Such is the nature of the vital consciousness — it can be temporarily satiated but never permanently satisfied.

Another important vital attribute is impatience, which stems from the energetic dynamism that is inherent in vitality. The significance of impatience is inextricably linked with the sense of time-urgency, which is a pervasive problem in modern life. We are always rushing, always in a hurry. Our entire relation with Time could be described as a chronic dyschronia. Sri Aurobindo commented that to the ordinary consciousness "Time appears as a resistance, for it presents to us all the obstruction of the forces that conflict with our own." (10) However, this is only so because we are unaware that time is also an instrument of the soul and that

there is an equally significant dimension of timelessness supporting our ordinary perception of time. As the Mother cautioned,

> "Men have a feeling that if they are not all the time running
> about and bursting into fits of feverish activity, they are doing
> nothing...This illusion of action is one of the greatest illu-
> sions of human nature. It hurts progress because it brings on
> you the necessity of rushing always into some excited move-
> ment...Stand back from your action and rise into an outlook
> above these temporal motions, enter into the consciousness
> of Eternity. Then only you will know what true action is."
> (11)

Our inability to appreciate the real value of time leads to the sense
of time-urgency that haunts the workaholic and Type A personality, who are more prone to coronary problems and other stress-
related conditions. The spiritual paradigm teaches that Time can
also be a friend, medium or instrument of the soul.

Dalal describes that the vital is also the source of fear. Though
all human beings are subject to fear, very few are aware of its presence as a continual undercurrent, or that anxiety is simply "fear
spread thin". (12) Fear is not merely an apprehension in the mind
but also a feeling of recoil in the vital. Mind-body medicine has
paid much attention to the stress response and techniques for
calming it (such as meditation and relaxation training), but it has
largely missed the important mediating effect of the vital, which
stands between the mental and physical planes of consciousness
and has a great influence on their interactions. Sri Aurobindo noted that many of the attributes associated with the stress response
actually originate in the vital. While making a distinction between
the emotions and lower vital movements, he commented:

> "Anger, fear, jealousy touch the heart no doubt just as they
> touch the mind but they rise from the navel region and en-
> trails (i.e. the lower or at highest the middle vital). Stevenson
> has a striking passage in *Kidnapped* where the hero notes that

> his fear is felt primarily not in the heart but the stomach.
> Love, hope have their primary seat in the heart, so with pity
> etc." (13)

Here, Sri Aurobindo observes that emotions such as love, hope, and pity are associated with the "heart" chakra (higher vital), while anger, fear, and jealousy arose associated with the navel chakra (lower vital). Though arising from the vital, fear can influence both the mind and the body. The fear of death is a basic vital weakness (14) which brings in pessimism and makes an illness chronic or even refractory. The Mother explained that fear opens the door to all contagion and has to be dealt separately at each level of consciousness. (15) Mental fear can be dealt through a cognitive-behavioural approach, but vital fear requires a more subtle control with a resolute will power, and physical fear at the cellular level is very resistant to usual interventions unless a veritable yoga is undertaken.

Dalal also explained how allied to fear is anger, as many people react with anger when they get frightened. (16) It is interesting that anger has become an increasingly prevalent problem in clinical therapeutic and counselling settings in clinical practice. Anger can not only be a symptomatic expression of psychopathology, it can be just a personality characteristic without any other psychopathology.

Readers who are interested in learning more about how Sri Aurobindo mapped various drives, emotions and other psychological characteristics (such as willpower) to the chakras are referred to his fascinating comments in the Letters on Yoga. (17) However, be forewarned that since Sri Aurobindo is always nuanced and complex, one has to learn his terminology in order to follow his thought. He observed interaction zones among and between the various chakras where the consciousness of one plane could influence another, and vice versa. This led him to use a series of two-word terms to describe these interaction zones. The key to grasping these is to understand that the second word in the pair is the primary plane of consciousness being observed and described, while the first word is modifying force or influence from another plane. Thus, the "vital physical", described next, is the zone of the physical which is influenced by the vital.

The Vital Physical and Psychosomatic Disorders

The vital-physical (known as the nervous being in yogic parlance) is the zone of the physical consciousness which is influenced by vital energy. It is the zone where the inertia and resistance of the physical are acted on by the thrust of the vital force. It acts as a link between the subtle and the gross dimensions of the being, between the mind and the body and this link is modulated through the neuro-physiological apparatus. The friction of the vital energy with the inert substrate of the physical causes stress and pain. Moreover, the vital energy operating at the level of the vital physical and modulating the physical substrate gets sustenance from the universal vital energy. Sri Aurobindo explained that:

> "there is a constant dynamic energy in movement in the universe which takes various material forms more or less subtle or gross, so in each physical body or object, plant or animal or metal, there is stored and active the same constant dynamic force; a certain interchange of these two gives us the phenomena which we associate with the idea of life." (18)

If this commerce between the individual vital and the universal vital is affected or restricted, the physical substrate can be insecure resulting in the stress response. Perhaps this is similar to what Heidegger, in a different worldview postulated that we are anxious when our natural, fluid engagement with the world is disrupted. (19) It is no wonder, therefore, that the stress response system with its sympathetic and parasympathetic components, as well as pain with its myriad presentations, arise in the vital-physical matrix. Sri Aurobindo explains that the vital physical is:

> "largely responsible for most of the suffering and disease of

mind or body to which the physical being is subject in Nature." (20)

The vital-physical underlies ailments like somatization disorders, psychosomatic diseases, hypochondriasis, migraine, chronic urticaria. The vital-physical modulates the signs and symptoms of anxiety neurosis and related neurotic disorders like panic attacks and phobias. It is also the underlying plane where withdrawal symptoms of substance abuse and alcoholism manifest. Following is a case that illustrates the vital physical:

> In India, where arranged marriages are common, a 30 year old woman was married to a 45 year old banker who had been under treatment for paranoid schizophrenia for the last ten years. He could do his office work reasonably well under medication. Just before marriage, he had stopped his medication. After the marriage he became delusional and made a sacrificial pyre. He sat in a meditative pose in front of the pyre and went on muttering indecipherable Sanskrit hymns for three days at a stretch without sleeping or eating and only at intervals re-igniting the pyre if the flame went off. His newly wed wife who had not known about her husband's illness, stood agonized and terror-struck and within three days, the fingers of her hands became dramatically distorted by rheumatoid arthritis. Her physical plane of consciousness was adversely influenced by her emotional distress that had affected her vital. Her vital energy succumbed to her husband's weird display and her physical consciousness reacted by producing the deformity.

This is an example of how the physical plane can be adversely affected by the vital plane to produce a somatic presentation with underlying psychological conflicts.

The Physical Vital and Hedonistic Traits

The physical-vital is that zone of the vital consciousness that is under the influence of the physical consciousness and submits to its inertia and recurrent habitual patterns. In other words, it is the zone where our atavistic past is dominant and the vital has to succumb to the physical and serve the demands of the senses. This is the plane where hedonism originates. The ordinary human being seeks happiness not from high sources like aesthetics, creativity or spirituality but from the small petty satisfactions of the senses that are often "varnished over with some conventional moralism and idealism as a concession to the mind and higher vital." (21) It is due to the physical-vital that despite the mind not wanting, the body cannot shrug off dependence on drugs or alcohol. It is due to this zone that lusts, greed, petty sensual satisfactions, dwarf desires and perversions get sustenance. Sri Aurobindo succinctly explained that "it is the physical vital that seeks after happiness", though other zones of the vital (the higher parts of the vital) may desire power, prestige, fame at the expense of happiness. (22) He elaborates, "That (seeking enjoyment) is the attitude not of the whole vital but of the physical vital, the animal part of the human being." (23)

Sri Aurobindo also explained that there are two groups of people where the physical-vital gets forcefully subjugated to other influences. In one group "this part of the being is gripped and subordinated to the mental or the higher vital aim, forced to take a subordinate place so that the mind may absorb itself persistently in mental pursuits or idealisms or great political or personal ambitions (Lenin, Hitler, Stalin, Mussolini)" while in another group, the "ascetic and the Puritan try to suppress it mostly or altogether." (24) In either case, suppression of the physical-vital is not the ideal way of dealing with it and can lead to disharmony, undesirable personality attributes, and even psychopathology.

An extreme example of the vital being stimulated by the atavistic habits of the physical is the case of the infamous Nithari killings in Delhi in 2005 where the perpetrator had sexual relations with youngsters he killed followed by devouring of their body parts. A pleasure was being sought not primarily by emotions but by a perverted atavistic habit of the physical forcing the vital to toe its line.

The Vital Mind and Bipolar Disorder

The vital mind is that zone of the mental consciousness which is strongly influenced by the vital plane. Thus, via the vital mind, the vital influences the thinking apparatus with desires, passions and ambitions, compels the reason to be swayed by emotions, and invests the mind with turbulence, impulsivity and volatility. The vital mind prefers to dream and imagine rather than being realistic and calculative. Its intrinsic nature is to resonate to the wave of dynamism which has spectacular upsurges but also phenomenal recoils. The upsurges of the vital mind represented through the mood might get so exaggerated as to manifest the manic phase of bipolar disorder, which is marked by grandiosity, over-activity, unusual extravaganza and aggression. Likewise the recoils of the vital mind can lead to loss of vitality, low self-esteem, hopelessness, helplessness and a plethora of related attributes that finally get expressed as depression. As the vital is the repertoire of conflicting and contradictory emotions, it is not surprising that the ingredients of bipolar disorder are both simultaneously present, and that both manic excitement and depression can emerge from the same matrix. In children, where the ability to cognize has not reached an optimal level, it would not be improbable for depression to be represented through aggression (one might also argue that depressed children can introject their emotions and be outwardly aggressive). The main thing to note is that as conflicting emotions reside in the repertoire of the vital, depression has as much chance to manifest as manic excitement or aggression.

When it is unable to follow the Truth of life or unwilling to surpass its characteristic limitations, the vital mind can make compromises with reality in the form of defense mechanisms which have been enumerated by psychoanalysts. Working through these defense mechanisms has a clarifying but limited effect in psychological well-being, as it cannot give full mastery of the vital unless the vital is subjugated to a higher principle in consciousness. Defense mechanism provide some protection to the outer being that revolves around the ego, but they cannot serve the subliminal being or the psychic being.

Psychotherapeutic Interventions for the Vital

Different psychotherapies act at the level of the vital consciousness from different perspectives. The cognitive therapies attempt to modulate emotions by cognition, which is naturally successful up to a point because the mental consciousness is at a higher evolutionary poise than the vital consciousness. Psychoanalytic therapies work on the vital plane by working through defenses against experiencing negative, painful, or otherwise avoided emotions. However, the limitation of all standard forms of psychotherapy (including existential and family approaches) is that they use some aspect of the mental consciousness to try to understand and regulate the vital. Mindfulness-based approaches can go a little deeper by developing a witness stance from which to observe both the mind and the vital, and CBP can extend this orientation further by discovering the psychic being and the overhead planes of consciousness. In this pursuit, two things are discovered:

First, as one crosses from the outer being to the inner or subliminal being, one enters a zone of peace, calm, passivity, silence and stability that actually stands behind and supports the dynamism and turbulences of the outer being. Sri Aurobindo explained that power does not only spring from strength and dynamism but simultaneously and more effectively from silence and calm. The silence has to be cultivated at the level of the vital and values which are not dependent on time have to be presented in psychotherapy sessions.

Second, a further entry into the inner realms of consciousness moves the subject away from the realm of desires to come in contact with the psychic being (or through the overhead planes of consciousness to a transcendent awareness). As the contact with the psychic being is a fourth dimensional experiential perception, it is independent of the adversities and complexities of life and can be experienced even amidst the most trying circumstances.

The following vignette illustrates how a CBP orientation can help deal with the vital:

> A, a 22 year old post-graduate student in clinical social work presented with binge eating and bulimic episodes, the intensity of which varied with her mood fluctuations. Her mood fluctuations were quite discernible but not to the extent of being labeled as due to bipolar disorder. She responded partially to an SSRI, but what really helped her was her fieldwork as psychiatric social worker, which exposed her to situations that helped her to introspect about her own desires. The therapist, following this cue, helped her in systematic introspective exercises where she understood how to work through her own desires. She was given the spiritual hint of not fighting forcibly with her desires but submitting them to a Higher Power for getting redressed. Over time this had a calming and stabilizing effect on her vital.

Note that this approach can be integrated in work with clients who come from just about any spiritual worldview, and adapted to the forms and terms of their spirituality as needed. Following are some other exercises for the vital.

The Mother has suggested one technique that can be practiced daily at the end of the day. (25) One is told to project oneself in imagination as if upon a cinema screen and watch one's whole movements during the day. One must be non-judgmental in observing carefully all the unnecessary movements, the wrong advances, the inability to control impulses, the exaggerations which could have been avoided, and the bodily discomforts. One can then be aware of the vital movements in one's own being. Once there is a clarity, any therapeutic technique can be worked out in the vital realms. It is interesting that many NDE subjects have reported seeing such life-reviews while purportedly in comatose states. This validates that a mastery over the vital is an essential pre-requisite for a growth in consciousness.

Another powerful exercise at the vital plane is to practice the widening of consciousness. The Mother suggested an exercise where the subject, after being relaxed, is asked to imagine floating on a wooden plank in the middle of a huge water body and expanding oneself. (26) One expands and expands like a balloon and ultimately becomes one with the huge expanse of the water. Some subjects find it more comfortable to expand in an imagined Space among galaxies and stars. This movement of expansion helps one to be detached from the ego, from the vital as well as from the physical mind and have a feel of the cosmic consciousness.

Also, the vital can be patiently trained to deal with Time, as one of the greatest maladies of modern life is the competition with Time. Instead of viewing Time as an enemy or resistance, it can be viewed as a friend and collaborator. After one has practiced silencing the mind (see Chapter 14), one has to concentrate to bring this peace, silence and quietude into the vital so as to impart a sense of timeless stability. Note that such training to deal with Time should start in infancy and continue across the lifespan.

For example, parents should allow infants to have complete sensory experiences without losing patience. If adults are in a hurry, infants are left with incomplete sensory experiences that sow the seeds of impatience later in life. Winnicot stressed the importance of total happenings — experiences having a beginning, a middle and end. He described how a 10-month old child develops an interest in a spoon but after the first simple reaction temporarily withdraws his interest as if wondering if mother is going to approve his action. Then, by carefully sensing the mother's feelings, he allows his interest to return. He is tense, however, until he actually puts the spoon in his mouth and chews it thus making it "his own". Now he is confident and plays with the spoon. He also invites play by trying to feed his mother and others with the spoon, hiding the spoon and then rediscovering it, scooping up imaginary food from a bowl and then imaginatively eating his food. Now the baby drops the spoon. Does he like the sound of the spoon striking the floor? The spoon is picked up and handed to him but he throws it away. He is reaching out for other interests and the show with the spoon is over.

Winnicot explains, "It (the experience) corresponds to the mystery of the middle of the body, the digestive processes, the time between when the food is lost by being swallowed, and when the residue is rediscovered at the lower end in the faeces and urine". (27) Thus, the middle of things can be enjoyed (or tolerated if bad) only if there is a strong sense of start and finish. Winnicot adds that if adults are not in a hurry, the child is not deprived of an imaginative inner life: "We have watched the baby develop an interest in something, and make it part of himself, and we have watched him use it, and then finish with it…there could be a beginning, a middle, and an end to what happened: there was a total happening. This is good for the baby."(28) To be patient and allow the child to have a totality of sensory experience is a tough but worthy exercise for parents to undertake with their children.

Later in childhood, exercises that deal with time should be incorporated at school. Dowsett explains that Time should not be brought into learning activity as it breaks into concentration and interest, which are the chief pillars of the learning experience. He recommends that children should be introduced to values which do not depend upon the time-sequence or chronology. For example, sincerity, enthusiasm, and intensity are peaks of experience that are independent of time or sequence. Students should be encouraged to recognize these values in history, literature, music, poetry and the sciences. The cultivation of the aesthetic sense consolidates this process. (29)

Finally, there are more mundane steps for stabilizing the vital, but these are nonetheless important and helpful. First is the organizing effect of work. Having some regular work to do is very stabilizing for the vital, and via the method of karma yoga outlined in the Gita, work can become a bona fide spiritual discipline. For this purpose, "work" does not have to be for money — it can be volunteer work, parenting, community activism, creative or artistic work, or any other endeavor that provides structure to one's life and requires a regular and persistent effort across time to achieve a goal. For similar reasons of structure, regular times for exercise and study also help stabilize the vital. Listening to music and taking care of pets both also rejuvenate the vital, especially the higher vital, and these two common aspects of life have been formalized into music and pet therapy, respectively.

A separate topic is "transformation" of the vital by spiritual seekers who are practicing integral yoga, but that passes beyond the purview of clinical psychology and psychiatry and belongs to the realm of yoga proper. Readers who are interested in this are referred to Sri Aurobindo's *Letters on Yoga.*

Although the shaping god's tremendous touch
Is torture unbearable to mortal nerves,
The fiery spirit grows in strength within
And feels a joy in every titan pang.

Savitri, *pg. 444*

References

1. CWSA 28, pg. 175

2. CWSA 21-22. Pg. 552

3. Ibid

4. CWSA 31, pg. 103

5. Miovic, M: Integral Yoga Psychology: Clinical Correlations, International Journal of Transpersonal Studies,Vol.37(1),2018,pp 199-225

6. Dalal, A.S: Psychology, Mental Health and Yoga, Auroshakti Foundation, India,3rd Ed, 2012, pg. 102

7. Basu,S: Integral Health, SAIIIHR,Pondicherry,2nd Ed,2011, pg. 39-40

8. CWSA 23-24, pg. 350-351

9. Parkar, Shubhangi: Personal Communication; also mentioned in op. cit. Integral Health, pg. 148-149

10. CWSA 23-24, pg. 68

11. CWM 03, pg. 66-68

12. Op. cit. Psychology, Mental Health and Yoga, pg. 107

13. CWSA 28, pg. 193

14. CWSA 29, pg. 116

15. CWM 09, pg. 122

16. Op.cit. Psychology, Mental Health and Yoga, pg. 107-108

17. CWSA 28, pg. 229-247

18. CWSA 21-22, pg. 192

19. Fulford,KWM;Thornton,Tim;Graham,George:Oxford Textbook of Philosophy and Psychiatry, Oxford University Press, New York, 2006, pg. 38

20. CWSA 28, pg. 203

21. Ibid, pg. 195

22. Ibid, pg. 194

23. Ibid, pg. 195

24. Ibid,

25. CWM 04, pg. 38-39

26. Ibid, pg. 266

27. Winnicot, D.W: The Child, The Family and The Outside World, Penguin Books, England, 1985, pg. 77

28. Ibid

29. Dowsett, N.C: Psychology for Future Education, Sri Aurobindo Society, 1977, pg. 36-40

16
The Physical Consciousness

Caught in a blind stone-grip Force worked its plan
And made in sleep this huge mechanical world,
That Matter might grow conscious of its soul...

Savitri, pg. 101

The main characteristic of the physical plane of consciousness is that its operations are mechanical and automatic in nature, and thus normally not conscious of their own workings. One way to harness the power of the physical plane of consciousness is through medical science. In psychiatry, this has lead to treatments such as psycho-pharmacology, ECT, vagal nerve stimulation, TMS, and other emerging forms of neuro-modulation. CBP avails of these treatment modalities and is open to the great developments in genetic engineering and neuroscience that are anticipated over the coming decades. However, CBP would also add that there are other ways to explore the physical plane of consciousness as well. Medical science studies matter and biology through the reasoning mind — but this same territory can also be explored and infused with the consciousness of the psychic being, the intuitive or "overhead" planes of consciousness, and ultimately the Supermind. The evolution of consciousness in this direction is already foreshadowed by the existence of various types of healers and medical intuitives who use subtle energies and supra-rational cognition to diagnose and treat illness. Another example of occult factors in the physical is the Mother's description of how vital beings produced by the violence of WWI lead to the Spanish flu pandemic. (1) This is relevant to the recent global pandemic of Covid19, and in other talks the Mother commented that pathologic viruses are crystallizations of adverse forces that exist on the border between the subtle planes and the physical world. (2)

As one enters into the large domain that concerns the interaction between the physical and supra-physical planes of consciousness, it is important not to engage in either-or thinking and not to reject whatever science has managed to learn about the mechanistic operations of the physical world. Sri Aurobindo did not ascribe to such simplistic and dualistic notions of scientific vs. spiritual approaches to healing, and neither should we. The aim should be to synthesize the best of both worlds and ways of knowing, and in the following letter Sri Aurobindo brilliantly answered both rational skeptics who deny the reality of non-local phenomenon — but he also points out that medications can be used as an instrument to transmit a spiritual force or subtle energy:

> "In a case of cure of illness, someone is lying ill for two days, weak, suffering from pains and fever; he takes no medicine but finally asks for cure from his Guru; the next morning he rises well, strong and energetic. He has at least some justification for thinking that a force has been used on him and put into him and that it was a spiritual power that acted. But in another case medicines may be used, while at the same time the invisible force may be called for to aid the material means, for it is a known fact that medicines may or may not succeed — there is no certitude. Here for the reason of an outside observer (one who is neither the user of the force nor the doctor nor the patient) it remains uncertain whether the patient was cured by the medicines only or by the spiritual force with the medicines as an instrument. Either is possible, and it cannot be said that because medicines were used, therefore the working of a spiritual force is *per se* incredible and demonstrably false. On the other hand it is possible for the doctor to have felt a force working in him and guiding him or he may see the patient improving with a rapidity which, according to medical science, is incredible. The patient may feel the force working in himself bringing health, energy, rapid cure. The user of the force may watch the results, see the symptoms he works on diminishing, those he did not work upon increasing till he does work on them and then immediately diminishing, the doctor working according to his unspoken suggestions, etc. etc. until the cure is done. (On the other hand

he may see forces working against the cure and conclude that the spiritual force has to be contented with a withdrawal or an imperfect success.) In all that the doctor, the patient or the user of force is justified in believing that the cure is at least partly or even fundamentally due to the spiritual force. Their experience is valid of course for themselves only, not for the outside rationalising observer. But the latter is not logically entitled to say that their experience is incredible and must be false.

Another point. It does not follow that a spiritual force must either succeed in all cases or, if it does not, that proves its nonexistence. Of no force can that be said." (3)

Two points are worth emphasizing about this passage. First, it is clear that Sri Aurobindo is logical and understands the difference between correlation and causation, as well as the problem of frames of reference. Second, Sri Aurobindo thoroughly debunks either-or thinking, and describes *interactions* between spiritual forces and material substrates. To this day people still argue about healing in an either-or fashion, with skeptical doctors often defending only medical approaches and distrustful patients defending only "alternative therapies." Note well that Sri Aurobindo did not fall into this trap. His whole philosophy is about the *interaction* between Spirit and Matter, which lead to him see no contradiction between spirituality and science, and this synthetic view culminated in him feeling perfectly comfortable applying a spiritual Force to use "medicines as an instrument." Thus, for practical purposes CBP recommends using science to produce the best possible material instruments to treat disease and promote health, and using yoga to access the highest possible plane of consciousness to infuse these instruments and the healers who use them.

The most common example of how the physical plane of consciousness affects psychology is the stress response. One of mankind's stressful problems has become the stress response itself. When the human being was a hunter-gatherer, the stressor was predominantly a physical threat such as an attack by a wild animal. In that struggle to survive, nature endowed the human being with adaptive physiological mechanisms to combat stress. During this classical stress response, blood pressure increases, blood is shunted to the brain and large muscle groups, the reticular activating system increases alertness, and energy-producing compounds such as glucose and fatty acids are released into the blood while the immune and digestive systems are temporarily downregulated. When this stress response system evolved, there were usually two outcomes to the struggle: either one survived or died, or the resolution happened fairly quickly. However, today the character of our stressors has changed from being predominantly short-lived and physical to prolonged and psychosocial. Today it is not the tiger but the job, the family, the board examination, the lawsuit or the alcoholic spouse which is the stressor — and often this stressor is prolonged in time to months and years in duration. The problem is that our body today reacts to these psycho-social stressors in the same way as it reacted to the physical stressor in the past, such that the stress response which once had an adaptive survival value can now become maladaptive. As average life expectancy has extended due to technological and medical advances, this has led to a situation in which stress-exacerbated illnesses of all types now abound. Thus, we have seen the rise of conditions such as migraines, chronic pain, depression, anxiety, irritable bowel syndrome and other functional GI disorders, hypertension, asthma, eating disorders, etc. From the perspective of CBP, it is quite possible that if our bodies could learn to react to prolonged psycho-social stressors in a new way, we could greatly reduce the frequency and severity of a whole range of stress-exacerbated conditions. (4)

According to Sri Aurobindo and the Mother, this sort of evolution does not have to wait for the slow action of random genetic mutations and selective pressure. In fact, we can evolve much more quickly and consciously due to the existence of a subtle body-consciousness that can be aroused and activated. Sri Aurobindo and the Mother explained that the body has a consciousness of its own, and this body-consciousness can be developed to such a extent that it can obey the mental will or even act independent of the will (5). The body-consciousness in most human beings is currently quite dormant and strongly influenced by the inertia of the Inconscience. However, a patient and persistent development of the body-consciousness can break the resistance of the physical consciousness. As the inertia is progressively lifted, the body-consciousness is more and more awakened and at an optimal point can start responding to what is willed and to positive mental formations. Such positive mental formations can be used in healing both physical illnesses per se as well as psychosomatic disorders. The responsiveness of the body consciousness to positive mental formations is conducive not only for the purpose of healing but also for those who aspire to offer the body as a template for evolutionary progress:

There are many healing methods that attempt to connect with the body consciousness in some way. Here is one example:

> A consciousness-based therapist working with chronic shoulder pain that was not abating for many years concentrated to receive a message from the client's body. She put her hand on the affected part of the shoulder and meditated over the course of three sessions. The therapist subsequently dreamt of somebody falling down in the midst of a horse-ride. She inquired and discovered that the client had actually fallen during a horse-ride as a child and hurt her shoulder many decades back. Unravelling this incident gave a new impetus to her counselling, which was now directed to work through the client's body consciousness. (6)

There is also the famous case reported by Dr. Paul Pearsall, in which a 10 years girl received the heart of an 8 years old who had been murdered. After the transplant, the 10 years old recipient had nightmares of how the donor was killed, which provided vital clues to track down the assailant. (7) In this case, it is not clear whether the cells of the heart retained the memory in a sort of "cellular memory", or whether a telepathic phenomenon prevailed. However, the case clearly shows that there was a "remembrance" that lies beyond the scope of the brain and mental memory, and which outlived the life-span of the donor. These and many other cases show that the body has wonderful capacities which remain usually unexplored and untapped.

In fact, modern research is now confirming what yogic wisdom asserted long back, which is that the gut exhibits behaviour independent of the brain. As it turns out, 90% of the fibres in the vagus nerve (the primary nerve regulating the gut) carry information from the gut to the brain and not vice versa. About two thirds of the activity of the immune system is consolidated in the gut itself. Thus, the "gut brain" in combination with the effects of microbiomes in the gut, can partially determine our mental/emotional state and play a key role in many diseases. (8) Sri Aurobindo has explained that the Inconscience is not only mental but also vital and physical. If that is so, then the subconscious of the gut can store repressed memories of uncontrollable cravings that can surge up to cause gastro-intestinal diseases even without primary interference of the mind, just as repressed psychological conflicts in the mental subconscious can surge up as neurotic illnesses.

All these developments show that consciousness-based treatment has to give as much importance to the "body consciousness" as to cognition and emotion. Indeed, just as each individual has to become aware of his or her own unique thinking style and emotional patterns, similarly each has to discover his or her own body consciousness. For example, during relaxation sessions it is common to find that that parts of the body which can relax spontaneously were the ones that had been worked on consciously in the past (whether via sports, body work, music, dance, yoga, tai chi, martial arts, or other sort of body training). All the planes and parts of consciousness are interconnected; we have only divided and analyzed them for convenience of understanding. As Sri Aurobindo commented , "But when we speak of the mental, we take the mind working on its own plane, so to say.But all the parts are interconnected and the mind is working from above right down to the lowest plane of consciousness; and so it is with every principle. It is only for the convenience of understanding, that we classify them". (9)

Finally, note that body work can be essential in cases where spiritual seekers develop psychological maladies, sometimes called "spiritual emergencies" in transpersonal psychology. Cortright echoed the Mother's contention that the body offers one of the best protections against psychological disturbances during spiritual pursuits.

> "Many times in spiritual emergency the person is relatively disconnected from the body and lost in a ferment of experiences on an inner or astral plane. Clinical experience confirms that grounding spiritual emergency in the body allows the process to proceed in a more assimilable way." (10)

Cortright added that in cases of spiritual emergency, diet, physical exercises and bodywork may all need to be combined for optimal effect. (11)

Practices to develop the body consciousness:

Exercise 1:

The following exercise shows that the body has its own form of memory. Participants are instructed to repeat this session daily for some time till the whole body can feel the touch of the air. One is then spontaneously ready to learn how to relax.

In a group session if everybody is instructed to close eyes and concentrate to feel the touch of air generated by ceiling fans in the room, almost invariably, the same result is obtained. The participants are told to feel the air touching the whole body, sequentially from head to feet. They are told to ignore the areas where the touch is not felt and to concentrate where they can. After some time if they are asked to provide feedback, each participant will talk about different areas of the body where they felt the touch. Actually people can feel the touch of the air only on those parts of the body which have been properly exercised, worked upon or which have been habitually used in a regular way. This makes that part of the body receptive to forces that induce relaxation. The teacher would feel it more spontaneously on the head, the painter and computer professional in the hands, the weight-lifter on the shoulders.

When a middle-aged person told he could only feel it in his legs, the therapist asked him how he exercised with his legs. The participant paused for a while and then remembered that till twenty years back, he was a regular football player. He had stopped playing and even exercising his lower limbs for two decades and yet his lower limbs retained the memory of being exercised and having been worked upon.

Exercise 2:

The body consciousness can be developed to increase the efficacy of the organs. Sri Aurobindo has described how in a transformed body, the organs will have subtler ways of action. The following exercise, inspired by Sri Aurobindo's sonnet –"The Golden Light" (12) can be modified to have a more extensive meditation on the organ systems:

Subjects are instructed to meditate on a Light (preferably golden — the colour of transformation) systematically permeating the whole brain substance — concentrating on the functions of the medulla (controlling the mechanical functions of the body like heart-beat, respiration), the cerebellum (controlling equilibrium), the mid-brain (controlling reflex actions connected with senses, touch, seeing and hearing) and cerebrum (the centre for consciousness, conscious remembrance of the past, awareness of the present, reason and intelligence as well as future planning). Alternatively, the subject can bring the light onto a neuron in the centre of the brain, focusing on the cell-body, on dendrites that receive signals, the axon that sends out signals and the synapse — the junction between two nerve cells.

Subjects can then focus the golden light to any other organ that needs attention or whose functioning is disturbed. One can visualize the whole organ and permeate it with the light or alternatively can focus on the typical structural and functional unit of that organ (cardiac myocyte in case of the heart, hepatocyte in the case of liver, nephron in case of kidney, islets of Langerhans in case of pancreas, etc.). Meditating with the organs improve their functioning and gives a deeper inkling of the body consciousness.

Exercise 3:

This is a powerful exercise based on a seed-idea in Sri Aurobindo's *The Synthesis of Yoga*. (13)

The subject is placed in a comfortable posture and helped to feel relaxed. If this is difficult, a simple relaxation technique is employed. The subject is then told to visualize oneself in another body behind the present body. For some it may be difficult and might have to proceed by visualizing a part of the second body behind one's physical body. Once the second body is visualized or felt behind the physical body, the subject is told to transfer all normal sensations (like hunger, thirst, fatigue) and disturbing sensations like slight twitches, pains, aches, stiffness, abdominal distension, tightness in chest, tremors or even palpitations and other unpleasant body movements to the body behind. These sensations are felt "as if they were experiences of some other person with whom it has so close a *rapport* as to be aware of all that is going on within him". (14)

There can be a dramatic response, such as a sudden relief from habitual pains, aches or stiffness. This exercise can be practiced at regular intervals as it gives a clarity to the subject about the body's functionings. One can appreciate the point of disharmony within oneself. This exercise breaks the physical inertia and gives glimpses to the subtle workings of the body.

> *Mind flowed unknowingly in the sap of life*
> *And Matter's breasts suckled the divine Idea.*
> *A miracle of the Absolute was born;*
> *Infinity put on a finite soul,*
> *All ocean lived within a wandering drop,*
> *A time-made body housed the Illimitable.*
> *To live this Mystery out our souls came here.*
>
> Savitri, *pg. 101*

References

1. Agenda 1V, pg. 116-117
2. CWM 7, pg. 144
3. CWSA 29, pg. 180-181
4. Basu,S: The Reaction to Stress, Srinvantu, Vol.XXXVII,No.4; Vol. XXXVIII, No.1, Nov.1989-Feb.1990
5. CWSA 28, pg. 176
6. Basu,S: A Journey Through Pain – A personal therapeutic saga, Namah-The Journal of Integral Health, Vol.23, no.3, 2015, pg. 21-27
7. www.thearrowsoftruth.com/tag/dr-paul-pearsall
8. Ibid
9. Evening Talks, pg. 452
10. Cortright, B: Psychotherapy and Spirit, SUNY, New York, 1997, pg. 175
11. Ibid, pg. 175-176
12. CWSA 02, pg. 605
13. CWSA 23-24, pg. 345
14. Ibid

17
The Subconscious

Yet in the exact Inconscient's stark conceit,
In the casual error of the world's ignorance
A plan, a hidden Intelligence is glimpsed.
                                          Savitri, *pg. 658*

The "Subconscious" described by Sri Aurobindo is related to the Freudian "unconscious," but is a larger and deeper reality than Freud conceived. According to Sri Aurobindo, the subconscious is both individual and universal in character. It contains all that is rejected from conscious awareness. It contains materials that are unconsciously repressed or consciously suppressed or rejected. It is the ante-chamber of consciousness. The subconscious is responsible for relapse and recurrence of illnesses, for the rigidity of character-structure, and for carrying over parental antecedents. The subconscious cannot be controlled by the reasoning mind or by the mental will. There is little guarantee that whatever lies in the subconscious will not re-surface. Waves arising from the subconscious can invade the conscious awareness, wreak havoc, precipitate distress and turmoil, and retard progress. Sri Aurobindo summed up the subconscious as follows:

"In our Yoga we mean by the subconscient that quite submerged part of our being in which there is no wakingly conscious and coherent thought, will or feeling or organised reaction, but which yet receives obscurely the impressions of all things and stores them up in itself and from it too all sorts of stimuli, of persistent habitual movements, crudely repeated or disguised in strange forms can surge up into dream or into the waking nature. For if these impressions rise up most in dream in an incoherent and disorganised manner, they can also and do rise up into our waking consciousness as a mechanical repetition of old thoughts, old mental, vital and physical habits or an obscure stimulus to sensations, actions, emotions which do not originate in or from our conscious thought or will and are even often opposed to its perceptions, choice or dictates. In the subconscient there is an obscure mind full of obstinate sanskaras, impressions, associations, fixed notions, habitual reactions formed by our past, an obscure vital full of the seeds of habitual desires, sensations and nervous reactions, a most obscure material which governs much that has to do with the condition of the body. It is largely responsible for our illnesses; chronic or repeated illnesses are indeed mainly due to the subconscient and its obstinate memory and habit of repetition of whatever has impressed itself upon the body consciousness. But this subconscient must be clearly distinguished from the subliminal parts of our being such as the inner or subtle physical consciousness, the inner vital or inner mental; for these are not at all obscure or incoherent or ill-organised, but only veiled from our surface consciousness. Our surface constantly receives something, inner touches, communications or influences, from these sources but does not know for the most part whence they come." (1)

There is currently no specific treatment approach that directly deals with the subconscious. So-called "dream work" in the psychoanalytic or Jungian sense is insufficient, as are all existing forms of psychotherapy, body work, and energetic therapies. All of these methods can be helpful for symptoms and for personal growth, but the progress achieved can be undone by a sudden upsurging of the subconscious. Also, note that it can be risky to explore the subconscious unless one has strong contact with the psychic being and the overhead planes of consciousness. In a letter to a disciple who actually tried psycho-analytic treatment in the 1930s, Sri Aurobindo articulates not only a cogent critique of Freud's method of making Oedipal interpretations, but offers sound advice on how to change subconscious patterns of thought, feeling and behavior. He expresses his insight in yogic terminology, but once one understands the worldview of CBP, it is clear that Western psychology went on to learn this lesson the hard way, and reached the same conclusion many decades later:

"Your practice of psycho-analysis was a mistake. It has, for the time at least, made the work of purification more complicated, not easier. The psycho-analysis of Freud is the last thing that one should associate with Yoga. It takes up a certain part, the darkest, the most perilous, the unhealthiest part of the nature, the lower vital subconscious layer, isolates some of its most morbid phenomena and attributes to it them an action out of all proportion to its true role in the nature. Modern psychology is an infant science, at once rash, fumbling and crude. As in all infant sciences, the universal habit of the human mind — to take a partial or local truth, generalise it unduly and try to explain a whole field of Nature in its narrow terms — runs riot here. Moreover, the exaggeration of the importance of suppressed sexual complexes is a dangerous falsehood and it can have a nasty influence and tend to make the mind and vital more and not less fundamentally impure than before.

It is true that the subliminal in man is the largest part of his nature and has in it the secret of the unseen dynamisms which explain his surface activities. But the lower vital subconscious which is all that this psycho-analysis of Freud seems to know — and even of that it knows only a few ill-lit corners, — is no more than a restricted and very inferior portion of the subliminal whole. The subliminal self stands behind and supports the whole superficial man; it has in it a larger and more efficient mind behind the surface mind, a larger and more powerful vital behind the surface vital, a subtler and freer physical consciousness behind the surface bodily existence. And above them it opens to higher superconscient as well as below them to lower subconscient ranges. If one wishes to purify and transform the nature, it is the power of these higher ranges to which one must open and raise to them and change by them both the subliminal and the surface being. Even this should be done with care, not prematurely or rashly, following a higher guidance, keeping always the right attitude; for otherwise the force that is drawn down may be too strong for an obscure and weak frame of nature. But to begin by opening up the lower subconscious, risking to raise up all that is foul or obscure in it, is to go out of one's way to invite trouble. First, one should make the higher mind and vital strong and firm and full of light and peace from above: afterwards one can open up or even dive into the subconscious with more safety and some chance of a rapid and successful change." (2)

Here, Sri Aurobindo's main point is that the conscious parts of the psyche should be well developed before one delves into the analytic "unconscious," which CBP calls the subconscious. Today, as we look back on the developments in Western psychology that transpired after Sri Aurobindo wrote this letter, it is striking how much psychotherapy has evolved in precisely the direction he recommended. Psychoanalysis has become something of a clinical dinosaur that very few practice, and the few who do no longer use Oedipal interpretations. Stimulated by a host of developments in psychology and culture at large, contemporary analysis is much more reality-based, focusing on issues such as attachment, object relations, Kohut's self-psychology, and developing more stable ego functioning. Transference and defense mechanisms are still analyzed, but a much more relational approach frames the whole endeavor and the impacts of real developmental events such as trauma and neglect are understood. Also, psychoanalysts have shed the fiction of objectivity and accepted the reality of relativism that comes with post-modernity, which in analysis is termed "inter-subjectivity," meaning the analyst and analysand are two subjects who interact with and influence each other in the analytic relationship. (3) Furthermore, within the larger field of psychotherapy as a whole, the vast majority of therapies delivered today are not regressive in the sense of breaking down ego defenses, but rather focus on conscious awareness and developing more adaptive functioning in the present. Thus, psychotherapy has steered towards CBT, problem-solving therapies, interpersonal and family-system approaches, DBT, acceptance and commitment therapy, etc. Even trauma therapies that address complex PTSD devote great time and attention to stabilization and developing effective coping skills before trying to reprocess traumatic memories.

All of these developments are consonant with Sri Aurobindo's recommendation to "make the higher mind and vital strong and firm," before delving into the subconscious. As for his yogic references to higher ranges of consciousness and things such as "light and peace from above," contemporary Western psychology and psychiatry are also now moving in this direction, too. The last decade has seen an explosion of interest in mindfulness, meditation, breathing exercises, hatha yoga, and other spiritual practices (such as chanting mantras), and research now shows these to be helpful for everything from eating disorders to depression, anxiety, and PTSD. (4)

Trauma Therapy

One of the cardinal developments in clinical practice over the last 40 years has been the rise of trauma therapy, which focuses on the negative impacts of real traumatic events such as rape, war, witnessed tragedies, and other forms of abuse or neglect. Since the Vietnam War and the women's rights movement put a spotlight on trauma, the advent of post-traumatic stress disorder (PTSD) as a diagnostic and explanatory tool has had a profound impact both on clinical work and culture at large. Culturally, it has led to a growing awareness of the negative mental health impacts of physical, sexual, and verbal abuse of children. This has helped to change attitudes about the use of physical discipline by parents, and in economically developed countries to mandated reporting to government agencies of cases of abused or neglected children or elders. More recently, revelations about the prevalence of sexual abuse by priests in the Catholic Church has slowly placed pressure on the Vatican to implement reforms; and the same sorts of revelations have led to reform within the Boy Scouts. In adults, the growing awareness of PTSD helped to fuel laws against sexual harassment in the workplace, as well as the recent "Me Too Movement." Obviously, abuse of both children and adults is still far too rampant, but the formulation of PTSD as a clinical problem has been central to appreciating — and measuring — the global burden of suffering attributable to trauma.

Clinically, treatment of PTSD has been difficult because discussing severe traumas often makes patients feel worse initially (by triggering traumatic memories), and medication treatments are often less effective than for other conditions such as depression, bipolar disorder, schizophrenia, and panic disorder. These limitations in treatment have led to much experimentation with novel psycho-therapeutic techniques, including treatments that can have spiritual dimensions. Some of these approaches are now mainstream (such as mindfulness methods), while others are still emerging but not controversial, such as a recent study that using a mantra can be as effective as other methods of therapy for PTSD. (5) However, trauma work can, at times and with certain clients, lead into areas that lie completely outside the purview of conventional psychology. In the West, this type of work is being done more in private practice, where clients and clinicians have the freedom to select each other for openness to this type of work, not in clinics where care is more standardized and subject to regulatory review.

The following case from Dr. Basu's practice of illustrates how, in CBP, the "triggering" of traumatic memories represents the subconscious can rising up and disrupting the outer being:

B was a 6-year old boy who left his home when his father killed his mother by hanging her and burning their shanty. B boarded a train, wandered aimlessly, and went without food for a couple of days before being finally picked up by the police and sent to a correctional home in an Indian city. He had many traumatic experiences in this facility, including being sodomized by older boys to the point of anal bleeding. When he was 12 years old, he was selected for adoption in Norway. As a preparatory measure, he was shifted to a short-stay home before being sent to Norway. During this time, B often disturbed the female nurse by attempting to molest her. His behaviour dramatically improved when he was sent to Norway. He liked his foster parents and their children, adapted himself to his new country, school and religion (he was converted), and picked up the language. Things were proceeding well until he was 16 and it was time for assuming an independent, adult role in an alien country. His old traumatic memories surged up from the subconscious and caused recurrent nightmares. He felt alienated and depressed. He was miserable and demonstrated spells of crying and fits of anger. He was diagnosed to be suffering from severe PTSD.

While biological, psychological, and energetic treatments can all be helpful for complex PTSD and disrupted attachment, as clinicians working in this arena know, this work can be long and hard, and traumatic memories can surge up at any point in a person's life. In B's case, the four years of warm nurturing by his foster parents could not counter his subconscious memories at a critical point of his life when he was supposed to take on an adult role. In fact, for children like B such phenomenon are common.

On the other hand, just as much as the subconscious can store traumatic memories, it can also store more helpful formations of consciousness that one has imbibed at some point in life. For example, the following case illustrates how the subconscious can also store positive and healing potentials:

S, an 18 year old youngster from a rural background, was now expected to move to a city for higher learning. Appalled with the fast-paced rat race of city life that contrasted with his easy going village life, he sought refuge in inertia that was reinforced by taking recourse to heroin abuse. Heroin gave him a zombie feeling which made him happy to be cut off from the rat-race where he would have to take responsibilities. He also smoked cannabis which made him more amotivational in life. When his father passed away, he attended the funeral services in an inebriated state so that he was spared the customary rituals.

He had been admitted several times for detoxification and rehabilitation but nothing worked out for he always loved to lapse into inertia with drugs. His desire to enjoy his inertia was so strong that he preferred to deal with the pain of his heroin withdrawal not by rational therapy but by taking more drugs to drive again into inertia. It was as if his inertia was too profound to let him cognize about his own plight or take a decisive movement to enforce his willpower.

It was only when all doors of help to maintain his bare sustenance in life were closed that he himself woke up to the necessity of overcoming his inertia by his willpower. He had been brought up in a stable, religious and cultured family whose values he had imbibed and so long were dormant in his subconscious. At a time when all other avenues in life were blocked, these higher values surfaced to motivate him to get over his habit of inertia. This was a point that was also worked through in his counselling sessions. A focus on cultural values steeped in spirituality took precedence over the focus on cognitive techniques. The early results were so encouraging that his determination increased and he took up his studies which he had abandoned. Within a few years he established himself as a professional financial expert.

This case illustrates the general approach CBP takes to the subconscious, which is not to go digging for it but to develop the higher planes and parts of the being first, while being cognizant of the existence of the subconscious and its periodic upsurges. In another letter, Sri Aurobindo explained his advice as follows:

"About the subconscient — it is the submaterial base of the being and is made up of impressions, instincts, habitual movements that are stored there. Whatever movement is impressed on it, it keeps. If one impresses the right movement on it, it will keep and send up that. That is why it has to be cleared of old movements before there can be a permanent and total change in the nature. When the higher consciousness is once established in the waking parts, it goes down into the subconscient and changes that also, makes a bedrock of itself there also. Then no farther trouble from the subconscient will be possible. But even before that one can minimise the trouble by putting the right will and the right habit of reaction on the subconscient parts". (6)

Finally, it has to be acknowledged that negative occult forces stand behind much perpetration of trauma, and this can lead to much complexity in the interactions between physical and supra-physical factors in trauma therapy. From the perspective of CBP, the same hostile vital powers that influenced Hitler and Stalin to kill millions of people stand behind not only ongoing global conflicts and tragedies, but also behind the smaller scale interpersonal traumas of rape, assault, and abuse of children and elders. These forces find any possible avenue for expression and exploit that, and heavy substance abuse opens the "gateway" that Sri Aurobindo speaks of to invasion by these negative vital beings and forces. Thus, in the clinic we see a pattern in which child abuse and neglect unfolds in the context of previously traumatized adults who abuse substances and perpetrate abuse, and thus create children who are biologically, psychologically, and spiritually more likely to repeat this pattern and transmit trauma across generations. Of course cases are varied and this pattern is not the explanation for every situation, but it is important to recognize this common presentation of interaction effects.

Following are several cases of trauma therapy that take such occult factors into consideration, contributed by Dr. Susan Curtiss, who works in the United States. (7) To place these cases in context, it is important to understand that this type of work takes years, and that clients often will not disclose their occult experiences unless and until they feel the therapist believes them. Because severe trauma fragments ego functioning, which can lead to the phenomenon of dissociation or what used to be call "multiple personality disorder," the therapist has to be skilled in both standard methods of supporting ego integration and be open to considering spiritual approaches to treatment. Thus, the integral trauma therapist must work on both outer and inner issues simultaneously. These are long treatments that can take years of therapy totaling 20-40 hour long sessions per year, and sometimes more.

Some of the outer issues to deal with include addressing substance abuse, managing triggers and alleviating symptoms, restoring physical balance, resolving emotional dysregulation, developing attunement, and building attachment and more healthy interpersonal relationships. However, at the same time, the integral therapist has to be aware of the possibility of past-life influences, the role of possession and/or hostile forces in the creation of the traumatic sequelae, and the way in which divine support is experienced during the traumatic events and subsequent treatment. The presence of subtle dimensions of consciousness may be experienced directly with the use of treatments that create abreactions as memories are re-processed. The therapist's own spiritual orientation and development can be crucial in acknowledging what is at play. If the clinician does not have the consciousness to recognize the exact nature of what is involved in the unfolding of the traumatic events, it is helpful, if not imperative, to seek consultation from spiritually developed people to interpret what is happening and possibly intervene in the treatment.

Case 1

A married businesswoman and mother of two entered treatment ostensibly to deal with her relationship with her husband and her frequent and extremely debilitating migraine headaches.

Lucy was one of 8 children and grew up in a devout Roman Catholic family. Her father had intended to go to seminary but married a woman who also thought of becoming a nun. The father became very alcoholic; the mother periodically beat and abused all the children and they were forced to watch her cruelty to their siblings. Lucy's mother would then "switch" and seem to have no recollection of her behavior. She herself had been brought up in a violent and extremely abusive family where there also was alcoholism. As treatment progressed it became clear that Lucy's mother had survived her childhood trauma by dissociating to such an extent that she could be diagnosed with multiple personality disorder, so severe that her parts had no knowledge of one another. Although Lucy's husband was a successful senior executive in an insurance business he was often dissociated and repeated himself over and over in ways that infuriated Lucy. It soon became clear that her husband, who had a rejecting and abusive family background, was also switching from one personality to another with no recognition of the shift. Lucy worked through much of her own developmental traumas and was able to raise her children and tolerate her husband's difficulties despite how enraging they were to her.

Lucy's spiritual orientation was critical to her successful treatment. During some of the most difficult periods of her recovery she began her work day at a large old Roman Catholic Church where she prayed and had vivid dialogues with God. These "conversations" were very sustaining to her and she credits them with feeling able to uncover and tolerate the knowledge of the abuse she had sustained. A turning point was reached when Lucy decided to leave the business world and enter a prominent theological seminary with the aim of eventually becoming ordained. The night before her first day at the seminary, she experienced a descent of luminous and loving consciousness which entered her crown chakra and remained for several hours. This served as confirmation that she had made the correct choice despite her fears that her background might make her unfit for this profession. The memory of it sustained her during the challenges that this training involved. She graduated with honors and became a hospital chaplain at a facility that treated alcoholics and drug abusers. She was highly successful with this population and received much recognition for her work. Throughout her treatment and studies she felt the presence and guidance of the spiritual realms. The therapy encouraged her to listen to these descents of spiritual force and to trust their presence and support. It is interesting to note that Lucy is the only one of the eight siblings who did not develop a substance abuse problem of some form. And she is the only one whose longing for God contact reached such a tangible form, although it was certainly a factor in her family of origin. One might look to the influence of the psychic being as an explanation for her progress in her recovery.

Case 2

Allie, a successful vice president of a large US corporation in her early 30's, sought psychotherapy to deal with blackouts and flashbacks triggered by blood, violence or deep grief. Over the next six years she quit three executive positions to focus on her new job #1 - the soul. Her father was her main perpetrator. His functioning deteriorated right after her birth when he lost a valuable consulting job and was never able to work at a high level again. There were six children in the family; at times the three oldest boys were physically violent with their younger siblings and parents. Allie was repeatedly sexually violated and physically abused by her father when she stood up to him. He broke her nose and fractured her back. He had raised her as a boy and seemed fascinated by her stoicism. When Allie was six, her father said she was "too big for [her] britches." So, he carried her into the woods behind their home and brutally sodomized her. She nearly completed a plan to hang herself but was resilient enough to go on and survive by cooling to him, while cultivating connections with her mother and the parents of friends.

After seeing some of her flashbacks, Allie's acupuncturist referred her to a gifted psychic to help her understand why she had endured so much suffering. The psychic's conclusion about the horrific dynamic between Allie and her father - "true" or not - was that her father was seeking revenge on her for murdering him in a previous life. Allie took this information in stride and it helped her continue to avoid falling into a victim stance. Instead , she saw her struggle in a larger light - and she persisted to meticulously document and reprocess all the traumatizing incidents.

The most terrifying flashback Allie had involved seeing on television a man's eyes shining from behind an African mask. The "look" was so reminiscent of her father's when he abused her that she let out a scream that "sounded like someone being killed" and drove 65 miles to a friend's home. Parenthetically, her older sister shared that she, too, had seen such a "look" in her father's eyes at age 12 when he became enraged and assaulted her after she said that she "could marry a black man" if she wanted to. The event prompted this sister to go to her bedroom and "stare at the wall for three days." The exact nature of what was seen in the eyes of the mask is not known but its effect verged on the demonic. Conversely, when Allie was remembering and reprocessing some of the more horrific early events, she relived vivid dialogues with the Archangel Gabriel who appeared to her at the time and comforted her.

In sum, in this case there appears to be action perpetuated by some hostile entity that the father was subject to, owing to some confluence of childhood abuse he likely suffered, coupled with his fragile state and decompensation. And there was the sustaining presence at crucial times of an "angelic" being that appeared to protect and support the child Allie.

Allie is highly intelligent and has a compassionate and "pure" nature and great integrity. After becoming symptom -free from PTSD, Allie set out to write an account of her healing couched in a sophisticated cultural analysis. She had cultivated deep knowledge of the latest research and understanding of trauma, its causes and treatments. But when she shared her plan to write this book to help others, her siblings decided to thwart her in every way to stop publication. Her computers, phones and cars were hacked, her sleep was disrupted using sophisticated microwave technology, and her activities constantly surveilled. Even the therapist's phone and computer were hacked. The techniques used by the family to stop the writing were validated through consultation with a notable

Indian swami whose advice and protection were sought by the therapist. Allie's book will be published and the family violence brought to justice according to this reading.

Case 3

Sally entered therapy in her late 40's when she started having memories of being raised in a satanic ritual abuse cult. Her childhood experiences were compounded by being used in U.S. government-sponsored mind control experiments carried out by her father, who was in the military. The cult was multi-generational; her grandparents as well as her parents were members. The practices in ritual abuse cults are extreme and involved all manner of sexual abuse, pornography, human trafficking, ritual deaths and incarceration in coffins, both real and feigned murders of babies and adults, cannibalism and torture. Children are manipulated to believe they are the perpetrators or cause of all these deeds. In short, Sally was tortured and traumatized to an extraordinary degree and survived this abuse by having her ego fragment into hundreds of parts connected to these experiences. These parts, referred to as "kids", were repressed during her early adult life and she was able to attend college and graduate school and function in a relatively normal way. As she strengthened, the "kids" began to speak to her triggered by a myriad of aspects connected to seasonal activities and places wherever there were gatherings or events that had ritual aspects. These voices in her head frequently berated her for her lack of protection, her bad choices, their traumatic experiences ; she was told she was responsible for the horrors they had been subject to and she should kill herself.

A different scenario emerged in the consulting room. To be with Sally there was to be in a luminous and crystal - clear expanded consciousness that was generated and held both client and therapist as she processed these experiences. Sally chose spiritual parents to replace the abusive ones she had had. The therapy then became listening to and acknowledging the returning parts, hearing their complaints, and tolerating the knowledge of their experiences. Safety for them to share what had happened to them was done by calling in imagined temples of truth and justice and love and peace. Sally would go into trance and channel messages of consolation and healing from her spiritual "parents" and by hearing out the parts they could "return" to consciousness and be settled and calmed.

Sally's experiences evoked both hostile forces and anti-divine presences as well as spiritually benevolent and loving beings in the subtle realms. Although it has been a long process dealing with these traumas and torture, Sally's prognosis is good. She is increasingly able to enter her body consciousness and settle the "kids" as new ones still continue to present themselves. The palpable illumined consciousness, possibly the result of the relative emergence of the psychic being, made Sally able to hold her horrific history in a larger spiritual light. Although the embedded hostile forces create an overwhelming challenge in ritual abuse settings, those who survive the many psychological and physical assaults have developed a radiating inner consciousness. The challenge for the clinician is to validate and embrace the conscious expression of both the divine and anti-divine realities.

From the perspective of CBP, it is important to understand the negative cyclical interactions among hostile forces, substance abuse, socio - political processes, and trauma. Hostile forces propagate their influence via substance abuse, which is often associated with the perpetration of rape and violence in the home. This creates traumatized children, who are both neuro - biologically and psychologically more fragile and injected with occult forces, which makes them more likely as adults to engage in substance abuse and the perpetration of further traumas on their children, or if not physical perpetration then inter-generational transmission of psychological stress via impaired parenting as well as, at times, a lingering aura of negative occult forces in the home. At the same time, these hostile forces are also influencing social and political processes that cause further trauma (such as wars), or prevent societies from properly acknowledging and addressing the traumas that have already happened or are ongoing. Examples of this latter process include resistance within the Catholic Church to addressing the problem of sexual abuse perpetrated by priests, global resistance to the "Me Too" movement, and resistance in the United States to fully address the historical traumas of slavery and aggression against Native Americans. CBP sees all of these forces and factors as continually interacting : individual and social , local and non - local, physical and supra-physical.

An awful Silence watches tragic Time.
Pain is the hand of Nature sculpturing men
To greatness: an inspired labour chisels
With heavenly cruelty an unwilling mould.

Savitri, *pg. 444*

References

1. CWSA 28, pp. 216-217

2. CWSA 31, pg. 612-613

3. Mitchell, Stephen A & Black, Margaret J: Freud and beyond : a history of modern psychoanalytic thought, Basic Books, 1995

4. www.eatingdisorderhope.com> Eating Disorder Hope Blog, December 4, 2019

5. Bormann, Jill E et al: Individual Treatmentof Post-traumatic Stress Disorder using Mantra Repitition: A Randomized Clinical Trial, American Journal of Psychiatry, Vol.175:10, 2018, pg. 979-988

6. CWSA 28, p. 221

7. Curtiss, Susan: Personal Communication, May 1, 2020

18
The Inconscience and the Future

I saw the Omnipotent's flaming pioneers
Over the heavenly verge which turns towards life
Come crowding down the amber stairs of birth;
Forerunners of a divine multitude,
Out of the paths of the morning star they came
Into the little room of mortal life.
I saw them cross the twilight of an age,
The sun-eyed children of a marvelous dawn..

Savitri, *pg. 343*

The Inconscience is the original nescience from which evolution begins. There is no equivalent for Sri Aurobindo's concept of the "Inconscience" in Western psychology, however, one can compare and contrast it with Jung's notion of the "collective unconscious." Jung's description of the collective unconscious was derived from his dream of a house where a descending series of floors, representing bygone eras in history, finally ended in a low cave cut into a rock. In the thick dust of this cave lay scattered bones and pieces of broken pottery, and two human skulls from a pre-historic past. Based on this dream, Jung deemed that Freud's description of the unconscious actually pertained to the personal unconscious, which is a reservoir of suppressed or repressed material that was once conscious, while his own description of the "collective unconscious" contained the accumulation of psychic structures and archetypal experiences of both the individual *and* humanity as a whole. However, it should be noted that it was Jung's *interpretation* of his dream that gave rise to the concept of the collective unconscious. (1) Thus, humans inherit unconscious memory traces linked to mankind's earliest experiences.

In contrast with this dream interpretation that lead to the *idea* of the collective unconscious, Sri Aurobindo and the Mother described not one but two different levels of consciousness that are associated with collective memories of the past, and both of these can be directly experienced via yogic methods. One is a subtle or supra-physical plane of consciousness that holds the terrestrial memory of world (often called the akashic record by occultists), and the Mother explained that one can acquire a special ability to contact this terrestrial memory:

> "There is a very interesting fact, it is that somewhere in the terrestrial mind, somewhere in the terrestrial vital, somewhere in the subtle physical, one can find an exact, perfect, automatic recording of everything that happens. It is the most formidable memory one could imagine, which misses nothing, forgets nothing, records all. And if you are able to enter into it, you can go backward, you can go forward, and in all directions, and you will have the "memory" of all things – not only of things of the past, but of things to come. For everything is recorded there."(2)

It is possible that Jung's dream about the collective unconscious arose, in part, from a veiled perception of this terrestrial memory. However, his dream may also have been a symbol of something even deeper and older, which is the Inconscient itself. The Inconscient is actually a sub-physical plane of consciousness that provides the primordial potential from which matter emerges. The Mother described her yogic vision or experience of the Inconscient as follows:

> "In this hole…I went down into a fissure, as it were, between two steep rocks, rocks made of something harder than basalt, black, metallic at the same time, with edges so sharp that you had the impression that were you simply to touch them, you would be flayed. It was something that seemed to have no bottom and no end, and it became narrower and narrower like a funnel, so narrow that there was almost no room left even for the consciousness to pass. The bottom was invisible, a black hole and that went down and down and down, with-

out air, without light, only a kind of glimmer, like a reflection at the peak of the rocks, a glimmer that came from beyond, from something that could be the heavens, but something invisible. I continued to slide down the fissure and I saw the edges, the black rocks, cut with scissors, as it were, shining like a fresh cut, the edges so sharp that they were like knives. Here was one, there another, there another, everywhere, all around. And I was dragged, dragged, dragged down, -- I went down, down, down and there was no end to it, it became more and more oppressive, stifling, suffocating." (3)

While the subconscious can be accessed psychologically, the Inconscience needs a deeper yogic probing than is accessible by any psychological method. It is because of the constant and persistent influence of the Inconscience on the evolving psyche that it is always vulnerable to psychopathology. The Inconscience is not only beyond the purview of conventional psychology, but beyond the purview of any plane of consciousness or type of cognition below the Supermind, which alone has the power to radically transform the Inconscience. However, because the Inconscience was created by the involution of the Supermind, it also contains the dormant potentialities of the Superconscience waiting to reveal themselves through an evolution of consciousness. Thus, the Inconscience carries in it not only the past of the entire material universe, but also the dormant seeds of a future that has yet to manifest, the potentiality of a new consciousness and new creation that has yet to evolve in matter. (4)

There is no currently available method of treatment for dealing with the Inconscience, but its influence can and should be noted, as illustrated in the following case studies:

S, a 45 year old bachelor who was under treatment for the last 20 years for paranoid schizophrenia, was quite stabilized in social settings. He helped his mother to run a kindergarten school where he managed the accounts. He was deeply spiritual and attended weekly study circles. He was adherent to his medications and had a strong therapeutic alliance with his psychiatrist. He had been clinically examined at different points of time and never exhibited any homicidal intent. It was therefore surprising that when his mother was on her death-bed, he suddenly attempted to stab the 17 year-old daughter of his cousin's brother, ostensibly with the idea that if his mother died, his property (including the school) would be grabbed by his cousin. The girl lived and S was both relieved that his victim survived and yet sad that he could not accomplish his mission. His mother died within a few days of this incident.

S was sent to a rehabilitation home for over a year, where he underwent prolonged counseling sessions and was given ample time for introspection. This helped him to get back to his usual stability, and he resumed his spiritual pursuits and got back to managing his kindergarten school, which he continues to do. No specific psychological or psychiatric explanation was ever found to explain his sudden homicidal impulse. Psychometric tests and clinical reviews at different intervals of his life never revealed subconscious homicidal wishes, nor was anything found during his year of residential treatment. From the perspective of CBP, it was due to the influence of the Inconscience, which lies below and beyond the purview of our psychometric tests, so any delusional idea springing from there can be difficult to understand. This might be the reason why delusional behaviour can be quite unpredictable at times.

On the other hand, as the Inconscience contains the dormant potentialities of the Superconscience, a redemption can also have its origin there. For instance, the following case illustrates how a vulnerable subject who was caught up in a mob frenzy suddenly sank into the terrestrial Inconscience — only to be reborn from this fall years later:

At age 30, K impulsively stabbed to death one of his close associates during a street riot, an act which was not planned and about which he was deeply remorseful. Previously, K had always been a peaceful and composed person who got along well with his peers, and he had never had problems with aggression or impulsivity. All this made his murderous action inexplicable both to himself and to those who knew him.

When the author met K in jail, K was informally nursing psychiatric patients who had been imprisoned for various reasons. K told the author that he had read the *Tales of Prison Life* by Sri Aurobindo, a book which was available in the jail library. K wanted some more books by Sri Aurobindo to read. He never discussed this spiritual interest with his jail mates and rather maintained an introspective mood. He had decided with firmness that he should change his mind-set not by ruminating on his feelings of guilt, but rather by sincerely dedicating himself to spiritual growth. The author obliged, and K spent his years in jail studying Sri Aurobindo.

When K was discharged after fourteen years of incarceration, he involved himself with creatively designing engineering tools. He visited the author, who was impressed by K's new-found confidence. Sri Aurobindo had described in his tale of prison-life how his own incarceration on charges of sedition had become a gateway to many transformative spiritual experiences. Inspired by this example, K had used his time in prison to find a new sense of spiritual meaning and purpose in life.

In the terms of CBP, K's sudden and inexplicable act of violence was due to falling into the terrestrial Inconscience, which is the ultimate root of such murderous impulses. K's fall into the Inconscience was not willed or conscious, but the Mother has described how she consciously plunged into the depths of the Inconscience to discover how the fountainhead of the Superconscience lies dormant there, waiting to be activated. (3, 4) Thus, in falling unwittingly into the Inconscience, K might have come into contact with this dormant Superconscious that holds the seeds of the future concealed in darkness.

The Future: Towards a Greater Psychology

In this book, we have explored how the worldview of Sri Aurobindo and the Mother is relevant to clinical psychology and psychiatry. To summarize, they changed the aim of classical Indian yoga from the search for a static awareness that transcends the world, to a dynamic process of transformation that embraces life in the world and promotes the evolution of consciousness in both individuals and social collectives. This change of focus validates the *raison d'être* of psychology and opens up new vistas for the development of supra-rational cognitive capacities, the growth of the inner or subliminal being, and the bringing forth the psychic being (evolving soul) as the central principle of consciousness that organizes and guides the development of the entire outer being (i.e., ego structure.) An integrative psychology that embraces all of these different planes (dimensions) and parts of the being, both inner and outer, would be a truly whole-person psychology.

Some of the highlights of Sri Aurobindo and the Mother's consciousness-based view of life and psychology include:

A new cosmological description of Consciousness as the cause and creator of Matter, and as the driver of the evolution of life forms in matter

The discovery of the Supermind, the non-dual creative power of the Infinite that becomes a graded series of worlds or planes of consciousness via the descending process of involution, and then returns to its origin via the ascending process of evolution.

The elucidation of an evolving soul, or psychic being, which is the delegate of the Supermind in the evolution of consciousness on Earth that guides the development of the psyche in all its various parts and dimensions, both inner and outer.

The description of involved, non-material, non-evolutionary planes of consciousness that account for a wide range of phenomenon from mythology, folklore, and possession states.

The characterization of supra-rational matrices of cognition, which include the Higher Mind, Illumined Mind, Intuitive Mind, and Overmind

The description of an inner or subliminal being that supports the outer being (the ego structure of the biopsychosocial model), opens to the cosmic consciousness, and accounts for many paranormal phenomenon studied in parapsychology and transpersonal psychology.

The characterization of the Inconscient, a densely involved form of the Supermind that resists the evolution of consciousness and is the root cause of all forms of both physical and psychological pathology.

The development of a cellular yoga that has the potential to transform the body and even to evolve post-human forms of life.

Taking all of these propositions together, Sri Aurobindo and the Mother formulated an "integral yoga" that encompasses the past and present strivings of the evolution of consciousness as it moves towards its future potentials on Earth. Over the last century, the mainstream of psychology and psychiatry have evolved to the point that they are now ready to open to this new, consciousness-based perspective. The first step of this process is already evident in the diffusion of mindfulness practices across both clinical and research settings. We expect the next step to unfold gradually, as people become aware of different planes or dimensions of consciousness and feel a growing need to turn to CBP for insight. In fact, even now one already sees a shift in the focus of mindfulness towards CBP. For instance, while Buddhism in India originally focused on transcending the cycle of karma and rebirth, most people who use mindfulness and related Buddhist practices today, do so to achieve peace and compassion *in this world,* and there are many ongoing efforts to integrate meditative practices with psychotherapy. Thus, the general focus of contemporary Buddhist psychology is on transforming problematic aspects of ego functioning and/or traumatic experiences, and this aim of transforming consciousness while yet remaining engaged in the world is entirely consonant with CBP. Why this shift in orientation happened is not entirely clear: it may be due to the influence of Western culture on Buddhism, the general evolution of consciousness on Earth, and/or the influence of the Dalai Lama, who has focused his teaching on the practice of compassion. (5) However, whatever the cause of this shift in emphasis, Sri Aurobindo and the Mother would agree that it is a good thing, and that the only way to change the world is to transform one's own consciousness. For that, in summary, is the whole point of CBP.

As we look towards the future, three aspects of CBP stand out as being especially useful for clinical psychology and psychiatry. First and foremost is the fact that CBP sees no contradiction between science and spirituality, which is essential given the current and coming advances in medical science. Because of CBP's focus on the spiritual consciousness of matter and the yoga of cells, it can naturally absorb developments in biology and neuroscience without any qualms or quandaries.

The second advantage of CBP is its focus on the inherent growth potential of all human beings. Because long-term psychotherapy is too expensive to deliver at a population level, and its outcomes have been unimpressive in any case, to work at a large scale mental healthcare must find an approach that is based more on self-development on the part of clients. Whereas medical science can already transplant whole organs and is likely to develop tissue-regenerating technologies in the future, it is highly unlikely that we will ever be able to transplant the whole CNS and much less that mysterious mixture of tissue and subjective experience that we call "personality." The closest that psychology and psychiatry may ever come to such whole-person transplant procedures would be conscious rebirth in a new body, and then we have landed squarely in the lap of yoga. Thus, whatever clinical innovations come in mental health, they will have to depend on the inherent growth-potential of the client as much or more than on the knowledge of clinicians. Fortunately, CBP sees this situation not as an inherent barrier to what can be achieved in real life, but as the very wisdom of the process through which consciousness grows. Because the same supreme Consciousness that created all the worlds and planes of existence also created the individual psychic being, this means that the knowledge and power of the Infinite is lodged deep in every human soul, and hence self-development and self-growth are not only possible but in the very nature of things inevitable. The role of the clinician is therefore not to give clients what they lack, but rather to help them find and bring forth what they already have within.

The third advantage of CBP is cultural. While the major religious traditions of the world have patriarchal roots that they have yet to outgrow, this is not so for integral yoga. The shared work of Sri Aurobindo and the Mother created a progressive model for female-friendly spirituality that still belongs more to the future than to the past. The Mother was one of the great women leaders of the 20th century, and Sri Aurobindo supported matriarchal spirituality both in theory and practice. In fact, some of his prose and poetry about the Mahashakti or Supreme Goddess is unrivalled in the literature of any culture in the world. For example, already in the 1920s, decades before Western academia became interested in matriarchal religion, Sri Aurobindo had already set forth a new theology of the Divine Feminine in a little booklet entitled *The Mother*, in which he wrote with sweeping vision and soaring language:

"The one original transcendent Shakti, the Mother stands above all the worlds and bears in her eternal consciousness the Supreme Divine. Alone, she harbours the absolute Power and the ineffable Presence; containing or calling the Truths that have to be manifested, she brings them down from the Mystery in which they were hidden into the light of her infinite consciousness and gives them a form of force in her omnipotent power and her boundless life and a body in the universe. The Supreme is manifest in her for ever as the everlasting Sachchidananda, manifested through her in the worlds as the one and dual consciousness of Ishwara-Shakti and the dual principle of Purusha-Prakriti, embodied by her in the Worlds as the Planes and the Gods and their Energies and figured because of her as all that is in the known worlds and the unknown others. All is her play with the Supreme; all is her manifestation of the mysteries of the Eternal, the miracles of the Infinite. All is she, for all are parcel and portion of the divine Conscious-Force. Nothing can be here or elsewhere but what she decides and the Supreme sanctions;

> nothing can take shape except what she moved by the Supreme perceives and forms after casting it into the seed of her creating Ananda." (6)

What can one say to that, other than "wow"? And from there Sri Aurobindo goes on with his memorable evocation of the four great powers of the universal Mahashakti, which are Maheswari (wisdom, majesty and compassion), Mahakali (force, will and strength), Mahalakshmi (sweetness, beauty and harmony), and Mahasaraswati (skill, knowledge and perfection in work). Friends, even if Sri Aurobindo is wrong and there is no such Goddess, it is still true that some girls need super-heroes like Wonder Woman to give them confidence, and that those girls will become women who may still need the "Four Powers of the Mother" to help them face life's challenges. And why, by the way, should not boys and men also benefit from these healthy symbols of the Divine Feminine? For all the discussion of pre-egoic and trans-egoic causes of mysticism that psychology has engaged in, in fact much of mythology and religious iconography can be interpreted as being simply egoic, as images of the ego-ideals to which people aspire both individually and collectively. We all want to be more brave and wise and beautiful and effective, and we find examples of this everywhere in comic books, video games, and the movies. From this purely pragmatic perspective, Sri Aurobindo should be thanked for having given the world such potent and positive feminine symbols of the Divine. And if his metaphysics are right, then the world needs his invocation of the Divine Mother not only because it is psychologically useful, but even more because it is spiritually true.

Furthermore, in addition to writing *The Mother* plus an epic poem with a female heroine (Savitri), Sri Aurobindo also showed Western culture how to heal its deeply dysfunctional relationship with mysticism. And he did this not by preaching to the West about the wisdom of the East, but by appreciating the roots of Western culture itself. For what is unique about Sri Aurobindo as compared to other Eastern teachers and traditions is that he had a profound knowledge and even love of Western culture. Though Bengali was his mother tongue, he was schooled in England and he was trained in the Western classics and read ancient Greek in the original. These interests lead him to compose an epic poem, *Ilion*, in which he described the fall of Troy as seen by the Gods, using his own novel method of adapting the ancient Greek hexameter into modern English. (7) For Western psychology, the importance of this literary masterpiece is that it heals the shame and disconnection of historical trauma that Western culture has inflicted on itself for about 1,500 years. Ever since Emperor Justinian gave the Catholic Church the legal power to eradicate paganism and heretics in the 6th century CE, (8) the West has marginalized and at times even oppressed its own mystics. The Church dogmatically rejected the spirituality of ancient Greece, and confined even Christian mysticism to narrow officially sanctioned channels. Indeed, so deep and severe was this rejection of indigenous European mysticism that one could even float the psychological interpretation that Christianity's colonial oppression of indigenous "heathens" around the world was, in classic fashion, simply a traumatic repetition of the very same aggression it had previously perpetrated in Europe itself. Unfortunately, the rise of scientific materialism which ultimately challenged this religion in the West only found new reasons to stigmatize mystics yet again, because they did not accept the dogma of materialism either. The impact this had on the development of Western psychology is discussed further in the Appendix, but what Sri Aurobindo offers the West in *Ilion* is the golden opportunity to embrace its own cultural roots and celebrate indigenous European mysticism.

For Western mental health professionals, this re-connection with ancient Greece leads directly to a re-examination of the origins of modern psychotherapy. Every Western psychologist and psychiatrist has to learn about Freud's famous Oedipus complex in the course of training — but few are taught the full story about the origin of this term, which came from the ancient Greek tragedy, *Oedipus Rex*, by Sophocles. If we now go back and re-read that story in the light of CBP, we will find that central to the plot is a prophecy from the Delphic Oracle that Oedipus will kill his father and usurp the throne, which comes true when Oedipus kills Laius at a crossroads on the way to Delphi. Freud's work explores the themes of subconscious sexual and aggressive impulses in *Oedipus Rex*, but he completely overlooked the theme of the Superconscious represented by the Delphic oracle. As students of history know, the Delphic Oracle was dedicated to the God Apollo, as was the Hippocratic oath, and in these two facts we find the clues for how Western psychology can reclaim its own spiritual roots. As Sri Aurobindo showed in *Ilion*, Apollo and the other Gods and Goddesses of ancient Greece never died--what died was the receptivity of the West to its own heritage. Thus, every healthcare professional who considers themselves to be in some way connected with the Western tradition would do well to re-read the introduction to the Hippocratic oath not in the traumatically purged version used today, but in the original:

> I swear by Apollo Healer, by Asclepius, by Hygieia, by Panacea, and by all the gods and goddesses, making them my witnesses, that I will carry out, according to my ability and judgment, this oath and this indenture. (9)

And there you have it — the first breath of Western medicine was not science but yoga, and it is time for the West to reclaim these roots. Even today one can still go on a pilgrimage to Delphi and feel the golden shining presence of Apollo, and meditate on the yogic dictum of "Know Thyself" that used to be inscribed over the entry to his temple there. In fact, many grottos and temples in Greece are still imbued with the presence of the Gods and Goddesses, and these overmental beings and forces are still very much alive to the yogic experience. Thus, from perspective of CBP, the Oedipal myth is a tale about the facets of not seeing. There are things in the subconscious that we do not want to see, and Freud's work reflects on these; but there are also things in the superconscious that we have yet to see, and in the end these are the most important because they frame the whole course and meaning of life. *Oedipus Rex* ends in tragedy, as tragedy is indeed the inevitable outcome of the lower consciousness; but a higher denouement is possible if one accepts the truth of Delphi and commits oneself to the path of yoga, to the quest for a higher consciousness and source of knowledge. Western medicine and psychology have neglected so much of their own heritage, and it took the healing touch of a Bengali mystic named Sri Aurobindo to bring these ancient roots back to life. The West ought to be profoundly grateful for this gift.

In conclusion, and to return to the beginning, Sri Aurobindo's work is a treasure that belongs not just to India, but to the whole world. His transformational vision points the way out of humanity's tragic past and confused present towards a much greater future for each and all. In this book, we have attempted to trace out the many ways in which his richly detailed view of the cosmos and human consciousness is relevant to the concerns of contemporary psychology and psychiatry. While his manner of expression can be admittedly complex, his message can be boiled down to the simple proposition that growth in consciousness is the very essence of existence. We can call that wisdom or philosophy or religion or spiritual science or whatever one wishes — or we can just take a cue from Sri Aurobindo and say that, in the final analysis, "Yoga is nothing but practical psychology." (10)

> *For ever love, O beautiful slave of God!*
> *O lasso of my rapture's widening noose,*
> *Become my cord of universal love.*
> *The spirit ensnared by thee force to delight*
> *Of creation's oneness sweet and fathomless,*
> *Compelled to embrace my myriad unities*
> *And all my endless forms and divine souls.*
> *O Mind, grow full of the eternal peace;*
> *O Word, cry out the immortal litany:*
> *Built is the golden tower, the flame-child born.*
>
> Savitri, *pg. 702*

References:

1. Holroyd, Stuart: Dream Worlds, Aldus Books, London,1976, pg. 26

2. CWM 4, pg. 110-111

3. CWM 15, pg. 361-363

4. Ibid, pg. 365

5. Dalai, Lama: Closing Address to the Global Buddhist Congregation, 2011, New Delhi, 30th November, 2011

6. CWSA 32, pg. 14,15

7. CWSA Vol 2, pp. 333-473, see especially Book VIII, "The Book of the Gods"

8. https://en.wikipedia.org/wiki/Justinian_I

9. https://en.wikipedia.org/wiki/Hippocratic_Oath

10. CWM 23-24, pg. 44

Appendix

Of Mystics, Mothers, and Madness

In Chapter 1, we touched on the controversy about mystics and "madness" in passing but did not delve into the history of this debate in psychology. While some of this debate stemmed from Western cultural bias against mystics, it does have to be admitted that the relationship between mysticism and mental illness can be complex, that it is possible to see manifestations of both in the same person, and that even the lives of great mystics may have moments that can be misinterpreted. For example, a psychologist meeting the Buddha in the middle of his most ascetic phase might have misdiagnosed him as having an eating disorder. Similarly, Sri Ramakrishna went through a phase of cross-dressing that might have been misdiagnosed as a gender identity problem, and Sri Ramana Maharshi went through a period of such prolonged samadhi (trance) states that he might have been misdiagnosed as having a dissociative disorder. And yet all three of these great spiritual figures went on to become extremely stable teachers who gracefully bore hardships that most human beings cannot. Thus, a more accurate and useful way to think of such exceptional individuals is to compare them to elite athletes or military personnel who are able to undergo intense physical training that the average person cannot. And just as heart rate and blood pressure rise to "abnormal" levels during heavy exercise, so too can certain psychological symptoms arise in the course of intense yogic efforts, but these are demand-related phenomenon that resolve after the goal of spiritual discipline is achieved.

Sri Aurobindo and the Mother belong to this class of extraordinary human beings, and their biographies reveal that they were both resilient and had excellent mental health. However, since the history of misdiagnosing mystics with madness still haunts the discourse on mental health, we will explain here why Sri Aurobindo did not suffer from mental illness, as the question has been raised. Let us begin with the biographical data and then proceed to the analysis.

Sri Aurobindo

Born Aravinda Ackroyd Ghose in Kolkata, on August 15, 1872, the boy who was to become Sri Aurobindo was the third son of Dr. Krishnadhan Ghosh and Swarnalata Devi. His father was a doctor who believed in the rationalism of Western science. His mother, sadly, had bouts of mental illness during which she was unable to parent, and sometimes became aggressive or even violent. It is impossible to establish a firm diagnosis today, but the illness was progressive and she was later kept in a bungalow with spacious gardens at Rohini near Deoghar, a popular health resort. (1) Due to his father's wish that Aurobindo receive a Western education, he was sent to England at age 7, along with two older brothers, and remained there until age 20, when he returned to India. It was, no doubt, a difficult childhood as Aurobindo lived with stern landladies, faced isolation and cultural discrimination, and sometimes went cold and hungry as his father fell behind on remittances. Nevertheless, Aurobindo excelled at language and literature, and graduated from Cambridge at the top of his class in classics. While his brothers were social, Aurobindo kept to himself and read avidly. He had a photographic memory and read widely not only in English, Latin and Greek, but also in French, Italian and even some German. By the age of fifteen, he became interested in the status of his homeland and joined a group supporting Indian nationalism. At the end of his stay, he failed the Civil Service exam because he intentionally did not show up for a horse riding test. He later admitted that he felt no inner calling for the Civil Service, and so maneuvered to get himself disqualified without himself rejecting the Service, which his family would not have approved as such a job would have guaranteed him financial security for life. (2)

Upon his return to India at age 20, Aurobindo joined the Baroda State Service, took up administrative work and later began teaching French and English. He started to have initial experiences of a spiritual nature, however, this interest stayed in the background for many years. Instead, Aurobindo focused his energies on the normal concerns of young adulthood, work and relationships, plus the ongoing constant reading of both Indian and Western literature that his extremely high IQ demanded. Since his mother continued to be chronically ill and his father had died just before his return, Aurobindo reunited with his siblings and cousins during his vacations whenever he visited Bengal, and in his free time joined the cause of Indian nationalism. He taught himself Bengali and Sanskrit and proceeded to absorb virtually all of Indian history, philosophy, and literature. He eventually married Mrinalini Bose who hailed from an orthodox Hindu background, but they were to spend limited time living together as Aurobindo became a leader in the freedom movement. After not seeing him for almost a decade, she died of influenza in 1918 just before she was scheduled to travel from northern India to join him in Pondicherry in the south.

In the early 1900s, Aurobindo wrote galvanizing essays on Indian nationalism, and became the first person to publicly call for complete independence from Britain. He was a central figure in the Bengali Renaissance, and he and his friends were involved in what the British called "terrorism" but what any American revolutionary would have called legitimate resistance against colonial oppression. In the wake of a foiled bomb plot developed by his brother's revolutionary group, Aurobindo was arrested and put in jail for a year. It is most likely that Aurobindo knew about the plot, and disapproved it but he remained silent on the subject. However, in a trial that was sensational in India, he was acquitted while his brother was sentenced to hard labor in the Andaman Islands. After he was freed, Aurobindo stayed back at Kolkata, but the British were looking for the least reason to arrest him again, as they considered him to be the most dangerous man in India. Thus, in 1910 he moved to the French territory of Pondicherry (now Puduchery), in Tamil Nadu. There, surrounded by British spies and facing financial hardship, he slowly withdrew from political activity and became a spiritual teacher, and came to be known to the world as Sri Aurobindo.

For in 1905, in the middle of the fight for national freedom, Sri Aurobindo had quietly taken up the practice of yoga and become a master. He experimented with pranayama (breathing) and various other yogic techniques, and reached a major turning point in January 1908, when a yogi taught him meditation. In only three days, Sri Aurobindo attained Nirvana, which is traditionally considered the final goal of Buddhist and Hindu spiritual practice. However, rather than giving up political life at that point, he had continued on with his busy schedule, as he believed from the start that yoga is worthless unless it can be applied to life in the world. It was not until that life forced a new direction for his energies that he set about his greatest work, which was to re-vision the ancient tradition of Indian yoga. From May 1908 to May 1909, he used his time in jail to explore the heights of mystical consciousness, and subsequently in Pondicherry he delved deeply into the entire history and methods of yoga. This period of intensive sadhana (yogic discipline) led to the development of his new approach to yoga which aimed at a supramental transformation of consciousness on Earth. In 1914, Sri Aurobindo was visited by a French couple, Mirra Alfassa and Paul Richard, who came to learn about Sri Aurobindo's philosophy. These meetings led to him launching a monthly journal, the *Arya* (1914-1921), in which he expounded his novel view of consciousness and evolution in a flood of writing that encompassed philosophy, yoga, Indian history, poetry and literary criticism, sociology, politics, translations of ancient texts, and an entirely new interpretation of the Vedas. Sri Aurobindo's intellectual accomplishment in each of those topics was exceptional, but to do this for multiple topics simultaneously was genius.

As Sri Aurobindo's reputation as a visionary yogi slowly grew, more people came to visit this unusual master in Pondicherry, and a few stayed and became disciples. As Sri Aurobindo gradually withdrew from political activity, he let the Indian freedom movement take on new leaders (such as Gandhi). He never viewed this change in focus as a retreat, but rather as an advance: he was confident that India would eventually win its freedom, and he had moved on to a bigger enemy (human nature) and a larger cause (the transformation of consciousness on Earth). This was his own view of his life and work, though of course external observers may have different opinions.

In 1920, Mirra Alfassa returned to Pondicherry to work with Sri Aurobindo. He had tremendous respect for Alfassa's spiritual development and always considered her to be an equal. In 1926, the Sri Aurobindo Ashram was finally launched, which was considered to be a laboratory for transforming human nature rather than an ashram in the traditional sense. By this point in time, he had come to refer Alfassa as "the Mother," which she preferred to the role and term of guru. In recognition of the Mother's extraordinary ability to organize people and teach yoga in practical ways, Sri Aurobindo turned over the day-to-day management of the Ashram to her. From that point on, he retired to his room to focus on what he called "bringing down the Supermind", and appeared publicly only on "darshan days" when disciples could see him briefly as they filed by in silent meditation. However, he continued to keep up active written correspondence with his disciples, from which we have his four volumes of *Letters on Yoga*.

The Ashram was unconventional from the start, and at times the center of controversy. For example, in the 1930s, Sri Aurobindo predicted the rise of Hitler, and took a public stance in favor of the Allies during World War II — a stance that was not popular in India. In the early 1940s, he urged India to accept the Cripps proposal to accept commonwealth status in exchange for sending troops to support the British. Some viewed this as treason against the cause of independence, but history soon proved Sri Aurobindo right, when the dreams of a united and free India ended in the bloodbath of Partition, which could have been avoided by accepting commonwealth status.

After Sri Aurobindo settled in Pondicherry, he turned down multiple requests to rejoin politics. He was even nominated for the Nobel Prize in literature. In the last year of his life, he completed work on Savitri, an epic poem in English blank verse that stands as one of the great works of 20th century literature — and is the single greatest example of yogic poetry since the time of the Vedas. Sri Aurobindo left his body on December 5, 1950, and it is a documented fact that his body lasted five days in the Indian heat before showing any signs of decomposition. Many who came to pay their last respects also commented that the body seemed to glow with light. (3, 4, 5)

The Mother

Born Blanche Rachel Mirra Alfassa in Paris, in 1878, she came from a bourgeois family that had recently emigrated from Egypt. Her father was a banker of Turkish descent who told colourful stories and let birds fly free in his bedroom, while her mother was of Egyptian background, quite serious, and was a staunch materialist. Both parents were non-practising Sephardic Jews. From a psychological perspective, Alfassa's biography reveals remarkable emotional stability, willpower, and freedom from convention. She had mystical experiences and trances from an early age, but had the good sense not to discuss these with her mother, who was considered such things to be a sign of "brain disorder". Her mother adored her older brother, who went on to become the governor of French Equatorial Africa, but was stoical with Mirra. (6) However, Alfassa later appreciated the discipline she learned from her mother, was fond of her brother, and there is no hint of jealousy, low self-esteem, or self-pity in her descriptions of childhood and youth. (7) She developed interests in music (she played piano), painting, and tennis that she maintained for the rest of her life. At age 19, Alfassa married a painter, Henri Morisset, and the couple had a son. She trained as a painter with some of the luminaries of her era, and later studied occultism with a teacher in Algeria. Her recollections of the social circles in which she moved during this period make for interesting historical reading. For example, she was friends with Alexandra David-Neel, knew Matisse, and no less than Rodin asked her advice on how to handle the jealousy between his wife and his model! (8, 9)

Alfassa was twice married and twice divorced, but from her comments, it is evident that understanding of her own life is so divergent from the norms by which conventional biographers judge people, that it is better to suspend judgment and admit that there are things external observers simply cannot know about a subject. (10,11) However, what one can conclude from her various comments about marriage and divorce (12), as well as her visible actions, is that she did not believe in traditional moral or social conventions. She clearly thought that women have the same abilities and rights as men, and her life shows that she was an independent woman who created her own values. Her progressive views on gender equality were later demonstrated again, when she had the girls in her Ashram wear shorts and play sports just like the boys — which was very unusual in India during the 1950s and 1960s.

When Alfassa first met Sri Aurobindo in 1914, he considered her to be his equal from the start. By the end of 1926, he had come to call her "the Mother" and turned over the management of their Ashram to her, as previously explained. After he left his body in 1950, the Mother continued to develop the Ashram with extraordinary skill and energy until she left her body in 1973. In 1968, she also launched the international spiritual community of Auroville just north of Pondicherry, and her pioneering work in education and collective yoga is described in Chapter 6. In short, rather than viewing spiritual communities as a place to retreat from the world, she approached community as a means to advance one's ability to express the soul in life, work, and action. Still, while she was always focused on innovation and progress, she was sensitive in how she dealt with individual and cultural variations in personal preferences. The Mother's style of teaching was warm, personal, and intimate, although she could be frank if needed. The tales of her solicitude and sweetness abound in the Ashram's literature, and she said she always felt students and disciples to be her spiritual children. Among her many contributions to yoga, two that stand out were her emphasis on the psychic being (evolving soul) and her development of cellular yoga in the last two decades of her life. Sri Aurobindo credited her focus on bringing forth the psychic being as radically changing his method of teaching, and while he left many hints in his writings about the consciousness of the cells, it was the Mother who quite literally fleshed out this new branch of yoga.

Now, the first thing that stands out about these two intertwined biographies is that Sri Aurobindo and the Mother were both extremely talented individuals who had leadership abilities, an international perspective, and progressive views on a host of issues that were far ahead of their time. Indeed, if not for the fact that they were mystics, they would be seen as two of the most remarkable figures of the 20th century. However, because they were mystics, inevitably the questions arise. This is especially true for Sri Aurobindo, due to his adverse childhood and having had a mother with mental illness. Thus, it has been asked whether his spiritual visions and experiences might be due to bipolar disorder or psychotic illness? Or was he a cult leader? And what is all this business with "the Mother"— did he have some sort of regressive mother complex?

Based on our reading of the biographical data, the authors think the answer to all these questions is "no." We would also point out that this cluster of questions stems from the long history that Western psychology and psychiatry have of confusing mystical experiences with mental illness, and thus unfairly pathologizing mystics and doubly stigmatizing mystics with mental illness. As we discussed in Chapter 11, there are mystics who have mental illness — but this was not the case for Sri Aurobindo and the Mother. Furthermore, the fact that some mystics have had mental illness does not invalidate them as people nor lessen the importance of their contributions to human culture; nor does the fact that some gurus have been involved in scandals, corruption, and exploitation invalidate yoga and mysticism any more than these same problematic behaviors invalidate other fields where they have occurred, including in science, business, education, democracy, Christianity, and scouting.

The next issue to understand is how psychiatric diagnosis has evolved over time. Due to the fact that psychoanalytic diagnoses were not objectively definable and had poor inter-rater reliability, and because psychoanalysis wrongly pathologized women, gays and lesbians, in the 1970s psychoanalysis started to fall out of favor. A major turning point came in 1980, with the publication of the DSM-III, in which the psychiatric diagnoses were replaced with more behavioral and objectively definable criteria. We now use the DSM-5 in clinical practice, but the basic paradigm remains the same, and in this the definition of mental illness hinges upon inability to function in important areas of life such as school, work, and relationships. Also, in order to be deemed pathological, a person's spiritual beliefs and experiences must be abnormal for their culture or sub-culture. Thus, using current diagnostic criteria, there is no evidence that Sri Aurobindo was psychotic or delusional, because his level of psychosocial functioning was consistently high, he showed none of the cardinal signs of schizophrenia, and his interest in yoga was within the norms of Indian culture. His biography reveals no evidence of major depressive episodes or bipolar disorder, no seizures to suggest temporal lobe epilepsy, no interpersonal turbulence and affect dysregulation to suggest borderline personality disorder, and no evidence of pathological narcissism, antisocial traits, or dependent personality disorder. He was not socially anxious or avoidant, and his mystical beliefs expressed the yoga tradition rather than the magical thinking of schizotypal personality disorder. Finally, it is abundantly clear that his writings demonstrate the complex yet cohesive thought-form of a genius, not the concreteness or disorganization of a thought disorder. Thus, overall there is no reason to think that Sri Aurobindo had a major mental illness, mood disorder, or personality disorder.

This narrows the differential diagnosis down to just the psychodynamic question of neurosis: did Sri Aurobindo have pathological issues due to being separated from his mentally ill mother at a young age, and were his mystical experiences regressive? Now, this debate about mystics, mothers and madness goes back to the early 1900s, and involves some of the founding figures of Western psychology. In *The Varieties of Religious Experience*, William James concluded that sometimes mystical and spiritual experiences are psychologically healthy. In contrast, after reading Romain Rolland's biography of the Indian yogi, Ramakrishna Paramahamsa, Freud took the opposite point of view. In *Civilization and Its Discontents*, he interpreted what he called the "oceanic feeling" of the mystic as a regression to a pre-Oedipal state of fusion with the mother. Rolland disagreed, and the two continued an amicable debate on the topic for years, which Parsons has analyzed lucidly in his sophisticated presentation of how to blend contemporary depth psychology with religious studies in a non-pathologizing way. (13) At the end of this debate, in a letter dated January 19, 1930, Freud admitted that mystical intuition could be "highly valuable for an embryology of the soul when correctly interpreted" and conceded that he was not an "out and out skeptic," for "there are some things we cannot know now." (14)

In the meantime, while Freud spent decades cogitating, Jung went on to develop his own model of psychology that accepted transpersonal states of awareness as potentially healthy. For most of his life, Jung interpreted transpersonal experiences from his perspective of archetypes, which is agnostic about the ultimate nature of reality. However, at the end of his life Jung finally decided that there is a spiritual reality independent of the physical world, and that some sort of spiritual essence of people survives the death of the body. (15) Subsequently, with the development of transpersonal psychology and Wilber's nifty labelling of the "pre/trans fallacy," which entails wrongly attributing a trans-egoic experience to a pre-egoic etiology, Western psychology was finally able to pronounce that the transpersonal experiences of mystics may not be caused by regression to pre-egoic states of functioning. (16) Of course, the determination of whether or not a given individual is having transpersonal experiences that are due to pre-egoic causes, trans-egoic causes, or a mix of the two, is a clinical judgment for which there is no universally validated test. The relationship between mysticism and psychiatric symptoms can be complex, and was addressed in Chapter 11.

From a psychodynamic perspective, the most significant and interesting thing about Sri Aurobindo was not his mentally ill mother, but the healthy adult relationship he had with the Mother. Modern history may have no equivalent example of a spiritual community that had two such accomplished parental figures who demonstrated mutual respect for each other, shared an equal balance of power, promoted equality among the genders, and gave both males and females many ways and symbols to fuse psychological growth with spiritual practice. This is not psychopathology, this is an amazing demonstration of mental and social health. Freud famously said that the goal of psychoanalysis is "to love and to work," and by that standard both Sri Aurobindo and the Mother succeeded admirably.

In fact, the tools of contemporary thinking now allow us to go one step further and interpret Sri Aurobindo's relationship with "the feminine" as pioneering. It is important to note that he came from Bengal, which has a long and vibrant tradition of worshipping the Divine Mother, as evidenced by Ramakrishna's faith, the Kali Temple in Dakshineswar, the Durga puja, and the existence of other female spiritual teachers such as Anandamayi Ma. In addition, growing up in England he learned of Mother Mary, as well the powerful female figures of Queen Elizabeth I and Queen Victoria of his own time, monarch of a global empire on which the sun never set. All of these varied cultural inputs, plus the traditional role of women as homemakers, provided Sri Aurobindo with symbols of the feminine that were both soft and strong, nurturant and warrior-like, in the home and in command. Combine this with his healthy experience as an adult with Mirra Alfassa, and we find the ingredients for a wide-ranging view of "the feminine" as having many modes and powers. And note that he referred to her as the Mother, perhaps because he considered her to be an embodiment of the Divine Mother. Besides, she herself preferred that title to the word "guru," which she felt was too distant and authoritarian to describe the closely connected relationship she had with her disciples.

That is what can be said of Sri Aurobindo's view of human women. As for his metaphysics and theology of the Divine Mother, these cannot be reduced to psychological causes and Sri Aurobindo should be appreciated for having made major contributions to the resurgence of matriarchal spirituality, as was previously explained. Thus, we have now set straight the record on Sri Aurobindo's mental health, and we conclude that he had exceptional resilience and was able to use his own experience of adversity in both childhood and adulthood to increase his empathy for the suffering of others, and to dedicate himself to the healthy goals of "generativity", a term coined by psychoanalyst Eric Erikson to denote a concern for establishing and guiding the next generation. As for dismissive critiques of the Mother as being nothing more than a cultish colonial dominatrix, we shall not even bother with these because they are so obviously biased by a combination of patriarchal prejudice against women, reductionistic materialism, and ignorance about the facts of her life as well as the spiritual traditions of India.

Having thus resolved the past, we may now return to that old debate about mystics, mothers, and madness and see it in a new light. Let us recall where all this controversy began — which was with Sri Ramakrishna, not Sri Aurobindo. It was Sri Ramakrishna who set Swami Vivekananda on the path that lead to the Parliament of World Religions in Chicago, in 1893, and via that opened up the West to meditation and yoga. And it was Sri Ramakrishna who worshipped the Divine Mother with all of his protean emotion, intuitions, and passionate rush into every form of religion he could find, be it Eastern or Western. In retrospect, we can forgive Freud for not knowing what to make of this "mad" mystic because many of his own countrymen and contemporaries were baffled by him as well. Even the young Vivekananda initially thought Ramakrishna's yogic trances were due to hallucinations, though he came in time understand otherwise. In answer to the skeptics who thought there was something lunatic about the man, Sri Ramakrishna once gave this pithy reply:

> "My friends, the whole world is a lunatic asylum. Some are mad after worldly love, some after name, some after fame, some after money, some after salvation and going to heaven. In this big lunatic asylum I am also mad, I am mad after God. If you are mad after money, I am mad after God. You are mad; so am I. I think my madness is after all the best."
> — Sri Ramakrishna (17)

No one has ever framed the debate about mystics and madness better than this, and even a cursory look around the world today proves that Sri Ramakrishna was right. We do live in a madhouse — we live in an international asylum of corporate greed, political corruption, violence, rape, racism, religious fanaticism, sex addiction, substance abuse, militarism, crime, drug cartels, human trafficking, nuclear armaments, irrational rejection of science, and the looming threat of a global climate crisis. In such a world of normalized insanity, Sri Ramakrishna's madness really is a better option — and, slowly, psychology and psychiatry are coming around to this fact. So if today it is the Buddha's agnostic model of mindfulness that holds sway, tomorrow it may well be the rainbow-colored view of the Supreme Goddess championed by Sri Ramakrishna and Sri Aurobindo that leads the way. It is to the hope for such a better and brighter world that we dedicate this quest for a greater psychology that embraces not only who we are and what we have been — but most importantly, who and what we can yet become.

References

1. www.aurobindo.ru.Personalia/Swarnalotta Ghosh nee Bose + Swarnalata

2. CWSA 36, pg. 31

3. Iyengar, K.R. Srinivasa: *Sri Aurobindo: A biography and a history*. SAICE, Pondicherry, 5th Edition, 2006

4. Heehs, Peter: *The Lives of Sri Aurobindo*, Columbia University Press, USA, 2008

5. Sethna, KD: The Passing of Sri Aurobindo [Its Inner Significance and Consequence], Monograph, Mother India, Jan 9, 1951, pg. 20

6. Vrekhem, Georges Van: *The Mother, the Story of Her Life*. Rupa Publications, New Delhi, 2004, pg. 3-14

7. Nahar, Sujata: *Mother's Chronicles*, Book 1, by Sujata Nahar, Institut de Recherches Evolutives: Paris, 1985

8. Op. cit. *The Mother, the Story of Her Life*, pg. 15-36, 37-70, 79-84

9. Op. cit. *Mother's Chronicles, Book 2*, 1986, pg. 78-93.

10. *Agenda II*, pg. 370-374

11. Op. cit. *The Mother, the Story of Her Life*, pg. 75-79,84-86,205-207,214-216

12. *Agenda Vol. 1*, pg, 506, footnote

13. Parsons, W.B: *The Enigma of the Oceanic Feeling: Revisioning the Psychoanalytic Theory of Mysticism*, Oxford University Press, 1999

14. Freud, Ernst: *Letters of Sigmund Freud*, New York, Basic Books,1960

15. Miovic, M: "An introduction to spiritual psychology: Overview of the literature, East and West", Harvard Review of Psychiatry, 12(2), 2004, pg. 105-115

16. Wilber, Ken: "The pre/trans fallacy, The Journal of Humanistic Psychology", 22(2), 1982, pg. 5-43

17. Vivekananda, Swami: *Complete Works, Vol. 3*, 1989, Advaita Ashram, Kolkata, pg. 100

Index

International Publications

Auroville Architecture
by Franz Fassbender

Auroville Form Style and Design
by Franz Fassbender

Landscapes and Gardens of Auroville
by Franz Fassbender

Inauguration of Auroville
by Franz Fassbender

Auroville in a Nutshell
by Tim Wrey

Death doesn't exist
The Mother on Death, Sri Aurobindo on Rebirth
Compiled by Franz Fassbender

Divine Love
Compiled by Franz Fassbender

Five Dream
by Sri Aurobindo

Vision
Compiled by Franz Fassbender

Passage to More than India
by Dick Batstone

The Mother on Japan
Compiled by Franz Fassbender

Children of Change: A Spiritual Pilgrimage
by Amrit (Howard Shoji Iriyama)

Memories of Auroville - told by early Aurovilians
by Janet Feran

Featured Titles

Divine Love

The texts presented in this book are selected from the Mother and Sri Aurobindo.

"Awakened to the meaning of my heart. That to feel love and oneness is to live. And this the magic of our golden change, is all the truth I know or seek, O sage."

Sri Aurobindo, Savitri, Book XII, Epilog

A Vision by the Mother

On 28th May 1958, the Mother recounted a vision she once had of a wonderful Being of Love and Consciousness, emanated from the Supreme Origin and projected directly into the Inconscient so that the creation would gradually awaken to the Supramental Consciousness. The Mother's account of this vision was brought out a first time in November 1906, in the Revue Cosmique, a monthly review published in Paris.

A Dream – Aims and Ideals of Auroville
the Mother on Auroville

50 years of Auroville from 28.02.1968 - 28.02.2018

Today, information about Auroville is abundant. Many people try to make meaning out of Auroville – about its conception, to what direction should we grow towards, and, what are we doing here?

But what was Mother's original Dream and what was her Vision for Auroville back then?

Matrimandir Talks by the Mother

This book presents most of Mother's Matrimandir talks, including how she conceived the idea for this special concentration and meditation building in Auroville.

Memories of Auroville - Told by early Aurovilians

Memories of Auroville is a book about the very early days of Auroville based on interviews made in 1997 with Aurovilians who lived here between 1968 and 1973. The interviews presented in this book are part of a history program for newcomers that I had created with my friend, Philip Melville in 1997. The plan was to divide Auroville's history into different eras and then interview Aurovilians according to their area of knowledge. Our first section would cover the years from 1968 till 1973 when the Mother was still in her physical body.

The Way of the Sunlit Path

May The Way of the Sunlit Path be a convenient guide for activating this ancient truth as a support for a Conscious Evolution.

May it illumine the transformation offered to us in the Integral Yoga.

A Dream Takes Shape (in English, French, Hindi)

A comprehensive brochure on the international township of Auroville in, ranging from its Charter and "Why Auroville?" to the plan of the township, the central Matrimandir, the national pavilions and residences, to working groups, the economy, making visits, how to join, its relationship to the Sri Aurobindo Ashram, and its key role in the future of the world. This brochure endeavours to highlight how The Mother envisioned Auroville from its inception, some of the major achievements realised over the years, and some of the difficulties currently faced in implementing the guidelines which she gave.

Mother on Japan

I had everything to learn in Japan. For four years, from an artistic point of view, I lived from wonder to wonder. And everything in this city, in this country, from beginning to end, gives you the impression of impermanence, of the unexpected, the exceptional... ...everything in this city, in this country, from beginning to end, gives you the impression of impermanence, of the unexpected, the exceptional. You always come to things you did not expect; you want to find them again and they are lost – they have made something else which is equally charming.

Auroville Reflected

On 28 February 1968, on an impoverished plateau on the Coromandel Coast of South India, about 4,000 people from around the world gathered for a most unusual inauguration. Handfuls of soil from the countries of the world were mixed together as a symbol of human unity. Why did Indira Gandhi, the erstwhile Prime Minister of India, support this development for "a city the earth needs?" Why did UNESCO endorse this project? Why does the Dalai Lama continue to be involved in the project? What led anthropologist Margaret Mead to insist that records must be kept of its progress? Why did both historian William Irwin Thompson and United Nations representative Robert Muller note that this social experiment may be a breakthrough for humanity even as critics commented, "it is an impossible dream"?

A House For the Third Millennium
Essays on Matrimandir

Nightwatch at the Matrimandir...
A cosmic spectacle; the black expanse above, the big black crater of Matrimandir's excavation carved deep into the soil. The four pillars - two of which are completed and the other two nearing completion - are four huge ships coming together from the four corners of the earth to meet at this pro propitious spot...

Passage to More than India

This book is a voyage of discovery. In 1959 the author, Dick Batstone, a classically educated bookseller in England, with a Christian background, comes across a life of the great Indian polymath Sri Aurobindo, though a series of apparently fortuitous circumstances. A meeting in Durham, England, leads him to a determination to get to the Sri Aurobindo Ashram in Pondicherry, a former French territory south of Madras.